"To Write the Lips of Sleepers"

The Poetry of Amir Gilboa

Warren Bargad

Hebrew Union College Press
Cincinnati

Library of Congress Cataloging-in-Publication Data

Bargad, Warren.
"To write the lips of sleepers" : the poetry of Amir Gilboa / by Warren Bargad.
p. cm. — (Monographs of the Hebrew Union College ; no. 17)
Includes bibliographical references and index.
ISBN 0-87820-416-4
1. Gilboa, Amir — Criticism and interpretation. I. Title. II. Series.
PJ5054.G5Z585 1994
892.4'16 — dc20 93-49756
CIP

Composition by Kelby Bowers, COMPublishing, Cincinnati, Ohio
Printed on acid-free paper
Manufactured in the United States of America
Distributed by Behrman House, Inc.
235 Watchung Avenue, West Orange, NJ 07052

Monographs of the
Hebrew Union College,
Number 17

"To Write the Lips of Sleepers":
The Poetry of Amir Gilboa

An I. Edward Kiev
Library Foundation Book

Monographs of the Hebrew Union College

1. Lewis M. Barth, *An Analysis of Vatican 30*
2. Samson H. Levey, *The Messiah: An Aramaic Interpretation*
3. Ben Zion Wacholder, *Eupolemus: A Study of Judaeo-Greek Literature*
4. Richard Victor Bergren, *The Prophets and the Law*
5. Benny Kraut, *From Reform Judaism to Ethical Culture: The Religious Evolution of Felix Adler*
6. David B. Ruderman, *The World of a Renaissance Jew: The Life and Thought of Abraham ben Mordecai Farissol*
7. Alan Mendelson, *Secular Education in Philo of Alexandria*
8. Ben Zion Wacholder, *The Dawn of Qumran: The Sectarian Torah and the Teacher of Righteousness*
9. Stephen M. Passamaneck, *The Traditional Jewish Law of Sale: Shulḥan Arukh, Ḥoshen Mishpat, Chapters 189^{8}240*
10. Yael S. Feldman, *Modernism and Cultural Transfer: Gabriel Preil and the Tradition of Jewish Literary Bilingualism*
11. Raphael Jospe, *Torah and Sophia: The Life and Thought of Shem Tov ibn Falaquera*
12. Richard Kalmin, *The Redaction of the Babylonian Talmud: Amoraic or Saboraic?*
13. Shuly Rubin Schwartz, *The Emergence of Jewish Scholarship in America: The Publication of the Jewish Encyclopedia*
14. John C. Reeves, *Jewish Lore in Manichaean Cosmogony: Studies in the Book of Giants Traditions*
15. Robert Kirschner, *Baraita De-Melekhet Ha-Mishkan: A Critical Edition With Introduction and Translation*
16. Philip E. Miller, *Karaite Separatism in Nineteenth-Century Russia: Joseph Solomon Lutski's Epistle of Israel's Deliverance*
17. Warren Bargad, *"To Write the Lips of Sleepers": The Poetry of Amir Gilboa*

To the memory of the
Pomerantz family of Kostopol
and the Wicnudel family of Rovna

Dr. I. Edward Kiev
1905–1975
Distinguished Rabbi, Chaplain, and Librarian

In September 1976 Dr. Kiev's family and friends established a Library Foundation bearing his name to support and encourage the knowledge, understanding, and appreciation of books, manuscripts, and other efforts of scholars in Judaica and Hebraica. In cooperation with the Publications Committee of the Hebrew Union College Press, the Foundation presents the present study by Warren Bargad as an I. Edward Kiev Library Foundation volume.

Contents

Preface

My interest in Amir Gilboa's poetry began in the late 1970s when Stanley Chyet and I were preparing the manuscript for *Israeli Poetry: A Contemporary Anthology.* Gilboa's oeuvre, the first to appear in that book, was quite a puzzle. His earlier works had a strong, traditional tenor to them, while his later works seemed very contemporary and blatantly modernistic. At once his poetry—its lexical aspect, at least—reflected the works of poets such as Shin Shalom, Ya'akov Fichman, Zalman Shneour, Yitsḥak Lamdan, and even the turn-of-the-century master, Ḥayim Naḥman Bialik, while his later works resembled the utterly modernistic poetry of the late Yona Wollach, the youngest and last-entered poet in the anthology. The mystery of this stylistic dichotomy proved enduring: Did Gilboa represent the denouement of an extended "Age of Bialik," or was he part of the new modernistic trend?

Later, in the mid-1980s, when I held a National Endowment for the Humanities Fellowship, I began to explore these issues in depth. A number of Israeli professors, critics, and poets added another dimension to the puzzle: Why was it that Gilboa was generally recognized as a leading Israeli poet, and yet few had ventured to pen thorough discussions of his works? (Just after I had committed myself to write this study, Prof. Hillel Barzel of Bar Ilan University published, in Hebrew, his *Amir Gilboa: A Monograph,* and Ida Tsurit's *Spheres of Life and Emanation* followed soon thereafter.) Most of the individuals I consulted agreed that Gilboa surely merited the attention and thus urged me to take on the task of chronicling the development of the poet's body of work from his teen-age Yiddish poetry in the Ukraine to his eighth and final volume, published in Tel Aviv after his death. My intention has been to convey a comprehensive and palpable understanding of Gilboa's poetic texts and a sense of the artistic vicissitudes of his long career. My main goal, however, has been to solve the enigma of Gilboa's dual poetic image and the ambiguity of his place in the modern Hebrew poetic canon. Gilboa's poetry, however, is often unwieldy and difficult to classify. Even after years of research—involving nearly two hundred critical articles, biographical writings, interviews, and the two book-length studies noted above—the questions are still not completely resolved.

Debts of gratitude have accumulated over the years during which this study was conceived and shaped. First of all, I would like to thank Gabriela (Gabi) Gilboa, the poet's widow, for her assistance. I am grateful for her kind permission to reprint more than 1300 lines of Gilboa's poetry in this study and for providing photos and poetic artifacts for inclusion in this book. She also has been graciously hospitable each time I visited her—especially so when I asked to meet with her only a month or two after Gilboa's death, in September 1984.

I also want to express my gratitude to Stanley Chyet for reading through the early stages of the manuscript; to Stanley Nash for his incisive suggestions; to Arnold Band, who early on supported my continuing work on poetry and also made many helpful comments on the manuscript; to the late Dan Pagis, who encouraged my work in general and the study of Gilboa in particular; to Amalia Kahana-Carmon, who provided hospitality and collegiality during a six-week stay in Israel at the outset of the research on Gilboa; to Boaz Arpali of Tel Aviv University, who was kind enough to share with me the manuscript of his *Ha-peraḥim ve-ha-agartal: Shirat Amiḥai—Mivne, mashma'ut, poetica* (The Flowers and the Vase: Amichai's Poetry—Structure, Meaning, Poetics); and to Ory Bernstein, who conveyed his conviction that Gilboa was eminently worthy of a thorough study.

I also want to thank Alan Mintz and David Roskies, editors of *Prooftexts,* and Norman Stillman, editor of the *AJS Review,* for their permission to include parts of articles originally published in these journals in this study of Gilboa's works. Thanks also to the Genazim Literary Archives and to Menuḥa Brafman, who supplied additional photographs of Gilboa. A number of institutions and their staffs assisted me in the various stages of my research: the Judaica section of the Tel Aviv University Library; the Judaica and microfilm divisions of the National and University Library at Givat Ram, Jerusalem; Philip Miller and the Klau Library of the Hebrew Union College-Jewish Institute of Religion, New York; Dina Abramovich and the Yivo Institute for Jewish Research; Leon Gold and the Judaica section of the New York Public Library; the Judaica and microfilm divisions of the Harvard University Libraries; and Bob Singerman and the Price Library of Judaica at the University of Florida. Thanks also to Carlene Smith, Administrative Assistant of the Center for Jewish Studies at the University of Florida, for her help with the Gilboa manuscript and for her day-to-day devotion to the Center's multifaceted activities, especially through the years of the preparation of this book.

Further, this study could not have been accomplished without the resources provided by the following: a year-long fellowship and a summer

Travel to Collections grant from the National Endowment for the Humanities; a year's leave from Spertus College of Judaica; a grant from the Division of Sponsored Research at the University of Florida; and a year's leave provided by the College of Arts and Sciences at the University of Florida.

I am indebted to Michael A. Meyer, chair of the Hebrew Union College publications committee, whose wise counsel and helpful comments considerably improved the original manuscript and the final draft; to Ezra Spicehandler, who graciously undertook a comprehensive reading of the manuscript and made many suggestions and emendations which greatly enhanced its quality; and to Barbara Selya, managing editor of the Hebrew Union College Press, who worked expertly, unstintingly, and caringly to shape the manuscript into an articulate, coherent book. To these three I express my abiding appreciation for their professionalism, their dedication, and their true collegiality.

Finally, I thank Arlene for her forbearance during the intermittent research trips abroad and other lapses at home while this book was taking shape. Her encouragement, love, and support over the years have been the mainstays of my work and life.

Warren Bargad
Gainesville, Florida
April 1994

Chapter I

A Cultural Biography

From the Ukraine to Erets Israel

At a gathering of personal and professional friends in honor of his being awarded the prestigious Israel Prize in May 1982, Amir Gilboa reminisced about his aliyah (immigration to Erets Israel, the Land of Israel) from the Ukraine. Since Gilboa and his group of Jewish youths were traveling on forged passports and any sign of Jewishness would have given them away, their leader ordered that all identifying items be jettisoned before their train reached the Polish border. Sadly, Gilboa was forced to throw out the window all the poetry, in both Yiddish and Hebrew, that he had written throughout his teens. He arrived in Erets Israel in mid-January 1938, a poet bereft of his work.[1]

For Gilboa, this act of discarding old poetry and beginning anew was repeated, in a sense, in late summer 1940, when he met in Tel Aviv with the Yiddish poet and publicist Shlomo Spivak. Gilboa brought with him the mostly proletarian Yiddish poems he had written since his aliyah two years before, seeking Spivak's advice and recommendation for their publication. It seems that Spivak was quite frank about his negative evaluation of the works, and Gilboa set them aside. They were never published.[2]

Soon thereafter the Yiddish proletarian poet Berl Feldman became the Hebrew lyrical poet Amir Gilboa.[3] Once he abandoned Yiddish, Gilboa wrote and published only in Hebrew. His early nature lyrics, many of which were written while he walked through the Jezreel Valley region,[4] were later collected in his first volume, *La-ot* (For the Sign, 1942). His first published Hebrew poem, *Ki az etsak* (For Then I Scream), appeared in February 1941 in *Ha-shomer ha-tsa'ir* (Young Watchman), the ideological journal whose literary editor was Avraham Shlonsky (1900–1973).

Significantly, Amir Gilboa's linguistic and poetic development reflects Erets Israel's own cultural transitions. Not only did the poet's arrival coincide with the denouement of the Yiddish-Hebrew hegemony conflict in the Land and involve him in the vagaries of the Yiddish vs. Hebrew "intersystemic" relationship. He was also involved with the "intrasystemic" confrontation between the Palestinian Generation's *moderna*—Chana Kronfeld's term for the poets of the second wave of Hebrew modernism led by Shlonsky[5]—and the standardized style of Bialik and the traditionalists of the Age of Bialik.

By the early 1940s Shlonsky had reached the height of his powers as the mentor of the Erets-Israeli modernist movement. His work in the twenties and thirties on the journals *Hedim* (Echoes), *Ketuvim* (Writings), and *Turim* (Columns) and on the newspaper *Ha-arets* gave great impetus to the nonconformist ways of the younger poets, among them Natan Alterman (1910–1970) and Leah Goldberg (1911–1970). In the early 1930s his attack on the "national poet," Bialik,[6] and his struggle with the "old guard" of Hebrew letters strengthened his position of leadership. He also influenced the younger poets through his editorial role in the new publishing venture Sifriat Poalim (The Workers' Library), established by the *Ha-shomer ha-tsa'ir* organization. Shlonsky's own writings in the thirties—*Avnei bohu* (Stones of Chaos, 1934) and *Shirei ha-mapolet ve-ha-piyus* (Songs of Downfall and Solace, 1938)—solidified his image as the founder of an entirely new trend in modern Hebrew poetry.[7]

While the "young Turk" poets were ascendant in the late thirties—Alterman's *Kokhavim baḥuts* (Stars Outside) was published in 1938 and his *Simḥat aniyim* (Joy of the Poor) in 1941; Leah Goldberg's *Tabot ashan* (Smoke Rings) appeared in 1935 and her *Shibolet yerukat ha-ayin* (Green-Eyed Sheaf) in 1940—the "old guard" was still holding forth in the Hebrew Writers Association and its mainstream journal, *Moznayim* (Scales). From the mid- to the late thirties the familiar names of the well-established "generation of Bialik"[8] appeared regularly in *Moznayim's* conservative pages. These included Sha'ul Tcherniḥovsky (1875–1943), Ya'akov Fichman (1881–1958), Ya'akov Cahan (1881–1960), Zalman Shneour (1886–1959), David Shimoni (1886–1956), Ya'akov Steinberg (1887–1847), Yitsḥak Lamdan (1899–1954), and Shin Shalom (1904–1989)—among others—who were firmly attached to the Bialikian mode of romantic poetry.[9]

This dichotomy of styles is reflected in nearly all of Gilboa's poetry. Although he was impelled toward the traditional layers of Hebrew poetic expression and leaned heavily on his background of Bialik, Bible, the liturgy, and the classical rabbinic texts, he toyed from the very beginning with some aspects of modernist linguistic innovation and structure. In terms of a poetic language, his initial confrontation with Hebrew was with its "defective polysystem"—Itamar Even-Zohar's term for a dynamic, multiple linguistic system which has a standard language but not a developed, nonstandard colloqial mode of expression.[10] As Chana Kronfeld has pointed out, the early Hebrew modernist poets were forced to

> fill in the gaps . . . by inventing equivalents or compensations for non-existing slang, dialects, technical language. . . . This process became uniquely productive for the modernist poets. . . .[11]

Gilboa was part of this process of "deautomatization" (that is, going beyond the standard or "automatized" language). At the same time, however, his early poems evince a great measure of loyalty to the standard usages of the Age of Bialik. Even-Zohar has noted that as a consequence of the intense, intergenerational overlap—the old guard with the *moderna*—in the sphere of Hebrew poetry in the thirties and forties, "even the [poetic and linguistic] norms that [had] 'fallen away' [were] not immediately nullified." What remained was a "variety" (*ravgoniyut*) of norms, old and new. It is this variety of poetic and linguistic approaches which permeates nearly all of Gilboa's work.[12]

Until 1953, however, Gilboa was recognized by neither school. Because of his unsettled life in Erets Israel from 1937 to 1942 and his long stint (1942–1946) in the British Eighth Army and the Jewish Brigade in World War II, he did not become well-known as a poet. During the war years, he published a few poems in the Jewish Brigade's journals and a number of other works in Erets-Israeli newspapers and literary magazines. However, it was only after his return home in 1946 that he began to publish in earnest the works he had written during and after the war. No critical attention was paid to his 1942 self-published collection *La-ot,* and only a few reviews appeared even after the publication of *Sheva reshuyot* (Seven Domains) in 1949. Only in 1953, with the publication of *Shirim ba-boker ba-boker* (Early Morning Songs) was Gilboa accorded significant recognition—and his work subjected to critique and controversy.

Another factor which made it difficult to categorize Gilboa was his initial inclusion in the *Yalkut ha-re'im* (The Friends' Knapsack) group, whose founders included Moshe Shamir (1921–), Shlomo Tanai (1919–), Yehuda Amichai (1924–), and Ozer Rabin (1921–). Gilboa published several poems in both issues of their short-lived journal (1944–45) and for a time was associated with that literary society, whose avowed goal was to initiate a new age of a full-fledged "Israeli" literature. Soon thereafter, however, Gilboa unofficially disengaged himself from the group. He was never again identified with any specific clique or trend. His strongly idiosyncratic combination of traditional allusiveness and standardized vocabulary with the *moderna*'s neologistic effort and its varied poetic structures made him, as Shlomo Sheva later observed, *meshorer le-atsmo,* "a poet unto himself."[13]

Berl Feldman was born September 25, 1914,[14] the youngest of seven children, three sons and four daughters. All of the children except for Gilboa ultimately worked with their father as tailors in the home shop. The family lived in Radzivil (or Radzivilov, as the Jewish population called it), a small town in Volhynia Province in the western Ukraine, just across the Russo-Austrian border from the Polish-Galician town of Brody. Not only was the area one of mixed languages and cultures—Russian, Polish, German, Yiddish, and Hebrew—Gilboa was also raised in the mixed ideological and literary worlds of Yiddish and Socialism, Hebrew and Zionism. At the close of World War I, the area was rife with conflict. Anti-Jewish pogroms were perpetrated by the factional armies of Petlura and Denikin,[15] and ultimately Radzivil came under Poland's reborn sovereignty.

Although Yiddish was the language of everyday life among Jews in this area of eastern Europe, the Hebrew-oriented Zionist movement was strong. Many *tarbut* (Hebrew culture and language) schools were established, including one in Radzivil. According to Ida Tsurit, Gilboa was enrolled in the school's kindergarten and spent several years there. At age ten he composed a Hebrew play and began to keep Hebrew diaries. He even published a small journal with a schoolmate, telling his friends he wanted to be "Bialik's arms bearer"—that is, a writer like Bialik.

After transferring to a Polish school, Gilboa continued his Hebrew studies in a *ḥeder* (traditional Jewish elementary school), where he learned the traditional texts such as *ḥumash* (Pentateuch) with the medieval commentator Rashi. Although his teacher, Reb Abba, was a hot-tempered man, he had a creative and artistic side which appealed to young Berl. Later, Gilboa also had a private teacher, David Schneider, with whom he read Hebrew poetry and language texts by the contemporary Hebrew poets Ya'akov Fichman and Yitsḥak Katzenelson (1885–1944).[16]

To supplement his formal and tutorial studies, Gilboa borrowed avidly from the local *tarbut* library. According to his own recollections, he read Jewish history, kabbalistic and Ḥasidic texts, and contemporary Erets-Israeli literary-political journals and newspapers such as *Kuntres, Davar,* and *Bama'ale.* He was also drawn to stories of Zionist heroes and martyrs (for example, Ḥayim Trumpeldor), and articles, poetry, and fiction by Fichman, Yehuda Karni (1984–1949), and Yosef Ḥayim Brenner (1881–1921).[17]

Zionist social and cultural activities also influenced the boy. From the age of eight, Gilboa was a member of Zionist youth groups, first in *Ha-shomer ha-tsa'ir* and later in *He-ḥaluts ha-tsa'ir* (Young Pioneer). His brother Joshua, also fluent in Hebrew, was a member of the *He-ḥaluts* board in Radzivil. These youth groups would go on hikes and picnics and arrange other social and cultural activities, where "emissaries" of the movement often spoke to the young members about settling in the Jewish homeland.

By his mid-teens Gilboa decided he would not become a tailor in the family workshop. He would make aliyah[18] and become a Hebrew poet. As a first step, he left Radzivil in the summer of 1933 and joined the Klossova *hakhshara* encampment at Lutsk, where he and other young men and women were trained in the skills they would need for the varieties of labor to be done in Erets Israel. (Klossova was geared to quarrying and rock-splitting, useful for future road-building efforts.) Later, in the Verba and Bendin encampments, he was also active in literary activities and administrative affairs. He produced a wall newspaper (which included some poetry) at Lutsk and was elected as a representative to the *He-ḥaluts* regional congress. In 1937 Gilboa joined an aliyah group and bade farewell to his family. His parents, brothers, and sisters were murdered by the Nazis on the eve of Simḥat Torah, 1942.

The purpose of this study is to describe and interpret Amir Gilboa's poetic works at various stages of his career and to define his place in the tradition of modern Hebrew poetry. Spanning nearly fifty years and collected in eight volumes,[19] the poetry is examined both for its general meaning and for its aesthetic dimensions. The central focus of the study is Gilboa's poetic transition from a full-blown romanticist to what may be called a "romantic modernist." Initially writing in the Age of Bialik tradition, Gilboa toyed with innovative figurative structures in the forties, introduced new themes in the fifties, and experimented with new syntactic and semantic usages in the early sixties. Subsequently, in the late 1960s and for the rest of his career, Gilboa created a highly idiosyncratic blend of abiding romantic preoccupations and new modernist structures.

This study also seeks to delineate Gilboa's varying poetics—that is, the materials which the poet selects from the world around him, his ways of combining elements of reality with linguistic components, his "policies" of poetic production, and his values as a writer.[20] Gilboa moved from one set of poetics to another in the course of his long career. His early poetry is composed mainly of romantic themes and a lyrical style—the combined result of his leaving behind the strident tone of Yiddish proletarian verse, his attachment to the poetics of the premodernist romantics, and his fervid enthrallment with Erets Israel as a source of spiritual, ideological, and personal fulfillment. Later, Gilboa experimented with other approaches: the poetics of figurative profusion in the early forties; the poetics of ambivalence in his Holocaust poetry; the poetics of ideological lyricism in the early 1950s; and the poetics of ambiguity in his later, modernist phase.

Two additional dimensions of Gilboa's poetry are addressed: its multiple linguistic strata and its autobiographical nature. The language of Hebrew romanticism is traced from time to time—not simply to point out the sources of Gilboa's vocabulary but rather to show his abiding attachment to the modes of expression used by Bialik and his followers. But in all of Gilboa's poetry, the dominant narrative voice is the poet's own. He describes past experiences and everyday incidents—his frustrations, his delights, his sorrows. Even in his poems on biblical figures, from which he is the most distanced, a "live" image of the poet emerges. The result is an interweaving of autobiography—even if a mythical one—and ancient history. The poems on poetry and the poetic process go much further. They disclose a virtually unmasked autobiographical voice, a voice which provides much of the force, fervor, charm, and poignancy of Gilboa's unique style.

The Poetics of Romanticism: Gilboa and the Age of Bialik

Particularly in his early works, Gilboa presents a poetic world founded firmly on mythical, imaginary, dream-like, other-worldly realities. The sunrise or sunset is not merely the beginning or end of the day; it is a grand cosmic event which envelops the poet with its majesty. For him, the event creates an aura of magic, sacrality, and mystique which prompts him to rhapsodize about its effects. The poet and his emotive verbiage take up far more space than the object itself, and his personal, emotional response to the outer world becomes the focus of the poem.

Just as Gilboa's inner world continually flows into the outer, his perceptions and preferences are also the central forces of his poetic language. It is archaic (or archaized) and highbrow—hence, distanced; allusive (to classical, sacred texts)—hence, dually signifying; synonymic (or semantically doubled)—hence, emphatic; abstract and profusely figurative—hence, complex, ponderous, and emotive. This specially wrought language is linked with the poet's romantic perception of the world, and it provides the means by which he expresses his feelings about that world.

Gilboa is indisputably a romantic. In every period of his production the poems are infused with classic romantic themes, images, and modes of writing: an enthrallment with nature and its mystique; personal visions, dreams, and memories; a blend of reality, fantasies, and myth; the creative imagination and self-ruminations of the poet; a pensive, lyrical style; the idea and experience of spontaneity; and the instinctive effort to transmit the depths of personal feeling.[21]

Many of these qualities have been noted in recent studies of Bialik.[22] Dan Miron describes how, in the 1899 poem *Razei laila* (Night Secrets), the poet broke away from the Haskalah's neoclassical style of writing and moved toward a more personal and lyrical mode of expression. Miron cites such motifs as "the emotional-instinctual aspects of the individual," "the magic force of nature," and "the concretization of mythical symbols."[23] In another study, Miron discusses Bialik's "autobiographical myth," forged mainly in the poems *Shirati* (My Song) and *Zohar* (Splendor), and the poet's "frontal confrontation" with nature and "the immediate presence of the world of myth" in *Tsafririm* (Morning Imps [or Breezes]).[24]

Ziva Shamir echoes Miron's view of *Shirati.* She uses the terms "confessional," "sentimental," and "romantic" and points to the poem's childlike point of view to emphasize its innovative nature in the development of Bialik's oeuvre. Shamir also focuses on the romantic image of the dreamy, nature-loving, instinctual child in *Tsafririm* and in Bialik's autobiographical narrative *Safiaḥ* (Aftergrowth).[25]

Scenes, images, biblical allusions and diction, and other Bialik-like qualities abound in Gilboa's works. These include the dreamy child, the mystique of night, the preoccupation with the self as poet, the use of mythical situations, the dualities of elation and despair, beauty and grimness, and the ubiquitously fervent tone.[26] Beyond the romantic modes of expression noted above, Gilboa's intractable attachment to the traditional Hebrew lexicon also links him to the poets of the prior generation. There is ample evidence to demonstrate that it is Bialik himself to whom Gilboa felt closest.[27]

An Appendix (page 329) presents a selected list of lexical items common to both poets.

It is not that Gilboa's poems are entirely similar to those of Bialik. Indeed, Gilboa's works differ considerably in theme, style, and rhetoric. He does not presume to be the voice or conscience of the generation. Though he often uses the vocabulary of the Prophets, he rarely assumes a prophet-like posture. His forcefulness is transmitted mainly in the agony brought on by the Holocaust and not by a social or moral view of a grand national malaise. He dwells more obsessively on the theme of imagination and on the experience of expressivity than does Bialik. He writes far less than Bialik about the mythic roots and destiny of the nation, and he uses far more ambiguity, a broader and more varied range of metaphor, and more frequently incorporates ironic figures such as the oxymoron and clashing oppositional structures. These distinctions notwithstanding, the romantic resonances of Bialik and the romantic "residues" found in the Age of Bialik poets pervade much of Gilboa's poetry.[28]

Dan Miron's differentiation between the "Generation of Bialik" *(dor Bialik)* and the "Age of Bialik" *(tekufat Bialik)* is significant for this discussion of Gilboa's place in the Hebrew poetic canon. According to Miron, a Bialikian view of a literary period depends on a dominant "stylistic character" *(ofi ha-signon)* or "unified stylistic atmosphere." It also involves the idea of "successorship," based on Dov Sadan's reference to the poets of the Age of Bialik and "their successors in poetry" *(mamshikheihem be-shira)*. As one such "successor" to those poetics, Gilboa can be placed in the Age of Bialik tradition.[29]

Accordingly, the "dominant poetics" of a period can remain in force from one generation to the next even though there may be certain, even drastic, changes. This continuity, he adds, depends on "the creative potential latent in the poetics [and its] flexibility," even when the chronological "generations" of poets are quite different.[30] Miron sums up his views as follows:

> In general it may be said that the growth of this generation [of Bialik] (much like the "Palmach Generation" in the 1940s) in relation to the generation which preceded it was one of continuity and development and not one of breach and rejection. Many of the poetic potentialities which were merely suggested in the Generation of Bialik . . . came to full artistic fruition in the [next] turn-of-the-century generation. . . .Even so, the turn-of-the-century

> generation was different in its spiritual physiognomy. Thus, an understanding of the connection between the generations demands not only a marking of the points of similarity of the two but also, in equal measure, a delineation of the lines of departure.[31]

This is certainly the case with Gilboa. Although his early works bear the marks of his romantic mentors in theme, language, and poetics, the various stanzaic and metric structures of his poems through the early 1950s were largely influenced by the works of Shlonsky. Even in his early poems, however, Gilboa attempted to free himself from those dominating structures, especially Shlonsky's four-verse, *abab*-rhymed stanzas.[32] By 1953, with the publication of *Shirim ba-boker ba-boker,* Gilboa had established his own independent voice and continued, throughout his writing career, to experiment with different themes, structures, and styles. This study traces the relentlessness of that poetic experimentation, but it also seeks to demonstrate Gilboa's abiding devotion to romantic images, motifs, and subjects, even in his later, most modernist works.[33]

Gilboa's classification as a romantic poet may be further understood in the context of what Roman Jakobson has called the *dominant—*"the focusing component of a work of art: it rules, determines, and transforms the remaining components."

> It is the dominant which guarantees the integrity of the structure. . . . A poetic work [is] a structured system, a regularly ordered hierarchical set of artistic devices.

Clearly the "dominant" of Gilboa's art, these romantic devices are, of themselves, sufficient to define him as a romantic.

Brian McHale's interpretation of Jakobson's larger statement is useful in explaining Gilboa's later modernism. McHale suggests that

> the concept of the dominant is in fact plural. . . . Jakobson applies his concept of the dominant not only to the structure of the individual literary text and the synchronic and diachronic organization of the literary system, but also to the analysis of the verse medium in general . . . of verbal art in gen-

> eral . . . and of cultural history. . . . Clearly, then, there are many dominants, and different dominants may be distinguished depending upon the level, scope, and focus of the analysis. Furthermore, one and the same text will, we can infer, yield different dominants depending upon what aspect of it we are analyzing. . . . In short, different dominants emerge depending upon which questions we ask of the text, and the position from which we interrogate it.[34]

The concept of many coexisting dominants is particularly helpful in understanding a poet such as Gilboa, who, for the most part, eschewed the Hebrew Modernist trends of the day—Shlonsky's Futurism, Greenberg's Expressionism, Alterman's Symbolism. As did Leah Goldberg, Zerubavel Gilead, Benjamin Tenne, Avraham Ḥalfi, David Rokeaḥ, Levi Ben-Amitai and Ozer Rabin, among others, Gilboa opted for a continuation, in varied garb, of Hebrew Romanticism. Falling between the cracks of the Age of Bialik and the Age of Modernism and between the "Generation of Alterman" and the "Palmach Generation," Gilboa, in his idiosyncratic way, moved impatiently in pursuit of his own poetic path.[35]

From Yiddish To Hebrew

It is illuminating to consider Gilboa's somewhat naive first steps on the path to poetry. As noted, throughout his teen years Gilboa wrote in both Hebrew and Yiddish. A proletarian work poem entitled *Mir shpanen* (We're Striding) was composed in 1933 and preserved by his friend from Lutsk, Sarah Segal, to whom Gilboa sent the poem with the request that it be forwarded to Warsaw for possible publication in the Socialist Yiddish newspaper, *Dos Vort*.[36] The work is strident in tone and idealistic in content. Marching into the distance, working with machinery, preoccupied with iron, sweat, burning, hands, mouths, and singing—all are common images in this socialistic genre. The poetics of strength and determination are reflected by the poem's strong rhythm and rhyming couplets. The combination of hyperbolic rhetoric and the depiction of physical regimen expresses the workers' ideological fervor and the arduousness of their task.

A perusal of *Dos Vort* in the mid-thirties, however, shows very little poetry in its pages. The paper features a plethora of ideological and political articles—reports on the pioneer movement in Europe and the number of new immigrants to Erets Israel, news stories on the ominous growth of Nazism in Germany. Although young Gilboa's wish to have his poem published in *Dos Vort* indicates his ideological ardor and his commitment to the movement the paper represented, *Mir shpanen* was never published.

מיר שפּאַנען

אין דער מזרח רויטלעך בלייַך,
זונען־שייַן. מיר שפּאַנען גלייַך:
איינס און צוויי און דרייַ און פֿיר!
נישט אין שורה, נאָר מאַרשיר–
גיי פֿאָרויס! ווייַט־ווייַט העט דאָרט
בייַם טאַרטאַק פֿאַרנעם אַ אָרט:
לעבן מאַשינען אויף דעם פּלאַץ
יעדער פֿלינקער ווי אַ קאַץ,
יעדער שטאַרקער ווי אַ ריז,
זאָל דייַן בליק דאָ זייַן אַ שפּיז
זאָל דייַן האַנט זייַן אַ אייַזן־שטאַנג
און דייַן פֿוס – שטאַרק לאַנג, שטאַרק לאַנג.
מיט דעם מויל אַזוי פֿרייַ זינג...
און די קלעצער דוכט זיך גרינג
כאָטש ס׳עסט אַ שווייס די אויגן, ס׳מויל
ס׳ברענט פֿון אויבן אַ זון, אַ קויל....[37]

We're Striding

In the east, reddish, pale,
sunshine. We're striding straight:
One and two and three and four!
Not in a line, only marching—
Go forward! Far-far into the distance
taking our place at the sawmill:

By the machine in that place
every agile one like a cat,
every strong one like a giant,
may your look be a dart
may your hand be an iron beam
and your foot—long strong, long strong.
With your mouth singing so free . . .
and the logs seem so light
though sweat eats the eyes, the mouth
from above burns a sun, a coal. . . .

Ki az etsak, Gilboa's first published Hebrew poem, should be considered in the context of proletarian works like *Mir shpanen* and the poet's early ideological indoctrination. Despite its being his first Hebrew publication, *Ki az etsak* is a vestige of Gilboa's socialist-Zionist experiences and marks the end of a major period in his poetic development.

Soon after the publication of *Ki az etsak* in *Ha-shomer ha-tsa'ir,* four other poems appeared in various other Hebrew literary journals: *Zikhron ahava aḥat* (The Memory of One Love)[38] and *El ha-even* (To the Rock) in *Gazit* (Quarried Stone), Gideon Talpir's journal of literature and art; *Ha-na'ar ha-meshorer* (The Boy Poet) in Yitsḥak Lamdan's *Gilyonot* (Folios); and, on June 19, 1942, just as Gilboa enlisted in the British Army, *Gevishayikh la-helekh* (Your Crystals for the Wanderer) in the newspaper *Davar.*[39] Three of these—the exception is *Ha-na'ar ha-meshorer*—are similar in general content and message. Typical of contemporary Russian, Yiddish, and Hebrew romantic and nationalistic poetry, the works address Erets Israel as a female entity whose combined beauty and toughness are respectively praised and overcome, celebrated and accommodated. The speakers are builders or wanderers, images of newcomers and *ḥalutsim* who confront the difficulties of transformimg the harshness of the Land and, at the same time, are taken with its beauty. The language is variably of the Song of Songs—the Land is depicted as the beloved—or of the poetic, archaic, euphuistic diction of Isaiah, classical rabbinic literature, and the liturgy. *Piyut*-like repetitions of refrains and parallel-structured phrases abound, as in liturgical poetry. *Ha-na'ar ha-meshorer,* although different in content, is similar in form and language to the three other paeans-to-the-Land.

Ki az etsak is conspicuously different. It was the only poem Gilboa ever published in *Ha-shomer ha-tsa'ir,* and even though it appeared before the others, Gilboa did not include it in the original *La-ot* collection. It is also his longest poem—over three pages, a length never surpassed throughout his career. Its focus is somewhat ambiguous. Though the subject is war (most probably World War II in general without specific consideration of the Holocaust since reliable reports of its horrors were not forthcoming until the fall of 1942),[40] the first and next-to-last stanzas repeat the general theme: on some future "day of joy," the entire universe will be like "a Temple on a holiday." With eyes both tearful and fiery, says the speaker, "then I will scream." In the anaphoric opening lines of four of the next seven stanzas, the speaker describes the various screams that will reverberate on that great, triumphant day. These are "the scream of the beaten dogs," "the scream of nights of curse," "the scream of the jubilant mornings," and "the scream of a memory of madness of awareness of people tumbling into the abyss." The "beaten dogs," then, are the victims of war; and the screams reflect individual suffering caused by the war. The remaining three of these seven stanzas and two later stanzas contain additional screams described more figuratively here than in those before.

וָאֶצְעַק –
בַּחֲלִילֵי אֲבִיבִים לְאֵין סְפוֹר, וּבְרֹדֶם עַרְבוֹת שֶׁלֶג תְּכֻלֵּי זִיו.
בְּדִמְמַת צָהֳרֵי חֹם דְּחוּסִים וְלֵילוֹת צוֹנְנִים בְּקֹר.

And I scream—
in the pipes of numberless springs, and in the slumber of blue-lit
   steppes of snow
In the silence of oppressive noon heat and nights chilled with cold.

וָאֶצְעַק –
בִּגְלוֹם קוֹלוֹת נְצָחִים שֶׁנִּתְאַדּוּ מִתְעַלְּפִים בְּחֻבֵּי יַלְדוּתִי....
וְעַל שֶׁלֹּא חָיִיתִי אֶלֶף אַלְפֵי פַּעַם וְכַמִּסְפָּר הַזֶּה לֹא מַתִּי.

And I scream—
In the muffled sounds of eternities which have vaporized, fainting in

the recesses of my childhood. . . .
And because I have not lived thousands of times nor died this many times as well.[41]

The screamer and protester here is clearly a romantic: a sensitive, ecstatic observer, concerned and entwined with nature and the cosmos. Rather than dwell on the suffering, he evokes nature's loveliness and the sweet memories of childhood. But these figments of the imagination have little effect on the gods of war. The speaker sends "voices on high like nightingales," but instead of mollifying the gods, the voices "fall, corpses, from on high onto my head."

Later in the poem the speaker, in a dreamlike but moralistic tone, describes the fate of a peasant.

...צְבָא קַלְגָּסִים זָר הִתְפָּרֵץ לִשְׂדוֹתָיו
לַעֲרוֹךְ מִלְחָמָה לֹא לוֹ. וְנִדְרַךְ וְכֻסָּה וְחָרַב
חֲזוֹנוֹ לְאוֹר יוֹם.

. . . his fields are invaded by a foreign army of soldiers
to wage a war that's not his. And he's trampled and buried
and his dream is destroyed in the light of day.

The peasant-farmer's dream provokes the speaker's unremitting rage. The voice is embittered, frustrated by being outnumbered by the invading forces, helpless in the face of superior numbers, ready to fight back even with wooden planks. "We're behind you," comes the call from the speaker and his cohorts, and the penultimate stanza repeats again the opening vision of victory and joy. At the end, the poet speaks triumphantly for the world. The powerful poetic voice—the visionary, mythic, irrepressible screams of poetry—will beat back the oppressive foe and ring in the day of glorious victory, and screamless days of peace and tranquillity will follow.

וְרוּחוֹת זַעְמִי יְטַאטְאוּ תֵּבֵל
וּלְשׁוֹנוֹתַי אֵשׁ יְלַחֲכוּ הָרַע עַד קֵץ

the winds of my anger sweep the universe
and the tongues of fire lick at the evil until [its] destruction

כָּל אָדָם יִהְיֶה בֶּחָג.
וְלֹא עוֹד אֶצְעַק.

every being will be in celebration.
And no longer will I scream.

The uniqueness of *Ki az etsak* among Gilboa's other Hebrew works written and published from 1940 to 1942 lies in its monolithic moralistic perspective. But the poem reflects a dualistic poetics, the rhetoric and syntax of a political diatribe and the figurative allusiveness of a personal confession. The syntactic density—usually strings of construct phrases—and a plethora of metaphorical figures, such as personification and synesthesia,[42] add both lyrical and hyperbolic dimensions to the already heightened language. On the one hand, this is proletarian, political poetry: Consider its rhetoric of indignation and outrage; its strident tone; its emphasis on the themes of oppression and helplessness in the face of evil; its use of anaphoric phrases and emphatic, chorus-like tag-verses ("—For the tramplers are many!". . . . "—And they'll keep driving us out!". . . . "—We're behind you!"); and its long, semantically repetitious lines, replete with bombastic, high-diction phrasing.[43]

From another perspective, however, the poetics which shape this work also reflect a turning inward as the speaker depicts himself as a victim of personal hostility. The use of figurative language and an emphasis on the natural, cosmic effects of the war give the poem a visionary quality. The language becomes mythical, as if to say that human history echoes with repeated episodes of victimization.

וְהָיְתָה זוֹ צַעֲקַת זֶכֶר שִׁגְעוֹן הִתְפַּכְּחוּת בְּמוֹט אִישׁ תְּהוֹמָה –
אָז נָמוֹג הַחֲלוֹם, וְאָבְדָה גַּם פַּת לֶחֶם.
הַבָּר – מֵעֵבֶר לְאֵלֶם־רְאִיָּתִי נֶאֱגָר, בִּפְנִים הַחוֹמָה.
וְנֶגַּסְתִּי גַּם מֵחֲלוֹם בִּכְאֵב, כִּמְטַּבּוּר, בְּהָגִיחַ יֶלֶד מֵרֶחֶם.

And this was the scream of a memory of madness of awareness of
 people tumbling into the abyss—
then the dream evaporated, and even a crumb of bread disappeared.
The grain—it was gathered beyond my muteness-sight, inside the wall.
And I was also torn painfully from a dream, as if from the placenta, as
 the child emerges from the womb.

In the less bombastic stanzas which frame the poem, the language is more muted, more lyrical, more Hebrew than Yiddish-engendered.

בְּיוֹם הַגִּיל כִּי יָחִיל.
הֶחָלָל לְהֵיכָל יִהְיֶה בֶּחָג.
כָּל עַיִן אֲבוּקָה. וְכָל בָּבָה – פְּתִיל.
כִּי אָז אֶצְעַק:

On the day of joy when it arrives.
The Temple's space will celebrate.
In our eye the pearl of light will bring a tear.
For then I will scream.

With its predominant tone of moral and political indignation, *Ki az etsak* must be viewed as an anachronistic work. By the time it was published, Gilboa had moved away from the style of his earlier Yiddish poetry and, as we shall see below in *La-ot,* was experimenting with a more lyrical poetics.

One must bear in mind, however, that in this period Yiddish poetry also featured a strong lyrical trend which coexisted with Hebrew romantic poetry. Gilboa's shift may be partially attributed to the influence of other poets whose works provided motifs and both stylistic and metrical usages for his early work.

One such influence was Joseph Papiernikov, who wrote both political and lyrical poetry throughout his career. His 1929 volume, *Royt oyf shvarts* (Red on Black), consists mostly of strident proletarian poems ("Masses, masses—/Freedom's masses"), interspersed with lyrical nature poetry. In later collections such as *Goldene zamdn* (Golden Sands; Warsaw, 1932), written in Erets Israel, Papiernikov turned to landscape scenes and paeans to the Land's beauty. In *Mizrekh-nekht* (Eastern Nights), for example, the speaker, awake late at night, looks out over the "dreamy houses" and takes in the "silver-white nights."

און גוט איז מיר
אַז מײַנע אויגן זענען אָפֿן
ווי צוויי בעכער פֿון קריסטאַל
און איך טראָג זיי אָנגעגאָסן מיט לבנה־ליכט
הימל איבער זיי.

It's good for me
that my eyes are open
like two crystal goblets
and I carry them brimming with moonlight
above them the sky.

The general ambience of this poem recalls Gilboa's early nature lyrics, such as *Ba-sheki'a* (At Sunset) and *Ba-emek* (In the [Jezreel] Valley). As noted below in the discussion of *La-ot,* several recurring images in Gilboa's early poetry are unmistakably similar to Papiernikov's: open eyes, goblets, crystal.[44] In addition, the poet's identification with his poetry, a major romantic theme in Gilboa's works,[45] calls to mind Papiernikov's *Mayn lid* (My Song),[46] whose second stanza begins:

מײַן ליד – בין איך, און איך – מײַן ליד.
וואָס טראָגט מיט מיר אין צער און אין פֿרייד.

My song — is I, and I — my song.
It carries me [like a pregnant woman] in sorrow and in joy.

The works of Gilboa and Papiernikov display certain stylistic tendencies common to much Yiddish, Polish, and Russian poetry: for example, a frequent repetition of adverbial phrases, which gives the verse a languid, melancholy tone. Thus a love poem collected in Papiernikov's *Iberblaybn* mourns the lost beloved: *Zi'z avek, avek* (She's gone, gone); in *Feld* (Field), the speaker looks longingly out the window and says: *Vi veyt, vi veyt* (How far, how far); another love poem declares, *kh'shtay, mayn libste, far deyn fenster/shoyn lang, shoyn lang* (I stand, my beloved, before your window/so long, so long).

Another feature common to Yiddish and Russian lyrical poetry is the syntactical use of the adjectival appositive. When Papiernikov, in *Iberblaybn*, describes the beloved as a bridge and the lover as a ship, the phrasing is typical:

און ברענגן, אָנצובינדען עס בײַ דיר
אין דײַנע וואַסערן ד י ר ו י ק ע

And to bring, to intertwine with you
in your still waters, *the quiet ones*

Interestingly, these stylistic tendencies were also common to Hebrew poetry of the 1920s and 1930s and are examples of Yiddish-Polish-Russian cultural crosscurrents rather than specific stylistic influences of individual Hebrew poets. The adjectival appositive, for example, abounds in the works of Shlonsky, Alterman, and Raḥel. Beyond its stylistics, Papiernikov's Yiddish poems on Erets Israel evoke the same idealized tone as those of contemporary Hebrew poets[47]—for example, the idyllic Hebrew works of Fichman, Raḥel, Ben-Amitai, and Gilead.

The stylistic dimensions of Gilead, in particular, seem to have influenced Gilboa. A prolific if somewhat naive writer, Gilead, under the name "Zerubavel," published a continuous flow of romanticized visions in the journals and newspapers read by idealistic pioneering youth in both eastern Europe and in Erets Israel. Not unlike the adverbial repetitions noted above, his verbal repetitions lend a tone of melancholy and poignancy to the already fervid context, as illustrated in these excerpts from *Efshar* (Perhaps)—a not-so-subtle allusion to Raḥel's famous poem, *Ve-ulai* (And Perhaps).[48]

אֶפְשָׁר כִּי יִשָּׂא הַנּוֹדֵד אֶת עֵינָיו
לַמֶּרְחָב הַקּוֹפֵא וּלְנְתִיב כּוֹכָבִים

וְזָכַר־וְזָכַר אֶת אַרְצוֹ וּבֵיתוֹ. . .
וְהֵלִיט אֶת פָּנָיו וּבָכָה וּבָכָה.

Perhaps when the wanderer lifts his eyes
to the frozen distance and to the path of stars
and remembers-and-remembers his land and his home . . .
And he'd cover his face and cry and cry.

Gilboa's first collection, *La-ot,* displays many of these linguistic, rhetorical, and stylistic usages as he strives to find his poetic voice in Hebrew.

Chapter II

Nature and the Poetic Self

La-ot/For the Sign, 1942

La-ot, which Gilboa published privately before volunteering for the British Army,[1] presents three genres of poetry which are basic to his early—and later—repertoire: nature poetry, "songs of self," and poems on poetry.

The nature poems are steeped in the imagery and vocabulary of myth. Their tone is one of enthrallment and devotion, their language archaized, their diction heightened by the traditional phraseology of the prayerbook and the Bible. All of these elements combine to create a sense of the ritualistic and the mystic. Everyday occurrences are magnified into mythic events, filled with rapture, wonderment, and a sense of cosmic ceremony. *Halelu Yah* is a typical example.

הַלְלוּ יָהּ

כַּטַּל וְכַמָּטָר אֶרְחַץ כָּרֵי הַיְּרָקִים
לְעֵת דּוּמָם הַבֹּקֶר יַצִּיל פָּנָיו לָאוֹר
מִצֵּל.
וְנִיד רֶגַע, מוּל אוֹרוֹת פַּנָּסַי, כְּזִיו יָמִים אֲרֻכִּים,
שֶׁעוֹמְדָה שִׂמְחַת לָבְנָם גַּם בַּכְּחוֹל הַמִּתְעַגֵּל.

הוֹד הָרֶגַע בְּזִיו בֶּקַע רִאשׁוֹן מֵעַל לְרֹאשְׁךָ!
הוֹרֵד הַבַּד, וְגֹל הַיְרִיעָה. קַבְּלֵהוּ בְּנֵצַח־גִּיל וּבְאֹשֶׁר־הַהוֹדָיָה.
גְּרוֹף הַשָּׁעוֹת מִפִּיחַ כּוּר וּמֵעֹמֶק בְּאֵר אֲשֶׁר חָשְׁכָה,
וּבְתַחְתִּיתָם – אֵשׁ מַזָּלוֹת וְגֵץ כּוֹכְבֵי־הַהֲוָיָה.

Halleluyah

Like dew and rain I wash my green meadows
while silently morning rescues its face for light
from shadow.

A moment's tremor against my lantern lights, like the luster of long
days,
whose whiteness joy stands even in the rounding blue.

The moment's splendor with the luster of first gleam above your head!
Lower the shade and roll up the curtain. Greet it with glee-everlasting
and gladness-thanksgiving.
Rake the hours from an oven's soot and from the depth of a darkened
well
and at their bottom—the fire of planets and the spark of Creation's
stars.[2]

Gilboa engenders a heightened aura of other-worldly splendor for the sunrise by attributing to the enthralled speaker a role in the creation of the new day. As if participating in that creation, he "wash[es his] green meadows" with dew and rain and brings forth the light with his "lantern lights." After the predawn scene is set, the second stanza opens with an ecstatic description of the day's "first gleam." In the lines that follow, both the speaker-observer and the reader become active participants in the mythical changeover from the night. Through the use of the imperative, all who experience the dawn are urged to become involved in the process of creation and to be initiated into the cosmic mysteries of light's heavenly sources.

The poetic and somewhat archaized language—*omda* (stands, line 5), *kablehu* (greet it, line 7), *be'er asher ḥashkha* (a darkened well, line 8)—colors the scene with a tone of lyricism and myth. Sacral allusions abound: "dew and rain" *(tal u-matar)* (from the morning *amida* service of the daily prayerbook) adds a mood of solemnity and divine grace.[3] "Roll up the curtain" *(gol ha-yeri'a)* is reminiscent of the daily evening prayer *(ma'ariv),* in which God is described as "rolling (or rotating, *golel)* light before darkness and darkness before light." The word used for "curtain" *(yeri'a)* refers to the curtain of the ark in the ancient Holy Tabernacle.[4] The words for "oven" *(kur)* and "rake" *(grof)* are taken from biblical and rabbinic contexts of sacrificial rite, purification, and holiness.[5]

With regard to the use of sacral terms in a secular context, the primary influence is Shlonsky, whose works of the late twenties and thirties related to nature and the Land borrowed heavily from traditional sources. In the midst of archaic usages and allusions, Gilboa inserts the contemporary-sounding *yamim arukim* (long days, line 4), familiar from Raḥel's *Ve-ulai.* This interpolation lends a modicum of pathos, but much like the contemporary term *beka* (gleam, or literally crack, as of the "crack of dawn," line 6), the allusion to Raḥel evinces a polysystemic blend of linguistic and intertextual materials. Other linguistic elements contribute to the mythical romantic tone. In lines 2–3 the syntactic inversion (which forms the rhyme of *mi-tsel* (from shadow) and *ha-mitagel* (rounding, lines 3 and 5) creates both a "poetic" and an archaic touch. *Le-et dumam* (while silently, line 2) adds an air of initial quietude and anticipation, while the combination words *netsaḥ-gil* and *osher-ha-hodaya* (glee-everlasting and gladness-thanksgiving)[6] engender an emotive contrast of hyperbole.

Adding to the poem's tone of enthrallment are its lush imagery and profusion of metaphors, especially personification, a usage found copiously throughout Gilboa's works. The first is of "green meadows" being washed by the early morning dew and rain, much like a person washing his or her face to greet the new day. Another follows in lines 2–3: the morning "rescues its face for light/From shadow." Other metaphors—"the luster of long days," time measured by the fire's ashes, and the length of night likened to a deep dark well—exemplify the poem's predominant stock romantic images.

The dualistic or oppositional structuring of certain images and motifs and the phraseology of equivalence or semantic doubling also confirm the poem's romantic roots. Images of opposition are central: water (dew, rain, wash, well) vs. fire (ashes, oven, fire, spark); light (luster, splendor, gleam, fire, spark, stars) vs. darkness (shadow, shade, curtain, soot, depth, darkened, well, bottom); the earthly (dew, rain, meadows) vs. the cosmic (planets, stars); the real (meadows, morning, gleam) vs. the mythic (lanterns, shade, curtain, oven); the concrete (rain, morning, shadow, white, blue, gleam) vs. the figurative (wash, rescues, face, well). At the same time, neutral non-oppositional words—joy, splendor, glee, gladness—unite those oppositional images in a burst of celebration of the new day's coming.

The frequently used phrases of equivalence include: "dew and rain" *(tal [u]-matar),* the traditional phrase for good rainfall; "lower the shade" *(hored ha-bad)* and "roll up the curtain" *(ve-gol ha-yeri'a),* both of which refer to the transformation of night into day; "glee-everlasting" and "gladness-thanksgiving," which are more semantically emphatic than strictly synonymic; "from an oven's soot" and "from the depth of a darkened well," phrases which also are not strictly synonymic, but denote the dark recesses of these objects; and "the fire of planets" *(esh mazalot)* and "the spark of creation's stars" *(gets kokhvei-ha-havaya)* underscore the sense of fiery heavenly bodies. This frequent use of semantic doubling adds to the language's emotive intensification—conveying not a simple narration of an event but its epiphanic experience.

Halelu Yah reflects several aspects of Gilboa's early poetics. Interpolating the usages of the Shlonsky *moderna* style, it draws upon the romantics' traditional vocabulary. Although it generally conforms to modern contemporary models in other ways, Gilboa's use of meter and rhythm here and in most of his early works is somewhat freer than that of Alterman, Shlonsky, and Goldberg and is more similar to his use of meter and rhythm in the Yiddish poetry he wrote during his teenage years.[7] Falling under the rubric of "limited free verse," a term coined by Benjamin Hrushovski (Harshav),[8] Gilboa's poems of this period display a variable structure from verse to verse and within each stanza by which he, like Raḥel, gravitates toward a more natural speech rhythm and avoids the sing-song effect often present in the works of Shlonsky and Alterman.

By way of comparison, note the following excerpt from Shlonsky's 1935 poem, *Ha-yad ha-iveret* (The Blind Hand):

Ze-khu-KHIT ra-a-VA be-o-RE-ha mu-FE-zet
me-E-ver mi-SHAM-ma—re-ḤOV.
Me-E-ver mi-PO yad i-VE-ret ḥo-RE-zet
be-FA-am ha-E-lef: makh-OV.[9]

Here the dominant foot patterns are the anapest (- - +) and the amphibrach (- + -). Typical of Shlonsky is the combination of metrical "feminine endings" (lines 1 and 3), which continue the anapestic rhythm into the following amphibrachic line (zet/me-E: - - +). The second half of line 1 may also be scanned as a paeon-amphibrach combination (be-o-RE-ha mu-FE-zet: - - + - - + -), thus providing an entree to the amphibrachic rhythm of line 2. In either option the effect is an unbroken rhythm throughout the stanza, with the exception, of course, of the truncated amphibrachs which end lines 2 and 4 (re-ḤOV)/makh-OV: - +/- +).

Similarly, consider this excerpt from Alterman's *Kol* (Voice):

ha-LAY-la im-EM biz-khu-KHIT ve-a-SHAN
sha-me-MA ha-ki-KAR ha-so-ḤE-ret.
Ve-sha-MA-yim hal-KHU im ne-RAM ha-ya-SHAN
min ha-IR ha-a-ḤAT
el ir a-ḤE-ret.[10]

With the exception of line 5, Alterman maintains an amphibrachic meter throughout. (Lines 2 and 4 end with truncated amphibrachs.) The phrase *el ir* in the closing line may be read only as an iamb *(el IR:* - +), which completely disrupts the established rhythm. (Had Shlonsky composed the stanza, he surely would have written *el a-ḤE-ret* [- - + -] to parallel *ha-so-ḤE-ret* in line 2.) Clearly, Alterman wanted to emphasize the word *ir* (city), much as he does the word *kol* further on in the poem. Except for the exercise of poetic license here (and in a few additional places where he uses emphatic iambs), Alterman follows metrical patterns similar to those in the Shlonsky excerpt.

Gilboa's *Halelu Yah* differs in several ways from these standard patterns.

Ka-TAL ve-*kha*-ma-TAR er-ḤATS ka-RAI ha-*ye*-ru-KIM
le-ET du-MAM ha-BO-ker ya-TSIL pa-NAV la-OR
mi-TSEL.
Ve-NID RE-ga, MUL o-ROT pa-na-SAI, ke-ZIV ya-MIM a-ru-KIM,
she-om-DA sim-ḤAT lov-NAM GAM ba-keKHOL ha-*mit*-a-GEL.

HOD ha-RE-ga be-ZIV BE-ka ri-SHON me-AL le-rosh-KHA!
Ho-RED ha-BAD, ve-GOL ha-*ye*-ri-A. Kab-LE-hu be-NE-tsaḥ-GIL
  u-ve-O-sher — ha-*ho*-da-YA.
GROF ha-sha-OT mi-PI-aḥ KUR u-me-O-mek be-ER a-SHER
  ḥash-KHA,
u-ve-*taḥ*-ti-TAM — ESH ma-za-LOT ve-GETS kokh-VEI
  ha-ha-va-YA.

Although the dominant metrical foot is iambic, Gilboa intersperses counter-rhythmic amphibrachs and trochees at random *(ha-BO-ker,* line 2;

RE-ga, line 4; *BE-ka,* line 6; *kab-LE-hu,* line 7). Quadrisyllabic paeons, though placed mostly at line ends (lines 1, 4, 7, 9) and mid-line pauses (ha-*ye*-ri-*A,* line 7) in effect counterbalance the strong accents of both iambic and amphibrachic feet. Gilboa also varies the placement of accents in the paeonic feet. While most of the paeons resemble an iambic pattern by having a secondary accent in the second syllable of the foot (e.g., ha-*mit*-a-GEL, line 5), several paeons have amphibrach-like accents in penultimately accentuated nouns (e.g., *u-ve-O-sher,* line 7, and *u-me-O-mek,* line 8).

It is no coincidence that Gilboa chooses similar nominal patterns in these cases. He also places them at nonpausal points, so as to emphasize their rhythmic difference. Anapests appear in various parts of the poem (lines 4, 5, 6, 8, 9): their random occurrence contributes to the work's relatively free rhythmic structuring, which is reinforced by three additional techniques. First, not only does Gilboa use trochaic feet to offset the iambic rhythm, he also juxtaposes the two in order to stress the dissonant accents (e.g., *ve-NID RE-ga,* line 4, and *be-ZIV BE-ka,* line 6)—rather than simply following an amphibrach with a trochee, which would engender a pattern of similarity. Again the parallel nominal and construct patterns are selected to highlight these metrically variant phrases. Second, in a few places Gilboa uses accentuated monosyllabic words which create automatic pauses in the meter: *hod,* line 6; *grof,* line 8; *esh,* line 9. Two of these monosyllables are followed by anapests and one by an amphibrach, a variability which again reflects Gilboa's avoidance of secondary rhythmic patterns. Third, there is a discrepancy between the number of feet in the verse line and the number of stresses: of the nine lines only two, lines 2–3 and 6, have an equal number of feet and stresses; and line 7, for example, has twelve metrical feet and eight stresses.

These prosodic aspects of Gilboa's early works do not differ radically from the standard versification forms of Hebrew poetry written in Erets Israel in the 1930s. In general, however, and increasingly so through the forties, his works display a greater freedom from the conventional norms used by his modernist contemporaries, Shlonsky and Alterman. It bears repeating that Gilboa's familiarity with Yiddish poetry undoubtedly influenced this freer metrical style.[11]

Gilboa, Shlonsky, and Alterman

Beyond their prosody, Gilboa's early poems differ from the works of Shlonsky and Alterman in other ways. These differences in romantic stylistics can be demonstrated by a comparison of Gilboa's *Ze yomi* (This is My Day)[12] with Shlonsky's *Be-laila ka-ze* (On a Night Like This) and Alterman's *Kol,* already considered for its metric characteristics. Gilboa wrote *Ze yomi* while serving in the British Army in North Africa in 1942–1943. Annotated "El Daabe" and published after the war in *Yalkut ha-re'im,* the poem depicts a sunrise scene near the battlefield.

זֶה יוֹמִי

הַבַּהַר נֶאֱחַז בַּבָּבוֹת
וּמַבְהִיק אֶת הַכָּר הַנִּפְחָד.
זֶה יוֹמִי לֹא נְתַתִּיו בַּעֲבוֹט.
זֶה יוֹמִי שֶׁלִּוַּנִי לִקְרַאת
שֶׁפַע יָמִים שֶׁל זְוָעָה וְלֹבֶן
קוֹרֵעַ צָעִיף מִשְׁחוֹרוֹת.
וּבָא מַחְשׁוֹפָם רָבוּץ רֹבֶד עַל רֹבֶד
אֶת אוֹר יוֹמִי זֶה הַגָּדוֹל לִכְרֹת.
וּבָא עֵירֻמָּם הַנָּדוֹן לְאִפּוּס
לְהַבְחִיל הַמָּרָה בְּרֶטֶשׁ הֲוָיָתָם.
וְאֶת אוֹר שְׁעָתִי זוֹ הַגְּדוֹלָה
מוֹבִילִים לְאֵבוּס
שֶׁבִּדְמֵי עוֹלָלִים נִכְתַּם.

This is My Day

The brightness is snared in my pupils
and illumines the frightened field.
This is my day, I've not given it as a pawn.
This is my day, it's brought me to a plenitude

of days of horror and whiteness
tearing a veil from blackness.
Their bareness lies layer upon layer
to slash the light of this, my great day.
Their nakedness, fated for oblivion,
thickens the gall with the crush of their being.
And they lead the light of this,
my great hour to a trough
stained with infants' blood.

The poem is filled with the conflicting dualities so prevalent in Gilboa's works. Words denoting bright light—for example, *bahar* (brightness), *mavhik* (shining), *loven* (whiteness), and *or* (light)—contrast with terms denoting darkness—for example, *sheḥorot* (black) and *nikhtam* (stained). The larger dramatic and emotional dimensions of the poem are also clashing ones. The day is great, yet it leads to "a plenitude/of days of horror"; the brightness of the "great day" is "slashed," its splendor destroyed. The brightness becomes "bareness" and "nakedness," uncovering too much of the war's fearsomeness. The "great hour" leads only to the tragic image of "infants' blood" in the trough, normally a place of respite and nourishment. Typical of Gilboa's oppositional style, these semantic juxtapositions create an undertone of irony through lines 9–10. Up to this point entirely metaphorical, the poem closes with a climactic image of unmitigated vulnerability and terror.[13]

Rhythmically, the use of several bisyllabic words with penultimate accents—*BA-har, SHE-fa, LO-ven, RO-ved, RE-tesh* (brightness, plenitude, whiteness, layer, crush)—disrupts the predominant amphibrachic meter, thereby emphasizing both the rhythmic difference of these words and, by extension, their ironic, or in the case of *RE-tesh,* violent purport. Similar dualities are reflected in some of the rhymed pairs of lines: *bavot/ba'avot/sheḥorot/likhrot* (pupils/as a pawn/blackness/slashes); *nifḥad/likrat* (frightened/to); *ipus/eivus* (oblivion/trough).

Ze yomi demonstrates Gilboa's early attempts to assume control of language, structure, and irony. Though there is some multiplicity and overstatement, Gilboa uses pointed restraint in the poem's images and metaphorical usages. With its combination of emotive diction, strong but constrained repetition, and succinct, trimeter lines, it projects much forcefulness. Its dualistic tone of jubilance and dismay emphasizes the poignant disparity between a conditioned, triumphant view of battle and the actual terror and vulnerability one feels at the front.

Ze yomi differs from Shlonsky's *Be-laila ka-ze* in several ways. Gilboa presents a well-defined specific time and place for the dramatic situation: the dawn of the morning after a battle ("the frightened field"). By his heightened diction ("this is my day" and "this my great hour") and bountiful alliterative usages (ha-*B*ahar . . . Ba-Ba*V*ot, Ne'e*ḥ*az . . . ha-*N*if*Ḥ*ad, u-ma*V*hi*K* . . . ha-*K*ar), Gilboa magnifies the experience of dawn's light into a momentous soul-searing experience. In contrast, *Be-laila ka-ze* presents a dark night—it could be any dark night—which serves only as a clever premise for a not-so-momentous social-moral message. While Shlonsky playfully uses the image of darkness as a metonymy for the world's wants, Gilboa fervidly heaps metaphor upon metaphor to express the conflicted emotions of an individual who is at once enamored of the dawn and dismayed at the horrors it bares. Shlonsky is gently philosophical; Gilboa is highly disquieted. Shlonsky is distant, cool, witty; Gilboa is engaged, temperamental, dismayed. Ending with a chiding jest, *Be-laila ka-ze* offers a fairly transparent idea; closing with a grim discovery, *Ze yomi* dramatically depicts a fearsome experience.

בְּלַיְלָה כָּזֶה

אָזְנִי הַחֵרְשָׁה לֹא הִטֵּיתִי לִשְׁמֹעַ.
עֵינַי הַסּוּמוֹת לֹא פָּקַחְתִּי לִרְאוֹת.
יֵשׁ לַיְלָה קָשֶׁה, אָטוּם וְגָבֹהַּ
שֶׁבּוֹ מִסְתַּלְּקִים הַמַּרְאוֹת.

בְּלַיְלָה כָּזֶה גַּם הַיָּד הַנִּמְתַּחַת
נִקְפֶּצֶת לְפֶתַע־פִּתְאֹם וְקוֹפֵאת:
רָפָה הִיא בְּלַיְלָה כָּזֶה מִלָּקַחַת,
עַל כֵּן מְהַסֶּסֶת לָתֵת.

הָאֵלֶם רוֹבֵץ עַל הַפֶּתַח כְּנֶדֶר.
קְפוּאָה, כִּגְזַר־דִּין אֲפֵלָה בֶּחָלָל.

סְתָם־כָּךְ תְּסוֹבֵב הַכַּפְתּוֹר שֶׁבַּחֶדֶר,
וְלֹא יִדָּלֵק הַחַשְׁמַל.

On a Night Like This[14]

I didn't incline my deaf ear to hear.
I didn't open my blind eyes to see.
The night is dense, opaque and high,
in it the visions withdraw.

On a night like this even a hand extended
suddenly jumps and is still:
On a night like this it's too weak to take,
and so it hesitates to give.

Muteness lies at the door, a promise.
Darkness, gelid, a decree in the air.
Just turn on the switch in the room,
and the light will not come on.

Though Shlonsky speaks of a dark, silent night, by the second stanza he offers a kind of moral message. When the night—symbolically, the world—is so "dense, opaque and high [i.e., deep]," there is no possibility of human contact or succor, no way to ask for or to offer help. The third stanza accentuates the symbolic nature of the poem with two similes: *ke-neder* "like a promise [or vow]," which I have truncated in the translation; and *ki-gezar-din,* "like a decree [that is, God's severe judgment or punishment]." These moralistic terms have a dual role: They connote a feeling of expectancy—Will the promise be fulfilled? Will the judgment be severe? And they enjoin the reader to light up the night, to fill the world with goodness and caring, not darkness and need. As the last line intimates, however, it cannot be done simply by turning a switch; that alone will not bring on the light.

In sum, Shlonsky uses the cover of night as a mini-morality play, a poetic existential statement. Because of descriptive words such as "dense," "opaque," and "darkness," the depiction of this particular night appears realistic and unique. However, "muteness," "high," *gavo'ah*—one of Gilboa's favorite metaphorical adjectives[15]—and the personifications "the visions withdraw" and "muteness lies at the door" give the night both human and symbolic dimensions. The message is serious, certainly, but the tone is just as playful as it is pathetic, a typical Shlonsky-Russian combination. Along with the smoothly flowing, unvaried meter and rhyme, the opening and closing pairs of lines, with their respective double ironies and casual prank (the broken light switch), highlight the poet's success in creating both a cleverly wrought and a morally evocative work.

One of the major differences between *Ze yomi* and Alterman's *Kol* (where the use of imagery is typical of that poet's early works), is the disparate use of metaphor. Like Shlonsky, Alterman regales in abstract metaphorical figures.

קוֹל

הַלַּיְלָה עִמְעֵם בִּזְכוּכִית וְעָשָׁן
שָׁמְמָה הַכִּכָּר הַסּוֹחֶרֶת.
וְשָׁמַיִם הָלְכוּ עִם נֵרָם הַיָּשָׁן
מִן הָעִיר הָאַחַת
אֶל עִיר אַחֶרֶת.

בַּדְּרָכִים הָרֵיקוֹת קוֹל דִּבֵּר וְנָדַם
וְהָיְתָה אָזְנְךָ הַשּׁוֹמַעַת
מַה גְּדוֹלוֹת הַמִּלִּים שֶׁנּוֹתְרוּ לְבַדָּן,
נְתוּקוֹת מִתְּשׁוּבָה וָדַעַת –

מֶה חָזְקוּ, מָה הִבְהִיקוּ עַד אֵין לְהַכִּיר!
מַה יָּפְתָה חֶפְשָׁתָן בְּצִיּוֹת הַקֹּר!
לְבָבְךָ הַנָּסוֹג,
הֶהָדוּף אֶל הַקִּיר,
אֶת נָגְהָן הַמַּקְפִּיא יִזְכֹּר!

Voice

The night grew dark in glass and smoke
desolate was the mercantile square.
And the heavens walked with their old candle
from one town
to another.

On the empty roads a voice spoke and was silent
and your ears would hear
how great were the words which remained alone,
cut off from response and understanding—

How strong they were, how wondrously lustrous!
How lovely their freedom in the wastelands of cold!
Your retreating heart,
pressed to the wall,
will remember their freezing gleam![16]

Thematically parallel to Shlonsky's poem, *Kol* offers an eerier and more palpable image of night than does *Be-laila ka-ze.* The opening scene reflects desolation and mournfulness, both of which are engendered by the image of the "old candle," perhaps the sunset or a memorial candle, a symbol of death. The imagistic figure of the night's growing dark "in glass and smoke"—an image of an industrialized urban landscape—also suggests the aftermath of violence, perhaps a pogrom. The heavens moving from one town to another is ambiguous; it may represent the spread of darkness as the sun sets or the spread of violence, without heaven's intercession, from one community to the next. This is often the case in Alterman's poetry: the simultaneous delineation, through unseemly or distant metaphors, of both a concrete and a symbolic dramatic situation.

The second stanza enlarges the scene to the roads outside the town. Here the situation is even more desolate; but there is a voice and its words, though brief, intimate the presence of an auditor. This is the speaker, a lonely wanderer who has left the town—a familiar folkloristic image in Alterman's works—and becomes enraptured by the voice's words, themselves a lonely entity, "cut off from response and understanding." The voice's description and its effect on the wanderer are again dualistic: on the one hand, it is tremendously impressive; on the other, it seems competely ineffectual in its communication. In either case the ambiguity of the voice enlarges the sense of wonderment and uncertainty created in the first stanza.

The third stanza offers a paean to the voice's words—an ironic one in view of the heightened ambiguity of the voice in the prior stanza. The exclamatory diction further accentuates the ambiguity: the words' attributes—"strong," "fantastically lustrous," "lovely," and possibly "freedom"—clash with the images that follow: "the wastelands of cold," the wanderer's "retreating heart/pressed to the wall," and the "freezing gleam." In itself an oxymoron, the last-noted image again highlights the ambiguous nature of the voice. The phrase *ma hivhiku ad ein lehakir* (line 9) also connotes an ironic message; literally, it translates as "how the words shone unto unrecognition."

With these multiple aspects of ambiguity and irony, *Kol* presents quite a puzzle for the reader. A closer look at its several dimensions may help to clarify its meaning. First, it suggests a dichotomy between the town and the open road. The town reeks of desolation, industrialization, mercantilism, aging, possibly violence and death. By virtue of the rhetoric which describes it, the open road is a source of liberation. Here the emptiness is welcome, for it is here that the voice and the words may be heard. Further, precisely because they are uncommunicative, the words symbolize the essence of freedom; they are not spoken for a concrete purpose, for a particular "response," or for understanding *(teshuva va-da'at,* line 8). Instead, the words in themselves become "lustrous," the experience of the freedom of the open road unforgettable. The wanderer revels in the voice's detachment from the city, from purposefulness. Though "retreating" and "pushed to the wall"—these descriptives may connote an actual liberation from the city and its strictures—the wanderer is overwhelmed by the ironic beauty of the words' intangible meaning. Alterman may be implying a larger connotation, namely, that the words depicted here are those of the modernist poet: moving beyond the usual pale of poetic tradition, the freedom can be exhiliarating.

The metaphors in *Kol*'s first stanza (lines 1 and 3–5) are not just abstract, they are surreal: the image of the heavens "[walking] with their old candle/from the one town to the other" is reminiscent of many Chagall paintings. In contrast, the metaphors in *Ze yomi* tend to be concrete, with personification the key mode of figurative expression. The field is "frightened," the days "[have] accompanied" the speaker to many moments of crisis, the whiteness of the days "[tears away] a veil from blackness," the days' bareness "[slashes] the light." In general, Alterman's imagery is distanced and cognitively demanding ("the words . . . cut off from response and understanding"), while Gilboa's is concrete and visually affirming ("the brightness is snared *[ne'eḥaz]* in my pupils").

Instead of a series of abstractions, Gilboa offers a series of equivalences—repetitions and synonymic words and phrases which continually accentuate both the graphic and the emotional aspects of the poem. These include "brightness," "illumines," "whiteness," "bareness," "nakedness," "light," "my day," "days," and "my hour," and the various phrases of illumination and baring of the day's realities. Contrasting expressions abound in both poems, but Alterman's dualism is derived more from the larger thematic dimensions of *Kol,* while Gilboa's is shaped by an effusive spate of antonymic verbiage.

Finally, much like the bulk of Shlonsky's poetry, Alterman's works generally come across as impersonal and nonautobiographical, suffused with unreal, symbolic worlds whose meaning must be sought beneath the surface of the poems.[17] In the case of Gilboa, the surface is replete with markers of reality, individual personality and emotionality, all of which are accompanied and shaped by a sharply heightened diction and an overflow of emphatic sound patterns.[18]

Ze yomi also reflects the blend of poetic and stylistic usages inherent in the context of Hebrew as a linguistic polysystem. The three-word opening line in itself transmits to the reader at least three levels of style: *bahar* (brightness) is a Shlonsky-like neologism, formed as a segolate from the word *bahir* (bright); *ne'eḥaz* (an allusion to the Binding of Isaac story in Genesis 22, where the ram which replaces Isaac as Abraham's sacrifice is "snared in the bramble bush" *[ne'eḥaz ba-sevakh])* creates a resonance of both sacrality and trauma for the dualistic image of the coming of the dawn; and *bavot* (eye pupils) is used by both traditional and modernist poets.

Most of *Ze yomi's* lexicon is standard, but the work contains two additional terms which demonstrate Gilboa's blend of traditional and new vocabulary usages. The term *ipus* (line 9), which I have translated as "oblivion," is derived from *efes* (zero or nothing). Gilboa uses the term in a metaphorical context: by speaking of the "whiteness" *(loven)* and "bareness" *(maḥsof)* of the war days, he conveys the glaring horrors that each sunrise brings. When he adds that the days' "nakedness" *(eirum)* is "fated for oblivion" (or nothingness), he is synonymically intensifying the message that the sights in war are always of repeated horror and death. However, the word *ipus* (in the sense of zero) is also a military term referring to the particular conditions on a rifle range or battlefield. Though Gilboa may have chosen *ipus* to rhyme with *eivus* (trough, in line 12), the term plays a dual role in suggesting the technological aspects of warfare. In addition, like *ipus* and *bahar,* the neologism *retesh* (crush) stands out in its modernness. While *retesh* highlights the acute violence of the war, *ipus* accentuates the poem's central irony—that the usually captivating experience of sunrise is undone by its revelation of those who died during the night.

The Allure of Nature

Of the thirty-five poems in the original 1942 *La-ot* collection, Gilboa retained only twenty-one in *Keḥulim va-adumim,*[19] to which he added eight new works. Among the retained originals were seven which present nature either as the main topic or as a strong secondary subject. Fully one third of the *La-ot* poems which Gilboa included in his major 1963 collection are his earliest nature poems, while only two of the fourteen not included in *Keḥulim va-adumim* are of this genre. In making these selections, Gilboa certainly demonstrated his abiding attachment to the poetics of romanticism.

The four nature poems which follow *Halelu Yah* are varied in situation, in style, and in the image of the speaker. In *Ba-emek* (In the Valley) the speaker is a homeless nonentity who, despite his feelings of sadness, smallness, and loneliness, wants to rebound and overcome his fate. Samson-like, he cries, "and I'll yet embrace the columns of mountains," an allusion to Samson's suicide as a heroic act.[20] He ends with a fervent vow.

וְאֶשְׁלַח עוֹד רוּחִי עִם אִוְשַׁת הֶעָלִים
אֲשֶׁר בָּעֵמֶק יוֹם יוֹם שִׁיר־יוֹם־רִאשׁוֹן
שָׁרִים.

And I will yet send forth my spirit with the rustling of the leaves
which is sung in the valley each day as the
first Psalm-of-the-week.

The language of *Ba-emek* ranges from the biblical *ve-od elpot amudei harim* (and I'll yet grasp columns of mountains) and *ve-ha-bika mele'a atsmot ḥayim* (and the valley is full of the bones of the living), to the talmudic *lo mi-kan ve-lo me-hatam* (literally, I am not from here nor from there—that is, a stranger or wanderer), to the liturgical *shir-yom-rishon* (first Psalm-of-the-week), and to the Alterman-like abstract metaphor *u-nekuda ketana nemasa ka-etsev* (and a small point dissolves like sadness)—to which Gilboa adds a romantic touch: *ha-ne'eḥaz be-vein ha-arbayim* (which is snared in the twilight). As in his other early works, the range of linguistic layers and poetic usages demonstrates Gilboa's simultaneous devotion to the romantic spirit and the modernist style.

In *Ba-sheki'a*,[21] the end of day receives the same sort of grand, mythological treatment as does the sunrise in *Halelu Yah*. The mythohistorical scene depicted is of the ancient Temple ruins, completely desolate and empty—a metonymy for the desolation of the Land. The speaker proclaims himself "wondrously adorned [like a priest],"[22] as he oversees the setting of the "sun of royal-purple into the sea." His hands grow tired as he "shades his [tired] eyes that shone for a moment." In the vein of "the glory that was Rome," the speaker-poet, engaged in a fantasy of ritual grandeur, disappointedly notes the reality of the situation: the Temple rites are not renewed, "the blood of broken-necked heifers is not sprinkled about." His imaginative act of reconstruction does not overcome the real desolation. Much as he cannot suspend the sunset, so is he unable to reconstitute the grandeur of the past.

By invoking the ancient scene with extravagant archaizations—*shevilim . . . reiku me-adam* (paths . . . emptied of people), *bi-sheko'a shemesh argaman ha-yama* (as the sun of [royal] purple set into the sea)—and the language of sacrificial rite and miracle (the allusion to Moses's hands in Exodus 17:8–16), Gilboa infuses the sunset with the aura of mythic demise.[23] Daytime's last rite, projected onto a scene of discontinued ritual, engenders a sense of unequivocal finality. Moreover, by combining the natural phenomenon of sunset with the barren Temple grounds, Gilboa imagistically redefines the passing of day as a symbolic embodiment of an ancient ceremony which has been forever lost. While it combines myth, history, ritual, and nature, *Ba-sheki'a* embodies more a mythopoetic depiction of a place than a rendering of a natural event.

Although the usage is muted, Gilboa injects a "modernism" into the archaized text in the last line: *ve-lo hitnagen me-elav laḥan ha-dam asher la-ma-*

grefot (and the tune of the [ritual] shovels' blood did not ring out by itself). The word for "sound" or "ring out" *(hitnagen)* is a fairly modern term. *Laḥan,* "tune" or "melody," has medieval origins, but with its Shlonsky-like segolate character *(LA-ḥan)* it has been fully adopted in the modern Hebrew lexicon.

Ru'aḥ-erev (Evening Wind), also reminiscent of *Halelu Yah,* is far more evocative in its imagery and less heavy-handed in its use of allusive language and mythological themes.[24]

רוּחַ־עֶרֶב

גַּלִּים, גַּלֵּי רוּחַ מְדַפְּקִים אֶל גְּבִיעַי הֶהָפוּךְ –
אָהֳלִי.
כְּסַאַן מִשְׁבָּרִים בְּיָם סוֹעֵר, פָּתוּחַ,
שֶׁמְּמַלְּטִים סוֹדָם אֶל אִי.
וְרַעַשׁ בָּם נִצְנַף עַל שׁוֹאַת מֶרְחַקִּים
וְתַחֲנוּנִים מִלֵּב יְתַנּוּ חֲרִישִׁית
עַל בְּתוּלֵי מִזְמוֹרִים שֶׁלְּנוֹגְנָם מְחַכִּים,
בְּשַׁרְבִיטוֹ יִגַּע וְיִתְגַּל פֶּלֶא הָרֵאשִׁית.

Evening Wind

Waves, waves of wind rap at my overturned goblet—
my tent.
Like the clamor of swells in a stormy, open sea,
that casts its secret onto an island.
And in them flowed a noise of distant destruction
and heartfelt prayers quietly proclaim
virginal psalms that await their player,
he wields his wand and the wonder of creation is revealed.

This is less a poem of enthrallment with nature than a treatment of nature's inspirational role in the creation of poetry—a significant theme throughout Gilboa's oeuvre. Here the poet depicts the speaker alone in the evening while "waves of wind" beat at his tent. The noise of these "waves" gives rise to "whispered supplications," which in turn spawn "virginal psalms that await their player." The player is presumably the poet, who, like a conductor-magician—a parallel but less sacral image than the speakers in *Halelu Yah* and *Ba-sheki'a*—"wields his wand," and "the wonder of creation is revealed."

The poem's romanticism is unabashed in its poet-nature scenario, in its images of wind and waves, poetry and prayer, shipwreck, and magical rescue through the creative process. The language is fairly archaic and allusive—three terms, *nitsnaf* (flow), *yetanu* (proclaim) and *ve-yitgal* (reveals) are traceable to Bialik[25]—and generally identifiable with the standardized usages of the Age of Bialik poets. An interesting exception is the word *sa'an* (noise), a modern term usually associated with the rustling sound of standing grain.[26] Gilboa uses the term here in connection with the sound of a wave, the same image that Bialik uses in *Ba-sade* (In the Field), where the speaker is so taken by the sight of the standing grain that he "drowns" in the sheaves and is "pulled into the flow of their waves." (It is in Bialik's description of the sheaves "flowing like the waves of the sea from the hill to the valley" that he uses the term *nitsnafu* noted above.) The intertextuality of *nitsnafu* and the metaphorical contexts of grain and waves once again demonstrate the blend of lexical ingredients which characterizes Gilboa's early poems.

The central motif of *Ru'aḥ-erev* is sound or noise. Both *ra'ash* and *sa'an* mean noise, but *sa'an* connotes a more intense sound. Other sounds include rapping *(midapkim),* the stormy sea, and the closing, unheard music of the psalms. At the same time, however, it contains several motifs of quietude. The prayers are described as "whispered" *(ḥarishit)* and the waves cast "their secret" *(sodam)* toward an island. Like *Halelu Yah,* the poem reflects the use of clashing entities, a convention to which Gilboa was continually drawn.[27]

The secondary image, the speaker's tent as an "overturned goblet," has a dual function: it personalizes the actual dramatic situation—the speaker is trapped in a fragile tent during a raging storm—and adds a measure of irony to the poem. The wine goblet *(gavi'a),* a recurring motif in Gilboa's early poetry, is an image of blessing or celebration, while here it is "overturned," a symbol of blessing-turned-misfortune. It is only through transformation to a player-poet that the speaker can be rescued and renewed, and thus *Ru'aḥ-erev* evokes the transcendent power of poetry in the face of adversity.

Songs of Self

While Gilboa's early nature lyrics overflow with romantic enthrallment and mythic transformations, most of the personae in *La-ot* are lonely and frustrated, struggling for self-definition and acceptance. In the tradition of stock romantic themes, they find a palliative in the embrace of nature. The landscape, the wind, the sunrise, the sunset—all give them a sense of belonging and the strength to face a bleak future. In *Ru'aḥ-erev,* the speaker, mired in the storm, becomes the "player" of the psalms; he sets them to music and brings on the "wonder of creation" with his wand-baton.

Gilboa forges a close connection here between nature and poetry. Both are sources of salvation, especially for the downhearted. The lonely poet-speaker's motto is *Ani ra'ev ve-shar*—"I am hungry and sing [that is, write poetry]."[28] But like nature, poetry is merely an idealized palliative. As already noted, Gilboa achieved neither recognition nor acceptance in the early years of his creativity, and the poetics of his works were shaped by both his passion for nature and poetry and his painful awareness of himself as a poet apart. His "songs of self" cycles aptly illustrate this combination of enthrallment and dejection.

The short four-poem cycle *Ha-na'ar ha-meshorer* represents Gilboa's imagistic entry into the exploration of poetic creativity. Typical of his works in this early period, these poems combine the components of nature poetry, mythological imagery, and the "song of self" genre.[29] The narrative voice in the title poem describes the different stages in the young poet's Bildung from his ingenuous investiture to his assumption of a mature poetic sensibility. Surely autobiographical—in later interviews Gilboa often shared his painful memories of want and rejection in this formative period[30]—the narrative tells of a young poet-persona who, though flooded with inspiration, remains unappreciated.

The persona moves figuratively through four stages of encounter: 1) While "the jewel of dawn burned with a deep and cold light," "the tall boy" naively drinks from the goblet of poetry and is fatefully burned by its fire. 2) While "the tips of sapphires stretched to the lips of a young day," "the sleeping boy" is beset by vision and sound. 3) While "the heart of day raised [copper columns] to support the heavens," "the wakeful boy" is a loner who struggles for his poetry's recognition. 4) While "the granite mirror, the pool of the ancient sun's reflection, grew pale," "the aged boy," threatened but no longer fearful, confronts the world—but at the same time becomes a confirmed wanderer.

Two other "songs of self" cycles in *La-ot* explore this state of simultaneous affirmation and frustration. In *Ba-derekh ha-ola* (The Ascending Path),[31] the road taken by the poet represents both his experience of aliyah and his decision to become a poet.[32] The path metaphor, fraught with duality, is expressed in oxymorons: it is "dangerous in its rest" *(mesukenet be-nuḥa);* it "sleeps [but lies] upon mines"; those who walk on it are doomed by the friendless but ambiguous fate of "the blessed sickliness" *(ha-ḥolaniyut ha-brukha).* Dualistic figures of speech create perceptions of both aliyah and poetry as laudable enterprises but fatal neuroses. On the one hand, the path is "like the Queen of Night"—a gothic, web-entangled creature, a cursed, pain-wracked witch. On the other, it is a Mother Earth figure, "to [whom] the world is bound with a rope. Like twins at birth."

Expressing both wonderment and frustration, the *Ba-derekh ha-ola* cycle depicts this ironic dilemma in a series of images. The poet is a naive Samson-Narcissus whose vision is threatened by the archetypical traitor-seductress Delilah, described as both "the stealer of light" and "the inspirer of light." The poet is young, daring, joyous; he forgets all past woes. His path seems clear and promising; but soon he is abandoned. The path turns into a "clamorous fire," yet he presses on toward the "diamond that calls [him] to despondence." The metaphors' blatant dualities clearly express Gilboa's ambivalent feelings toward his aliyah experience.

The cycle ends with a paradoxical image of inspiration and pain, both redolent with mythological connotations. On the one hand, in part three of the five-poem cycle the poet's voice is heard in "deep sounds" of inanimate objects. A primitive, natural source, the sounds lead the poet to an understanding of the great mysteries: "the sign engraved in stone," "the secret revealed to the child," "the cry of the nearing storm." These revelations bring him even greater magical powers. He knows the inner thoughts of colors, the mysteries of the fabled curtain *(pargod)* that shields the Divine Presence. He has the power to purify the unclean.

On the other hand, the poet-persona is seen in deterioration. In the closing poem he is dressed in filthy rags. Like the traditional Christ-like figure of the Jewish Messiah, he stands freezing in the cold, covered with wounds, wishing for death.[33] But the image of poetic power beats back his despair, and joy prevails in his love of "the sweetness dripping from plants," "the quiet that spreads through the hours." Poetic inspiration, that sudden, romantic force which forms the poet's inner expression, soothes the pain that accompanies him on his difficult path.

The second "songs of self" cycle, *El ha-ata ha-aḥer* (To the Other You),[34] is composed of six separately titled poems, each of which is based on a condition or attribute of self which is shaped by the behavior or attitude of others toward the poet. As such, the poetic personality and sensibility are defined both internally and socially. Once again the poet sees himself as an outcast, ridiculed by those who cannot understand his mission. Wounded and ragged, racked by hunger, rejected as ugly, laughed at and cursed, the boy-poet persists, saying, "I still sing and hunger before you." He vows "a day of revenge that is near," retains his "purified look," and awaits the opportunity to grasp "the moments of power."[35] He knows full well the frustration of "the buried dream." His voice is undone by the "noise" of the streets, his "tablets are broken," his "cry has been silenced on the roads." Powerless, voiceless, and vulnerable, the poet resigns himself to the lonely life of social and artistic rejection. In later works, including the Holocaust poems of the 1940s and the modernistic poems on poetic process of the late 1960s, Gilboa returns again and again to the themes of the powerlessness of the poet and the essential fragility of the poetic experience.

Visionary Images

Within the larger themes, Gilboa establishes in these early writings a network of motifs which also pervade much of his later poetry. Predominant is his repeated use of eye imagery. In *Ki az etsak,* eye images are related to fire and light or to their extinction, in both concrete and figurative usages. When Gilboa writes "and piece by piece the battlefield ashened with extinguished eyes," the metonymy conveys a vivid, horrible spectacle—presumably a World War II scene—filled with corpses. The figure turns inward, however, relating more to the emotional response of the speaker-screamer. Shock and despair are conveyed by "my muteness-sight" and by "fire, kindled in my eye, [which] has gone out." When the voice rises in muted but hopeful tones toward the end of the poem, the images are again of the eyes: "Every eye a torch. And every pupil—a wick." From the very earliest of Gilboa's writings, eyes are the mirrors of emotions, the absorbing and reflecting instruments of feeling.

Also reflected in eye imagery are the themes of renewal and revival. In *Basheki'a,* as if in a symbolic rite of futile stop-time, the priest-figure's hands "grow heavy as they shade my eyes/which sparkled for a moment/and they are tired."[36] The fleeting spark of light from the eyes figuratively gives renewed life to the antique scene—a replay of sorts—as it does to the dying light at the end of day.

Parallel uses of the eye motif appear in other poems of this early period in connection with holy acts, holy figures, and images of fire or light. In *Yadati, be-onyi esha'er* (I Knew, In My Poverty I Shall Remain),[37] the speaker is desperate, at wit's end. At dawn, like a lover responding to the intoxicating smells of the sun-beloved, he is revitalized. But at night, the voice reveals, "I feel/the terror of the creepings of the moon/trembling like the rings of fire in the pupils [of the eyes, *ishonav]* of a prophet/conjuring among spirits, at night, in the midst of a forest." The night itself, the dying of the light, is a metonymy for the speaker's despair; but the "terror" actually derives from the visionary fire in the prophet's eyes. It is the visionary poet's unrelenting imagination which causes his artistic trepidation. Fearful of the very nature of poetic inspiration, the reluctant poet is continually beset by visions imprinted on his mind's eye—visions over which he has no control. This terrifying fire is a recurring image throughout Gilboa's works.

The eye imagery in *Bo ha-erev ba-parvar* (Twilight in the Suburb)[38] presents yet another recurrent theme—the poet's perception of and allusion to moral issues in addition to aesthetic ones. Posing as an artist, the speaker here tries to capture the scene, which is immersed in sounds of anger and despair. Instead, he falls into a reverie, apparently brought upon him by "golden-shored islands [which] blind him under the shutting of his eyelids *[afapayim].*" The reverie is broken by the rapping sound of crutches: an old lame man totters by, holding the hand of a little blind boy. "He saw," says the poet-observer, "in the socket of the child's pupils burns the fire of agate." The speaker then closes his own eyes and decides to walk along with these figures—shutting out romantic reveries, as it were, and feeling the suffering he sees in real life. His is to be an earth-bound, concerned poetry, he seems to be saying, not simply a recording of stylized, myth-like images.[39] This issue is encountered frequently in *La-ot*[40] and reflects Gilboa's early confrontation of the question of aesthetic direction: Is he to be the artist-poet, painting sweet images of nature—or the engaged socially conscious poet, committed also to allaying human despair?

The depth of emotions derived from Gilboa's inner perception of moral issues in *La-ot* is accentuated by the variety of his eye imagery and frequent use of parts of the eye: *afapayim* (eyelids), *ishonim* and *bavot* (pupils), *risim* (eyelashes) and *sheka* (socket). The emotive quality of the imagery is intensified by the accompanying motifs of blindness and blinding, the opening and closing of the eyes, and the various forms and terms for light or fire.[41] The extensive use of this imagery—and accompanying sub-motifs such as blindness/clear-sightedness—contribute much to the figurative style of Gilboa's later poems.[42]

The Innovative Impulse

Shiri ha-paru'a, which closes the *La-ot* volume, shows how distinctive and innovative Gilboa was, even in his early work. Here, the duality of poet and poetry parallel the theme of the self vis-à-vis the other in the *El ha-ata ha-aḥer* cycle. A masterful statement of self-affirmation which proclaims the poet's sardonic victory over his adversaries, *Shiri ha-paru'a* is a paean to poetry, an ars poetica manifesto, and a psychological portrait of the poet in relation to his art. His rubric "wild poetry" reflects Gilboa's awareness that he used meter, rhythm, and rhyme more freely that his contemporaries. In addition, it most likely expresses his reaction to rejection by the poetry establishment.[43] As already noted, Gilboa published *La-ot* privately, without the assistance of any of the established publishing houses in Israel. The collection elicited no published review and no critical opinion. It was only with the publication of *Sheva reshuyot* (1949) that Gilboa began to establish his reputation.

In the same vein, very few of the poems collected in the original 1942 edition of *La-ot* were published previously in journals or newspapers, as is most often the case with volumes of collected works. Of the thirty-five poems gathered in the 1942 edition, only seven were previously published, and all of these were placed in the opening section of the volume.[44] Moreover, as already noted early in this chapter, when Gilboa edited the *"La-ot"* section of *Sheva reshuyot* for the volume's publication, he dropped fourteen of the original thirty-five works and replaced them with eight different ones, some new and some previously published but uncollected. These include Gilboa's first published poem, *Ki az etsak,* which was added as the lead poem of *Sheva reshuyot.* Therefore, even from the perspective of Gilboa's later editing of

Sheva reshuyot, it may be surmised that *La-ot* was seen as a somewhat immature offering and not given much attention by the reading public.

שִׁירִי הַפָּרוּעַ, עוֹד אֶחֱזֹר אֵלַי וְאֵלֶיךָ.
עוֹד אֶחֱזֹר לָאֶחָד. כִּי שְׁנֵינוּ אֶחָד.
אַדְבִּיקוֹ עוֹד בַּדֶּרֶךְ, אַדְבִּיק אֶת חֲלֵכָה.
שֶׁדְּבָרוֹ פָּרוּעַ כְּאַדַּרְתּוֹ – הַמַּטְלִית.
שֶׁדְּבָרוֹ נָטוּעַ כַּעֲטַרְתּוֹ שֶׁל שַׁלִּיט.
וְצַוּוֹ שֶׁעוֹד לֹא הָשְׁבַּת.

לֹא אֶטְשֵׁךְ הַשּׁוּרָה הַבְּשׂוּמָה וּמְפֻלֶּמֶת.
לֹא אַנִּיחֵךְ הַבְּשׂוֹרָה הַגְּשׁוּמָה וְנִרְגֶּמֶת.
שֶׁכָּל תָּג כְּתַלְתַּל. וְכָל קַו מְבֻדָּר.
וּבַיִת מִבַּיִת מַחֲלִיף קַרְנוֹתָיו.
כִּי אֵין, לֹא הָיָה עוֹד עוֹלָם מְסֻדָּר.
כִּי הֵן, זֶה הָיָה הַהוֹד שֶׁבַּשָּׁוְא.
כְּחֵן שֶׁל פְּסוּל־גְּבִישׁ, כְּסוֹד הַטָּרָף,
שֶׁנָּפַל וְנִרְסַס,
שֶׁנֻּגַּע וְהוּא עָף.

לָכֵן, שִׁירִי, לֹא אַלְבִּישְׁךָ עוֹד בְּשַׂק.
לָכֵן, נִירִי, לֹא אוֹבִישְׁךָ בְּשָׁרָב.
כִּי הֵן נִירִי רָחָב וּמִתַּעְתֵּעַ.
כִּי הֵן לְעִירִי רַק אָז אֶצְעַק.
וּבְנֵי עִירִי יֶהֱמוּ מֵרָעָב.
וְנִירִי מַצְמִיחַ בַּסְּתָו.
וּסְתָוִי אָבִיב פּוֹרֵחַ.
וַאֲבִיבִי לָרָעֵב
לֶחֶם זוֹרֵעַ.

My wild song, I'll yet return to me and to you.
I'll yet return to the one. For the two of us are one.
I'll yet overtake it, overtake the wretch.
Whose word is wild as its coat—a rag.
Whose word is implanted as the crown of a king.
And its command not yet denied.

I'll not abandon you, [my] perfumed and moist line.
I'll not leave you, [my] rained on and stoned [i.e., attacked] tidings.
Whose every jot is a curl. And every mark is scattered.
And one stanza exchanges its corners with another.
For there is no, never was, an ordered world.
And yes, that was the splendor of futility.
Like the charm of the crystal-flawed, like the secret of prey
that's fallen and shattered,
that's injured but flies.

And so, my song, I'll not yet wear you as mourning cloth.
And so, my field, I'll not scorch you with a desert wind.
For my field is broad and confounding.
For only then will I scream for my city.
The people of my city moan with hunger.
And my field gives forth bloom in the fall.
And my fall is a blossoming spring.
And for the hungry my spring
sows bread.[45]

Declaring his loyalty to his "wild song," the speaker acknowledges and defends his increasingly aberrant poetic endeavor. His feelings for his song, however, are more intense than loyalty. His return "to me and to you" and his statement "the two of us are one" in line 2 delineate a unity between them, a deeply psychological emotion, a nearly physical cohesion. The unifying act of returning to "the one" evokes a spiritual tone of monotheistic dimensions. For Gilboa, loyalty to his art is indeed a devotional, spiritually enhancing ideal.

At the same time, however, the poet seems to demean the poetic endeavor, calling it *ḥelekha,* "impoverished" or "wretched," a term often used for the unfortunate historic fate of the Jewish people. The speaker also refers to poetry as "wild" (i.e., "disheveled"), ragged as an impoverished person's coat (line 4). Here, too, is a mixed message: the term *aderet* often refers to a fancy, expensive coat, and just as often to the mantle of the prophet, especially Elijah's.[46] Moreover, *aderet* is a homonym meaning "splendor" or "beauty," much akin to "the crown of the king" in line 5.

The second stanza embellishes the speaker's fidelity to his art and simultaneously amplifies a sense of irony toward his particular method of poetic production. Referring indirectly to its "wildness," he claims (line 10) that his poetry reflects the true disorder of the universe. Its "wildness," though perceived as nonconformism, is a far more honest reflection of the way things are. "For there's no, never was an ordered world," he claims (line 11). His poetry embodies "futility's splendor" and "the charm of the crystal-flawed *[pesul-gevish]"*; these are oxymorons which combine conflicting attributes of beauty, charm, futility, and imperfection.[47] It is also akin to "prey" *(taraf)* which has been "injured but flies" (line 15), a fairly transparent metaphor for his persistence in creating art which might be considered aberrant.[48]

In the final stanza the poet-speaker turns away from mourning and celebrates the victory of his brand of poetry *(shir)* over the "hungry" (i.e., unsated) people of the city *(ir)*. His is an unconventional, productive field *(nir)*[49]—the repetitious internal rhyme is emphatic—which blossoms even in the fall, giving nourishment to the hungry. It could bring forth much bread, were it not for the cultural snobbishness and rejection of the "city" people, who have no notion of or need for beauty. Thus the poem ends with the classic dichotomy of countryside versus cityscape—a metonymy for Gilboa, the upstart, determined newcomer versus the smug and rejecting poetry establishment. Beauty's nurturing is abjured by the hungry but recalcitrant, self-deceiving city dwellers. The poet's loneliness turns into a sense of superiority; his rejection becomes self-affirmation.

The poetics of *La-ot* are comprised of five interconnected components which shape Gilboa's later works as well. First, a pain-filled personal dimension reflects his life as a young immigrant caught between Zionistic idealism and the poverty, loneliness, and rejection he experienced during his first years in the Land. He is beset by loss and aloneness *(she-khol hinḥani)*, utterly degraded, vilified and abused *(hem deḥafuni . . . ba-bivim)*; his self-esteem is entirely vitiated *(ata mekho'ar u-mityape)*; he is "naked and freezing" *(eirom ve-kofe),* wounded, in constant pain, emotionally bleeding; his scream is muted, unheard, his eyes "know weeping-profusion" *(rav-bekhe),* and he is completely at the end of his rope *(higati le-tav).*[50]

But the second component acts as a powerful emotional counterforce—his enthrallment with the nature and landscape of the Land. Indeed, the Land is his "one love" *(ahava aḥat);* and his heart overflows with scenes of its idyllic landscape. The mornings and evenings, the brooks, the fields, the rocks, the rain—all these capture his unbounded ardor. At the same time the Land is personified as Delilah, her face "dark and angry" *(lutim ve-zo'afim),* her eyes likened to "cats on the thresholds/waiting in ambush to pounce and spray the blood."[51] Thus the Land is two-faced: loved and yet feared, adored but flawed by the disappointment it invariably brings.

A third component is Gilboa's recurring usage of mythological or cosmological themes, language, and phraseology. The mythological catalogue includes such items as *pargod* (in the Midrash and Jewish mystical texts, the heavenly curtain behind which the divinity is hidden); dreams and ladders (Jacob's experience in Genesis 28); images of Moses, priestly officiants, prophetic figures, and "live bones"; and a variety of allusions to artifacts in the Holy Temple of Jerusalem. Parallel motifs include the spices and landscape of the Song of Songs and several allusions to the legal or spiritual state of sinfulness. Cosmological references include various stars, planets and comets, cosmic forces such as winds and storms, and dimensions of the heavenly firmament.

The fourth component is the theme of poetry itself, intertwined with the experience of being a poet. In *Ba-emek,* for example, the poet hears the leaves singing "the psalm-of-the-first-day." In *Ru'aḥ-erev,* the poet describes the noise of the sea and storm as intermeshed with the "virginal psalms" of the poet. In *Ha-na'ar ha-meshorer,* he sees the "gem of the firmament burning . . . with a deep and cold light"; he is dressed in the veil and moon-jewel of the young shepherd; "his fire blazes with the marble-glare of song"; and he yearns for "the good news of sound."[52]

The last component is Gilboa's varied use, even at this early stage, of a broad spectrum of linguistic sources and prosodic configurations. These include allusions to biblical, rabbinic, and liturgical texts;[53] archaisms which create a tone of sacrality or epiphany; extensive borrowings from the traditional lexicon of the Age of Bialik; neologisms, some generated by Gilboa but mostly taken from Shlonsky; and metrical and stanzaic structures which range from less-than-conventional to innovative.

In sum, in *La-ot* Gilboa dramatizes his inner consciousness into a poetics of oppositional forces—forces which ultimately shape the rhetorical and stylistic aspects of his later art. In the process he creates a personal poetry which is at once intimate in its self-revelatory character and definitive as a marker of his locus in literary history: at the transition between the Age of Romanticism and the Age of Modernism.

Chapter III

Poems of War and the Holocaust

Sheva reshuyot/Seven Domains, 1949

Sheva reshuyot presents a poetic chronology of Gilboa's experiences from 1942 to 1949. The volume is divisible into three sections: 1) poems written in North Africa, Malta, and Italy when Gilboa served in the British Eighth Army and the Jewish Brigade; 2) poems on the Holocaust, including personal elegies on the poet's murdered family, most of which were written after the war; 3) poems written from 1946 to 1949 during Gilboa's postwar activities in Italy, France, Austria, the Netherlands, and Belgium and after his return to Erets Israel.[1]

Some of the works are based upon childhood memories or soldiering experiences; others ponder the role of poetry and the poet in the grand scheme of human vulnerability. Still others, mainly the poems written in 1948–1949, attempt to recapture, if momentarily, the ecstasy and comfort of nature, love, and the imagination. Throughout, Gilboa continues to express the inner life shaped by his experiences and to experiment with language and structure as he broadens his range of aesthetic expressivity.

"Sefer ḥayei olam" (The Book of Eternal Life)

Written while Gilboa served in the Jewish Brigade from 1942 to 1945, the first "book" of *Sheva reshuyot* takes its name from the familiar call-to-the-Torah blessing, *ve-ḥayei olam nata be-tokhenu*—"[You, God] have implanted in us eternal life." Gilboa no doubt uses the phrase ironically. These poems are not about the promise of eternity at all, but about the harsh realities of life in this world—suffering, death, the agonies of the war, and the Holocaust.

After a short epigraph about loss and the affirmation of memory, the book opens with an untitled elegy about the death of a person alternately identified as "the wondrous," "the guest," "a friend of mine," "my brother," and "a beloved brother."

הוּא נוֹפֵל. מָת. צוֹנֵחַ.
הוּא עַל סַף הַשְּׁעָרִים.

הוּא הַפֶּלְאִי, הָאוֹרֵחַ,
בָּז לַמָּוֶת גְּלוּי עֵינַיִם.

הָאוֹרֵחַ הוּא לִי אַחָא.
אָח שֶׁלִּי הוּא. אָח אָהוּב.
מִי פִּלֵּל שֶׁנִּפְגֹּשׁ כָּכָה –
הוּא נוֹפֵל. וַאֲנִי טָרוּף.

He falls. Falters. Drops.
He's at the threshold of the double gates.
He is the wondrous, the guest
scorning death open-eyed.

The guest is a friend of mine.
He is my brother. A beloved brother.
Who ever thought that we'd meet like this—
He falls. And I am torn apart.[2]

At the end the speaker identifies so closely with the "beloved brother" that when he "falls," the speaker himself feels as if he himself is killed, "torn apart [*taruf;* like prey]." The obvious impression is that Gilboa is mourning here the death of his brother and mentor, Joshua, murdered by the Nazis with the rest of his family in Radzivilov. This reading, however, is problematic. In May, 1982, when Gilboa spoke briefly at the Israel Prize celebration in his honor, he recounted how he had scribbled the short poem *Po lo she'arim* (Here There are No Gates)[3] on a cigarette pack on the eve of Simḥat Torah in 1942. He was stationed at the time near the Bitter Lake in Egypt and later discovered that was the very day on which all the Jewish adults of his home town, including his parents and siblings, were murdered.[4] When the elegy was composed, in the spring of 1942, Gilboa was not yet aware of his family's deaths or of the extent of the Nazi persecution. The "beloved brother," then, may refer to an army friend killed in battle or to the Holocaust in general. In any case, the poem sets a mournful tone for the entire *Sheva reshuyot* collection.

The first group of poems in *"Sefer ḥayei olam"* contains a blend of genres. While it includes Gilboa's first poetic responses to the war in North Africa, in this period Gilboa seems also to have experienced a renewal of inspiration after one of the recurrent bouts of writer's block he suffered throughout his career. In *El kadmon* (To the Primeval)[5] he considers himself to be the same young rebellious poet *(na'ar mored)* that he was once was. Feeling that "nothing's been lost of the imagination that's returned," the poet prays that his "flawed song" *(ha-nigun ha-nagu'a)* will become transformed into a poetry of renewed hope *(ha-nigun ve-sivro).*

But in a more pervasive way, the terrors of war loom large in these works and begin to dominate Gilboa's artistic imagination. Though *Li af peraḥ-anan* (Not Even One Flower-Cloud)[6] is also about the creative process, its contents blatantly state that the blood and ashes of war sweep away all the niceties of poetry. "Never did I pick a cloud-flower on the roads," says the speaker in the opening line.

Lines 8–9 describe what the poet actually had to deal with in the fire of battle.

וּשְׂעָרוֹת זָעֲקוּ מֵרָאשִׁים כִּנְעֹרֶת
מֻצֶּתֶת בְּאֵשׁ וְעוֹלָה עִם הַיַּעַר.

And hairs screamed on heads like chaff
set on fire and burnt with the forest.

His dreams and memories help the poet overcome some of those horrors (in *Zikhron ha-tov* [Memory of the Good],[7] he rises every morning with renewed happiness and a feeling of "human majesty")—but the day brings only piles of bodies and blood. In most of these poems the poet-speaker vacillates between hope and anguish, between an idealized view of the world and the relentless realities he confronts on a daily basis.

For Gilboa, poetry was also a victim of those realities. Witnessing the fighting at Tobruk, El-Daabe, and Bengazi, he wonders whether he will even live to write again. In the prayer-poem *Tefilat azkara* (Memorial Prayer)[8] he pleads for time itself to stop; he feels like a man drowning in a gigantic, uncontrollable wave. He wants the opportunity to remember, to look back and write about his experiences, and "to sow the seed of tomorrow,"[9] — that is, to continue to be a productive poet.

"Sefer ḥayei olam" is based on the same dual consciousness found in *La-ot.* Drawing on his war experiences here, Gilboa simultaneously explores his inner life with many of the same motifs used earlier in his poems of nature and the Land. Once again the language is heightened and hyperbolic, often archaic in diction, tone, and phraseology. The battlefield replaces the natural landscape as the background for these works, but the poetics remains the same.

In *El kadmon,* for example, the vocabulary is borrowed from several traditional sources: the "anvil" or source of poetry has had "its spirit breathed into it" (Genesis 2:7); the poet prays for a poetic spirit "mightier than [the prophet's] screech (*sherika,* Jeremiah 18:16); the day of renewed poetic vigor is sacralized as *ve-yitkadesh yom,* literally, "may the day be sanctified" (from the liturgical phrase which announces the beginning of a holy day; its plain meaning is "let the day begin"); and, from the fervent language of Bialik, time is solicited to "gather in a mound the splendor-slivers [of light] *(zohorei-shevarim).*" The yearned-for day of creativity will be onc of "the beauty of the battle of luminaries *[milḥemet shemashot]* of the future" — a grand mythological, cosmic event, akin to the classic midrashic clash between the sun and moon for the rule of day.[10]

Similarly, the emotive romantic themes of *La-ot* continue in the motif designs here: light, day, brightness, splendor, gold, sun, red, darkness, night, and blue. Water images also predominate: waves, sea, depths, streams, flooding, splashing, overflowings. Also abundant are the familiar motifs of eyes, pupils, and sight; fire, burning, and ashes. To these, Gilboa adds dominant new themes of time and memory, both of which reflect his preoccupation with the possibility of his own imminent death.

The Poetics of Profusion

In these first World War II poems, personification predominates as the major metaphorical figure with phrases such as "yesterday waits for a conquered step [of territory]," "[O time,] stop your movement," "the flawed [or wounded] song," "thus the earth will not be silent," "[memories] cover the mouth of caves." Gilboa also uses synesthesia and hyperbole: "the flagration of the scream" *(taverat ha-tsa'ak)*; "ten thousand feet are walking"; "a host of eyes"; and stock romantic and mythological images: the anvil, spirit, secret, stone, sun, memory, the primeval *(kadmon)*.[11]

But the figurative language grows more complex in this opening section of *Sheva reshuyot*. Here Gilboa develops a style which may be dubbed "metaphorical (or imagistic) doubling," featuring a secondary metaphor which is attached or closely juxtaposed to the primary figure. An example from *El kadmon* reads as follows:

הָמֵסְנָה רַצֵּי הַקּוּרִים שֶׁהֶאֱפִילוּ
עַל סְדַן אוֹר דָּמָיו....

[O my years,] dissolve the strands of webs which have brought darkness
upon the anvil of the light of [imagination's] blood. . . .

This technique occurs in the overlapping phrases "the anvil of light" and "the light of [imagination's] blood"—that is, the poet's lifeline of creativity. The dual image combines the graphic image of a blacksmith's anvil with the mythical idea of the shaping source of creativity. The second figure personifies the imagination as a living entity. The dual impulse of concretization and abstraction gives the notion of creativity both a worldly and otherworldly quality; and the poetics is of a continuous envisioning, a ceaseless process which blends the inner and outer worlds of the poet.[12]

Zikhron ha-tov contains a similar figure.

בָּבוֹת נֶאֶסְרוּ אֶל תַּבְעֵרַת הַצַּעַק–

Eye pupils are tied to the flagration of the scream—

The image "flagration of the scream" refers to the shrieks and fires of the battlefield. When the poet says that his "eye pupils are tied to" these graphic sounds and images, he means that he cannot take his eyes off the terrible scenes to which he is witness. Through his staring eyes, the outer world of war is absorbed into his feelings. The metaphorical complexity continues to develop even further in Gilboa's later poetry, where its effect is to intensify already heightened images in order to express his overflowing emotions in even more innovative ways.[13]

In *Tefilat azkara,* Gilboa refers specifically to this metaphorical profusion. The poem presents a particularly poignant expression of his fear of death and his wish to be spared in order to continue to write. The opening stanza sets the emotive tone of figurative prolixity. The poet voices the hope that he will not reach the point of emotional saturation. He tries to stop the flow of feeling, but his wish is to hold onto as much of it as possible and control it without letting it overwhelm him—an oft-recurring but seldom-resolved tension in Gilboa's poetry.

אַל תִּשָּׂאוּנִי, רַגְלַי, לָרְוָיָה הַמְקֻלֶּלֶת.
אֲנִי מִפָּנֶיהָ בּוֹרֵחַ.
אֲנִי אֶל הַשֶּׁפֶךְ מִפִּתְחוֹ שֶׁל הַלֵּב אֶגְהַר
לַעֲצֹר בְּעַד פַּס הַכֹּסֶף הַנִּגָּר
וּבְאֶצְבְּעוֹתַי עֲוִית, רְתֵת הָרָצוֹן
לְהֵחָלֵץ מִן הַשִּׁבֹּלֶת
כְּטוֹבֵעַ.

Do not carry me, my legs, to the accursed plenitude.
I am fleeing from it.
I crouch over the outpouring of the heart's opening
to put a stop to the line of flowing desire
and in my fingers a trembling, the quiver of a wish
to escape from the wave
like a drowning man.[14]

The plethora of synonymic terms for water and flowing adds to the sense of metaphorical profusion: *revaya* (slaking of thirst), *shefekh* (outpouring or mouth of a river), *nigar* (pouring forth or flow of water), *shibolet* (wave or whirlpool), and *tove'a* (a drowning person). These images continue in the second stanza with "night slid forward *(higlish)* its broad hours" and "casts the streams of effulgence's redness *[zirmei odem ha-nehara]* beyond this place." Similar phrases occur in the remainder of the poem: "waterfall crossings," "the depths," "the abyss," "dew." The effect is a surfeit of expression, which, on the one hand, impresses the reader with the genuineness of the poet's emotional outpouring, and, on the other, invites critical assessments of verbosity.[15]

For the poet himself, the combination of forces in *Tefilat azkara* implicitly threatens to limit his creative powers. In effect Gilboa creates a mythology of the poet as one who "contains" a finite number of images—images which may overwhelm and exhaust him and cause him to lose control of the very inspiration that feeds his creativity. In his mind, this is the dilemma: how to remain the master of one's creative process and not become its slave or its victim.[16]

The second section of *"Sefer ḥayei olam"* contains a variety of short poems written in various locations during the North African campaign in late 1942 and 1943, the period of tragic discovery for Gilboa. In late fall of 1942 his works attest to a full awareness of the Holocaust; by the end of the year, to learning his family's fate. But the first few poems in the section are still innocent, expressing his feelings about being at the front and the place of poetry in his battlefield existence. In *Gedola mi-shira hi ha-re'ut* (Greater Than Poetry Is Seeing)[17] Gilboa continues to ponder the function of poetry in the world, positing the idea that in times of war, vision, feeling, and escapist fantasies are more important than art. In the second half, however, he affirms the act of writing. Even though it is peripheral—he calls it *katnut,* smallness or pettiness—even though the poetic hand can capture only "one-thousandth of the storm of burning reality," the act of writing is still an act of courage; and it is only through the written word that the poet's natural instinct can be fulfilled. *Gedola mi-shira hi ha-re'ut* is Shlonsky-like in its focus on one idea, its aphoristic mode, and its use of colloquial verbiage: *kakha, stam, le-lo ḥashash* (like that, just like that, undoubtedly).

More heightened emotions propel *Po lo she'arim,*[18] the visionary poem written, as noted above, on a cigarette pack on Simḥat Torah, 1942. After opening with a desolate landscape description, the speaker immediately moves into an imaginary, mythic mode.

פֹּה לֹא שְׁעָרִים מִבַּרְזֶל.
לֹא מֵעֵצִים פּוֹרְחִים.
אַךְ אֲנִי בְּאֶגְרוֹפַי דּוֹפֵק

עַל שַׁעַר הָרְבָבָה.
כִּי הִכְרִיחַנִי אֵים הַיְבָבָה.

וּשְׁעָרִים אֶרְאֶה בַּכֹּל.
וּשְׁעָרִים לִי מִסָּבִיב.
אַךְ עוֹבֵר הוֹרֵס אֵלַי הַקּוֹל.
וְעֹז־שֶׁל־דִּין בּוֹ –
הוּא קוֹלוֹ שֶׁל אָבִי.

Here there are no gates of iron.
Not of blossoming trees.
But I pound with my fists
on the ten thousandth gate.
For I'm compelled by the terror of wailing.

And everywhere I see gates.
And gates are all around me.
But the voice rises striving towards me.
And in it is the force-of-law –
It is the voice of my father.

Immersed in hallucination, the speaker hears the voice as it "rises striving toward [him]." The jarring juxtaposition of asyndetic predicates, the seemingly inappropriate preposition, and the hyphenated description of the voice accentuate the poet's intensified state of mind. Here already one sees Gilboa's use of innovative structures, "ungrammaticalities" which appear with increasing frequency over the next several years and, beginning in the late sixties, become the central force in his poetry.[19]

The images in *Po lo she'arim* follow Gilboa's usual patterns of allusion and mythic resonance. Taken from the Yom Kippur liturgy, pounding on the gates evokes the mythical image of atonement prayers knocking at the heavenly gates for admittance to the Divine Presence.[20] Gilboa heightens the image by using multiplicity in "the ten-thousandth gate." (Variations of "thousands" and "tens of thousands" occur regularly in his work.) The mythological hyperbole combines with syntactic, grammatical, and punctuational techniques to convey a palpable intensity which culminates with "It is the voice of my father." The knocking, the voice, and the notion of divine judgment all lead the reader to understand the poem as one of self-expiation, echoing Yitsḥak Lamdan's guilt-ridden poetry of lament.[21] The Simḥat Torah holiday may have evoked for Gilboa his immeasurable distance from the traditional holiday celebration in his ancestral, now threatened, home. The war and its traumas surely have intensified his feelings of loneliness and vulnerability. With its images of barrenness, atonement, and disquieting parental sternness, *Po lo she'arim* conveys a psychological state of terror, remorse, and irresolution.

The Holocaust: First Responses

Each of the remaining works in *"Sefer ḥayei olam"* is a poetic response to the Holocaust. The first blatant image of slaughter, in *Akhshav mul yom* (Now Facing the Day),[22] is a high, red (i.e., bloodied) column of water, and inside it the outline of an axe, "shattering my brethren's [bejeweled] crowns of splendor." Another poem greets the new day as "merciless . . . opaque/and strange"—a far cry from the romantic, rapturous dawns Gilboa described in more innocent days.[23] Similarly, in *Bekarim bi-me'urati* (Mornings in My Hovel)[24] he expresses anger and despair by depicting the mornings as "a drawn bayonet/whose lit-up point blinds the scrolls of rage."[25] A traditional poetic motif, the image of ancient scrolls *(gevilim)* is also used here to convey his outrage. Borrowed from the Martyrology segment of the Yom Kippur liturgy,[26] the image combines with the theme of blindness in a figurative depiction of a tragic, incomprehensible morning.

Other images and motifs are familiar ones: flowing, pouring, broken crystal, secret, shadows, infants, eyes, blues and reds, the abyss, the beloved, mornings, dreams, and blood. Ironically typical of their romantic style and function, the same motifs and emphatic word structurings serve both Gilboa's lyrical nature poems and his agonized Holocaust works. As in *La-ot,* segolates and word repetitions convey the fervidness of his emotions: *O-tem ha-BA-hal* (the pit of panic), *ḥofei ha-MA-al* (the shores of betrayal), *SHE-ga el tokh sod sodotav* (madness [poured] into [the night's] secret of secrets);[27] *siyut sakinim she-shaḥatu shaḥatu* (a nightmare of knives that slaughtered slaughtered); *ve-ḥaron/ve-ḥaron* (and rage/and rage); *ḥarada! ḥarada!*

(horror! horror!); *lu yakholti amod./Lu yakholti lamut [mul penei aḥyotai]* If only I could stand it./If only I could die [in the presence of my sisters].[28]

Since their images contrast directly with the fervid enthrallment of the earlier poems, these first Holocaust poems are antithetical in their entirety to Gilboa's prior works. In *Lo ekra la-boker shem* (I'll Not Call the Morning by Name)[29] the speaker makes the following angry declaration:

לֹא אֶקְרָא לַבֹּקֶר שֵׁם
כִּי לֹא אֵדַע.
עֵינַי בּוֹ חֲלוּלוֹת
כִּי אֲנִי בּוֹ
וְהוּא תוֹכִי לֹא בָא.

I'll not call the morning by name
for I do not know.
My eyes are hollow in it
for I am in it
but it does not come into me.

Familiar with images of the poet's formerly rapturous self-immersion in the dawn, the reader cannot help but grasp Gilboa's agonized distancing from these Holocaust-tainted mornings. Unopened and unreceptive, his eyes are not merely closed but *ḥalulot,* hollow, devoid of any cogent perception. The sense of alienation is total. He feels nothing of the morning; he cannot devise a name for it; he cannot even see it. For him it now exists merely as a dimension of time. In the same poem, however, the speaker remembers how mornings once held wondrous moments, with birds singing Psalms "like the blessed dew" on the roofs and fences. Now this experience is but a memory, empty and destroyed like a broken, flattened birdcage—a symbol of the poet's irretrievable loss of innocence.

The heightened contrast in these works simultaneously denotes both difference and equivalence. Gilboa's enthrallment and his anger derive from the same source—his acute perception, whether celebrative or tragic, of human experience. His oppositional poetics comes into play in yet another dimension: When he writes that he "will not call the morning by name," he is abnegating the very act of poetic invention and creativity. This is as radical a declaration of self-denial as is the wish, in *Ze tsili* (This Is My Shadow),[30] to be twenty again, in order to die in the slaughter with "the most beautiful among women," his beloved sisters. In *Ani rotse lashir* (I Want to Sing [i.e., poeticize or write poems]),[31] the poet-speaker mourns the death of a young fellow soldier. "Perhaps," he writes, "the hand will recoil as it paints his name/in chalk on every cliff/and sings *[ve-tashir]*."

In stating his refusal to write romantically about the dawn, Gilboa of course fulfills the act of doing so. As with the theme of profusion versus the loss of poetic images, Gilboa's rejection of the beloved morning becomes an impassioned act, one which derives from his dualistic poetics of the inner and outer self. This is the poetics which impels him to express his most deep-seated sentiments at all times and at all costs and thus serves as an affirmation of his commitment to his art.[32]

The most evocative work of this group is *Hine va-akhabehu [et ha-ner]* (Behold, I Extinguish It [the candle]),[33] in which Gilboa, for the first time, poetically mourns the loss of his immediate family. The poem evinces, as Aryeh Anavi has noted, the tension between "the wish to escape" and "the burden of memory"—the emotional dichotomy which lies at the center of much of Gilboa's work.[34] Should the poet extinguish the flame of memory and try to forget, or should he keep the flame alive, an ever-present reminder of the death of his dear ones?

הִנֵּה וַאֲכַבֵּהוּ
אֶת הַנֵּר.
לֹא רַק נֵר נְשָׁמָה הוּא –
הוּא נֵר הַגּוּף הַמִּתְעַוֵּת
שֶׁל אַבָּא, שֶׁל אִמָּא,
שֶׁל אֲחוֹתִי הַקְּטַנָּה,
שֶׁל אֶסְתֵּר.

הִנֵּה, הִנֵּה הָאָיֹם מִתְבַּהֵר –
הַנֵּר בּוֹכֶה בְּלִי הֲפוּגוֹת

חֶלְבּוֹ נָמֵס
וְעִגּוּל הַשְׁקַעֲרוּרִית סְבִיב הַפְּתִיל
תּוֹסֵס
בְּדָם וּדְמָעוֹת.

בָּבוֹתַי, בָּבוֹתַי הַבּוֹעֲרוֹת,
הַגֵּדְנָה!
הַאֲכַב אֶת הַנֵּר
שֶׁשָּׂרִיד קָדוֹשׁ לֹא יִתַּם?
אִם בִּזְוָעָה קַדֵּשׁ עַד סוֹף
אֶת אֵלֶּה דְמָעוֹת,
אֶת זֶה הַדָּם?

Here I extinguish it
the candle.
Not merely a memorial candle—
it is the candle of the twisted body
of my father, of my mother,
of my little sister,
of Esther.

Here, here the horror comes clear—
the candle cries ceaselessly
its wax melts
and a circular hollow around the wick
bubbles
with blood and tears.

My eyes [pupils], my burning eyes,
tell me!
Should I put out the candle
so that the holy remains will not be consumed?
Or sanctify with horror to the end
these very tears,
this very blood?

The key motif in this drama of mourning, memory, poet and poetry is holiness (lines 17–18). Like the memorial candle and the sacredness of memory, the act of poetry (represented by the candle, with its bubbling groove of blood and tears) is also perceived as holy. Parallel to the burning weeping candle, the poet himself is represented through his personified "burning eyes" *(bavot)*, Gilboa's established metaphor for the poet's perception, imagination, and fervor.

The poem's final question is a rhetorical one. Although he will do so "with horror," the poet will continue to memorialize his family, in order to preserve as sacred both their blood and his tears. Here Gilboa charges himself with the poetic mission as a holy task, a means of sanctification, if not in substance then at least in style, diction, and tone.

In these initial Holocaust poems, Gilboa expands his poetics of fervor with the pervasive use of intensely archaic, euphuistic, often manifestly inarticulate linguistic choices and by experimenting with the spasmodic articulation of his most fervid verbal sources.

The title poem of part three of *"Sefer ḥayei olam," Ru'aḥ ba-midbar* (Wind in the Desert),[35] seems to be an exaggeratedly romantic nature poem, even a parody of such a poem. The language and syntax of the work are archaized beyond any similar usage Gilboa has demonstrated before. The first stanza of the opening section illustrates these somewhat bizarre and overstated features.

הֵי הֵילִילִי רוּחַ בְּעָצְמַת רְאוּתֵךְ הַחוֹלֶפֶת.
זִלְפִי בַּעֲתַר שְׁלוּחוֹת עַד יִתַּם גַּרְגֵּר רוֹגֵעַ.
פֹּה לֹא טַאטֵא לָךְ יֵשׁ מַרְצֶפֶת
וְלַחְשֹׁף בְּרַק מַטְבֵּעַ –
כָּךְ שֶׁלָּךְ תֵּרוֹם הַנֶּפֶשׁ
וּתְבַדֵּר עֶרְגוֹן רַקֶּפֶת
בְּשָׂרִיגַת אָדְמִי פּוֹרֵחַ.

So weep, O wind, with the force of your fleeting sight.
Spray the abundance of plants till the calm seed is gone.

Here's no broom for you there's a tile [mosaic] floor
and discovering the glint of a coin—
So you must lift your soul
and scatter the anemone's longing
in the vine of my blossoming redness.

The title itself, *Ru'aḥ ba-midbar,*[36] prepares the reader for a wasteland nature poem, similar, one might expect, to *Ru'aḥ-erev* in *La-ot.* The opening line does nothing do dispel this expectation, especially with the opening phrase, *hey heylili ru'aḥ,* which sets a jaunty tone. The words *otsma[t]* (force) and the personification of the wind through *heylili* (weep) and *re'ut[ekh]* ([your] sight) support the initial perception of a typically Gilboan nature lyric. On the other hand, the verb *heylili,* despite its playful sound, denotes weeping or a mournful wailing *(yeleil).*

Line 2 is replete with archaic vocabulary selections: *zilfi* (spray) and *yitam* (gone) are not terribly esoteric, but *atar* (in the secondary meaning of "abundance")[37] and *sheluḥot* (plants) are words used rarely even in poetic Hebrew. It is the stringing together of all four of these words in one verse that makes blatant the archaic and esoteric nature of the line. In lines 3–4 it is especially the syntax which appears archaic, especially in its elliptical character. From here to the end, the language comes across as a half-articulated, primitive tongue, reminiscent of some of the more difficult passages of the Book of Psalms.[38]

Because of the ambiguity of the language, the imagery here is entirely opaque, but a paraphrase may read as follows: The speaker tells the wind that in its flight over the desert wasteland areas, beyond where berries still grow, it need not sweep the desert floor clean to find a mosaic tile or an ancient coin (since these ancient objects lie close to the surface). This should make the wind happy, so that it might move on to uncover a lonely cyclamen on the speaker's vine of "blossoming red," another ambiguous image.

The poem's second stanza evinces the same sort of archaic, elliptical, or partially articulated linguistic manipulation.

בַּעֲדִי, מֵחוֹל מִסְגֶּרֶת,
לְבֶן עֶצֶם חוֹפֵן נֶצַח
לְעוֹבְרֵי מְגַלֵּי־שְׁמָּא.

וּפַחְדָּם אָז מִכָּל מֵצַח
מוֹרִישׁ אֶל לֵב אֶת טִיף הָעֶצֶב:
הֵם שֶׁמֵּתוּ וְלֹא קָמוּ –

For me, out of a sand frame,
the whiteness of bone scoops up eternity
for passerby revealers-of-perhaps.
And their fear then from every forehead
bequeaths to the heart a drop of sorrow:
those who have died and have not risen—

To paraphrase, the speaker has a vision which the supposedly happy, fleeting wind does not possess. It is a white, skeletal bone in a frame of desert sand, grasping in its hand a piece of eternity for passersby to see and perhaps thereby to make some discovery. Something indeed is revealed to make them afraid and bring sorrow into the heart as an inheritance—the understanding that many have died and will not rise again.

In many ways, *Ru'aḥ ba-midbar* may be read as a latterday version of Bialik's *Metei midbar.* Indeed, there are several oblique allusions to the Bialik work in this closing stanza: the bones in the sand; the passersby who discover the dead Israelites buried there; the use of *metsaḥ* (forehead), which Bialik uses in his descriptions of the dead heroes of the Exodus; and, of course, the dramatic resurrection of the Israelites, which is reflected ironically in the last line, "those who have died and have not risen."

Parts 2 and 3 confirm the impression formed by the closing of part 1. This is an "antiromantic romantic poem,"[39] which—through radically heightened, archaic, euphuistic, elliptical, psalm-like language—flaunts its romantic hyperbole, only to end with an abrupt, anticlimactic articulation of the tragedy. In part 2, for example, the speaker chastises the wind by telling it that it always has led him to "the aromatic streams of the spices of spring" *(palgei ha-reiḥot she-le-vosmei ha-aviv)*, those distant places of youthful innocence *(ofkei terem ḥet).*

The first stanza of part 3 continues the hyperbole with phrases such as "restful grass, green," "flowing stream" and "splendor of song," only to end the stanza with "and into the flowing stream with splendor of song/flows the blood of the decapitated head/of my brother my own." Typical of the antiromantic romantic poem, the closing stanza completes the traumatic climax with the very same images and metaphors used previously by Gilboa for the pleasures of nature and its beauty: eyes, overflowing, imagination, flames, sparks, and blue. In a conscious projection of the antithesis of these previously perceived pleasures, Gilboa ends the poem with a lament for the imagination, now forced to focus on the terror of the Holocaust, and with a wish for blindness "till the flame sparks in the blue of madness."

The poems that follow reflect some of the same romantic themes, images, and language seen in *Ru'aḥ ba-midbar.* These include motifs of the imagination, the inability to hear or to see, lying alive in a grave,[40] the cosmos in disarray, the hyperbolic use of "thousands," and a new, ironic motif: the laugh. Especially moving and romantically antiromantic is *Demama* (Silence),[41] in which the speaker imagines himself lying in an empty grave in an open field with wheels—perhaps the mythological wheels of Ezekiel's chariot or of the cosmos itself—spinning all around. In this fearsome setting, the speaker fears not death but the loss of all the things he "once loved."

לְחִישַׁת הַכְּחוֹלִית שֶׁבָּאֵשׁ.
מִלְמוּל הַגְּוִיָּה הַנִּדְבֶּקֶת.
אִוְשַׁת הַשַּׁלֶּכֶת בְּקִמֹּרֶת וְרֻדָּה.
וְצַהַל חָבוּי רוֹעֵף סוֹד
חֲגִיגַת נִיסָן טְלוּל הַשֶּׁקֶט –

The whisper of blue flame in the fire.
The murmur of a clinging corpse.
The rustle of leaf fall in a violet arc.
And a hidden joy raining the mystery of
Nisan's holiday dewed with quiet—

The list mournfully acknowledges the loss of romantic subjects for his poetry: lyrical perceptions of the world of love, beauty, nature, holiday joy and peace.

In *Galgal ha-ḥama* (The Wheel of the Sun)[42] Gilboa returns to the themes of myth and the cosmos, both of which have now gone awry.

Instead of the lovely sunrises and reenactment of scenes of empowerment, the sun now penetrates the atmosphere and threatens the world.[43] The speaker himself holds the wheel of the sun, who asks him to guide it. "But all this is a joke and just a game," says the speaker. On the other hand, should "the sun penetrate until it melts—/I'll no longer laugh." The language of the poem combines mythical and colloquial verbiage, as if to replicate a child's nightmare, an oft-repeated motif in Gilboa's later works. Because the disaster has already occurred, Gilboa knows that to laugh—to perceive the universe frivolously or romantically—is no longer possible.

The next section of *"Sefer ḥayei olam"* opens with *Yetom* (Orphanhood),[44] which sets the tone for many of the poems written while Gilboa was at the front in Malta and Italy. Its theme is the pitiable fate of the poet forced to live in two emotional worlds, the world of personal sorrow and the world of the soldier fighting for victory and the joy of final triumph.

יְתוֹם

מַה מַּאֲפִיל וְלוֹחֵץ עַל הַלֵּב וְהָאוֹר?
–זֶה הַגִּיל הַגָּדוֹל הַפּוֹרֵץ וּמְבַשֵּׂר
בְּקוֹלֵי הַקּוֹלוֹת אֶת בּוֹאוֹ.
מַה כּוֹבְדָה הַנְּשִׁימָה מֵחֶדְוָה גוֹרֶפֶת גְּבוּלוֹת?
–תְּחִלַּת נָגְהוֹ שֶׁל הָאוֹת!
וּמִי מַכֶּה עַל עֵינַי בַּכָּתוּב בִּשְׁמֵי רוֹם?
–זֶה הַיּוֹם–

What grows dark and presses on the heart and the light?
—It is the great joy bursting and bearing the news
loud and clear of its coming.
Why is the breath so heavy from the joy that moves boundaries?
—The beginning of the splendor of the sign!
And who beats upon my eyes with that which is written in the heavens?
—It is the day—[45]

In this poem, structured on a Hamlet-like series of rhetorical questions to himself, the speaker wonders what it is that presses on him so heavily, nearly to the point of suffocation. The answer, of course, is obvious, but it comes to him only at the end: *Ani yatom,* "I'm an orphan." His happiness about the victory in North Africa is logically understandable, yet troubling. Gilboa cannot reconcile the unseemly coexistence of the height of joy with the depth of sorrow. "Who beats upon my eyes" has the ring of Gilboa's familiar motif of poetic perception and self-awareness. The instrument of this beating is "[what is] written in the high heavens," meaning the divine declaration as to the ordering of earthly events. And "the day," which does the beating, connotes the daily realization on the part of Gilboa that mixed emotion will forever be his fate, as will the combination of poetry and loss, mentioned again in the closing stanza.

אֵיכָה כְּסוּס פֶּרֶא לֹא אֶדְהַר קַלִּילוֹת,
לֹא אַמְרִיא אֶל עֲלִילוֹת,
בְּזֹהַר טֵרוּף אֶל מוֹשְׁכוֹת הַיּוֹם
אַגָּדוֹת לִרְתֹּם?
אֵיכָה לֹא אֲרַו הַשִּׂמְחָה עַד תֹּם?

אֲנִי יָתוֹם –

How is it I can't gallop like a wild horse,
nor fly toward great deeds,
nor hitch with the splendor of madness
great legends to the reins of day?
How can I not quench happiness to the end?

I'm an orphan—

Both the fascination with nature of the early poems and the deep despair in his poems of loneliness and rejection are mirrored here in the oxymorons of conflicting emotions ("the breath so heavy" vis-à-vis "the splendor of the sign"; "the splendor of madness"; *ze ha-yom* vis-à-vis *ani yatom).* These rhetorical usages move easily from the world of abstraction to artistic alienation to the harsh real world of death and destruction. Gilboa's poetics of heightened perception works well in shaping his ambivalent responses to the poetic impulse in these works. He has the urge to write of the great adventures, the legendary deeds, the victories of the day, to be the poet of triumph and record his overflowing joy. But he cannot; he is a Holocaust orphan.

In the poems of 1943–1944, "war reportage" intermeshes with the poet's personal feelings; themes of guilt, sin, memory, and silence predominate. In *Yiḥud* (Unity),[46] the sounds of battle, much like a beautiful woman's body, seem to "entrance" and are "consumed in the mystery" of war. The main feeling, however, is fear, which "pours into me from the rage of parchment scrolls/which may catch me forgetting them." The speaker protests this alleged "sin" of forgetfulness, claiming that it happened unintentionally *(be-shogeg)*. To overcome any feeling of guilt, he cries out in the form of a prayer-poem, which allows for the victory of the "whitening light of day" over the "night of blood." Once again, the act of poetry here is an act of both psychological and artistic salvation, a means of expressing both Gilboa's unrelieved personal pain and his fervent commitment to his art.

The Holocaust poems in the next section of *"Sefer ḥayei olam"* are particularly beautiful and hauntingly wrought. *Elem pinot* (Corner Muteness)[47] is a dream-description of a return home, the poet's fantasy quest for reunion with his loved ones. What confronts him as the door opens wide is complete silence, not the greetings he expected as an antidote for the pain of "thousands of sorrowing mornings." *Ir zokheret* (A City Remembers)[48] presents a portrait of a city destroyed by battle and abandoned, its ruins listening to the song of the departing soldiers, the mined roads leading away from it perilously silent. In *Im benei dami* (With My Blood Brethren)[49] the background description of Ancona, including a "wide-eyed rooster"—the poem was written on the eve of Yom Kippur, 1944[50]—is combined with a dream-confrontation with Gilboa's murdered brothers, Moshe and Joshua. The evocative eeriness contrasts with the sounds of the triumphant clinking of glasses in the officers' tent.

Once again, a good deal of the linguistic energy in these three poems is expressed by way of contrasts and semantic doubling. A primary example is the clash between sounds and silence, with numerous synonyms and motifs used for both. Sounds are expressed by *sa'an* (noise), *shir* (poem or song), *yishma* (hear), *hedim* (echoes), *zimzum* (hum), *lesaper agadot . . . she-pot-setsu* (to tell legends . . . that have burst), *ra'ash* (noise), *tslil* (sound or note), *hishtaksheku ha-kosot* (the cups clinked). Silence is represented by *elem* (muteness), *ha-pinot lo tagedna me'um* (the corners won't tell anything), *kevishim yishketu . . . ve-yishtoku* (roads will be silent . . . be silent), *sheket* (silence), *domemim yaldei ha-bayit* (the children in the house are silent), *ha-ra'ash shoket* (the noise is silent), *agala . . . dom overet* (a wagon . . . silently passes by), *ha-ra'ash gove'a* (the noise is dying), and *loḥashim* (whispering).

As in the early nature poems, these works display an abundant use of personification, which engenders here a kind of Gothic frightfulness of being surrounded by unseen, hostile powers. Corners "are silent" or "do not tell anything"; a city "remembers"; the noise "is dying"; the ruins "listen"; the darkness "remembered"; the courtyard "dies"; the noise "turns pale"; the hours "stare." Images of empty houses, destroyed cities, distant echoes, a wide-eyed rooster, a wounded child, a moving, horseless wagon, and ghostly voices of the dead all create a world fraught with spirits, a haunting poetic vision of the post-Holocaust world.[51]

Most of the works in this group are love poems addressed to a female beloved. On one level, their diction, grammar, and syntax echo the Song of Songs. At the same time, however, Gilboa injects an insistent tone and oppositional structure which create a mood of disquietude and, often, a resonance of violence and death. With their patterns of dualistic images—references to flame, betrayal, blood, distance, bereftness, and the grave alongside the language of love and longing—the poems reflect an intensely erotic love gone awry or betrayed by powerful external forces. Lovers' delight soon turns to anger and anguish.

The dualism is reminiscent of some of Bialik's love poetry: In *Eineha* (Her Eyes), *Ha-einayim ha-re'evot* (The Hungry Eyes), and *Rak kav shemesh eḥad* (Only One Beam of Sunlight), Bialik also projects the duality of innocent love and beauty as against the intensity, even evil, of lust and its accompanying feelings of sinfulness and guilt. These works, however, are meant to exacerbate the lover's dilemma; they are romantic indicators of the depth of passion, revealed under a calm surface of innocent attraction.

Gilboa's dualism is different. It is expressed not only in the poems' contents but in their very genre, which is not love poetry at all but symbolic works which pit sensual love against images of its absence, an absence caused by violence, distance, betrayal, and death. Not only do these poems reveal love's antithesis through their abrupt suggestions of malice and doom. They also evoke the loss of potential love, the demise of all lovers and loved ones. The Holocaust dead are both lovers and beloved; their passion is realized in the remembrance of those who survive and express love so passionately for the dead.

A significant aspect of this symbolic representation is Gilboa's identification of love and passion with poetry. His dilemma lies in the very thought of continuing to write while mourning his murdered loved ones. In *She-etse mi-ma'avai* (Should I Leave My Longings)[52] the poet posits that if, because of the Holocaust, he were to abandon his love—that is, his poetry, he would become completely divorced from the source of his creative inspiration—and of his solace.

שֶׁאֵצֵא מִמַּאֲוַי
לֹא יִהְיֶה עוֹד אוֹר
וְלֹא יוֹם אַחֲרָיו
לֹא חוֹמָה לְסְתֹּר
לֹא יַיִן לִשְׁתּוֹת
וְלֹא שִׁיר אֲשֶׁר מֵחֲלוֹם
אֵלַי שָׁב –

לֹא דִמְעָה מִן הַלֵּב עַל אֲשֶׁר־נִצְחִית־
לֹא־נִתְפָּס
לֹא פָּרֹכֶת כְּאֵב
עַל עָמְקוֹ שֶׁל הָרָז
לֹא מַיִם גּוֹאִים שׁוֹפְעִים מִשִּׂמְחָה
לֹא יַעַר־לֵילוֹת בְּנַהַם שְׁמָהּ
לֹא מַבָּטַי אֶל גְּבָהִים
אֶל כִּתְרֵי הָרַי
לֹא מִצְעֲדֵי עֲרִירִים בִּרְחוֹבוֹת עָרַי.

Should I leave my longings
there would be no more light
and there would be no day following it
no wall to break down
no wine to drink
and no poem which from a dream
would return to me—

No tear from the heart for that-which-is-eternally-ungraspable
no *parokhet* [ark-cover] of pain
upon the depth of the mystery
no water rising flooding with joy
no night-forest with the hum of her name
no looks of mine toward the skies
toward the crowns of my mountains
no steps of mine bereft in the streets of my cities.

Poetry is Gilboa's essential life-giving source of pain and joy, love and anger. Without it he is bereft of emotion—or the means to express it. His lyrical "longings" for poetry allow him to express himself in both romantic directions: toward his "crowns of mountains," the inspirational sources of nature, and toward his "bereft steps," the terrible traumas of his life. For Gilboa, "love," "pain," and "poetry" have become coequal.

Mavet ba-aviv (A Death in Spring),[53] which closes this section, is more a war poem than a Holocaust work and is yet another example of Gilboa's antiromantic romantic poetry.

מָוֶת בָּאָבִיב

אוֹר עוֹבֵר כָּל גְּדוֹת
רַב מִדַּי אוֹר.
וְהוּא נִשְׁפָּךְ אֶל תְּעָלוֹת
וְאֶל כָּל בּוֹר.

וְהוּא מֵנִיב שׁוּב אַגָּדוֹת
וְלֹא נוֹתְנָן לָבוֹא.
וְאִתָּנוּ עוֹלֶה בַּמַּעֲלוֹת
חִידַת הַיּוֹם לִפְתֹּר.
וְכָל מִיתוֹת בּוֹ נִתְלוֹת –
אֶל קִנּוֹ רָצוֹת לַחְזֹר.

Death in Spring

Light flooding both banks
an excess of light.
Poured in ditches
into every pit.
Bringing forth more legends
but not letting them take place.
Mounting the stairs with us
to solve the puzzle of this day.
All deaths reliant on it—
rushing back to its shelter.[54]

Light has always been Gilboa's symbol of life, natural beauty, and spiritual, often sacred, uplifting. Here, in lines 2–3, the light is both overflowing and overbearing. The "excess of light" illuminates everything, even the things that one would rather not see.[55] That "all deaths [are] reliant on it" suggests that it would be better were the war deaths kept in the dark. Instead of bringing on new, enchanting days and stories of triumph, spring and its morning effulgences of light become solemn bearers of glaring, unremitting death.

Mavet ba-aviv also relates to the pervasive theme of poetry itself. When the light "mount[s] the stairs with us/to solve the puzzle of this day," Gilboa suggests that poetry embodies the attempt to understand the meaning of all these glaring deaths. The moment is numinous, oracular. The word for steps, *ma'alot,* refers generally to the steps leading to an altar or a throne.[56] More specifically, it refers to the steps in the Holy Temple, where the Levites would sing a "song of steps" *(shir ha-ma'alot)* as they mounted the Temple stairs. *Ma'alot* may also refer to the phrase *be-ma'alot kedoshim u-tehorim,* the "high places [namely, heaven] of the holy and pure [souls of the dead]," which appears in the Jewish memorial prayer *El male raḥamim* (God, Full of Mercy). Gilboa uses these multiple allusions to elicit a moment filled with ironic light, ironic discovery, ironic sacrality. Of course, all of these forces can never explain "the puzzle of this day." The meaning of "death in spring," the mystery of every war death and of each post-Holocaust day, can never be fathomed.

By regularizing the poem's structure and deregularizing it at the same time, Gilboa creates a poetic dichotomy which mirrors the dualistic nature of its contents. As in *Lo ekra la-boker shem,* the poem deceptively appears to be "regular"—that is, regularly rhymed, which it is, and regularly metered, which it is not.[57] The poem is carefully structured in short verses, with every odd line rhyming with the feminine plural suffix *-ot.* The even lines also rhyme, almost identically: *or-bor, liftor-laḥzor,* and a centered approximate rhyme, *lavo.* In all this exactitude, the metrical structure of the poem is quite mixed. The meter is based on an anapestic scheme: *kol ga-DOT, mi-dai OR, te-'a-LOT, a-ga-DOT, bo nit-LOT, el ki-NO;* but verse-leading iambs predominate too: *ve-HU* (twice), *ve-EL, ve-LO, ḥi-DAT, ve-KHOL.*

In almost every line, iambs appear within the verses as well: *o-VER, nish-PAKH, kol BOR, me-NIV, not-NAN, o-LE, ha-YOM, mi-TOT, ra-TSOT, laḥ-ZOR.* Other metric "irregularites" appear: *Or* in line 1 stands alone and accented, as does *rav* in line 2; both these evince the accentuated opening called *tiferet ha-petiḥa* (roughly, "splendid beginning") which occurs in medieval Hebrew poetry. *Shuv,* in line 5, also stands alone and is stressed, thereby emphasizing the repetitiveness of the futile act of triumphant story-telling; *el,* in line 3, reflects the same prominence. In fact, it is only the inclusion of regular rhyming, verse-ending anapests that gives the impression that the poem is basically anapestic.

The central work in the following section of *"Sefer ḥayei olam"* is *Boker selah* (Morning Selah), which is immediately followed by eight parts, beginning with *Ke-zimrat ma'asav shel avi* (Like the Melody of My Father's Deeds).[58] The larger work consists of Gilboa's personal reminiscences of his father, his childhood and his home, his musings on poetic efforts then and now, and his vision of the post-Holocaust world.

In the first poem, the poet's father wakes from a dream "which embraced the past." This, of course, is precisely what the poet himself is doing. Analogous to "the melody of [his] father's deeds" and to "his luminous waking from sleep" is "the poetry of his youngest child." Just as Gilboa's father dedicated his every act to his children and wakened from sleep to their presence, so the poet now tries at every turn to express his love and grief through poetry.

In the second part, the poet's vision as he dreams of standing at the threshhold of his home is an ironic apotheosis of the revelation at Sinai. The dream turns into disaster, the world has been set aflame, "and all the eyes see the fire"—a reversal of the biblical synaesthesia.[59] Whereas before the poet had the opportunity to see "the stars in their paths," a natural, regularized, controlled world, now, after the decree, "there is not anything" *(ein yesh!)* of the innocence and goodness that one might have enjoyed. The poet's eyes are oblivious to the paths of the stars—that is, to the brutal, ordered normality of a world out of control.

The main images in these poems deal with peripheries and edges, things being closed off or ended, and threats to poetry or its demise. In the dream the poet's father stands at the threshhold, as does the son in the present, watching the world being destroyed. For those, like the poet, who are distant from their town, the "door is closed." The poet even pleads: "close your doors in my face," for fear that one speck of "hidden light" (that is, any glaring testimony to the utter truth of the disaster) will reach him outside. "The house is destroyed before my eyes," he laments. Eyes and seeing, once the instruments of his enthralled vision, again represent the antithetical theme of death and loss.

The poet abandons the dream scene with "a final legend in my blood/of the kingdom's end." The notion of *malkhut,* "kingdom," a recurrent theme in Gilboa's Holocaust poetry, encompasses the personal reminiscence of a revered, forceful past, the hoped-for messianic "kingdom" to come, and the apocalyptic idea of the destruction of the world. Continuing in a mythological vein, Gilboa intones that "all the hems of curtains have fallen down to earth/and have hidden the vision from the eye of beholders." At this very moment "the word" *(ha-omer),* the key to expression, is being created; but the curtains remain in place and shield the eyes and ears from witnessing its birth.[60] Despite the dramatic irony, the apocalypse has completely enveloped and concealed the word.

Leaving the dream, Gilboa refers to his closing expression of feeling toward the apocalypse: "And my light will rhyme in my blood a final legend/on the end of the kingdom." At other points in these poems Gilboa notes imagistically that "arms stretch out to my strings/to tear them apart." His harp, personified, "is hurt [or afflicted, *nagu'a]* by fire."[61] His poetry is threatened by "the end of all melody [which] is a silent cry/endlessly consuming."

Thus the central theme of Gilboa's Holocaust poetry emerges: Confronting the horrors has led to Gilboa's fear of losing his poetic voice and of no longer being able to express his complex and far-ranging emotions through poetry. Even as he obviously succeeds in recording those emotions with all the considerable poetic powers at his command—images, motifs, allusions, oppositions, oxymorons, and personifications—the magnitude of the destruction, the depth of his sense of loss, the enormity of the poetic task confronting him cannot be contained in words. In the very act of sharing his fear of creative demise, he creates his uniquely personal poetic responses to the tragedy.[62] These works clearly identify Gilboa as one of modern Hebrew poetry's most poignant and eloquent Holocaust poets—a fact not often acknowledged, or at least not put forward very forcefully, by critics or historians of the literature.[63]

Compared to his contemporaries, Gilboa's lyricism and his poetics of reminiscence and lament have shaped a more emotive poetry of individual sorrow. Often distanced from a sense of direct personal involvement, the Holocaust poems of Shlonsky and Alterman are far less evocative. Shlonsky uses stock motifs such as a loss of words, muteness, primordial chaos *(bohu)*, the Binding of Isaac, slaughter, and conflagration. He also replicates the format of Yehuda Halevi's *Tsiyon ha-lo tishali* (O Zion, Surely You Would Ask) and the Kol Nidrei prayer to elicit a tone of mournfulness, with the overall impression being more formulaic than emotive.[64] Alterman comes to the Holocaust only by way of abstract, symbolic, and, in the case of *Shirei makot mitsrayim* (Poems of the Plagues of Egypt, 1944), mythological imagery.[65] Indeed, the modernistic modes upon which Shlonsky, Alterman, and Uri Zvi Greenberg are reliant—Futurism, Symbolism, and Expressionism—set poetic patterns which tend to deviate from the lyricism of personal expressibility.

Gilboa and Greenberg

Though there were many Hebrew poets who wrote on the subject,[66] the works of Greenberg are no doubt the most well-known. Greenberg perhaps considered himself *the* poetic voice of the Holocaust with declarations such as "I will not stray from the flame . . . it is with me. I am it. . . . Who else will/sing the song of fire in this generation?"—one among many issued in the pages of his magnum opus, *Reḥovot ha-nahar* (Streets of the River, 1950).[67] In contrast to the highly personal and memoiristic works of Gilboa, Greenberg's poems are predominantly visionary, political, sarcastic, defiant, and vengeful.[68] While both Gilboa and Greenberg use mythical themes related to nature and the cosmos and their chaotic state, Greenberg often adds dimensions of historical and cultural mythology. Gilboa also uses mythic images such as the "life" of the dead, but he typically understates the dimensions of myth and cosmic images, limiting them mostly to earthly depictions. Greenberg's orientation is quite different: He usually revels in grand expansiveness. For example:

כָּבוּ כָּל צִבְעֵי הַפְּלָאִים.
כָּל הַנְּתִיבוֹת בָּעוֹלָם –
חֹשֶׁךְ־וְדָם־בּוֹ כִּסָּם...

All the wonders' colors were extinguished.
All the paths in the world—
darkness-and-blood-in-it covered them . . . [69]

Greenberg's mythical expansion into history and culture is expressed in many ways. These include his use of phrases such as the Jewish "fate-of-exiles from the rivers of Babylon," "the End of Days—no sun or stars," and "the fear of [God's harsh] Judgment" *(eimat ha-din* and *gezar dinenu).* He also includes mythical references to the courageous Hebrews at the battle of Lakhish, the power of the Kingdom of Judah, the Sword of David, the "Lone Lamb" *(se levadad,* God's beloved but oppressed people), and the prophetic, cataclysmic era of Gog and Magog. In *Arba'a shirei bina* (Four Poems of Wisdom),[70] the history of Jewish persecution appears in a mythic guise.

מִיּוֹם שֶׁנִּצַּחְנוּ אֶת טֶבַע הָאֵשׁ וְהַמַּיִם...
הוֹלֶכֶת אַחֲרֵינוּ הָאֵשׁ...
הוֹלְכִים אַחֲרֵינוּ הַמַּיִם: כְּדֵי לְטַבְּעֵנוּ.

From the time we conquered the nature of fire and water . . .
we are followed by fire . . .
and water follows us as well: in order to drown us.

In further contradistinction from Gilboa, Greenberg mythologizes the entire history and culture of Mediterranean and Western societies into one beastly conglomerate *ha-goy ha-magor* (the Gentile Dread), a fearful Unmensch force, which, since the days of the Israelites' bitter enemy, Amalek, has aimed to destroy the Jewish people. Thus he dismisses all non-Jews as animals; only the Jews are made in God's image.

אֲנַחְנוּ לִמַּדְנוּ עוֹלָם: אָבִינוּ הַקַּדְמוֹן הוּא אָדָם
בְּצֶלֶם דְּמוּת תַּבְנִיתוֹ שֶׁל אֱלֹהִים...וְאוּלָם
בַּגּוֹיִים קָם מוֹרֶה וְלִמְּדָם: אֲבִי הָאָדָם הָיָה קוֹף...

We taught the world: Our ancient ancestor was Adam
in the image and form of God . . . while
the gentiles had a teacher who taught them: Humanity's father was the ape. . . .

הִנֵּה נִרְאֵהוּ – אֶת הַגּוֹי: אֵירוֹפָּה יַעַר: שַׁלִּיט הַקּוֹף.

אֶת הַיַּעַר הַזֶּה עָלֵינוּ לַעֲקֹף
עַם אַבְרָהָם יִצְחָק וְיַעֲקֹב –

Behold and see — the gentile: Europe's a forest: ruled by the ape.

This forest we must avoid
[we] the people of Abraham Isaac and Jacob —[71]

In his more personal, lyrical style of memorializing the Holocaust, Gilboa eschews these larger dimensions of myth and phobic accusations. (Only once, toward the end of *Shir ke-migdalekh ha-gavo'ah* [A Poem of Your High Tower],[72] does Gilboa point an accusatory finger at God.[73]) Nor does he include graphic depictions of the horrors of the Holocaust. In contrast, Greenberg writes of the camps and gas chambers, of Jews lining up for extermination — the book's title, "Streets of the River," in part captures these images. In the larger context of Holocaust literature, Gilboa may be compared to the Israeli novelist Aharon Appelfeld (1932–), who purposely abjures such details, while Greenberg's poetry is more similar to the fiction of KaTzetnik (Karol Cetynski, 1917–), which contains graphic descriptions of deprivation, torture, and slaughter.

In spite of their radically different poetics, there are some similarities between Gilboa and Greenberg. Greenberg has his personal, lyrical moments:

אֲנִי נוֹתַרְתִּי אֶחָד מִזֶּה גַּן הַפֵּרוֹת שֶׁכֹּרַת...
אֵיךְ אֶפְשָׁר שֶׁאָבִי כָּתַב פַּעַם אֵלַי: ,בֵּן פּוֹרָת!׳?

I alone survived from the orchard that was cut down. . . .
How is it possible that my father once wrote to me: 'My beloved son!'?

אֵיךְ אֶפְשָׁר שֶׁאִמִּי לִבְּבַתְנִי: ,בְּנִי הַזּוֹרֵחַ!׳?
וְיָדְעוּ שֶׁבְּיוֹם אֵיד לֹא יַעֲמֹד עַל סִפָּם כְּמָגֵן
זֶה הַבֵּן
הַבּוֹרֵחַ:

How is it possible that my mother lovingly called me: "My radiant son!"
And they knew that come the catastrophe this son of theirs
a runaway [i.e., an *ole* to the Land of Israel]
would not stand at their door
as a shield.[74]

And Gilboa has his more effusive moments:

עַתָּה יָדַעְנוּ כָּל מַבּוּלֵי מַרְאוֹת
נוֹצְצִים בְּתַאֲווֹת עַל צִפָּרְנַיִם.
וְטֶרֶם בָּא פַּחַד אָהַבְנוּ לִרְעוֹד
כִּרְעוֹד לְחַיָּיו הַמָּוֶת.
וּנְטִיפוֹת שֶׁל זָהָב עִנַּדְנוּ לַשָּׁמַיִם
שֶׁיִּהְיוּ גְּבֹהִים עַד מָוֶת.

זֶה שִׁיר בְּלֵילוֹת גְּבֹהִים עַד מָוֶת
וּלְעֵת שַׁחַר צוֹרֵחַ נֵפֶל עַל אָרֶץ.
(אֵין דָּבָר! בַּעֲבוֹר יוֹם הוּא יִשְׁאַג כְּאַרְיֵה מוּל חֲלוּדַת שָׁמַיִם,
,עֲקָרָה׳, ,עֲקָרָה׳ יְגַדֵּף בְּשִׁקְרוֹ שֵׁם אִמּוֹ הַבּוֹרֵאת.)

Now we knew all the floods of visions
sparkling in lusts upon fingernails [or claws].
And before fear came we loved to tremble
like the trembling of Death for its life.
And [with] drops of gold we decorated the sky
so they'd be high unto death.

This is a poem on nights high unto death
and at dawn a stillborn [child] screams on earth.
(No matter! Another day and he'll roar like a lion at the rusting
of heaven.
"Barren," "barren" he'll revile in his lie the name of his creating
mother.)[75]

Gilboa's effusiveness, however, is metaphorically based. Though he often felt that his overwrought style in his early works was problematic, his imagistic profusion in the Holocaust poems is unquestionably effective.[76] Greenberg's style is also highly effusive, but his poetic exposition is for the most part realistically descriptive, hence metonymically oriented.

There are smaller commonalities in theme, image, and phraseology: the metaphoric use of tears as dew (common in Hebrew lyric poetry); the use of the verb *higir* for the flowing of blood and water; and the image of ancient scrolls to evoke both the world and the longevity of Jewish tradition. More visible in the works of both poets is the use of hyphenated combination words. Greenberg's use of them is most prominent in *Reḥovot ha-nahar,* but they are also abundant in his 1937 collection *Sefer ha-kitrug ve-ha-emuna* (The Book of Accusation and Faith). Gilboa, who knew Greenberg and his works well,[77] probably borrowed the usage from him—though it is not very prominent in Gilboa's later works. Another shared image is the use of the traditional tune *(nigun, zemer,* or *zimra),* which both poets relate to memories of their parental homes.[78]

There are other common usages. Greenberg's Holocaust poems are filled with such phrases as "my dead [ones]" *(metai),* "my slaughtered [ones]" *(tevuḥai),* "my burnt ones" *(serufai),* "my Jews" *(Yehudai).* Gilboa also uses this type of word-phrase at times—especially *metai* and *yeshenai* (my sleepers)—when he refers to the Holocaust dead, mainly his own family.

By coincidence or by borrowing, both poets use the same descriptive adjective *ha-zore'aḥ.* Gilboa incorporates it in his plaintive, elegiacal poem about his murdered nephew: *Yossi, Yossi ha-katan, ha-zore'aḥ* (little Yossi, the shining one). Using the same term, Greenberg, in *Kinat ha-ben be-vorḥo mi-beit aviv ve-imo* (excerpted above) remembers his mother calling him *beni ha-zore'aḥ* (my shining son).

Probably the most striking textual similarity involves the short opening elegy to *"Sefer ḥayei olam,"* Gilboa's dream-poem about the fall of "the brother," discussed above on p. 48. Gilboa uses the uncommon term *tsone'aḥ* to describe the envisioned death—the same term Greenberg uses in *Ba'ei ba-maḥteret* (Those Who Come By Stealth), the opening poem of *Reḥovot ha-nahar,* where the subject is also a brother. Set in 1931—the subtitle is "Vision of a Summer Night, 1931"—the poem refers to a "survivor" *(palit)* who brings rumors of the slaughter of Jews. "With these shoes that's how I passed through the blood, with my body all alone the fire." In the poem's second stanza the speaker tries to convince his brother to steal out of town and seek refuge is a safer place; the brother agrees.

וְהִנֵּה הוּא שׁוֹתֵק. הוּא צוֹנֵחַ לִישֹׁן. הוּא נוֹחֵר.
פִּיו פָּעוּר. פִּיו תְּהוֹם. חֲצוֹת לֵיל. הַיָּשֵׁן זֶה אָחִי.
מָחָר אוֹר...יַכִּירֵנִי וַדַּאי, אֶת אָחִיו.

Look, he's silent. He's falling *[tsone'aḥ]* asleep. He's snoring.
His mouth is open. His mouth's an abyss. Midnight. The sleeper's my brother.
Tomorrow morning . . . he'll surely recognize me, his brother.

That both poets include the same rather uncommon word in the beginning of their collections of Holocaust poems and a dream or vision involving the physical "falling" of a symbolic brother seems to point to an intertextuality rather than a coincidence. All such convergences aside, however, the two poets perceive their roles as Holocaust poets in vastly different ways. Gilboa takes on this writing as a personal and artistic commitment, as a way of memorializing the lives of his family and assuaging his self-consuming grief. At the same time, he is constantly—painfully—unsure of his ability to maintain the emotional energy required to put the enormous trauma into words.

Greenberg is anything but ambivalent. He speaks through an open wound; his works are poetic tirades. He regards himself as the Holocaust's prophet; his ordained role is to expose and curse as inherently bestial and evil the entire gentile world, its roots, its history and culture. He blasphemes God for abetting the beast in its slaughter of His people. While the works do memorialize his murdered parents, Greenberg relates mostly to the larger, impersonal categories of Jew vs. gentile, murderers vs. victims, animal vs. spirit. His venom is fanatic; his stance, radical. Where Gilboa is sorrowful, Greenberg is enraged; where Gilboa is personal, Greenberg is monolithic; where Gilboa is figurative, Greenberg is factual; where Gilboa is metaphorical, Greenberg is metonymic; where Gilboa is relenting, Greenberg is unrepentant. Gilboa's worldview is from the center of his poetry, in the very act of producing the poem. This uneasy artistic involvement is a recurring dramatic situation in Gilboa's works:

הִנֵּה עָמַדְתִּי בְּתוֹךְ הַשִּׁיר
וְנִכְלַמְתִּי בְּכֹחַ.

Here I stand in the midst of the poem
and I am completetly overcome.[79]

Greenberg, on the other hand, stands *with* his poem "in the center" of a grand mythical design: a vast historical, social, cultural, ethical, even genetic conflict between Jews and the world:

וּבַתָּוֶךְ – אֲנִי וְשִׁירִי
עִם מַאֲוַיֵּי אָדָם נִשָּׂאִים –

And in the center—I and my song
with the lofty cravings of humanity—[80]

His vision is political, global. In a sense, he moves beyond the poem, beyond poetry.

Gilboa's dichotomous theme of nature/beauty/normality versus death/blood/fear is reflected in the final section of *"Sefer ḥayei olam."* Presumably written on the Italian front and published, in part, while Gilboa was still in Europe, these works lack the fervid personal tone of the previous group of works.

The subject of *Mi-dibur hi niset* (It Is Borne By Speech) is courage *(ha-gevura)* and its derivation from speech.[81] The poem begins, "Courage is borne by speech, by the speech of one friend to another." What follows is a sequential tracing of speech from its sources in both everyday and mythical realms. Its role, says Gilboa, is to engender a peaceful calm, which then creates more words, more happiness, and more courage.

The act of speech is derived from "sayings of belief *(dibrot emuna)* which [a friend] has gathered in the corner of a field and at the corner of a street/and in the rungs of the ladders by which every infant goes up to heaven."[82] These "sayings of belief" are to be found both in common everyday encounters and in visionary scenes of death and deliverance. They are magical entities, sent either by heaven or by nature, which provide the strength to overcome the sorrow brought on by the death of so many children. The hopeful "sayings" are envisioned as follows:

הֵן דִּבְּרוֹת אֱמוּנָה זְרוּעוֹת עַל פְּנֵי אָרֶץ
הַנּוֹפְלוֹת מִמִּזְרֵה הָרוּחַ וְנִשְׁבָּצוֹת כִּפְנִינִים בִּירִיעוֹת הַקַּרְקַע
לִשְׂמֹחַ עַל אָשְׁרָם בַּקַּיָּם.

[They are] sown upon the earth
falling from the wind's pitchfork and set like pearls in the
  curtains of the ground
to rejoice at the happiness of that which exists.

The poet is struggling here to cope with his sorrow and to summon the courage to speak or write about the Holocaust; his romantic visions become poetic words of healing. His apparent success is demonstrated by the poem's outpouring of idyllic images and scenes: The revitalization and fructification of dried-up land, the youthful greening of "the boulders of silent life," the watering of furrows in spring and winter, "their quiet song [borne] upon a thousand musical instruments and song." All this, so that humankind will discover more expressions with which to greet each other in the field; so that grandfathers "will stretch out [their] hands and gather blessings on the heads of grandchildren"; so that the eyes of young girls will sparkle and young men "will blossom in their youth like the branches of trees in the avenues."

The images are rustic and pastoral: fields, earth, greenness, the entrance to a village inn, the harvester amidst his standing grain. The overall impression is one of close-to-the-earth innocence — a vision of settling the Land — a palliative, perhaps, for all the Jewish suffering. The vision is meant to assuage the poet, the survivors, even the dead. The combination of idyllic scenes and the motif of expressivity shows once again how dependent Gilboa is on the poetics of romanticism for the continuing vitality of his poetic voice.

Typically, however, Gilboa soon renounces the cogency of romantic vision and embraces despair. *Elul* (September)[83] opens with a picture of day'send quietude and signs of "the holiday of fall." At the same time, the speaker envisions "the blood flowing from life to life screaming with the redness of pain." The horrible image becomes mythological: it flows "upon the blood wells for generations of children/who have sunken into the abyss without a sound." The twilight's beauty and calm — the beautiful and the lyrical in life — are meaningless in the face of the Nazi slaughter.

The last two poems in this group, *Kets ha-krav* (Battle's End)[84] and *Gan na'ul bo'er* (A Locked Garden Burning), reflect the same dichotomy — or equivalence — of the romantic and the realistic. Although different in their respective poetic configurations — *Kets ha-krav* utilizes a mythological mode of dramatic depiction while *Gan na'ul bo'er* presents a more lyrical, idyllic scene — both poems are more metonymic than metaphorical in their signifying structures.[85]

For example, *Kets ha-krav* amplifies the battle's end by depicting it as a cosmic, apocalyptic, stop-time event.

אוֹתוֹ רֶגַע וּבָרְחוֹבוֹת עָמְדָה מִלֶּכֶת
כָּל הָאֱנוֹשׁוּת.

At that moment all humanity stood still
in the streets.

אֵי־מִי גִלְגֵל רְעָמִים בַּמְּחִלּוֹת...

Someone rolled thunder through the caves . . . [86]

וְאֵד עָלָה מִן הַתְּהוֹם מִן הַדָּם הָרָב.
עֲרְפִלִּים כִּסּוּ אֶת עֵין הַשֶּׁמֶשׁ.

And a haze rose from the abyss and from the abundant blood.
Fog covered the eye of the sun.

These descriptions constitute a metonymy by substituting a mythological vision for a natural idyllic scene.

Gan na'ul bo'er, in contrast, is immersed in lyrical language, though there are mythical resonances here as well. The speaker describes a personal experience: he sees a lovely, private garden going up in flames; within a few minutes the entire garden is consumed. Musing on this incident, the mournful speaker relates the fire directly to the destruction of his town, *iri* (my city), as he calls it.[87] Even though the poem depicts a general war scene, the garden fire serves as a metonymy for the Holocaust. The poem's lyricism also expresses the emotional bond between the speaker-observer and the garden and is enhanced by mythic and metaphorical images: revitalized magic, birth, smoke likened to a great king with a crown of sparks, the smell of sacrifices.

אֵלֵךְ וְאָבוֹא בִּשְׁבִילָיו שֶׁל הַגַּן הַכּוֹבֵל בִּסְבָכָיו אֶת הָאֶמֶשׁ
וְעֵינַי תִּרְאֶינָה בְּעַנְבַּר הַשְּׂרָף אֶת נִטְפֵי הַהֶמְיָה הַמְשֻׁתֶּקֶת.
כִּי עָיְפוּ אִילָנוֹת מִסְּפִירַת הַשָּׁנִים בְּמַעְגְּלֵי גִזְעֵיהֶם בְּשָׂפָה אִלֶּמֶת
וּמִכִּלְיוֹן שָׁרָשִׁים עוֹרְגִים עַל הֵדֵי צְמִיחָתָם מִן הַשֶּׁקֶט.

I walk and come to the paths of the garden that binds the night before
in its shrubs
And my eyes see in the amber of resin the drops of its silenced
yearning.
For the trees have grown tired of counting the years in the rings of
their trunks in a mute tongue
And of the longing of roots lusting for the echoes of their growth from
the quiet.[88]

The work ends, however, on an anticlimactic note.

עַד הֶאְדִּים הַמַּרְאֶה אֶת בָּקְרִי מוּל עִיר הָאָדָם־הַצּוֹוֵחַ. . .
וּבֹקֶר עִירִי אֶל יוֹם בִּפְרָעָיו עוֹלֶה וּפוֹרֵחַ.
וְעִירִי בְּיָגוֹן וּבְחִיל אֶת עֲשַׁן הַשְּׂרֵפָה נוֹשֶׁמֶת.

Till the sight turned my morning red across from the town of the
screaming-man. . . .

And the morning of my town rises to the day and blossoms in its
destruction.[89]
And my city in sorrow and fright inhales the smoke of the fire.

The oxymoron of the city "ris[ing] to the day and/blossom[ing] in its destruction" expresses the full force of Gilboa's sorrow. Written toward the close of the war,[90] the poem demonstrates how Gilboa was able to "romanticize" the Holocaust by combining lyrical language with an overriding sense of tragedy.

The Experience of War: Poems of the Jewish Brigade

The first sections of *"Sefer mi-derekh"* (Book of the Road) are "soldier poems" written as the Jewish Brigade made its way from Italy to France. They were published after the war, between February 1946 and August 1948. Far more narratively structured than Gilboa's Holocaust-oriented works, they focus mainly on the feelings of soldiers at war and may be seen as the forebears of the works of poets such as Ḥaim Gouri and Yehuda Amichai written during and after the War of Independence.

The main themes are the typical situations and plaints of soldiers in active combat. They are weary, filthy, in need of rest; they collect and compare war souvenirs; they feel aged beyond their years; having come through dark days, they wonder how long they will yet survive; many die before their time; feeling abused, they look forward to the "great day" of final victory and peace.

Here Gilboa draws on his established repertoire of allusions and metaphors. Once again the most prominent motif is eye imagery, as the soldier-speaker describes the agonizing sights and sounds of the battlefield. "Our eyes flash [*borkot,* from *barak,* lightning] with the color of rust *[ein ha-ḥaluda],*" says the weary soldier in *Anaḥnu ba-derakhim* (We On the Roads), using an anticlimactic parody of Numbers 1:7, which describes the manna in the desert as having "the color of crystal" *(ein ha-bedolaḥ).*[91] In *Afar* (Dust) the speaker describes little children playing near the front as having "gold laughing in the pupils of their eyes *[ishonim].*" At night, he says, "our eyes are so tender/and the silver of the moon longs for them." More often, however, the sights are less dreamy and appealing. *Ne'um ha-*

govim lifnei yomam (The Speech of Those Who Die Before Their Time) laments that "even before we [have a chance to] smile we are dead"; the sights of death make "the pupil *[bava]* burn in our eyes."[92]

As before, the *bavot* motif accentuates the terror brought on by visual traumas at the front. "Who can separate the eye from the pupil," cries the dismayed, frustrated speaker in *Al ha-tsa'ar* (On Sorrow), fearing the response of strangers who detect the soldiers' Holocaust sorrow "which dwells and stings deep in our pupils." The last poem of this group, *Laila be-karaḥat ha-ya'ar* (Night in the Forest Clearing),[93] presents a dream sequence in which the Holocaust dead rise and gather before the sleepless soldiers. "We recognized them," the speaker says. "Yes. They are our elders *[avotenu]*. We recognized them by their pupils of fire."

The most ironic image in these works is laughter—except for the laughter of children, which is used to signify moments of happiness that shine through the fatigue and filth. In *Ne'um ha-govim lifnei yomam* it is the "great day" of triumph that laughs derisively at the soldiers: "And it laughed alone. And it laughed gold./And it—never reached us," says the unnerved speaker. In *Al ha-semaḥot* (On Happinesses [or "happy occasions"])[94] the speaker cautions his soldier-auditors "to recognize and deal kindly with happinesses," and not to "laugh so much about things/you've done and could have let pass and be forgotten/if only you could see in the eyes of strangers/the happinesses you've let flee from your shoulders."[95] Of course, the entire passage is ironic, for what follows and closes the poem is a litany of sorrows. There is so much sorrow, in fact, that "flowers cry in the tears that have fallen from your eyes." Even the good times themselves begin to weep. After the Holocaust and the war, laughter and tears—like other romantic dualities—are not very far apart.

The most salient feature of these poems is their narrative character and structure. *Laila be-karaḥat ha-ya'ar* tells of a night experience when the soldiers could not fall asleep. A dream of resurrected Holocaust survivors comes upon them. The rise of these ghostly images is described in detail, as are the impressions formed in the minds of the soldiers as they watch. The forest clearing is also described in a combined realistic-Gothic manner. In the last part of the poem the dreamers themselves rise and begin walking toward the ghosts, while the sounds of axes cut away at the trees. This is a pure story, a folk-narrative of a nightmare, told from beginning to end. There are nonnarrative dimensions of the poem, to be sure; but these dimensions are constituted mostly of metaphorical figures or symbolic background action and are also fraught with dramatic force.

The narrator of *Benei beli shem* (Sons With No Name)[96] tells of a number of encounters between Jewish soldiers and some passersby, probably war refugees, upon whom the soldiers play a joke. Suspecting the soldiers are Jews, the passersby do not bother to ask the soldiers' names. Sarcastically, the soldiers tell them that they are grand nobles, with elegant castles and stables. They invite the strangers to stay overnight, for "we are all brothers . . . our ancestors are the sons of one father." Through the voice of the narrator the soldiers call themselves constant "forgivers"—"O, forgivers were we from morning till morning" *(ho salḥanim hayinu mi-boker ad boker)*—and they have a good laugh. It is clear, however, that the Jewish soldiers themselves wish that they had a home—a double entendre, no doubt, in the context of the Holocaust experience.

Ḥalomot shelanu (Our Dreams)[97] focuses not on one particular dream but on the whole phenomenon of soldier-dreaming. The narrative structure of the poem combines effectively with its figurative, rhetorical, and dramatic dimensions to create a highly charged portrayal of the war experience, itself heightened by the Jewish dimension.

חֲלוֹמוֹת שֶׁלָּנוּ

אֶת הַלַּיְלָה עָבַרְנוּ גֵּאִים וּמֻכִּים.
שִׁבְרֵי חֲלוֹמוֹת נָשְׁרוּ אֶל הַחוֹל
כִּפְרָסוֹת שְׁחוּקוֹת, אֲשֶׁר הַסּוּס לֹא יִזְכֹּר
אֵי נַפָּח פִּרְזְלוֹ –
אַךְ שִׁבְרֵי חֲלוֹמוֹת עוֹד יָבוֹאוּ רַבּוֹת
חֲדָשִׁים וְזָרִים, מְלֵאֵי תֹקֶף.
אַךְ שִׁבְרֵי חֲלוֹמוֹת יַדְבִּיקוּנוּ פְּצוּעִים
קְלוּפֵי־מָאוֹר בִּצְלָב שְׁמָשׁוֹת
רִאשׁוֹנִים אֶל חֲלִין כַּאֲרֻחַת־בֹּקֶר.

אֲנַחְנוּ פְּשׁוּטִים כָּל־כָּךְ בַּיּוֹם.
אֲנַחְנוּ חוֹלִים כָּל־כָּךְ בַּיּוֹם.

אַךְ מִלַּיְלָה אֲנַחְנוּ צוֹעֲקִים אֶל גְּבוּרוֹת.
אַךְ בַּלַּיְלָה דָּמֵינוּ זוֹמְמִים סְעָרוֹת.
רָאשֵׁינוּ נוֹתְצִים הַקִּירוֹת וְהָאָרִיחַ.
וּבַיּוֹם אָנוּ יוֹדְעִים שֶׁחֲלַמְנוּ נְצוּרוֹת
וְחוֹלְמִים לִזְכֹּר אֶת הַחֲלוֹם –
הַמָּשִׁיחַ.

אֲנַחְנוּ גְדוֹלִים כָּל־כָּךְ בַּלֵּילוֹת.
אֲנַחְנוּ צוֹעֲקִים הַרְבֵּה בַּלֵּילוֹת
מִגַּנֵּי הַזְּוָעָה וְהַשֶּׁגַע.
וְאֵינֶנּוּ יוֹדְעִים אֶת כָּל־זֹאת
וְאֵינֶנּוּ זוֹכְרִים אֶת כָּל־זֹאת
לוּלֵא עוֹבְרֵי־הָאֹרַח בַּלֵּיל
הַמִּתְבַּהֲלִים מִן הַיְלֵל,
שֶׁמְּסַפְּרִים לָנוּ זֹאת
וְנִמְלָטִים מִפַּחַד
כַּעֲבֹר רֶגַע.

Our Dreams

Proud and beaten we've passed the night.
Slivers of dreams fell on the sand
like hooves worn down, the horse has forgotten
where the smith had shod him —
But slivers of dreams will keep on coming
new and strange and powerful.
But slivers of dreams will overtake us, wounded,
devoid of light, at the cross of sunlight,
first to something as simple as breakfast.

We're so simple by day.
We're so sick by day.
But at night we scream at glories.

But at night our blood plots storms.
Our heads break through the walls and tile.
And by day we know we've dreamt secret things
and dream to recall the dream—
Messiah.

We're so big at night.
We scream a lot at night
from gardens of dread and madness.
We don't know all this,
we don't recall all this,
if not for the passersby at night
terrified by our cries,
who tell us this
and run off in fear
a moment later.[98]

The poem begins dualistically. The soldiers pass the night "proud and beaten"—"proud," one presumes, because of their accomplishments during the day of fighting, and "beaten" because they are exhausted and because they are beset by dreams. The dreams themselves are not detailed, but the impression is that they are nightmarish. The soldiers come upon them "like hooves worn-down" of a horse that "has forgotten/where the smith had shod him"—an ambiguous image which conveys either a traceless source or a repetitious series of dreams which are fragmentary and quickly forgotten. Nevertheless, the "slivers of dreams" are numerous and always "new and strange and powerful."

The dreams "overtake" the soldiers, who feel "wounded"—perhaps because the dreams are "slivers," like shrapnel. The soldiers are also "devoid of light" *(kelufei ma'or)*, an ironic image, since they appear this way precisely at "the cross of suns," a reference to the convergence of moon and sun at daybreak. These are ordinary men, says the speaker; they are "first to something as simple as breakfast." However, the reader already knows that these soldiers are extraordinary, especially in the suffering and pain of their shrapnel-dream. (The use of the word *tslav*, "cross," in line 8, is significant in this sense.)

The narrator continues on this ambiguous tack in the second stanza. In the first two lines the conflicting conditions "simple" and "sick" are semantically incompatible. The connotation is that the days, relatively simple compared to the nights, are also emotionally complex. But the nights are unambiguously horrid. The soldiers "scream at glories," referring either to God *(ba'al gevurot,* "the purveyor of courage") or, sarcastically, to the glorious deeds in battle. At night their blood "plots storms" in preparation for the battles to come.

The ambiguity is resolved in lines 14–17. Because their sleep is deeply troubled, the soldiers scream and plot and bang their heads against the walls in fear, anger, and frustration. Filled with the day's violence and the hope of salvation, their dual dreaming bespeaks their wish for deliverance from both the days and the nights.

Like the first two, the third stanza has an oppositional opening. Gilboa's use of *gedolim,* "big" or "adult,"[99] is usually ironic, as in "our great day" *(yomenu ha-gadol)* in *Ne'um ha-govim lifnei yomam* or the similarly overstated use of *gavo'ah* (high) in *Rigei ḥesed.* But the anaphoric rhyming juxtaposition of *anaḥnu gedolim* (we're so big) with *anaḥnu tso'akim* (we scream) leaves no doubt that the soldier-dreamers are continually immersed in paradoxical "gardens of dread and madness *[shega].*" (The neologistic form *shega* for "madness" semantically accentuates the depth of the insaneness they have experienced.) The narrative ends with the soldiers saying that they "don't know" or "don't recall" anything of the night. They are told of their screams—*yelel,* used in the same segolate form of *shega,* conveys a mournful wailing more than a scream—by passersby who become frightened and quickly run off.

"Sofei devarim" (The Ends of Things)

"Sofei devarim" contains Gilboa's last poems about the Jewish Brigade experience. Most were composed in 1945–46 as the Brigade disbanded and its members helped bring Holocaust survivors to Displaced Persons camps in Italy and Austria. Gilboa also assisted in recording information on Brigade members killed in the war, and his research took him to France, Belgium, and Holland. He arrived back in Erets Israel on January 10, 1946.[100]

The opening poems reflect a tone of looking backward, remembering "all the nights we stood at the crossings of rivers." Their experiences are approached with ironic nostalgia, through a prism of time passing into memory.

הַחוֹל שֶׁנִּשְׁטַף מִן הַחוֹף אֶל הַיָּם
לָקַח סִמָּנֵי עִקְּבוֹתָיו שֶׁל אָדָם
וּפִזְּרָם בְּמֶרְחָב שֶׁל אֵין־סוֹף.

The sand that was washed from the shore to the sea
took the traces of people's footsteps
and scattered them into the vastness of the infinite.[101]

Of course, realities of the seemingly endless war counterbalance the nostalgia. The soldiers ironically wonder why they were not able to enjoy the good times when the days seemed to "spread out before us like burning/ brides for their lovers."

Memory is again the main theme. The speaker observes that old soldier friends seem to have forgotten members of the Brigade. "We'll not let you forget what you are obliged to remember," he says, referring simultaneously both to the relentless memory of the Holocaust and to the oblivion of war. His understanding of the memory lapse is less rueful than it is universally damning, "for we understood that we'd lost the privilege of the comprehensible" *(ha-zekhut el ha-muvan)*. The soldiers of the Jewish Brigade do not have the luxury of forgetting.

שֶׁמִּדֵּי בֹּקֶר לְאַחֵינוּ דָּם יִקְרָא עוֹד מִמִּפְתָּן
וְחֶשְׁבּוֹן כַּסְפָּם בַּסֵּפֶר שֶׁיִּהְיֶה מָחוּק מִדָּם.
שֶׁבְּפָרְשָׂם בְּרָכָה אֶל בֹּקֶר תִּוָּלֵד מִלַּת נָקָם.

Each morning blood cries out to our brothers from the threshhold
and their money account in the book, may it be erased of its blood.
For as they cast a blessing toward morning, may the word of vengeance
be born.[102]

El-erer[103] is an expression of their unequivocal feelings of revenge. It is a Gothic incantation poem, composed of a number of curses aimed at the enemy-murderers.

רָאשֵׁי אֶצְבָּעוֹת קָרוֹת יִנְחֲתוּ אָז עַל כְּתֵפְךָ הַלּוֹהֶטֶת.
בְּשִׁמְךָ נִקְרָא...
בְּאוֹתִיּוֹת מְתֻזּוֹת, חַדּוֹת, אֲיֻמּוֹת הַקֶּצֶב.
בְּכֵרַת רֵעִים יָזוּב יֵינְךָ כִּמְגֻלַּת מַכָּה –

Cold fingertips will come to rest on your fiery shoulder.
We will call out your name . . .
in battered letters, sharp, fearsome in their rhythm.
At a banquet of friends your wine will flow like pus from a
wound—

מְרוּקָּדִים בְּעִגּוּל נְשַׁכֵּל טְפִיפוֹתֶיךָ בִּבְעָתָה –
וְאֶל פַּחַד נְשַׁלְּחֵן לְדַרְדֵּר
עַד עַצְמוֹתֶיךָ תַּלְבֵּנָּה
עֶצֶם אַחַר עֶצֶם.

We will destroy your [dancing] steps with horror—
and we will send them off toward terror to roll about
till your bones turn white
bone after bone.[104]

In this final group of soldier "portraits," Gilboa attempts to sum up emotions the soldiers have felt during the difficult four-year journey from North Africa to Western Europe. Entitled *Signonot shonim* (Different Styles—that is, different ways of expressing feelings),[105] the prose-like poem is composed of a series of elliptical, nominal verses, each of which describes a different response. Of the nineteen lines, ten begin with *ze* or *zo,* the equivalent of "it's."[106] Five of the remaining nine begin with *El* (God), giving the poem a prayer-like tone. However, the word *El* simply stands at the start of these lines with no comma following it, so that instead of "O God," the reader hears a hasty, whispered, under-the-breath "God." The anaphoric use of the term strikes the reader more as a recurring expletive than a prayerful invocation. Among the emotions and experiences listed are the following:

סִגְנוֹנוֹת שׁוֹנִים. זֶה לַחַץ הַדָּם בְּלִבֵּנוּ הָעוֹלֶה וְיוֹרֵד.
זֶה יוֹמֵנוּ בְּתַהְפּוּכוֹת רְגָעָיו הַצּוֹרְבִים.
זוֹ מִלְחֶמֶת יְצָרִים עַזִּים שֶׁכְּמוֹ הַחַיִּים לָהֶם מָוֶת תָּמִיד אוֹרֵב.
זֶה קְרָב בְּמַעֲמַקֵּי הַיָּם אַךְ גַּבּוֹ הַשּׁוֹקֵט שׁוֹמֵר חִיּוּכָיו.

Different styles. It's the blood pressure rising and falling in our hearts.
It's our day with the deceptions of its blistering moments.
It's a war of strong passions always threatened, like life, by death.
It's a battle in sea-depths but its silent back preserves its smiles.

זוֹ נַפְשֵׁנוּ בְּכַפֵּנוּ הַנִּטְרֶפֶת וְטֵרוּפֵנוּ שֶׁעוֹלֶה בְּשִׁיר קָדוֹשׁ.
זֶה קֶשֶׁר טַבּוּרֵנוּ בַּנִּתּוּק הָאַכְזָר מִיקָר בֵּית־אָבוֹת שֶׁנִּכְרַת.

It's the ravaging of our threatened soul and our madness which rises in holy song.
It's the knot of our navel in its cruel severance from the grace of our butchered family home.

The impassioned rhetoric, strewn with familar images and motifs—fire, water, holiness, madness, home—fervidly disgorges the "different styles" of battle-weariness which beset the men. For the speaker the agonized verses are more self-defining than prayerful. The God-invoking lines express Gilboa's unabated anger and failure to comprehend. The soldiers' feelings are eminently clear. Yet an innocent, instinctive laugh hovers above their suffering—a moment of release and frivolity that is disconnected from experience.

The poem ends with a rhyming couplet which expresses the inevitability of continued pain for these soldiers. With sarcastic irony, Gilboa uses the language of *Shir ha-palmaḥ,* the Palmach hymn: *Tamid anaḥnu,* "We're always [first]," and *tsav [damenu/ha-dorot],* "the call of our blood/of history" (altered here to *tsav uvdot,* "the call of facts").[107]

סִגְנוֹנוֹת שׁוֹנִים. אַךְ הֵם תָּמִיד אֲנַחְנוּ, מַעֲרֻמֵּנוּ הַבּוֹהֵק אֶל כָּל עֵבֶר וְקִמְרוֹן.
זֶה עִמָּם נִחְיֶה בְּצַו עֻבְדּוֹת שֶׁל כָּל יָמֵינוּ עַד הַיּוֹם.

Different styles. But they're always us *[tamid anaḥnu]*, our nakedness
that shines toward every arch and way.
It is with them we shall live by the call of facts of all our days to this
very day.

The reference to *Shir ha-palmaḥ* underscores the soldiers' resoluteness to fight on for Erets Israel—and the nightmares which are their history and their destiny. *Signonot shonim*—much like *Shiri ha-parua*, the closing poem of *La-ot*—is about the search for a cogent poetic voice. In *Shiri ha-paru'a* Gilboa affirms the legitimacy of his own style of writing. In *Signonot shonim* he also affirms the reality of his view of the postwar, post-Holocaust world. It is one of ceaseless struggle with pain, revenge, and memory.

The Holocaust: Memory, Lament, and the Poetics of Ambivalence
"Sefer ha-almog" (The Book of Coral)[108]

Although love poems and nature lyrics are also included, Gilboa continues to come to terms with both the larger and more personal losses of the Holocaust in this "book." He also mournfully celebrates survival as he begins to recapture his earlier romantic predilections. The most frequent subgenre of these memory poems is the survivor's lament.

Eikh ze ba (How It Comes [or Happens]), which opens this group of works, operates on Gilboa's familiar system of binary oppositions. The typically Russian opening is used most often in nature poems of wonderment.[109]

אֵיךְ זֶה בָּא לַעֲלוֹת וְלִחְיוֹת
שׁוּב לְדַרְכְּךָ בְּאוֹר יָמַי וְצִלָּם
וְלִפְעֹם בִּנְהִיָּה אֲבִיבִית
מִזְּרִיחוֹת שֶׁעָבְרוּ לְעוֹלָם–
זֶה הַלֵּב שֶׁפִּצְעוֹ לֹא הִגְלִיד
הוּא זוֹכֵר, הוּא זוֹכֵר אֶת כֻּלָּם.

How it comes [upon you] to rise and to live
again to stride in the light of my days and their shadow
and to throb with a spring-like cry
of sunrises that have gone forever —
It is the heart whose wound has not healed
It remembers, it remembers them all.

The placement of "shadow" at the end of line 2 immediately changes the poem's direction. Instead of a celebration of rising, living, and recapturing the light, the poem evokes sad memories. With the poignancy of a Gilead-like repetition, the last line of the first stanza sums up Gilboa's sense of loss.

The second stanza expands upon those feelings and interweaves them with familiar eye metaphors of intense experience.

הוּא זוֹכֵר וְכוֹבְלָם בְּסִיבָיו
וְכוֹבֵל מִצְעָדַי מִוִּתּוּר
וְאוֹרֵב לְעֵינִי אִם בַּשֶּׁמֶשׁ
הִיא מַיְשִׁירָה הַבֵּט עַד סִנְווּר —
אָז יָגַח כַּחַיָּה הַנּוֹהֶמֶת
מִמְּאוּרָתוֹ הַלֵּב הַקָּבוּר.

It remembers and binds them in its threads [or web]
and binds my steps from surrender
and lies in wait for my eye should it peer
straight into the sun till blindness —
Then like a roaring beast from its den
the buried heart will spring forth.

The speaker is caught in a memory-web of the dead, and the intensity of his emotion is reflected in the somewhat disjointed and elliptical syntax, a style Gilboa begins to use more frequently in his postwar works. Similarly, in the Hebrew, "the buried heart" *(ha-lev ha-kavur),* the instrument of the act of memory (and the subject of the sentence), is placed at the very end of the sentence and stanza. The syntactic inversion accentuates the pent-up rage in the image of animal wildness and savagery.

The poem closes with a fearsome yet benign image, fraught with irony and semantic opposition.

הוּא בָּא בְּצִפָּרְנַיִם חַדּוֹת
לָשֵׂאת אֶת טַרְפּוֹ עַל הַדָּם
וּנְהִיָּתוֹ כָּאָבִיב חֲרִישִׁית
כִּזְרִיחוֹת שֶׁחָזְרוּ לָעוֹלָם.

It comes with sharp claws
to carry its prey on the blood
and its cry is soft as spring
like sunrises that have returned to the world.

Though savage and bloodied, the pouncing beast-heart has a cry which is "soft as spring." Despite the preying animal presence, the simile which follows refers to the return of nurturing sunrises.

Similarly, the poem's structure proceeds from an emotionally ambiguous memory of things forever lost to an unmistakably fearsome memory of things which can never be erased. The "sunrises that have gone forever" *(zeriḥot she-avru le-olam)* become the "sunrises that have returned to the world" *(zeriḥot she-ḥazru la-olam)*. The heart's "cry" [or "sob" or "lament," *nehiya]*, at first "a spring-like cry," becomes a cry "soft as spring" at the poem's end—precisely at the point of the heart's dramatic appearance. Infused with irony, the contrasting images and oppositional structures project a heightened experience of anguished remembrance. The poet's soul is torn by the polarities of death and survival, anguish and acceptance, memory at once relentless and unreliquishable.

The same sentiments are expressed more directly in the two poems which constitute *El rishon ha-orot* (To the First of the Lights).[110] In the first work, the poet, returning to nature, is enraptured by the sights. "Again the lakes rise up before my two eyes!" he exclaims. As if to celebrate the experience, he once again launches much of his repertoire of figurative images and recurring motifs: eye-pupils *(bavot)*, the mirror of water *(re'i)*, an evanescent blueness *(keḥol)*, the water visions growing tall *(gavhu)* and resembling precious crystal *(bedolaḥ yekarot)*, a bubble of laughter *(tseḥok)* bursting forth from them.

The romantic encounter prompts the return of poetry as well. The poem's final, single-line stanza opens with a Bialik-like idiosyncratic phrase of identification.[111]

וַאֲנִי שִׁירִי נוֹשֵׁם אֶל פְּנֵי רִאשׁוֹן אוֹרוֹת.

And I breathe my song toward the first of the lights.

The return—a rebirth, really—is to pure, natural poetry, a poetry free of the agony of memory or the rush of mournfulness. All is effulgence and beauty; the poet even tries to capture the scene by tossing "the lasso of my days toward the mirror of water." Nature, poetry, and the poet are one, and he does not want to let the moment escape. As he returns to the theme of poetry and the healing force of nature, Gilboa begins to revive his earlier preoccupation with his inner being and the aesthetic dimensions of his work.

Aha, et mi ekra (Alas, Whom Shall I Call),[112] the companion work to *El rishon ha-orot,* is also a poem of memory and survival, but despite its parallel opening

אֲהָהּ, אֶת מִי אֶקְרָא לִרְאוֹת עִמִּי בַּפֶּלֶא
אֵיךְ אוֹר רִכֵּז קַרְנָיו וְאֶל שִׁכְחָה צוֹחֵק

Alas, whom shall I call to see the wonder with me
How the light has focused its rays and laughs at oblivion

the second work turns the images of the first poem on their head. The light of rebirth and reconnectedness with nature and poetry turns savage. Its force mocks the poet's romantic memory loss; its cruel glare exposes "with the whiteness *[loven]* of sight" the yearning "for a heart crying to the distance." The first poem's sense of wonderment and innocence becomes in the second "a sad flute . . . celebrating the rebirth of the dead [sic] of its colors covering toward beginning." Entwined in the joy of poetic rebirth and rediscovery are the relentless mood of sorrow and the constant awareness of the person who "sees his life rise from destruction."[113]

In these works of the late 1940s, Gilboa's poetics reflects a coexistence of memory, mournfulness, and resignation. In addition, several stylistic features begin to come into prominence: asyndetic and otherwise "ungrammatical" syntax, ellipsis, and the use of metonymy. If not a bona fide leap into modernism, the new stylistic elements demonstrate Gilboa's expanding vision of composition. Still predominant, however, are the earlier conventions of profuse metaphors and oppositional structures.

Nishmat Yossi ben-aḥoti Bronia (The Soul of Yossi the Son of My Sister Bronia)[114]

This much-anthologized poem of memory and loss is one of Gilboa's most poignant and forceful works. What makes it such a powerful reading experience is, in part, the direct linkage between Gilboa and his murdered nephew. Presented as an autobiographical dream encounter in which the speaker addresses Yossi's ghost, the dramatic situation shapes this linkage into a fervid lament on the boy's tragic premature death.[115]

נִשְׁמַת יוֹסִי בֶּן־אֲחוֹתִי בְּרוֹנְיָה

כָּל הַלַּיְלָה נָפְלוּ כּוֹכָבִים אֶל חֵיקִי
וְלֵאָה מִסְּפוֹר צָחַקְתִּי יְחִידִי אֶל תּוֹךְ הַלַּיְלָה מְאֻשָּׁר.
וְכָךְ רָדוּם, וְכָךְ הוֹזֶה רְקִיעִים צָבְעוּ עֵינַי וּנְשָׁרִים צָנְחוּ לָעֲמָקִים.
אָז פָּקַחְתִּי עֵינַי אֶל הַחֲלוֹם. בָּא יוֹסִי הַקָּטָן וְגָאַל אֶת הַשִּׁיר. וְהָיָה
מְרַחֵף וְשָׁר.

קוֹל הַתּוֹר נִשְׁמַע בָּאָרֶץ. וְעַל אִבֵּי הַבֹּקֶר גֶּשֶׁם כּוֹחֵל וְיוֹרֵד.
לְמַרְגְּלוֹת הַר־טֶרֶם־שֶׁמֶשׁ אֲנִי כּוֹרֵעַ וְזוֹכֵר וְזוֹכֵר וְזוֹכֵר.
רֹאשִׁי בַּמַּיִם שֶׁמִּגְּבָהִים נוֹפְלִים בִּצְלִילִים יְרֻקִּים שֶׁל הַחֲלוֹם הָרָוֶה הַכָּבֵד.
אֲנִי שׁוֹמֵעַ אֶת כָּל שִׁירֶיךָ, יוֹסִי. יוֹסִי הַקָּטָן, הַזּוֹרֵחַ. יוֹסִי הֶהָרוּג בֶּאֱמֶת.
צְבָיַיִךְ הַתּוֹעִים עַל כָּל דֶּרֶךְ צָדִים הֵד קוֹלְךָ הַצּוֹחֵק.

אֱלֹהִים, אֱלֹהִים, כָּל הַבְּקָעִים מָלְאוּ אָז מַיִם.
וְאַחַר הַגֶּשֶׁם שְׁטָפָנוּ הַיָּרֹק וְשִׁכֵּר צְעָדֵינוּ.
וּמְלוֹא־כַּפַּיִם הֶחְוִירוּ פִּטְרִיּוֹת כְּסִפּוּר אַגָּדָה שֶׁרוֹמֵז בְּבָבוֹת שֶׁל אֶלֶף עֵינַיִם.
וְכָל הָעֵצִים הִדְלִיקוּ שְׁמָשׁוֹת בַּאֲמִירֵיהֶם לִכְבוֹדֵנוּ.

הוֹ יוֹסִי, הוֹ יוֹסִי! אֶת לַחֲשִׁי שָׁלַחְתִּי עִם מוֹצָאֵי הַלַּיְלָה אֶל פְּנֵי הָאֲגַם
וּבַרְוָזֶיךָ הַלְּבַנְבַּנִּים גִּלְגְּלוּ עַצְמָם לְהַעֲלוֹתוֹ כֶּתֶר לָאַדְווֹת.
אַךְ עִם שֶׁמֶשׁ שֶׁעוֹלָה גַּם אֲנִי עוֹלֶה כָּלִיל...וּבוֹעֵר מֵאֵשׁ עֶרְגָּה
לְנַשֵּׁק הֶעָפָר שֶׁל בְּחִיר הָאֲהָבוֹת.

The Soul of Yossi the Son of My Sister Bronia

All night long stars fell into my lap
and too tired to count I laughed alone into the happy night.
And so asleep and dreamy my eyes grasped the skies and vultures
[or eagles] plunged into the valleys.
Then I opened my eyes to the dream. Then came little Yossi and
rescued the poem. And he hovered and sang.

The voice of the dove was heard in the land. And on the morning ferns
rain turns blue and falls.
At the foot of a before-sunrise-mountain I kneel and remember
and remember and remember.
My head is in the water that falls from heights in green sounds of the
heavy sated dream.
I hear all your songs, Yossi. Little Yossi, radiant. Yossi truly murdered.
Your roes wandering on every path capture the echo of your laughing
voice.

O God, God, all the valleys then filled with water.
And after the rain the greenness engulfed us and intoxicated our steps.
Handfuls of mushrooms shone pale like a legend that winks in
the pupils of a thousand eyes.
And all the trees kindled suns in their crowns in our honor.

Oh Yossi, oh Yossi! I've cast my prayer at the turn of night onto the lake
and your white ducks turned about to lift it as a crown for the ripples.
But with the rising sun I too rise altogether . . . and burn with the fire of desire
to kiss the earth of the most favored of loves.

Dream-like, the poem opens with the stars falling into the speaker's lap. Reminiscent of an earlier poem, *Din yamim* (Judgment of Days),[116] the image immediately evokes a tone of loss and remembrance. Here, however, the child-speaker seems more playful, innocent. He has been counting the falling stars, but now, tired of the game, he stops, laughs "into the night," and seems happy and content. The scene is peaceful and idyllic despite the subtle irony. Star-counting is what God commanded Abraham to do—promising that his descendants would be as numerous as the stars of heaven (Genesis 15). Here the motif works to show the child-speaker's paradoxical innocence: The falling stars represent the fallen victims of the Holocaust. The divine promise has been symbolically thwarted.

The irony becomes clearer in lines 3–4, which focus on the speaker's ghostly dream of Yossi, the innocent, murdered child. As the child-speaker begins to fall asleep, his eyes perceive colors—the expectation, perhaps, of a happy, Technicolor dream. But toward the end of line 3 the downflight or diving of vultures into the valleys purports a more ominous development. However, line 4 holds the tragic moment in abeyance when little Yossi, Chagall-like, "hovers [above] and sings." Not simply a performance, it is an act of deliverance; for Yossi has "rescued [or redeemed] the poem." By injecting Yossi's ambiguous but apparently admirable act, Gilboa keeps the poem from moving too quickly into an elegiacal mode. This narrative strategy of holding back—like a musical ritard—is present throughout the poem.

As the narrative moves toward the ominous (the plunging vultures), the poem itself seems to be endangered either by an uncontrolled emotiveneness or by a premature revelation of its tragic intent.[117] Yossi, who "rescued the poem" from a ruinous fate, thus enters the work not just the subject of an uncle's lament but also as a catalyst which allows the poet to preserve his poetic duality of fond memory and heart-rending elegy. The structural duality in this case derives from a poetics of ambivalence; responding creatively to the Holocaust is a difficult task, often deterred by its own subject matter.

The second stanza continues the poem's opening idyllic mode, though much pathos is added toward the close of the stanza. Line 5 quotes and paraphrases the Song of Songs 2:12 and the reader is immersed in a romantic mode of beautiful springtime and soft "blue" rain. Line 6 has the speaker bow down "at the foot of a before-sunrise-mountain." The act is ritual-like, one of veneration or worship; the memory is emotionally and spiritually overwhelming, the timing portentous, reminiscent of numerous sunrises or sunsets in Gilboa's poetry. Here again the moment is one of enthrallment, but it is an enthrallment with memory, not with nature. The voice intones "and remember and remember and remember," a repetitive structure which is familar from devotional or emotive moods in earlier poems.

In the middle of the stanza (line 8), however, the mood changes. The speaker's head is suddenly covered by a mysterious shower or flow of "water that falls from heights in green sounds of the heavy sated dream." Something has gone wrong. The dream is weighed down with mysterious heavenly waters.[118] Yet these waters do not seem to threaten the speaker. In fact, they appear to enhance the communication with his nephew's ghost or soul. "I hear all your songs, Yossi," says the speaker. And precisely here, at the moment of total recall and closest binding with the dead child's spirit, the speaker expresses the full measure of his loss: "Little Yossi, radiant. Yossi truly murdered." And Yossi's loved ones, the symbolic deer of the Song of Songs who wander all the world's paths—like Gilboa, they are the survivors—now have become hunters who search for "the echo of [Yossi's] laughing voice."

The third stanza presents the speaker crying out in agony and anger toward heaven: "O God, God, all the valleys then filled with water." The dream is over; everything is muffled, flooded, destroyed. But the purposely ironic, binary structure of the poem turns again on its axis, and the scene turns idyllic once more. A fructifying spring rain (line 11) brings with it an effulgence of greenness which "engulfed us and intoxicated our steps." The idyll expands with an abundance of fairytale mushrooms which resemble "the pupils of a thousand eyes"—Gilboa's recurring symbols of euphoric perception and enchantment. Even the sunrise (or sunset) chimes in (line 14) with a personified celebratory image of "all the trees [kindling] suns at their crowns in our honor."

Here the poem reverts not only to the realm of nature but also to the mode of fairytale or children's story, much like the falling star dream at the outset of the poem. The turnabout also evokes an aura of innocence which accentuates the tension between sweet memory and the recognition of death—and reflects the psychological state of mixed emotions engendered by the poet's loving memories and their irrepressible redolence of unsuccored loss. The feelings of loss are expressed fully in the last stanza. "Oh Yossi, oh Yossi!" cries the speaker in his sorrow. Yet even at this point of externalized emotion the speaker sends his prayer for Yossi over the lake, and the ducks—he calls them "your [i.e., Yossi's] ducks," in parallel with "your roes" in line 9—make of it "a crown for the ripples."[119] At the close of the poem—though he appears to be an embodiment of the adult poet, distanced in time and place—the speaker still retains a firm touch of the romantic. With the portentous sunrise he "rises altogether" toward heaven and "burn[s] with the fire of desire/to kiss the earth of the most chosen of loves."

Nishmat Yossi ben-aḥoti Bronia is rife with Gilboa's network of heightened, often binary images and metaphors. To these he adds, as he has done in many other poems, the romantic and ironic tone of the Song of Songs. The image of the child is also familiar from other works, such as *Bo ha-erev ba-parvar, Ha-na'ar ha-meshorer,* and *Almog adom* (Red Coral).[120] What makes this poem unique is its play between an elegy and a children's narrative. After the dreamy, happy-child opening, Gilboa injects into each stanza images which confirm the poem's childlike framework. With its binary oppositional structure, the child's-tale mode constantly conflicts with the overriding elegiacal purport of the poem. It is this blend of oppositional features which gives so much force to the most poignant and pathetic lines in the poem: "Yossi truly murdered" (line 8), which is placed among several romantic images; and the closing lines (16–17), which with finality denote the poem's identity as a plaintive elegy.

Gilboa ends the *"Sefer ha-almog"* series of memory and loss poems with *Milim rishonot* (First Words).[121] Here once again he confronts the problems of uncontrollability, expressivity, and self doubt. The first section of the poem presents a series of three dreams, each of which involves a mythical or symbolic situation. The first is based on a combined terrestrial and earthly disaster.

שֶׁאָנוּ חוֹלְמִים נִשְׂרַף הַפַּרְגּוֹד.
כָּל הַבּוֹרוֹת מִתְמַלְּאִים שׁוּב חֵמָר.
שִׁכְבוֹת־בַּרְזֶל מִשְׂתָּרְגוֹת כִּמְטִילֵי־עֲנָק
אַחַת בַּשְּׁנִיָּה
וְכָל הַסּוֹדוֹת צוֹחֲקִים בְּגִלּוּי־לֵב
מִן הַנְּיָר.

As we dream the curtain is burnt.
All the pits fill again with clay.
Iron layers intertwine like giant chains
one with another
and all the secrets laugh openly
from the paper.[122]

The recurring image of the "curtain" in line 1 is the mythical (and later mystical) *pargod* which separates the Shekhina, God's "Divine Presence," from the hosts of heavenly angels. The term is also used to denote the boundary between the divine and earthly worlds. When the curtain is burned, a defined line between heaven and earth no longer exists, and the world is cast back into an ante-Creation state of chaos. Such is the case also with the clay pits in line 2 and the stark, primordial landscape of lines 3–4.

Lines 5–6 present an enigmatic aberration from this antediluvian picture. Syntactically, the "secrets" seem to be a part of this dramatic regression. Semantically, however, the addition of "secrets" foments a shift away from the grouping of curtain, clay pits, and iron layers. "Paper" is also not a feature of the primordial universe, but represents an abrupt shift to the theme of poetic expressibility which figures so prominently in the early poems of *"Sefer ḥayei olam."*

Gilboa's use of the "secret" *(sod)* motif is also familiar. At times it connotes the appealing side of nature, whose mysteries the romantic poet unlocks. For the most part, however, it refers to the ungraspable and tragic puzzles of death, war, and the Holocaust. In *Milim rishonot,* then, the injection of "secrets" is thematically consistent with the mythological subjects which precede it.

Less clear, however, are the motifs of laughter and the phrase "from the paper"—both used sardonically in these lines. In other poems laughter has come at times of sorrow—at the very moment the reader might expect a mournful response, the speaker uses laughter as a defense mechanism against the tragic message he must bear.[123] Other poems show the speaker reminiscing about happy childhood experiences and laughing to himself, as in the context of a poignant lament such as *Nishmat Yossi ben-aḥoti Bronia.* In *Milim rishonot,* however, Gilboa introduces the element of mockery to the motif: These cosmic mysteries, particularly the world's regressing to a state of primordial chaos, defy understanding and mock those who would try to explain their meaning—the poet, for example, whose own words mock him "from the paper."

Elaborating upon the mythical context of the first stanza, the second stanza presents a bizarre dream of infants flying through the heavens with stones tied to their umbilical cords "and all the voices in [their] mouths." The infants are apparently seeking entrance into heaven, but are confused by the great number of paths they find there. In addition, there are "a thousand flutes" right behind them, rushing to pursue their own paths. After the great catastrophe, the souls of unborn children, weighed down by stones, seek a resting place. The heavens, however, are crowded not only with the countless souls of victims, but also with the petty trappings of war. While other nations bury their martial flutes and hold celebratory parades at the close of war, the Jews mourn the deaths of future generations of unborn children.

The third stanza returns to a number of Gilboa's oft-used metaphors: crystal, eyes, doors and threshholds. This third dream is of crystals, which "throw their eyes to builders of worlds" *(bonei olamot).* As we have seen in Gilboa's early writings, "crystal" usually refers to the splendor of natural landscapes, especially the land of Israel.[124] The motif of "eyes," expressed as *einayim, ishonim,* or *bavot,* is used most often to convey a sense of heightened perception, whether visual, aesthetic, intellectual, or emotional. Here the poet combines the two motifs, but the combination is ironic. Instead of experiencing a deepened perception of the Holocaust, the personified crystals cast off their eyes. The sight is unbearable, says Gilboa, so in this case blindness is preferable to perception.

The tone is sarcastic throughout. We, the surviving witnesses, have no insights, no perceptions of or blueprints for a rebuilding. We are asked to share our understanding of the horror, but it is impossible to comprehend. We look into each beckoning doorway "and we see everything like the palm of our hand/but we never go beyond/the threshhold." We know intimately what happened, yet we cannot grasp it. The secrets laugh at us; how can we understand them. Heaven has so many paths; how can one choose the right one. It is best to give one's eyes to those who see the world and its rebuilding only as a practical task. We, the victims—the weighted-down infants, the eyeless crystals—are filled with an awareness which is impossible to share, for we are bereft of understanding.

Parts 2 and 3 of *Milim rishonot* continue the theme of knowledge or understanding. The context has changed, however, to a primarily realistic one. "A day will come," says the poet, "and we'll be aware of everything we wanted to know." He adds, however, that by then we may be "too tired." The implication is that comprehension of the Holocaust is still far off; even if it comes, however, we may not have the strength to absorb it.

In part 3 the already chimerical day of understanding is put off indefinitely. What follows is more a symbolic opportunity for mourning and remembering than an intimation of hope or despair.

עַד אִם נְגַלְגֵּל אֶת כָּל כַּדּוּרֵינוּ שֶׁפָּרְחוּ בָּאֲוִיר
וְלָאָרֶץ נָפְלוּ אֵין־אוֹנִים
בְּכָנָף לְכָנְפָם וּלְשִׂימָם עַל־יַד חַלּוֹן בַּיִת עָזוּב
וְעָקוּר מִבָּנִים
שֶׁיִּהְיוּ כְּמַעֲלוֹת הָאֶבֶן לַעֲלוֹת בָּן וְלַעֲבֹר,
לִפְסֹחַ אֶל תּוֹךְ חָלָל
בּוֹ קִמְרוֹנִים שׁוֹלְטִים עַל הַשֶּׁקֶט
וְלִשְׁכַּב אַפְרַקְדָּן בְּפִנָּה אַפְלוּלִית
וְכָךְ מִלְּבָבוֹת הוֹלְמִים טִפּוֹת רוֹתְחוֹת שֶׁל דָּם
אֶל הָרִצְפָּה לָצֶקֶת–

עַד אִם נְגַלְגֵּל כָּל כַּדּוּרֵינוּ שֶׁפָּרְחוּ בָּאֲוִיר
תַּאְדִּים טִפָּה אַחֲרוֹנָה
אִמְרָתֵנוּ רִאשׁוֹנָה
בְּשִׁיר.

Until we launch all our balloons that have sailed in air
and they've fallen helplessly to earth
to enfold them in a wing and to place them by the window of
an abandoned barren house
so they might be as stone stairs to ascend and move on,
to step into empty space
where arches reign over the quiet
and to lie supine in a dark corner
and to pour from pounding hearts boiling drops of blood
onto the floor—

Until we launch all our balloons that have sailed in air
the last drop will turn red
our first word
in a poem.[125]

The mythical imagery which follows is gloomy, disheartening, and purposely opaque. The motifs of barrenness and the loss of home are redolent with futility. The words of poetry fall helplessly to the ground in their inability to capture adequately the feelings of sadness and pain. In utilizing such a profusion of ambiguous, often incoherent images—the usage is similar in *Shir ke-migdalekh ha-gavo'ah,* discussed below[126]—Gilboa has returned to a poetics of inexpressibility. The syntax grows murky with the use of ambiguous, neutral infinitives: "to enfold," "to place," "to ascend, "to lie supine." Some verbs are transitive, others intransitive; their subjects overlap, creating an ironic unity of those who perform the verbal action and those who are its objects. The awkwardness of the language tends both to confuse and to involve the reader more intensely.

At least two interpretations are possible. The idea that the souls of the dead are both the subject and the object of the actions described flows more easily from the images Gilboa provides. A more plausible interpretation, however, is that the souls of victims are not the subject of these actions. (Certainly it would be unseemly that the dead could yet "pour from pounding hearts boiling drops of/blood onto the floor.") In this reading, therefore, the subject is the dashed dreams and hopes of the survivors, who now realize the full reality of the tragedy. It is the survivors who seek an ironic nirvana, a place of quietude where they may tell effusively of their sorrow.

Like the first, the last stanza begins with the image of balloons flying off. The opening dependent clause is repeated as well, implying that until we are able to realize what really happened in the Holocaust—and that may never fully come to pass—all we can do is to mourn. For the poet this means putting his feelings into poetry. This is the symbolic "last drop" of blood, which coincides with "our first word/in a poem."

Mi-shirei ha-yiḥud asher le-Meliselda (From the Songs of Praise of Meliselda)[127]

The Meliselda poems are set apart at the end of *"Sefer ha-Almog"* mainly by their symbolic thematics: the Gothic seductiveness of Evil ironically portrayed as Beauty. The name Meliselda is known from the historical episode of Shabbetai Zevi, false Messiah of the seventeenth century. Gershom Scholem has written that "Meliselda, the Emperor's Daughter," a Spanish love ballad, was a favorite song which Shabbetai Zevi sacralized and sang "to the mystery of the Sabbath." Scholem notes that the song "acquired great sanctity in the eyes of Sabbatian believers, who sang it at their meetings, as is proved by its inclusion in the hymnal of the Donmeh [Islamized Sabbatians] in Salonika." In Shabbetai Zevi's interpretation the ballad takes on a Song of Songs-like, allegorical meaning: the marriage of the bridegroom with the Torah or Shekhina. Shabbetai Zevi actually acted out this allegory in a mystical marriage ceremony with the Torah in Salonika.[128]

Intertwined with the Meliselda legend is the figure of Shabbetai Zevi's wife, Sarah, whom he married despite her reputation as a prostitute. There may also be some connection here with the general theme in Sabbatian thought of evil and sin being converted into blessedness and sanctity.[129] In any case, Gilboa's figure of Meliselda is derived from this mystical or allegorical blend of holiness, sexuality, and sinfulness.

In each of the three works which constitute the Meliselda cycle the speaker is Meliselda herself. The first of the three, *He-ḥazon* (The Vision), is a poem of investiture and identification. Meliselda addresses a multifaceted male figure: protégé, rescuer, visionary, comforter, rememberer, hero, coward, victim, poet. She proclaims his origins, shapes his identity through her own being, and praises his courage and saving acts. As a femme fatale, she also threatens him with her long, sharp, manicured nails.

Meliselda is an ambiguous, mythical persona, defined only by the information she gives us regarding the figure she is addressing. "From my suffering you have risen," she notes, informing the reader that her lot has been tragic. As the source of wood which her addressee has gathered "to set at the pyre," she is also the source of violence. Her hair "has called [him] to weave a rope"—a reference, perhaps, to the Rumpelstilskin fairytale—to rescue the drowning; thus, she is also the source of rescue. She is the source of his voice as well, for it is her word, in dybbuk fashion, which "has trembled from [his] throat." By the end of the first stanza, it is clear that Meliselda is the empowering source for everything her companion has done and said. He is a multifaceted person; she, his creator. He is a poet; she, his muse.

The second stanza makes the symbolic nature of this pair more explicit. Meliselda is the male figure's lover; she makes tracks in the mud to his tent. But he, the poet, fashions out of her footprints "a fixed vision" *(ḥazon matbe'ot).* Love and muck are dual sources of his poetry; a third is blood.

מִדַּם מוֹלִידַי טְבוּחִים בַּמְּצוּלָה, חָרַזְתָּ גְאֻלָּה לַדָּמִים.
אֲנִי שֶׁעֵינַי רָאוּ סַכִּינָם שֶׁל עַמִּים
מִפִּיךָ דִּבַּרְתִּי אֶל פַּחַד כְּגִבּוֹר שֶׁאֶת צִלּוֹ לַקְּרָב יָצָא לְלַוּוֹת.

From the blood of of my progenitors, slaughtered in the abyss, you
have woven revenge [lit., salvation for the blood].
I, whose eyes have seen the knife of nations,
have spoken from your mouth to fear, like a hero who wanted to
accompany his shadow to the battle.

As multifaceted as her addressee, Meliselda is his lover and protector; she is also a witness to the violence and the slaughter. (Here the reference to the Holocaust becomes clear.) And he, speaking with her voice—a kind of dybbuk—is the poet of the tragedy who composes his visions with the blood of the victims. She is both a protector and a suffering victim; he is a fearful but undaunted instrument-poet who "envisions and comforts and remembers." Both are rescuers in the sense of jointly creating the poems which commemorate the Holocaust and its victims.

The characterizations, explicit or implied, of Meliselda and her addressee are dualistic, as are the specific images conveyed of them. For example, the male figure rises from Meliselda's suffering, yet he is described as "a dream interpreted for salvation from captors." Meliselda's footsteps come from the muck of a chaotic abyss,[130] yet they are fashioned into a poetic vision. Their poem is a poem of salvation, yet it is shaped out of the blood of the slaughtered and is thus also a poem of revenge *(ge'ula la-damim)*. These dualistic images are so blatantly ironic that the reader perceives the dualism itself as a main subject of the poem.

He-ḥazon ends with a flourish. The poet flees "from the fright of [Meliselda's] nights" to "mountains of days"; he gathers the dispersed "to protect [him] in the night of horrors." He is then struck, cupid-like, with "an arrow that is launched at the right time," while Meliselda lurks threateningly in the background with her sharp nails. The poet seems to escape, but his protection is rather flimsy. Simultaneously, he is both wounded and marked for love; in either case, he is vulnerable.

Ironic, oppositional themes—love and vulnerability, suffering and salvation, fear and escape, rescue and threat—and their mythical framework, the Meliselda-poet love affair or muse-artist relationship, project a Sturm und Drang image of the poet's turmoil. The relationship with Meliselda is illicit yet unavoidable; the impulse to write poetry on the slaughter is daunting but uncontrollable; the poetry is formed out of blood yet offers a redemption, of sorts, through commemoration.

In this cycle Gilboa attempts to come to terms with grand taboos: the memorialization of a tragedy which is best deleted from memory; the illicit, guilt-ridden drive to write about the unspeakable; the very idea of an aesthetic response to the Holocaust. The next two poems in the Meliselda cycle reinforce this emotive message through dramatized situations. In the second, *Ha-dam* (The Blood),[131] the scene is an erotic love tryst in which Meliselda urges the poet-lover on to increasingly intense sensual delights. Both the love acts and the language of the poem, however, are entirely symbolic.

The poem opens with Meliselda's passionate praise of her lover.

אַתָּה טוֹב, אַתָּה טוֹב עַד בֹּקֶר!
יָדֶיךָ תִּפְרֹקְנָה אֶת עֻלָּם שֶׁל שָׁדַי הַכָּבֵד אֶל הַלֶּטֶף.

> You are good, you are good until morning!
> Your hands will throw off the heavy burden of my breasts to the caress [sic].

The language of lust soon forges a larger meaning. For example, line 3 reads: "Your blood which strives to flow in me *(damkha ha-hores bi iklo'aḥ)* will solve the riddle of my nights from darkness." The "blood which strives to flow in me" refers to the lover's semen. The sensual imagery makes explicit both the passionate and illicit nature of this relationship.

In consonance with the dualistic interpretation of the cycle, one might say that writing these poems is the act of a "Holocaust-lover." Gilboa attempts to plumb the meaning of the tragedy, to keep it at the forefront of our consciousness, to prevent it from passing into oblivion. Such commemoration, however, is destructive, for it results in the perpetuation of the trauma. In the Meliselda cycle, loving, on the one hand, connotes an ironic fructification, a continued nourishment or awareness; on the other, it expresses a paradoxical insidiousness, an overwhelming sense of dilemma and despair.

Like *He-ḥazon, Ha-dam* is suffused with dualistic images—intensified terms for darkness *(aletet, ofel)*, light *(shimshei tsohoray, tsefirei bekarav)*, and oppositional motifs such as thirst and slaking, fire and water, joy and moaning, rising and falling—which fit the context of a passionate love tryst but, symbolic of the mixed feelings of the poet, reflect a very different struggle.

In the third and final poem of the cycle, *Ha-kets* (The End),[132] both the language and the dramatic action become even more transparent. Meliselda calls herself "a bride among brides whose bridegroom has been destroyed" (literally, burned, *nisraf*). She points to "the last scroll which has turned its face into ash." She notes that while "facing the knives *[ma'akhalot]*[133] my ancestors also sang out [my name: 'Meliselda! Meliselda!']/, and I licked their blood in tears from the bread." Here Meliselda reverts to her role as a paradoxical protector, a Shekhina figure which can only bemoan the tragedies.

Meliselda also represents the quintessential beloved *in potentia,* a bride reminiscent of the Sabbatian bride-Torah-Shekhina combination. Because her bridegroom has been murdered, however, she is bereft and unloved. She calls out to her lover: "Oh gazelle *[tsvi*—a reference to both Shabbetai Zevi and the Jewish people], thou hast been desecrated upon my altars, and thou art beautiful! *[vatif]*."[134] The ironic juxtaposition of desecration and beauty again demonstrates Gilboa's poetics of ambivalence. Even the bit of comfort Meliselda musters for the poet is stated in dualistic imagery.

חֲשֻׁכֵי פָּנִים עוֹד יֵאוֹרוּ מִזִּיוֵךְ, כִּי אֲנִי לְמַעְיָנַיִךְ הַיְקוֹד.
וְכַחַתָךְ בַּבָּשָׂר הַחַי שֶׁבִּכְאֵבוֹ לֹא יַבְגִּד
לְדוֹרוֹת יַעֲמֹד זִכְרֵךְ כִּי אֲנִי הִשְׁבַּעְתִּיו.

Those with darkened [i.e., sorrowful] faces will yet be lighted by your splendor, for I am the flame for your springs [i.e., your source of inspiration].
And like a stab in the living flesh which will not betray its pain
for generations your memory will stand, for I have sworn it.

"Sefer sheti ha-yagon ve-erev ha-simḥa"
(The Book of the Warp of Sorrow and the Woof of Joy)

The lead poem of this grouping, *Shir ke-migdalekh ha-gavo'ah* (A Poem Like Your High Tower),[135] displays a consummate combination of poignancy and volatility—an ironic mix of lyricism, agonized memory, blatant rage, and call to vengeance.

שִׁיר כְּמִגְדָּלֵךְ הַגָּבֹהַּ הַמִּתְמַלֵּא צִלְצוּלֵי פַּעֲמוֹן
וְשׁוֹלֵחַ עִמְעוּמָם בָּעֲרָפֶל עַל פְּנֵי אֶרֶץ
לְכַסּוֹת עַל רָאשִׁים בְּחֻפָּה שֶׁל שָׁמַיִם.
שִׁיר כְּדֹק חֲלוֹמוֹת שָׁקוּף, זְגוּגִי, הַנִּמְתָּח
עַל שְׁמוּרוֹת וְעֵינַיִם
וּבוֹלֵם אֶת הַפֶּה לְמַלֵּט הַזְּעָקָה
שֶׁעַל פִּי הַתְּהוֹם הִיא נִצְוַחַת.
שִׁיר כַּיּוֹרָה הַקּוֹלְחָה אֶל מוּל מַבָּטֵךְ
וְהַכָּרַת הָאֵימָה שֶׁמֵּאֲחוֹרֵי גַּבֵּךְ נֶאֱנַחַת.

שִׁיר כְּפָנַיִךְ שֶׁעִסִּיתִי בְּאֶצְבְּעוֹתַי
וּכְרִקְמוֹת סִיבֵי עֵינַי שֶׁנִּשְׁזְרוּ בְּעֵינַיִךְ.

כַּלְּשׁוֹנוֹת שֶׁעִלְּעוּ דְּבָרָם בְּסִיגֵי אֵשׁ זוֹמֶמֶת כִּלָּיוֹן
אֶל רֵאשִׁית.
וּכְחֶשְׁבּוֹנִי הַקַּר וְלֵאֶה – אַחַר־כָּךְ – בְּעָמְדֵךְ
אַחַת מוּל שָׁ ל שׁ
וִהְיִיתֶן יַחַד –
אַ רְ בַּ ע.
(כָּל הַנְּעָרוֹת נוֹלְדוּ לָלֶדֶת –
הַכְּעוּרָה וְהַקּוֹרֵאת,
רַכַּת הָעַיִן
וַחֲשׁוּקַת הַמֹּתֶן.
אֲהוּבָתִי, עֵינִי צָרָה בָּךְ!)

זֶה שִׁיר הַגֶּשֶׁם עַל גַּגּוֹת הַפַּח
(גֵּרוּיוֹ הַמָּתוֹק שֶׁל הַיֶּלֶד).
זַרְזִיפוֹ בַּשָּׂדֶה הַפָּתוּחַ
(יוֹנֵק שְׁדֵי הָעוֹלָם).

זֶה שִׁיר הַחוֹבֵק גִּזְעוֹ הָאָזֹב שֶׁל אִילָן
בְּיַעַר עָבֹת
כִּסְגוֹר הַיָּדַיִם עַל בִּטְנָהּ הַמְגֻלָּף
שֶׁל הָעַלְמָה הָאַחַת
(בְּעִתָּהּ!)
בָּעוֹלָם.

עַתָּה יָדַעְנוּ כָּל מַבּוּלֵי מַרְאוֹת
נוֹצְצִים בְּתַאֲווֹת עַל צִפָּרְנַיִם.
וְטֶרֶם בָּא פַּחַד אָהַבְנוּ לִרְעוֹד
כִּרְעוֹד לְחַיָּיו הַמָּוֶת.
וּנְטִיפוֹת שֶׁל זָהָב עָנַדְנוּ לַשָּׁמַיִם
שֶׁיִּהְיוּ גְּבֹהִים עַד מָוֶת.

זֶה שִׁיר בְּלֵילוֹת גְּבֹהִים עַד מָוֶת
וּלְעֵת שַׁחַר צוֹרֵחַ נֵפֶל עַל אָרֶץ.
(אֵין דָּבָר! בַּעֲבוּר יוֹם הוּא יִשְׁאַג כְּאַרְיֵה מוּל חֲלוּדַת שָׁמַיִם,
,עֲקָרָה׳, ,עֲקָרָה׳ יְגַדֵּף בְּשִׁקְרוֹ שֵׁם אִמּוֹ הַבּוֹרֵאת.)

זֶה שִׁיר שֶׁכָּל הַקְּדָמוֹת לוֹ נְכוֹנוּ,
מִיתוֹת בְּאֵימֵי הַדְּרָכִים.
וִיצִיאוֹת לְלֹא פֵּשֶׁר אֶל תֹּהוּ
לִרְקֹד בְּמַקְהֵלֶת בּוֹכִים
בְּתִקְוָה שֶׁנּוֹגְנִים עַלִּיזִים
עוֹד מְעַט וְיָבוֹאוּ.

זֶה שִׁיר הָרוֹעִים שֶׁעוֹד מְעַט וְיָבוֹאוּ
אֶל דִּיר לְכַנֵּס וְלִפְקוֹד אֶת הַצֹּאן.
וְחָלִיל שֶׁנִּסְדַּק שׁוּב יֶאֱסוֹף נִגּוּנָיו
מִפְּעִיַּת זִכְרוֹנוֹת שֶׁל הַצֹּאן
עַל זְהַב
דָּמִים שֶׁנִּגַּר בַּשָּׂדוֹת
בֵּין הַיָּרֹק וְהַטְּחָב
וְחַיִּים שֶׁיַּעֲלוּ וְיָבוֹאוּ
כָּאוֹר בַּשָּׂדוֹת.

זֶה שִׁיר כָּל הַשְּׁקָרִים שֶׁרָצִינוּ לִשְׁמוֹעַ
עַל כֶּרֶס מְלֵאָה וּמַפְתֵּחַ בַּכִּיס.
זֶה שִׁיר כָּל הָרָעוֹת לְיַד אָח בָּן אִוִּינוּ
וְיַלְדֵּנוּ צוֹחֵק אֶל מַלְאָכָיו מִן הָעֶרֶס
וּמוּגָף הַתְּרִיס.

אַךְ יֵשׁ אֱלֹהַּ שֶׁל מַעַשׂ – לֵץ וְאַכְזָר! –
הַשְּׁקָרִים חַיִּים הֶרְאָנוּ

וְדִמְיוֹן הָפַךְ אֶל אֱמֶת
וְהָיָה הַכֹּל נָכוֹן וְיַצִּיב וּמוּזָר
וְ אָ י ם
עִם הַשֶּׁקֶר הַמֵּת
בְּפִתְחֵי הָרִיס.

A poem like your high tower filling with sounds of a bell
and sending their dimness in the fog upon the earth
to cover over the heads with a canopy of sky.
A poem like a curtain of dreams, transparent, glass-like, spread
over eyelids and eyes
and muzzles the mouth to let forth the scream
that is screamed over the mouth of the abyss.
A poem like a boiling cauldron toward your look
and the awareness of the terror which is sighed behind your back.

A poem like your face which I kneaded with my fingers
and like the weavings of the threads of my eyes that were interwoven
  with your eyes.
Like the tongues that stammered their word in the dross of a fire
  conspiring destruction
to beginning.
And like my cold and tired reckoning—later—as you stood
one facing *three*
and you together were—
four.
(All the girls were born to give birth—
the ugly one and the reader,
the one of the gentle eye
and the one with the belted waist.
My beloved, I envy you!)

This is a poem of the rain on the tin roofs
(the sweet excitement of the child).
Its drizzle in the open field
(suckling at the breasts of the world).

This is a poem of the embracer of the mossy trunk of a tree
in a dense forest
like the closing of the hands on the sculptured belly
of the one maiden
(in her season!)
in the world.

Now we knew all the floods of visions
sparkling in lusts on fingernails [or claws].
And before fear came we loved to tremble
like the trembling of Death for its life.
And [with] drops of gold we decorated the sky
so they'd be high unto death.

This is a poem on nights high unto death
and at dawn a stillborn [child] screams on earth.
(No matter! Another day and he'll roar like a lion at the rusting of
heaven,
"barren," "barren" he'll revile in his lie the name of his creating
mother.)

This is a poem for which all introductions have been prepared,
deaths at the terrors of the roads.
And departures without explanation for chaos
to dance in a chorus of weepers
with the hope that merry musicians
soon will come.

This is a poem of shepherds who soon will come
to the pen to gather and count the sheep.
And a pipe that's been cracked will yet gather its tunes
from the bleating of memories of the sheep
of gold of
blood that was spilled in the fields
between the green and the moss
and life which will arise and come
like the light in the fields.

This is a poem of all the lies that we wanted to hear
with a full belly and a key in one's pocket.
This is a poem of all the sorrows by a fireplace we lusted after
and our child's laughing to his angels from the cradle
and the shutter's closed.

But there's a God of deed — base and cruel! —
He's shown us the lies alive
and imagination's turned to truth
and everything's secure and firm and strange
and terrible
with the dead lie that dies
at the openings of the eyelid.

The poem is structured on a varying sequence of static and dynamic elements. The static elements consist of a list of definitions which attempt to denote the poem's parameters: its genre, contents, motivation, other sources, or aims of expressiveness. The dynamic elements focus on the poem's central stanza, beginning with "Now we knew" (line 33) and its closing stanza (line 63). Instead of the metaphorical expressions "a poem like" or "this is a poem of," these stanzas are metonymic passages which delineate what the speaker's world feels like after the Holocaust. In this poem pervaded at all levels by dualistic and oppositional interplay,[136] these dynamic elements provide another significant clashing entity.

The opening poetic definitions are given in the form of similes, as if the speaker is groping toward a cogent delineation of the poem being created. Lines 1–3 seem to refer to an idyllic place, a town perhaps, with a tower whose ringing but muffled bells "cover over heads with a canopy of sky." "Like your tower" *(ke-migdalekh)* and "a canopy of sky" *(ḥupa shel shamayim)* evoke a romantic, pastoral situation; the tone is one of love, quietude, security, with the place personified as a beloved female auditor. In lines 4–5 the next definition seems to continue the evocative, sentimental tone as well as the theme of muffled dimness: "A poem like a curtain [or membrane] of dreams, transparent, glass-like, spread over eyelids and eyes." The atmosphere of dreaminess or seeing through a curtain adds a nostalgic note of looking backward, remembering the hometown, envisioning it dimly. The poem is identified here as the instrument of this act of translucent dream-memory.

The images work on many levels. The tower is filled with the ringing of bells, but the canopy created by their ringing consists of a muffledness or darkness *(imum)* and fog *(arafel).* The dream-curtain covers the lids and eyes, but it is transparent and allows the speaker to see. Line 6 adds yet another dimension. The curtain "muzzles the mouth to let forth the scream/ that's screamed over the mouth of the abyss"—a jarring reversal marked by the blatantly ironic juxtaposition of *u-volem et ha-pe* (and muzzles the mouth) and *lemalet ha-ze'aka* (to let forth the scream). The virtual impossibility of a closed-mouth scream intensifies the agony of the speaker's awareness—the magnitude of the horror he is confronting is beyond expression. The powerful irony of this image forces the reader to "read the poem backwards"[137] and to confront the parallelism in lines 2–3 and 6. The rereading leads us to perceive the bell tower's "darkness" and the act of covering as omens of danger or a descent into sentimentality. The ringing of bells calls to mind other familiar poems *(Pa'amonim* [Bells] by Tcherniḥovsky, and Greenberg's *Taḥat shen maḥarashtam* [Under the Tooth of Their Plow], for example) which link the ringing of bells in church towers to anti-Jewish violence.

The closed-mouth scream also serves as an imagistic anchor, an abiding reference point or "matrix"[138] continually brought to mind as the reader moves through the poem and discovers similarly dualistic and blatantly self-contradictory situations, images, or tropes. Such would be the case in lines 46–47 with the juxtaposed images of "a chorus of weepers" and "merry musicians"; in lines 37–38 with the paradoxical combination of innocence and ominousness of "[with] drops of gold we decorated the sky," followed by "so they'd be high unto death." The dualities persist in lines 23–25 with nostalgic images of "the rain on the tin roofs" and "its drizzle in the open field," which are counterposed with "floods of visions" in line 33. The same is true of "our child laughing to his angels from the cradle" (line 61), an ironic image within the framework of harsh truths, stillborn children, barren women, and "deaths at the terrors of the roads."

Indeed, the image of "[muzzling] the mouth to let forth the scream" leads the reader to the perception of the poem's entire semantic apparatus as a structure of binary oppositions.[139] In the litany of definitions, for example, "a poem like a curtain of dreams, transparent" (line 4)—an image, though fleeting, of somnolent quietude—is counterposed with "a poem like a boiling cauldron (line 8), a vision of dire prospects; and "a poem like your face" (line 10), which evokes a loving scene, is contrasted by "like the tongues that stammered their word in the dross of a fire conspiring destruction" (line 12), a scene of fiery destructiveness.

In a syntactic vein, all the elliptical phrases in the first two stanzas beginning with the word *shir* (a poem) are contrasted with phrases entered later in the poem that begin with the words *ZE shir* (THIS IS a poem): *ZE shir ha-geshem* (THIS IS a poem of the rain, line 23), *ZE shir ha-ḥovek* (THIS IS a poem of the embracer, line 27), *ZE shir be-leilot gevohim* (THIS IS a poem on nights high, line 39), and *ZE shir she-kol hakdamot lo nakhonu* (THIS IS a poem for which all introductions have been prepared, line 43).[140] The change from *shir* to *ZE shir* is dualistic; it both denotes metaphors which are ardent: "This is a poem of the rain on the tin roofs" and the ecstatic "This is a poem of the embracer of the mossy trunk of a tree/in a dense forest"; and it also evokes their dire contrasts: "This is a poem on nights high unto death," and "This is a poem for which all introductions have been prepared." In these contrasting *ze* definitions, the specificity represents the equivalence factor of the metaphors, while their semantic content reflects their opposition.

At the center of the poem (lines 33–34) lies the point where metaphorical definitions cease for the moment and the speaker interjects a dynamic and explicit response to all these possibilities: "Now we knew *(ata yadanu)* all the floods of visions/sparkling in lusts upon fingernails." Just what is now known is not entirely clear. What *is* clear is that structurally this stanza divides the poem into two nearly equal parts. Semantically, too, the stanza, laden with a purposeful, multilayered ambiguity of images, metaphors, and tenses, dramatizes the poem's sustained oppositional structure. In lines 33–36, the sparkling "visions" that come to mind are qualified by uncontrollable "floods" of these visions; and the "lusts upon fingernails," which may be a memory of passionate loving—a theme continued by "we loved to tremble" in the following line—are qualified by the ironic, Alterman-like simile "like the trembling of Death for its life" *(ki-re'od le-ḥayav ha-mavet)*. The image leaves the reader with a fearsome shiver instead of a passionate love tremble.

The last two lines in the stanza (37–38) seem to describe a childlike, innocent act of decorating the sky with "drops of gold,"—play-stars, perhaps—

which make the sky look pretty and "high." But the metaphor "high unto death" destroys the innocence and turns the playfulness into a horrible Gothic nightmare. The death image returns the speaker to his primary task of seeking self-definition, of searching for purpose and response in the inner and outer worlds, both of which have gone awry.

Other binary oppositions pervade the poem. There are similarly structured verb phrases: *lirkod be-mikhelet bokhim* (to dance in a chorus of weepers) versus *lifkod et ha-tson* (to count the sheep); counterposed construct phrases: *hakarat ha-eima* (awareness of the terror) versus *rakat ha-ayin* (the one of the gentle eye), and *shedei olam* (the breasts of the world) versus *eimei ha-derakhim* (the terrors of the roads); phrases with one common part: *ḥupa shel shamayim* (a canopy of sky) versus *ḥaludat shamayim* (the rusting of heaven) and "fog upon the earth" versus "a stillborn [child] on the earth."

Individual word groupings are also counterposed: *zikhronot, rikmot, ne'arot, ḥalomot* (memories, weavings, girls, dreams) versus *ta'avot, mitot, yetsi'ot, ra'ot* (lusts, deaths, leavings, sorrows). The same may be seen in contrasting thematic motifs: "and muzzles the mouth" versus "he will roar like a lion; "the sculptured belly of the maiden" versus "a full belly"; "sound and firm" versus "strange and terrible"; "a stillborn [child] screams" versus "our child laughing"; "destruction" versus "beginning"; "imagination" versus "truth."

As is usually the case in works in which binary oppositions play a significant role, there are several words or images that embody both meanings of the oppositional structure. For example, *sade* or *sadot* (field, fields) is the setting of both a soft, gentle rainfall and a stream of blood; *einayim* (or *shemurot, risim,* or *sivim)*—eyes (or eyebrows, eyelids or eyelashes)—are the instruments of both unmitigated pleasure and ultimate pain; *yeled* (or *yonek* or *nefel)*—child (or infant or stillborn)—is the symbol both of innocence and new life, and of betrayal and death; *shekarim* (lies) connotes both a blissful state of prior innocence and a devastating reversal of God's trust. Even *shir* (poem)—the most semantically laden word in the poem—reflects at once both a sweet, pathetic celebration of memory and a bitter, unappeasable exclamation of agony and loss.

Built on these oppositional components, the larger images and themes in *Shir ke-migdalekh ha-gavo'ah* loom in their contrariness. The newborn versus the stillborn, the young pregnant woman versus the barren mother, lies versus the truth, innocence (of children or lovers) versus betrayal (most disturbingly, by God). In sum, there are two central categories of opposition into which all other mutually opposed entities may be placed—love, with all its ramifications of birth and life, and death, with all the loving and life which it precludes. In attempting to express the horrible truth of the Holocaust, Gilboa injects into the poem dualistic memories of all he once held most dear. And all of the poem's images, tropes, and structures fall into the subsuming dichotomy of love versus death.

Reconciliation, Renewal, and Romantic Return

The remaining poems in *"Sefer sheti ha-yagon ve-erev ha-simḥa"* were written between 1947 and 1949 and, in effect, continue the responses evinced in Gilboa's first Holocaust poems of 1942–1944. At times these later works bewail again the very knowledge of the disaster—as in *Shir ha-mefaḥed mi-da'at* (A Poem of One Who's Afraid of Knowing).[141] Gilboa also reverts to an old image, the wanderer *(ha-mehalekh ba-derakhim)*, the survivor who cannot stay put and in his sorrrow continues to move on, searching for new sources of sustenance. He acknowledges, however, that "we haven't said anything./We haven't yet said ourselves"[142]—once again using the theme of inexpressiveness to describe his profuse but unsuccessful efforts to move beyond the Holocaust.

Though professing to avoid sentimentalism, Gilboa turns to another brand of romanticism: the unbridled expression of a passionate, limitless despair—his verbal version, one could say, of the scream. While confessing the need for a more radical mode of expressivity, however, he continues to use familiar nature images and reverts to the style and vocabulary of his earlier works. For example, in *Sod she-lo nigla* (A Secret Unrevealed), the poet sees himself as an explorer who seeks *Tarshishim* (Tarshishes)—mythical, distant, exotic destinations—but is unable to consummate the journey. Because there is no sense of his having reached the "splendor" of far-off places, his wanderlust becomes an empty desire—a reference, perhaps, to his having left his ancestral home, a decision he, in retrospect, laments.

These later poems might be considered examples of antiromantic romanticism, where the modifications in Gilboa's style are not so much alterations as they are quantitative expansions of his romantic stylistics. These modifications include a plethora of literary and biblical allusions and a salient reversion to the standard lexicon of the Age of Bialik poets.[143] These minings from the prior poetic generation contribute to a jarring clash of contexts—romantic and antiromantic—whose effect is a resonant emotionality which cannot help but strike the reader with its deeply moving tone of exasperation and grief.

With the establishment of the State of Israel, however, Gilboa's tone turns euphoric for the first time in decades. In *Lefa'am ata merim patish* (At Times You Lift a Hammer),[144] he ecstatically pens a wish list for the new Israeli generation. His mournfulness has temporarily lifted, and in its place are joyous disorientation and a vision of normalcy and happy children.

אֲנַחְנוּ רוֹצִים שֶׁיִּקְרוּ הַמִּקְרִים רַבִּים וְשׁוֹנִים.
אֲנַחְנוּ רוֹצִים לַעֲלוֹת וְלָרֶדֶת בְּכָל הַשְּׁלַבִּים.
אֲנַחְנוּ רוֹצִים אַחֲרוֹנִים לִסְגֹּר אֶת הַדֶּלֶת
וַאֲנַחְנוּ רוֹצִים לְפָתְחָהּ רִאשׁוֹנִים.

אֲנַחְנוּ רוֹצִים לִגְרוֹס כָּל סְבָרָה מְקֻבֶּלֶת.
אֲנַחְנוּ רוֹצִים לַחֲשֹׂף הֶעָפָר מְנוּצֵץ.
וְלָלֶכֶת אֲנַחְנוּ רוֹצִים. וְלָבוֹא. וּלְהַגִּיעַ.
וַאֲנַחְנוּ רוֹצִים, אִם צָרִיךְ, אֶת חָבִית הַשְּׂרֵפָה לְפוֹצֵץ.

וּלְיַשֵּׁר אֲנַחְנוּ רוֹצִים. וְלִבְנוֹת. וְלִרְאוֹת בְּעֵינֵינוּ
אֵיךְ קָמִים הַבָּתִּים, הַגַּנִּים, הַבְּאֵרוֹת.
אֲנַחְנוּ רוֹצִים לִרְאוֹת אֵיךְ הֵם קָמִים לְעֵינֵינוּ
וְעַל כָּךְ אֲנַחְנוּ רוֹצִים לָרִיב וְלִשְׂמֹחַ בֵּינֵינוּ.

אֲנַחְנוּ רוֹצִים עַל מַצָּע שֶׁל פְּרָחִים וּסְלָעִים
לִזְרֹעַ צְחוֹק בְּבָנִים שֶׁיָּקוּמוּ.
אֲנַחְנוּ רוֹצִים לִלְחֹן עִם בָּנִים שֶׁיָּקוּמוּ
אֶת כָּל הַשִּׁירִים שֶׁהָלְכוּ וְעוֹד יָקוּמוּ.

We want many and all sorts of things to happen.
We want to go up and go down all the rungs.
We want to close the door last
and we want to open it first.

We want to take on every reasonable thought.
We want to uncover the dust from a glittering object.
And we want to go. And to come. And to arrive.
And we want, if we must, to explode the barrel of powder.

And we want to straighten. And build. And see with our eyes
how the houses rise up, the gardens, the wells.
We want to see how they rise up before our eyes
and for that we want to argue and be happy among ourselves.

We want on a bed of flowers and stones
to sow laughter in children that will arise.
And we want to sing with children who will raise
all the songs that have gone and are yet to arise.

Im pa'am be-ḥayekha (If For Once in Your Life)[145] is also quite different from most of the works Gilboa wrote between 1946 and 1949. Its predominant features are the use of a recurring refrain, a plethora of repetition and ungrammaticalities,[146] a colloquial diction, and a tone of personal communication. These usages are by themselves not new. Their combination in one poem, however, reflects if not a new style, then at least a reinvigorated aesthetic perspective.

וְאִם אוֹהֵב אַתָּה מְאֹד
אִם אֶת עַצְמְךָ אוֹהֵב אַתָּה מְאֹד
עֵינֶיךָ תִּזַּלְנָה אָז דְּמָעוֹת.
אִם אֶת חֲבֵרֶיךָ אַתָּה אוֹהֵב
עֵינֶיךָ תִּזַּלְנָה אָז דְּמָעוֹת.
אִם יָכֹלְתָּ פַּעַם לִצְחֹק וְלֹא צָחַקְתָּ
עֵינֶיךָ תִּזַּלְנָה אָז דְּמָעוֹת.

וְעַל הַרְבֵּה דְבָרִים אָז תַּחֲשֹׁב
שֶׁיָּכֹלְתָּ עֲשׂוֹתָם
וְלֹא עֲשִׂיתָם
וְעֵינֶיךָ תִּזַּלְנָה דְמָעוֹת.

And if you love very much
if it's yourself you love very much
your eyes will then flow with tears.
If it's your friends you love
your eyes will then flow with tears.
If once you could have laughed and didn't laugh
your eyes will then flow with tears.
And then you'll think of many things
that you could have done
but did not do
and your eyes will flow with tears.

A closely repetitive, nearly stammering style appears here, mainly in the first two lines (8–9) of this stanza, in which there is a sense of starting, pausing, and then starting again. The structural discontinuity may be an emphatic ploy, but it also reflects an inner pensiveness on the part of the speaker, who, in nearly a stream-of-consciousness mode, seems to be trying out a sentence before uttering it in completely finished form. This tentative sounding-out process seems to depict a poet struggling to express himself. His disjointed style, demonstrated only subtly here, is reinforced by the structure of the last stanza, which is based on the repetition of words, phrases, and motifs to form an enigmatic pattern.

מַסְלוּלִים רַבִּים תִּרְאֶה אָז בְּעֵינֶיךָ
מַסְלוּלִים שֶׁבָּם עָבַרְתָּ אֶלֶף בְּרָצוֹן
וְתִבְכֶּה עַל רַגְלֶיךָ שֶׁלֹּא שִׁמְּשׁוּ הַמַּטָּרָה
וְתִרְצֶה לְהַגִּיר עֵינֶיךָ שֶׁלֹּא רָאוּ הַמַּטָּרָה
וּלְךָ דוֹמֶה הָיָה שֶׁדְּרָכֶיךָ מוּל עֵינֶיךָ תָּמִיד רָצוֹת.

וְעֵינֶיךָ תִּזַּלְנָה אָז דִּמְעוֹת־
תַּחֲנוּן שֶׁפַּעַם בְּחַיֶּיךָ תָּרוּץ עוֹד.

Many paths then you'll see with your eyes
paths upon which you have passed a thousand willingly
and you'll cry for your legs that did not serve the goal
and you'll want to make your eyes flow for not seeing the goal
and it seemed to you that your roads are always running past
your eyes.
And then your eyes will flow with tears-
of-comfort that once in your life you will run more.

There are several repetitions here, including "paths," "the goal," and especially "your eyes" *(einekha)*, which appears four times. In addition, the verbal form "you'll" is repeated three times: "you'll see," "you'll cry," "you'll want" *(tire, tivke, tirtse)*. The repetitions, unambiguous as they are in themselves, are surrounded by ungrammaticalities—that is, by phrases or word combinations which do not follow the ususual conventions of grammar, syntax, or generally accepted modes of formal expression. In addition, unlike many other works Gilboa wrote during this period, the poem does not present the reader with complex metaphoric structures which communicate through abstraction.

The end of line 20, for example, seems completely ambiguous. What does it mean to pass by on paths "a thousand willingly" *(elef ba-ratson)?* Is Gilboa saying, in essence, "paths which you've walked on a thousand times before"? If so, why does he opt for an awkward, ungrammatical phrase? And why does he use the form *BA-ratson* (literally, with THE will), a non-idiomatic, malapropos version of *BE-ratson,* which denotes "willingly"? In addition, there is the apparently disjointed tense structure (line 23) with its combination of past (*dome haya,* it seemed) and present (*ratsot,* running past).

Of course, the ungrammaticalities are explicable, though the process takes the form of interpreting metaphorical language. Taking the last example first, it may be that Gilboa is suggesting that when one stops and finally takes a good look at oneself, one might conjure up all the paths or roads of the past which now, in the present, are passing before his eyes. The other example, *elef ba-ratson,* is also easily interpreted, as it is paraphrased above. But that is precisely the point: because of their strangeness, the reader is forced to confront and interpret these phrases. Why, then, does Gilboa use ambiguous, "ungrammatical" language when he could have stated things much more simply and comprehensibly?

The answer may lie in yet another compositional aspect of the last stanza: its structure. The first five lines (19–23) give the appearance of an incantation. Lines 19 and 20 begin with the word "paths" *(maslulim);* lines 21 and 22 end with "the goal" *(ha-matara);* lines 21 and 22 begin with the two parallel (and, in the Hebrew, rhyming) verb phrases "and you'll cry/and want" *(ve-tivke/ve-tirtse);* lines 21, 22, 23, and 24 begin with "and"; dispersed among the first six lines (19–24) is the four-time repetition of "your eyes," which is accompanied by a set of repetitive sounds, rhyming in the Hebrew: "your legs," "your roads," "your life" *(raglekha, derakhekha, ḥayekha).* To these repetitions are added the strangeness of the phrases "a thousand willingly" and "to make your eyes flow," the tense disjunction in line 23, the enigmatic reference to "the goal," and the closing-line repetition of the poem's opening verse. The result of all this is a fairly complex structure of subliminal, enigmatic meanings.

To borrow a term from the Russian Formalists, Gilboa seems to be "making strange" the language of this last stanza.[147] The effect is to immerse the reader in the very act that is being described: someone looking at himself, as if into a mirror, trying to grasp visually, intellectually, and emotionally, perhaps for the first time, what he or she is all about. The incantatory nature of the stanza, with its purposeful ungrammaticalities and ambiguities, attempts to reproduce this psychological process of self-perception and redefinition.

This is a deeply painful and halting process, especially for someone who has been torn apart emotionally by the loss of his family and much of European Jewry. Here he stands at the crossroads of a new beginning: the founding of the State and his own self-fulfillment as one of its pioneers. Gilboa is confounded, filled with the memories and tears and roads of the past and overflowing with the instinct of self-renewal in the present. Suddenly the world has changed. And just as suddenly—in this poem, at least—he abandons the profusely metaphorical imagery of pain and trauma and turns to more colloquial, disjointed, and enigmatic patterns of ungrammaticality. Glimpsed here in *Im pa'am be-ḥayekha,* the new—but not completely new—style brings Gilboa a step closer to the modernist mode which in expanded form becomes his hallmark in the late 1960s with the publication of *Ratsiti likhtov siftei yeshenim.*

Gilboa closes the *"Sefer sheti ha-yagon ve-erev ha-simḥa"* section with three multi-part poems. Each continues, in an oblique fashion, the theme of reconciliation.

The six-part *Shirim mi-gei ha-etsa* (Poems From the Valley of Counsel)[148] is composed of a series of vignettes which, by way of analogy or metonymy, dramatize a number of psychological and ethical messages: the world is not a perfect place; we should be less harsh with one another and less frantic about the achievement of our goals; we should accept our own humanity and seek some pleasure in life; we must let go of our pain and our rage and get on with the act of living. The images are varied: young children who try to pluck unripe fruit from trees but are read bedtime stories rather than punished; a horse who does not run off when unbridled and given food; a friend who is advised not to move mountains but to stay alive and climb one; persons in limbo between hopes and reality who are told to give up their unrealistic dreams and to savor the wonder of life.

Though the poem is didactic in nature, it reflects less an intrusiveness than a candid conversation between friends. The presence of the auditor is palpable here, and the same interactive tone predominates in most of the poem—except in part 5, where, in more of a soliloquy fashion, the poet speaks of casting off the nightmare and daring to "touch the wondrous."

In the final section, the poet turns completely inward. Quite conscious of this sudden change in structure and tone, he prefaces part 6 with the phrase, "And [here is] a poem to myself" and sets the entire section—the aesthetic version of his advice to others—in parentheses. Once again, Gilboa is dealing here with artistic control. He counsels himself to be less compulsive, less bombastic, and at the same time, more forceful in his future poetry. "Be simple and strong *(tamim ve-ḥazak),*" he says, in his usual contradictory way. On the one hand, he claims to want to simplify the poetry, to make it more natural, perhaps more down to earth, less polished and rhetorically lofty. On the other, he seems to be bent on impressing upon the reader a resounding message, a message borne by the strokes of a whip "without letup, without letup" *(beli heref, beli heref).* His new motto is "Don't poetize, don't poetize—arouse" *(lo leshorer, lo leshorer—le'orer).*

This avowed new poetics of strength and ceaseless impact is manifestly inconsistent with the general message of comfort, wonder, reconciliation, and gentleness Gilboa transmitted in parts 1 through 5 of *Shirim mi-gei ha-etsa.* One wonders whether he wishes to revert to the moralistic proletarian poetry of his youth or whether he is immersed in a dilemma of artistic direction in his self-perceived role as a Holocaust poet. The puzzle is resolved by Gilboa himself in the closing lines of part 6.

וְקַמְתִּי בַּבֹּקֶר וְשׁוֹפְעָה מוּלִי הַבְּאֵר.
וְקַמְתִּי בַּבֹּקֶר וְגִדְּלוּ הָעֵצִים עֲנָפִים
וְיוֹנִים מַהְגוֹת מֵאֹדֶם גַּגּוֹת רְעָפִים.
וְהָלַכְתִּי בָּעִיר לְשׁוֹטֵט
וְאֵין אַף בַּיִת אֶחָד מִתְמוֹטֵט
וְכָל יֶלֶד קָטָן אֵלַי בְּחִיּוּךְ מְצוֹתֵת.)

And I rise up in the morning and the well facing me is overflowing.
And I rise up in the morning and the trees have grown branches
and doves coo from the red of tile roofs.
And I walk in the city for a stroll
and not one house is toppling
and every little child greets me with an attending smile.)[149]

The strength and impact, the "thunder" and "lashes" Gilboa refers to in his new poetic credo connote the power of the idyll, the everyday scene of a benign nature and happy, smiling faces. This is how he wants to be reborn poetically, to seek out the wonders of existence and the effects of the beautiful. This is where he wishes to focus the power of his poetry, not in the raw, uncontrollable feelings elicited by the Holocaust.

Although a sense of renewal is Gilboa's apparent new goal,[150] he is also once again declaring his poetic independence, just as he did in *Shiri ha-paru'a* and *Signonot shonim.* Fearing he may have established himself in the eyes of his audience mainly as a Holocaust poet, Gilboa is attempting here to free himself from that image of awesome responsibility.

Moving away from the Holocaust, Gilboa displays a full-blown obsession with romantic nature images and scenes. In *Aviv* (Spring),[151] a pastoral depiction of a green chameleon and frolicking colts evokes themes of renewal and rebirth. But even in a poem which celebrates the excitement and enchantment of spring, hope is still tainted with blood.

Love is a central motif in *Aviv.* Light, passions, adventure, and forgetfulness enhance the romantic possiblities of springtime. The beloved, bearing a halo crown, is idealized as the Shekhina, the protective spirit of all living things. But the halo is flaming red—fire, burning, and flaming recur throughout the five sections of the poem—and by the end of day the lover is blinded by the flames. Even the day itself is elusive, "ungrasped" *(lo nitpas);* spring's passion and wonder cannot be sustained because of the relentless shadow of sorrow.

Aviv closes with images of a shattered mirror and a paired ring and rock. By alluding to the shattered mirror, Gilboa implies that the reality which the lovers wish to dissolve magically is indeed gone, never to return. In its place is a dual reality: the Holocaust will never disappear, and the idyllic is forever irretrievable. The ring, of course, symbolizes the lovers and the consummation, or potential consummation, of their love in marriage. The ring is "tossed from worlds [beyond]" and falls onto a rock. The ring is small, fragile, magical, mythical, other-worldly, unreal. The rock is mighty, hard *(barzilit),* earthly, only too real. Ironically, it is the rock that "weeps before the lovers/cursing." A symbol of ungiving reality, it cries and curses because it is static, earth-bound, incapable of flying off or moving from its place.

That place is Gilboa's place: a bedrock of sorrows assuaged at times by small transient flashes of love, beauty, and joy. *Aviv,* while celebrating these partial glimpses of renewal and recovery, conveys the feeling of unforgetableness precisely at the point of wishing to forget. In the midst of efforts to free himself from the past, Gilboa finds himself continually bound by the truth. His fate, essentially, is to be a romantic poet who, while seeking the solace of poetic nature and love, is constantly reminded of death and destruction.

"Sefer yom ha-tamid" (The Book of the Forever Day)[152]

The last group of works in *Sheva reshuyot* is based on the same emotional conflict that lies at the heart of *Aviv:* wanting to find a new beginning but being held back by a lingering "forever day" which does not allow one to move on without the looming memories of blood and death.

As in *Aviv,* the central images in this section are of the beauty of nature: flowers, a gentle wind, the coming of spring, a feeling of renewal. In each case, however, a sense of foreboding brings a fear of cosmic disaster. Spring is "cut off," voices are "dripping blood," a deer—the beloved, the symbol of spring—leaves "traces of blood."[153] Poetry itself is flower-like, a victim; for with the constant awareness of horror the only way a poem can be written is by "plucking [it] from the jaws of these days."

Concurrent with the motifs of nature, the imagery of these poems is visionary, mythical, and folkloristic. In *Lo bi-se'ara hi holekhet* (It [the Wind] Comes Not In a Storm)[154] the poet envisions "the steps of the Ancient One *[ha-kadmon]* rising before our eyes"; the entire cosmos is in flux. In *Agadat ha-ya'ar* (Legend of the Forest),[155] the forest's darkness is "an abyss-darkness" which hides the murderous thieves who seek to capture Sleeping Beauty. But the poem abruptly turns antimythical and becomes idyllic. By grasping nature's idyllic qualities, the memory-laden survivors are able to return to a normal life, to an enjoyment of beauty and love.

The mythical images in *Kol be-harim* (Voice in the Mountains)[156] also reflect a central dualism. The entire poem consists of a vision of earthly and cosmic forces in flux: the plummeting of things "into the abyss like hard stones," reminiscent of the drowning of the Egyptians at the Red Sea; "great waters," an oft-used phrase for the irrepressible, tragic forces of nature; and the mountains' ever-strengthening voice, which parallels the sound of the shofar at Sinai.

Through this plethora of mythical images and allusions, Gilboa gives expression to a psychological catharsis. The motifs are darkly portentous of apocalypse and death. The poem's ending, however, seems to contradict the traumatic mood: what might have been a "hill of scorpions" *(ma'ale-akrabim,* Numbers 34:4) has become a "hill of streams" *(ma'ale-afikim)*, an image which connotes redemption, peace, even love.[157]

Gilboa seems to be saying: We have survived. We nearly drowned. We have seen the victims falling into unmarked graves. We screamed day and night to proclaim and mourn the horror. But we have survived the apocalypse. Though the "voice from the mountains" will not go away, we also have begun to hear the trickle of streams and to feel the possibility of renewal.

Visionary and epiphanic modes of writing are central features in the poems at the end of *Sheva reshuyot.* As the reader has seen, nature, often in primeval forms of chaotic forces, dominates the dramatic action. But another, even more significant feature of these works of the late 1940s is Gilboa's developing style of ambiguity and ellipticalness. In *Ba-derekh min ha-har el ha-emek* (On the Road from the Mountain to the Valley),[158] the use of ellipsis creates a palpable ambiguity. The ellipsis is extended, however, into a sense of stammering, even inarticulateness. For example, the last two lines of part 1:

וְאֵין שָׂח אָדָם אֶל עֵמֶק שֶׁיָּרַד
אֶלָּא אֶת שָׁמַע מְעַט מֵהַרְבֵּה.

Translated literally, this reads as:

And a person says to a valley which he descends
only [what] he heard a little from a lot.

Gilboa probably means to say: And a person says to the valley into which he descends only a little of all that he has heard. One wonders, however, what poetic purpose is served by the incomprehensible syntax and blatant ungrammaticalities. The answer lies in the characterization of the speaker himself, whom Gilboa in effect presents as either overly pensive or, more likely, emotionally overwrought.[159] In these poems Gilboa has altered his earlier theme of inexpressibility and begins to reshape it as a poetics of inarticulateness. The speaker is not just bemoaning his inability to express his feelings; he appears physically unable to do so. His groping for speech (a condition seemingly akin to aphasia)[160] engenders an illusion of poetic trauma—the frustrated attempt to express outrage and disbelief. In the late 1940s Gilboa was still experimenting with this poetics of "distorted-language" which so effectively expresses those nondissipating emotions that are beyond ordinary language. In his next collection, *Shirim ba-boker ba-boker* (Early Morning Songs, 1953), the poet continues to explore new dimensions of theme, genre, and style while demonstrating his continual self-consciousness as a poet.

Chapter IV

New Beginnings

Shirim ba-boker ba-boker/ Early Morning Songs, 1953

Survival and the Return of Myth

The opening sections of *Shirim ba-boker ba-boker* are evocative both of the "recovery" poems in the later parts of *Sheva reshuyot* and of Gilboa's earliest nature poems. The works in the first section, *"Keḥulim va-adumim"* (Reds and Blues), project images of children and bridegrooms and the belief in miraculous rejuvenation and love. In the second section, *"Milḥama atika"* (Ancient War), Gilboa conveys childhood reminiscences of survival, youthful perspectives on nature, and themes of freedom, myth, legend, and dreams. The section closes, however, with an elegiacal poem on Gilboa's "heroic" brother, Joshua, whose "blood calls out from the ground." This blend of hope, nostalgic reminiscence, a return to nature, and tragic memory reflects the efforts of a poet attempting to pick up the strains of a career gone awry, a career which had stumbled on an unrelenting trauma.

"Keḥulim va-adumim" opens with *Huledet* (Birth).[1] The rain has stopped, yet the speaker is ecstatically immersed in its echoes: " . . . from the roofs and trees it still sings in my ears/and covers my head/with a bluish bridal veil." The veil accentuates the motifs of innocence and intimacy which dominate the poem. Along the same lines, the "birth" in the title is represented by the poem's central figure, a newborn child, an image which is highlighted by the recurring refrain:

אַשְׁרֶיךָ, אֱלֹהַי,
בְּרִשְׁתְּךָ נָצוֹד הַיֶּלֶד.

Happy are You, my God,
the child is caught in Your net.

The child, a primordial configuration of the romantic poet, proceeds poetically to "place one leaf on top of another/to see how one leaf covers another/and [how] the pieces blend together" *(u-mitmazgim ha-resisim).* He also serves as a catalyst for magical moments by calling "the swallows from my skies for marriage" (a continuation of the bridal theme) and by decorating "all my windows with flowerpots."[2] As if awakening from a dream, the child then "opens [his] eyes" and sees that "[his] land is very wide/it's all one piece of growths of green/blossoms." Enraptured by the landscape, he cries out, "Oh, my God, how we were embraced *[eikh hayinu ḥavukim]!"*—proclaiming his complete merging with the natural world in a symbolic state of innocence and love.

The metaphorical and thematic design of the poem incorporates several semantic layers: First, there is the language of nature. the rain "has passed"; it "sings [a tune]" *(mezamer);* leaves, birds, and flowers abound; blue and green color the scene. Then there is the language of love: the bridal veil, marriage (or "engagement," *kelulot),* and the lovers' embrace. Added to these are the usual biblical usages (e.g., *sisim* for swallows) and liturgical references, as in the phrase "caught in Your [i.e. God's] net,"[3] referring to the sinner caught in a forbidden act and implying, by contrast, the innocence of the newborn child.

The poems which follow *Huledet* incorporate similar themes of ecstatic wonderment and unity with the natural. In *Bi-sedei ha-ḥemar* (In the Fields of Clay)[4] the speaker finds himself immersed to his hips in water-soaked fields. Instead of being annoyed or frightened, however, he is bemused and even taken with the idea of being stuck in the mud. His advice to one who might find himself in a similar situation—"Say a blessing for the softened earth"[5]—implies that being thus intermingled with and protected by nature can be relished as a mythical state of bliss rather than tolerated as an aggravating mishap.

וּבְבוֹא הָרוּחַ מֵעֲשָׂבִים לְהִתְבַּשֵּׂר
תִּצְרֹר הִיא בִּכְנָפֶיהָ גַּם אֶת שַׂעֲרוֹת הָרֹאשׁ.

And when the wind comes up to hear the news
may it bind up in its wings the hair on my head.

The phrase "bind up in its wings" *(titsror bi-khenafeha)* is reminiscent of the *El male raḥamim* (O God, Full of Mercy) memorial prayer, in which the souls of the dead are "bound up in the bond of [eternal] life." Toward the poem's close the speaker is metaphorically transformed into a tree, and simultaneously the tree is animated into a human figure: "My [tree]top projects [into the] heights; [my] body is erect as a cypress." Nature and person become one, whether the individual is immersed in mud or standing erect like a tree. This intertwining is especially significant when one considers that Gilboa's taken first name, Amir, means "treetop."

In the closing poem, *Ba-kokhavim ḥatsavti* (I Have Hewn the Stars), the poet once again uses a mythical framework to express his feelings toward the "love" he has lost. Here, however, the "love" seems to be a catchword for all that perished in the Holocaust.

בַּכּוֹכָבִים חָצַבְתִּי

עָמַדְתִּי מַכֶּה עִם מַכּוֹשׁ בַּכּוֹכָב
מְנַתֵּז אֶת הָאֹפֶק הַמְאֹהָב
בְּכַסְפַּת כְּחוֹל הַשָּׁמַיִם.
וְכָל כָּךְ צָחַקְתִּי לָדַעַת שֶׁעַתָּה מַבִּיטִים
חֲבֵרַי שֶׁבַּדֶּרֶךְ בַּשְּׁבִיטִים
וְקוֹרְעִים הָעֵינַיִם.
חַה חַה! לוּ יָדְעוּ מִי עָרַךְ לָהֶם הָרַאֲוָה!

אֲנִי יָדַעְתִּי אַהֲבָה.

I Have Hewn the Stars

I stood striking the star with a pick
spraying the beloved horizon
with the silver blue of sky.
And I laughed so hard knowing that now my
friends in the path of comets were
watching and staring.
Ha ha! If only they knew who arranged the display!

I've known love.

The oft-used motif of laughter denotes here amusement at the idea that he is entertaining his dead friends by his mythic activity in the sky. His claim of taking a pick-axe to the stars—one must remember that Gilboa was a teen-aged member of the Klossova commune, which dedicated itself to rock-quarrying—becomes a metaphor of the romantic poet's self-definition. Enthralled with creation both in his writing and in his very being, Gilboa feels immersed in and creatively a part of the cosmos.

But in Gilboa's universe, laughter has a mournful side. Even as he sets about to please his friends, even as he depicts a mythical act of cosmic display, his amusement is a blend of joy and grief. The closing line, "I've known love," connotes both the wish for what is possible and the reality of what is not. Thus these opening sections of *Shirim ba-boker ba-boker* illustrate once again a poetic expression of conflicting dualities.

The several poems in *"Milḥama atika"* have a distinctive narrative bent. Each depicts an incident apparently connected to a pogrom which occurred in Gilboa's home town and blends the real with the impressionistic, a child-like tone with the retrospective view of an adult.[6] In the first, *Zera'im shel oferet* (Seeds of Lead),[7] the child-speaker offers a combined visual, aural, and emotional view of the situation.

זְרָעִים שֶׁל עוֹפֶרֶת

גַּג אָפֹר שֶׁל רְעָפִים.
מִשְׁפָּע.
כַּדּוּרִים נִדַּרְדְּרוּ מֵעָלָיו –
קְטַנִּיּוֹת.
צְמוּדִים אֶל הַקִּיר
שָׁכְבוּ אַבָּא וִיהוֹשֻׁעַ אָחִי
חוֹסִים עָלַי –
חוֹמוֹת מָגֵן.

שֶׁמֶשׁ עָמַד חָסֹן.
בָּרִיא אוּלָם. דּוֹמֵם כַּפָּר.

מֵאִיר בְּכָל פִּי הַצָּהֳרַיִם
שֶׁנִּמְתַּח מִגַּן הָאֲגָסִים
עַד לְמִשׁוּכוֹת הָעֻזְרָד.

הַבְּאֵר –
רֶחֶם פְּעוּרָה
קוֹלְטָה זְרָעִים שֶׁל עוֹפֶרֶת.

בַּבֹּקֶר בַּבֹּקֶר אֶתְחַמֵּק לִרְאוֹת
אֵיךְ בְּמַעֲמַקֶּיהָ
נוֹלָדִים הַכּוֹכָבִים –
כּוֹכְבֵי הַכֶּסֶף.

וּפְנֵיהֶם שֶׁל אַבָּא וִיהוֹשֻׁעַ אָחִי
כַּמֶּרְחָק –
פְּסָלִים בְּנֵי אֶלֶף וָעוֹד.

לְאַחַר שָׁנִים רַבּוֹת הֻבְרַר לִי הַדָּבָר
בְּגַנֵּי הֶעָרִים הַגְּדוֹלוֹת
וּבַמּוּזֵיאוֹנִים.

Seeds of Lead

A grey tile roof,
inclined.
Bullets rolled down it—
chickpeas.
Close against the wall
lay Father and Joshua my brother
protecting me—
walls of defense.

The sun stood strong.
Quite healthy. Quiet as a bull.
It shone in every noon space
that stretched from the pear orchard
to the rows of crabapple.

The well—
an open womb
gathering seeds of lead.

At break of day I stole out to see
how in its depths
the stars were being born—
silver stars.

And the faces of Father and my brother Joshua
[were] like the distance—
statues a thousand years old or more.

Many years later it all came clear to me
in the parks of large cities
and in the museums.

The scene, depicted elliptically, offers just enough detail to promote the child's ironic, contained experience. The sound of buckshot on the roof reminds him of chickpeas, the traditional Jewish dish usually served at holiday times or family celebrations. The domestic image contrasts sharply with the reality of the situation—an attack on his home. Similarly, the second half of the first stanza is also dualistic. Father and brother protect the child yet obviously are themselves both threatened.

From this point nearly to the end of the poem, the child departs from the immediate scene and drifts off into a reverie. Perceiving the sun as robust and "quiet as a bull"—another strong, protecting spirit—he evinces a perspective split between awareness of the threat and a naive, joyful view of nature's splendor. The dualism persists in his depiction of the well. Instead of a reflection of dread and vulnerability, he sees a fructifying birth event, the sparkle of stars. The innocence of this visionary child who sees forces of life in the shadow of death overrides the terror and brutality of the poem's main event and allows the work to become a rapturous reminiscence of childhood.[8]

As the poem closes, the adult Gilboa looks back nostalgically and sees the faces of his father and brother, who now resemble ancient statues. Like them, the childhood scene has become distant and mythological. Exacerbated by survival and the privilege of a life of culture, Gilboa's sense of distance and time turns the poem mournful, leaving the reader with impressions of both the forcefulness of his imagination and the tragedy of his loss.

Gilboa's use of childhood memory in the *"Milḥama atika"* section contrasts with the profusion of metaphors and heightened rhetoric of his poems of the late 1940s. The return to romantic nature poetry and resonances of childhood also signal Gilboa's attempts to recapture his own youthful poetic impulse. In the biblical-persona poems which immediately follow the *"Milḥama atika"* section, this sense of distance is underscored, with each work depicting a mythological scene and featuring an "autobiographical" portrait of the poet, who appears in both ancient and contemporary guises.

The closing work in this section, *Ve-aḥi shotek* (And My Brother Is Silent),[9] is set outside the reminiscence of actual events. The entire poem is a dream describing the speaker's older brother upon his return "from the field." There is no traumatic pogrom here, but rather the fear on the part of the child-speaker "that [his] dream will not come true *[yitbade]."* The fear grows more palpable when the speaker greets his brother and begins "immediately to count his wounds." The grim ghostly image is followed by the poem's recurring refrain (and title), "and my brother is silent." By the end of the first stanza, the work shows itself clearly as a poem of mourning. As it continues, the speaker empties his brother's uniform pockets and sifts through his belongings. Among them he finds an old bandage with a dried-up bloodstain and a worn postcard with a woman's name on it "under a drawing of poppies." With each object the speaker discovers "memory after memory."

הֵידָד, אָחִי, אָחִי הַגִּבּוֹר,
הִנֵּה מָצָאתִי אוֹתוֹתֶיךָ!
הֵידָד, אָחִי, אָחִי הַגִּבּוֹר,

אָשִׁיר גַּאֲוָה לִשְׁמֶךָ!
וְאָחִי שׁוֹתֵק.
וְאָחִי שׁוֹתֵק.

וְדָמוֹ מִן הָאֲדָמָה זוֹעֵק.

Hurrah, my brother, my brother *the hero,*
here I have found your signs!
Hurrah, my brother, my brother *the hero,*
I will sing praises to your name!
And my brother is silent.
And my brother is silent.

And his blood cries out from the ground.

In the child's mind, his brother is a heroic figure, bearing the stereotypical artifacts of a dead or wounded soldier: bloodied bandages and a love letter. At each stage of the speaker's discovery and investigation, the soldier-brother remains silent. The silence is redoubled after the praise of heroism is showered on him, so that the word "hero," emphasized twice in the text, rings hollow. The artifice of distancing through the dream framework and unreal detail are particularly effective ways of closing the *"Milḥama atika"* cycle. In the previous poems the use of metaphor provided some sense of consolation in the idea of creativity. Here, however, figurative language engenders only a lingering despair.

The poem may certainly be perceived as an elegy to Gilboa's brother, even though it is certain that Joshua was never a soldier. The brother image may also have been inspired by a friend killed in the War of Independence. If so, the composite of the martyred real-life brother and the fallen Israeli soldier forge a redolent blend of historical and contemporary mourning.

Biblical Theme Poems

The context of distancing is essential to an understanding of the four biblical-theme poems published approximately the same time as *"Milḥama atika."* Each is a dreamlike narrative; each includes a first-person speaker who is an active participant in the dramatic action (though the level of activity varies); each either mentions or alludes to the Holocaust or to another notable historical trauma; three of the four feature the figure of a naive or inept child; and each is woven around a biblical figure whom the speaker addresses with an air of apparent familiarity. The child-image theme engenders a dissonance between the monumentality of the occasion and the immaturity, triviality, or helplessness of the childlike figures. By humanizing events, the monumentality-triviality dissonance creates a bond of empathy whereby the reader identifies with the vulnerability inherent in these mythical traumatic moments. Gilboa creates here a sense of immersion in experiences which have deep roots in the culture and yet are emotionally just beneath the surface of everyday reality.[10]

In *Yitsḥak* (Isaac)[11] the child-speaker assumes the role of the biblical Isaac in the context of the "Binding of Isaac" narrative. The child tells about a rather innocent walk with his father in the forest,[12] but the tone changes quickly with the sudden appearance of a flaming knife among the trees and a vision of "blood on the leaves." The child calls out for his father to save him, "[so that] no one will be missing at lunchtime." The father's response constitutes the dramatic center of the poem.

זֶה אֲנִי הַנִּשְׁחָט, בְּנִי,
וּכְבָר דָּמִי עַל הֶעָלִים.
וְאַבָּא נִסְתַּם קוֹלוֹ.
וּפָנָיו חִוְּרִים.

It is I who am slaughtered, my son,
and my blood is already on the leaves.
And Daddy's voice was choked.
And his face was pale.

At the poem's end, the child-speaker Isaac wants to scream in disbelief. He wakes from a dream, and his right hand is numb [literally, "bloodless," *azlat-dam*].

Several interpretations of *Yitsḥak* relate the poem to the Holocaust,[13] but its particular autobiographical component should also be underscored. In this version of the Binding of Isaac, the boy is spared but the father is slaughtered. It is quite possible that Gilboa may be expressing the thought that he—the one who left home, traveled far, fought in the war—should have been sacrificed instead of his father.[14] In another vein, the poem may imply a contemporary context, as in *Ve-aḥi shotek,* related to the struggle and sacrifice of the War of Independence. Once again the nightmare of death haunts the Jewish people. The wishful dream of statehood, here depicted as an idyllic walk in the woods, is disrupted by the reality of continued strife.

The central image in *Yitsḥak* is the vulnerable, helpless child. His numbness symbolizes his impotence. Similar images appear in the three biblical poems which follow.[15] In *Moshe* (Moses),[16] the speaker seems at first to be quite an assertive adult. At the poem's end, he suddenly regresses to an ineffectual adolescent.

נִגַּשְׁתִּי אֶל מֹשֶׁה וְאָמַרְתִּי לוֹ:
עֲרֹךְ אֶת הַמַּחֲנוֹת כָּךְ וְכָךְ.
הוּא הִסְתַּכֵּל בִּי
וְעָרַךְ לְפִי שֶׁאָמַרְתִּי.

I went up to Moses and said to him:
Arrange the camps like this.
He looked at me
and arranged [them] just as I said.

The speaker is quite taken by this success and follows his own boasting with a list of admiring women he's known: "Sarah from my childhood," "the long-legged one from the women's cooperative," "Melvina from Rabat in Malta," "Dina from the Italian-Yugoslavian border," and "Riya from the coastal plain up north." One woman, a very enigmatic one, "whose name is truly engraved in mine," is missing from the list. The absence unsettles the speaker; he becomes diminished, uncertain of himself, and sulks off to sleep.

מֹשֶׁה מֹשֶׁה הַנְחֵה אֶת הָעָם.
רְאֵה, אֲנִי כָּל־כָּךְ עָיֵף וְרוֹצֶה לִישֹׁן עוֹד
אֲנִי עוֹדִי נַעַר.

Moses Moses lead the people.
Look, I'm very tired and want to sleep some more
I'm still only a boy.[17]

The sudden uncertainty might be due to the absence of the woman he truly loves, the one whose name is written all over him, as it were.[18] *Moshe,* then, can be read as a realistic portrait of the soldier in war. The speaker at first is all business, an inspired, if self-appointed advisor to Moses. Once he remembers his true love, however, he breaks down. By distancing the poem in antiquity, Gilboa implies that this is the way war has always been. Even those who appear to be larger-than-life heroes are in reality vulnerable victims of separation and loneliness. One can assume that the poet himself had first-hand knowledge of such feelings.

Sha'ul (Saul), 1950[19]

The context of *Sha'ul* may be a dream or an imaginary personal vision.

שָׁאוּל

שָׁאוּל! שָׁאוּל!
אֵינֶנִּי יוֹדֵעַ אִם בּוּשָׁה זֹאת הָיְתָה
אִם פַּחַד מִפְּנֵי רֹאשׁ נְטוּל־גּוּף –
אַךְ בְּעָבְרִי עַל פְּנֵי חוֹמַת בֵּית־שְׁאָן
הֲסִבּוֹתִי אֶת רֹאשִׁי.

אָז, בְּמָאֵן נַעַרְךָ לְהַגִּישׁ לְךָ הַחֶרֶב לְפִי שֶׁצִּוִּיתָ
עָמַדְתִּי אִלֵּם, נְטוּל הַדִּבֵּר
וְדָמִי זָב מִלֵּב.

אֲנִי בֶּאֱמֶת אֵינֶנִּי יוֹדֵעַ לֵאמֹר מָה אֲנִי בִּמְקוֹמוֹ
אִם נַעַרְךָ הָיִיתִי.

וְאַתָּה הַמֶּלֶךְ.
וְאַתָּה כְּבוֹד הַמֶּלֶךְ בְּמִצְוָתְךָ.

וַאֲנִי בֶּאֱמֶת אֵינֶנִּי יוֹדֵעַ לֵאמֹר מָה אֲנִי בִּמְקוֹמוֹ.

שָׁאוּל שָׁאוּל בּוֹא!
בְּבֵית־שְׁאָן בְּנֵי־יִשְׂרָאֵל יוֹשְׁבִים.

Saul

Saul! Saul!
I don't know whether it was shame
or fear of a disembodied head—
But as I passed by the wall of Beit She'an
I turned my head away.

Then, when your boy refused to hand you the sword as you had commanded
I stood mute, speechless
and my blood flowed from [my] heart.
I really don't know to say what I in his place
had I been your boy.

And you are the King.
And you are His Majesty the King with your command.

And I really don't know to say what I in his place.

Saul Saul come!
At Beit She'an the Children of Israel live.

The first stanza places the speaker at the ancient Mt. Gilboa, where the Philistines, vengeful in victory, display the head of the King on the walls of Beit She'an. Horrified at the barbaric exhibition, he calls out to Saul and tells how distressed he is to see his dead body so hideously maimed.

The second stanza focuses on another source of grief for the speaker: the behavior of the young arms bearer who did not obey the King's command to kill him with the sword before they were set upon by the enemy. Once again the speaker is thrust (or injects himself) into the dramatic death scene on Mt. Gilboa, where he was struck dumb—twice: *ilem,* "mute," and *netul ha-diber,* "speechless" (line 7)—and "[his] blood flowed from [his] heart," obviously connoting his state of shock at the arms bearer's inaction. When he confronts the dilemma of what he would have done if he were in the boy's shoes, his pain and trepidation are so excruciating that he can express himself only by an elliptical stutter.

> I really don't know to say what I in his place
> had I been your boy. (Lines 9–10)

The speaker's anguish and helplessness lead him to repeat the plaint in nearly the same words in line 13.

On one level, the speaker's overwrought response to the idea of not obeying the King underscores Gilboa's use of Saul as a symbol of majestic authority and power. This reading gains support in lines 11–12 and indeed seems to reflect the lingering tradition of Saul-as-tragic-hero as recorded in Tcherniḥovsky's classic ballad, *Al harei Gilboa* (On Mt. Gilboa).[20]

> And you are the King
> And you are His Majesty the King with your command.

The restatement of the speaker's dilemma in line 13, however, refocuses the poem on the figure of the observer himself, whose painful reactions replace the King's mutilation as the dominant image in the poem. Reading the work backwards,[21] one notes that the witness is even confused about the events surrounding Saul's death. For example, he says that he had to turn his head away from the sight of Saul's "disembodied head" *(rosh netul-guf)* nailed to the wall of Beit She'an. According to I Samuel 31:10, however, the

King was beheaded and his "body" *(geviyato)* was nailed to the wall of Beit She'an. Gilboa may have been alluding to the other version of Saul's death (I Chronicles 10:10), where the Philistines indeed nailed Saul's head to the wall. In that version, however, the head is nailed to the wall of Beit Dagon, not Beit She'an.

There are other discrepancies. The speaker, in addressing the ghost of Saul, notes that the King's arms bearer "refused to hand you the sword as you had commanded." There is no such command by Saul in either version of the story. In both versions the King says, "Draw your sword and stab me with it."[22] It is only after the boy fails to do his bidding that Saul "took the sword and fell upon it." Saul never asks the boy to "hand" him the sword, nor does the text state that the boy "refused" to do so. (Gilboa uses the verb *me'en,* "refused," while both biblical versions use the phrase *lo ava,* "did not wish to.")

While these incongruities may not be obvious, all of the poem's details draw the reader away from the already familiar figure of King Saul and focus more on the psychological portrait of the traumatized, helpless witness. As such, the poem becomes a metaphorical characterization of those who confront the Holocaust. It was impossible to save the King; the speaker arrived on the scene too late. He is a witness to the tragedy, but not an eyewitness. And what would—or could—he have done, had he been present at the death scene? The implication is: probably nothing. At this point of shame, shock and pain, all that the speaker can do is to look beyond the tragedy to a broader perspective: "Saul Saul come!" he calls out to the King's ghost. "At Beit She'an the Children of Israel live." The scene is contemporary; Jews have returned to Israel and settled in Beit She'an. Only this evidence of the Jewish people's survival and continuity can provide solace.

The inner dynamic of Gilboa's text broadens the symbolic projections of Saul as a historic figure and diminishes him as the tragic hero of classic balladry. Gilboa replaces the tragedy of the King's death not only with the contemporary catastrophe, but also with the trauma of our impotence—the realization that we were totally unable to prevent it. The new tragic hero is the witness-survivor who finds himself in the dualistic condition of despair and hope. By turning the theme of the tragic hero on its head—the anti-canonic act—Gilboa has created a cultural sign with which the Holocaust may be considered from a different perspective. This is the poem's outer dynamic. *Sha'ul* is the *parole* which presents the modern tragic hero through the medium of the *langue* of the survivor.[23]

Unlike the poems that immediately precede it, *Al naharot Bavel* (By the Waters of Babylon) does not focus on a particular biblical character. Instead, it depicts a familiar scene from the Babylonian exile, a scene in which the Jewish exiles are portrayed as weeping "by the waters of Babylon" as they remember Zion.[24] The common bond between this poem and the others is a young child as the main figure. Here that child protests the way the exiles are being treated. But the central theme of the poem is not death or renewal. It is language—more specifically, the familiar issue of expressibility. The child-speaker, who has hidden a small harp under his coat, complains that the guards who hold the exiles prisoner are "imitating our language in a stuttering way." The older exiles merely glance sadly at their harps, hung on the willows, useless. But the child rises up in anger and shouts at them:

מִי כָּאן נֶעֱלָג
פְּרִיצֵי הַחַיּוֹת, וְאֵיךְ תְּלַהֲגוּ אַתֶּמָּה?
הֲלֹא אֵין כִּלְשׁוֹנֵנוּ עוֹד לְצֶבַע וְקוֹל, לְעֹמֶק וּמֶרְחָק.

Who is the stutterer here
Wild animals, and how do you [dare to] stutter?
For there is none like our language in color and tone, in depth and breadth.

Toward the end the child himself becomes the instrument of expression when he grasps the harp and plays.[25]

In juxtaposing *Al naharot Bavel* with the biblical-theme poems, Gilboa demonstrates once again his continuing need to respond poetically to the Holocaust. Others within the camp, so to speak, may hang back, and outsiders may only mock his "stuttering" language. But the child-speaker keeps his instrument ready under his coat. Even if others rebuke him and are filled with anger, he still "plays a bit on [his] harp."

The "stuttering voice," i.e. the elliptical or ungrammatical style of the speaker, has already been noted in several poems toward the end of *Sheva reshuyot.* Gilboa uses the inarticulateness of the speaker—in *Al naharot Bavel,* the unheard voice of the child—even more frequently in the early fifties. By the late sixties, in *Ratsiti likhtov siftei yeshenim,* he becomes completely absorbed in the primal inarticulation of the poetic voice itself.

"Shirim al kiyum" (Poems on Being)

In the group of poems entitled *"Shirim al kiyum"*—*kiyum* may also be translated as "survival"—Gilboa continues to succumb to mournful memory and project the impression that all of his poetry is rooted in sources of sorrow. Bereavement haunts him at every turn: at holidays, when sighting a tree while walking down the street, waking from a dream, remembering his soldiering days, or viewing some minor damage in the garden.

In *Rabi Yisrael Ba'al-Shem-Tov al borot ha-ḥemar* (Rabbi Israel Baal Shem-Tov On the Pits of Clay),[26] the Baal Shem-Tov stands over the graves of the dead and recites the Kaddish. His tears fall onto the snow and "blossom into roses"[27] which take on several images.

וּדְמוּתָן כַּמִּקְדָּשׁ. וּדְמוּתָן כַּיּוֹנִים.
וּדְמוּתָן כְּחַנָּה עַל שִׁבְעַת הַבָּנִים.
וּדְמוּתָן כַּמְּנוֹרָה בַּת שִׁבְעַת הַקָּנִים.
וּדְמוּתָן אֲדָמִים אֲדָמִים בַּטַּלִּית
עוֹטָה הָעָם אֲשֶׁר אֶל אֵין־חֹמֶר
עָבַד בְּשִׂמְחָה
וְנָמוֹג בָּאַיִן.

And their image is like the Holy Temple. And their image is like doves.
And their image is like Hannah and her seven sons.[28]
And their image is like the candelabrum with seven branches.
And their image is the deep red of the talit [prayer shawl]
enveloping the people
who worshiped *in joy*
to *non-matter*[29]
and dissolved into nothingness.

The images combine themes of martyrdom and annihilation with themes of sacredness, transcendence, and joy. As in the biblical-theme poems, Gilboa links ancient and contemporary Jewish experience as a lachrymose series of struggles for survival. The talit is particularly effective in conveying the poem's tragic irony. Used first in the phrase "the plain of snow is enwapped like a talit" *(arvat ha-shelagim ota ka-talit),*[30] it appears later as a shawl, emblazoned with the rubies of the ancient High Priest. But the talit wraps "the people that worshiped *in/joy* to [sic] *non-matter* and dissolved into nothingness." Instead of reflecting security and divine majesty, the prayer shawl signifies the incredible demise of a civilization.

For the poem's final doleful depiction of the Baal Shem Tov's sorrow, Gilboa turns to Bialik.

דִּמְעָתוֹ רוֹתְחָה בָּעַיִן
וְנוֹפְלָה עַל בּוֹרוֹת הַחֵמָר.

וְאֶצְבְּעוֹתָיו לָשׁוֹת לָשׁוֹת בַּחֵמָר.

[The Baal Shem-Tov's] tear boils up in his eye
and falls upon the pits of clay.

And his fingers knead knead the clay.

The "boiling tear," from *Levadi,* depicts in combined mythical-romantic imagery the sorrow of the Shekhinah as she weeps over the Jewish people, who have abandoned her.[31] The image of "kneading" is similar to that in Bialik's *Shirati* (My Song), which describes the poet's mother rising early in the morning to bake Sabbath bread for her family. In her poverty and despair she weeps over the bread, and as her hand "kneads and kneads," her tears drip into the dough.[32]

The multiple images, allusions, and mythic resonances create a pervasive sadness which is simultaneously palpable and other-worldly. It is most down-to-earth when it depicts the snow enveloping "the one people in the Land" *(goy eḥad ba-arets),* implying that all the survivors who made their way to Israel—a "unique entity"—are still enveloped by tragic memory. In this sense, the poem is a sardonic allegory in the tradition of *hatrasa klapei ma'ala* (protesting God's harsh judgment).

Hilukh ha-aḥim (March of Comrades)[33] seems out of place in the "poems of survival." In place of mournful remembrance, it celebrates the soldiers' march, the camaraderie, the rhythmic song, the endless path, the cold, the sun, the morning. The heroic tone contrasts dramatically with the preceding poems, and the contrast, of course, is purposeful—emphasizing the dualistic quality, the heroic vs. the traumatic, that pervades even Gilboa's notion of memory.

חֲצוֹצְרוֹת תּוֹרְעוֹת שִׁירֵינוּ. וּטְוִי שֶׁל כֶּסֶף בֶּחָלָל.
בְּאֵרוֹת עוֹלוֹת מִשֶּׁפַע. מַעְיָנוֹת נֹחַם. וְאֵין אָבֵל.
הוֹ, לֹא יֵרֵד הַיּוֹם הָעֶרֶב. שַׂעֲרוֹתֵינוּ מָלְאוּ טַל.

Trumpets blare our song. And a weave of silver in the air.
Wells rise in plenitude. Springs of consolation. And no mourner.
Oh, the day will not end this evening. Our hair is filled with dew.

As he puts it in the poem, there is "no mourner" in this picture of happy young soldiers. The self-enthrallment is reinforced by Gilboa's use of repetitions, elliptical syntax, and phrases of limitlessness.

וְהָלַכְנוּ. וְהָלַכְנוּ. וּמִי לַדְּרָכִים יִמְנֶה מִסְפָּר?
וְזוֹ הַשֶּׁמֶשׁ, וְזוֹ הַשֶּׁמֶשׁ אֵיךְ מֵעֵינֵינוּ שָׁאֲבָה הָאוֹר!

And we walked. And we walked. And who could count the number of paths?
And this very sun, this very sun how it drew light from our eyes!

At the same time, he alludes to a contradictory dimension. The wellsprings of exuberance are "springs of consolation"; the memories of youth may provide some solace. Their actual effect, however, is to sharpen the trauma of the fall from grace. Gilboa hints at this message in the poem's opening lines.

אֵין שִׁירָה בְּלִי בֹּקֶר. וּמִי יִקְרָא חַיִּים לְנֶעְדְּרֵי בֹּקֶר?
וְזֶה הַשִּׁיר נִרְקַם בַּבֹּקֶר. כִּי הוּא אֵבֶר מִן הַחַי.

There is no poem without morning. And who will call alive those who are bereft of morning?

And this poem was woven in the morning. For it is a limb of the
living [flesh].

"Those who are bereft of morning" refers to the figures who populate his previous poems of survival. Here the poet, himself a representative of that bereaved group, still finds himself confronting the urge to write a poem ("a limb of the living [flesh]") in the morning. The connotation is that poetry is an instinctive or impulsive act. The poet cannot put aside the urge to write, for poetry is like one of his limbs, a piece of his flesh.[34]

Another connotation to *ever min ha-ḥai,* however, refers to the Noachic prohibition against eating a limb torn from a living animal—raw meat. Since for Gilboa writing poetry is an irrepressible act, the poem itself falls into the category of taboo. Viewed this way, the dissonant, heroic work strikes him as unseemly and explicable only in terms of the instinctiveness itself. Torn between retaining the memory-poem and letting it go, he opts to write it and include it in this particular context. Its very contrast with the other works further defines his identity as a romantic poet: one who lives simultaneously on oppositional levels of past remembrance and present impulse.

"Shirim al kiyum" closes with the brief elliptical *Mi-kol derekh* (From Every Path),[35] which also reflects Gilboa's view of himself as an artist.

מִכָּל דֶּרֶךְ

לְעוֹלָם תּוֹהִים
בְּעֵינַי יָצִיצוּ
מִכָּל דֶּרֶךְ וְזָוִית
שֶׁעִמִּי הָלְכוּ וְהִפְלִיגוּ
שֶׁעִמִּי הֶאֱפִירוּ וְהִתְרִיגוּ
שֶׁעִמִּי שָׁרוּ קֵץ
אֶל רֵאשִׁית.

From Every Path

Forever the bewildered
peer into my eyes
from every path and corner
who walked and sailed with me
who greyed and yellowed with me
who sang with me end
to beginning.

The "bewildered" appear to be Gilboa's companions and colleagues. Having spent a good deal of time with him, they peer into his eyes for understanding: What is he saying? What sort of person is this? In light of biographical information and certain critical essays, Gilboa seems to have been an enigma to many. How is one to comprehend poems such as those which immediately precede *Mi-kol derekh*—their dissonant images, their emotive enthrallments and diatribes, their conflicting innocence and worldliness?[36]

The answer: This is Gilboa, and this is his poetics. He draws on esoteric myth and familiar fairytales. He blends Bialik with the Baal Shem-Tov. He conjures up mournful ghosts and heroic youth. He is beset with bereavement and exalted with joyfulness. His eyes fill with tears and shine with sunlight. To understand his poetry, one need only to look into his eyes—and become more bewildered. Perhaps this is why, in *Mi-kol derekh,* he writes about those "who sang with me/end to beginning." Should it not be "from beginning to end"? No, for that would make him too conventional. In his own mind, at least, his work is impulsive, instinctive, elliptical, imagistic, unpredictable.

Every so often Gilboa reaffirms this commitment to his distinctiveness. He does so at the end of *La-ot* in *Shiri ha-paru'a* and again toward the middle of *Sheva reshuyot* in *Signonot shonim.* Here, he does it once more, resolute in his goal to be compulsively impulsive, devoted to the very idea of inspired creativity. This commitment is the focus of *"Shirim bodedim,"* the next group of poems in this collection and, indeed, a major theme in much of Gilboa's poetry over the next thirty years.

Poetry Re-viewed and Reclaimed
"Shirim bodedim" (Random Poems)

Ḥomer ha-shamayim (The Stuff of Heaven),[37] the first work in *"Shirim bodedim,"* opens with a motto poem which depicts a lonely king and his tenuous relationship to his people. Interpreted allegorically, the king becomes an image of the poet—remote, misunderstood, or not understood at all. As his readers passively observe his colorful show, the poetry takes on a life of its own—a very productive life at that. The king's imaginings flow regularly, even though the people are devoid of comprehension.

The king prefers a solitary life with no guests or visitors. Such is the nature of kings, implies the speaker, in the aphoristic opening line: *Simḥat melekh ba-ḥatserav,* "The king's happiness is within his court." The monarch has three basic characteristics: he is mighty *(kabir),* sad *(atsuv),* and bemused or playful *(meshu'asha).* The people outside the palace see in the sky "line [or flash, *pas]* after line lightning forth [sic: *mitbarkim]*/from his palaces in red." At this point, "the un-understood/in space sings by its own strength," and "tower after tower/rises and floats on high." The short, playful work is fairly sardonic, yet Gilboa is quite serious about his view of poetic power. As we have seen, he intermittently confronts his audience's response to his works and obliquely defends his right to create poetry that is justly individualistic, even if his critics have been confounded by its "difficulty." Here, by identifying with the king, he claims for himself the power to control his "stuff of heaven," an almost divine property owned only by the ruler. The analogy has limitations, however. The king-poet is not that majestic. He is both "sad" and "bemused," torn between the playfulness of creativity and the pain which creativity often causes. Gilboa further explores these issues in other poems in *"Shirim bodedim."*

In *Mi hirshif ha-laila* (Who Has Sparkled Tonight),[38] the first part of *Ḥomer ha-shamayim,* Gilboa turns once again to questions of poetic control. What motivates the poet to write? What is the source of his imaginings? As one might expect, Gilboa's response to these questions reflects his idiosyncratic poetics. Posing as a veritable victim of the poetic process, he beseeches unknown, seemingly divine forces.

מִי הִרְשִׁיף הַלַּיְלָה אֶת כָּל רְקִיעַי
וְהִבְזִיק אֶת מַפַּת הַנְּהָרוֹת עַל רֹאשִׁי
וְהוֹלִיךְ אֶת דְּבָרִי כַּמַּטֶּה הַנִּסְעָר
הַנּוֹבֵט בְּיָדִי בְּצִיצִים וּפְקָעִים
בַּמַּהֲלָךְ אֶל הַר מִשְׁכַּן הַנְּטוּשִׁים.

Who made all my skies sparkle tonight
and floodlit the map of rivers on my head
and guided my word like a stormy staff
that flowers in my hand with blossoms and buds
on the walk to the Mount of the Abode of the Abandoned.

By using terms of illumination, "made sparkle" *(hirshif)* and "floodlit" *(hivzik),* Gilboa equates the process of poetic inspiration with heavenly "flashes" that light up the night and illumine the mental terrain. The poet, however, is not in control of this phenomenon. The flashes simply come down "on [my] head." The allusions and metaphors here reinforce the familiar Gilboan theme of uncontrollability. The staff alludes to the staff of Aaron, which flowered as a sign of divine chosenness.[39] But the blossoms and buds refer to the carved wood decorations in Solomon's Temple[40] and connect with the "Temple of the Abandoned," a metaphorical expression of Gilboa's defenselessness and his ambivalence toward the adversarial nature of the poetic "gods." At once impelled and abandoned by the very same forces, he is their arbitrary victim.

Though he grows less obtuse in his figurative vocabulary and allusions, Gilboa goes on to complain effusively about the "dizzying abyss" of inspirations which defy any effort toward order, permanence, or the possibility of forgetfulness. He is so overpowered by "the hand of awareness" that he cannot differentiate between the "bread" and the "wine," the mundane and the truly inventive. As he has done before,[41] Gilboa describes here the psychological state of the romantic mind, which responds to the impulse for poetry in every visual and emotional experience. This time he reacts with sardonic laughter.

הִי, הִי הִי, סַפֵּר, סַפֵּר אֵי לִבָּם הַבּוֹכֶה
כַּאֲשֶׁר לְעֵינֵיהֶם גָּוַעְתָּ.

Ha, ha, ha, tell, tell where is their crying heart
when you perished right before their eyes.

שְׁמַע, נְכוֹנִים לְךָ הֵדִים בְּחַמּוּקָיו שֶׁל הַלַּיִל
לוֹטְפִים וְעוֹיְנִים כִּטְלָפָיו שֶׁל הַלַּיִשׁ.

Listen, the echoes are ready for you in embracing limbs of night
they stroke and threaten like the paws of a lion.

סַפֵּר, סַפֵּר. סַפֵּר אֶת עָדְפֵי הַיָּמִים,
אֶת עִקְּרֵי חִיּוּתְךָ שֶׁזָּרִיתָ אֶל רוּחַ.
סַפֵּר אַגָּדוֹת שֶׁבַּלַּיְלָה
עִם הָרוּחוֹת הַקָּמִים
סָעֲרוּ
עַד בֹּקֶר מְצָאָם
אֲפֹרִים,
גּוֹוְעִים בַּתֵּל הַתָּחוּחַ.

Tell, tell. Tell of the surfeits of days,
of the essences of your being that you've sown to the wind.
Tell of the stories of night
with the winds rising up
storming
till morning finds them
grey,
expiring in a soppy pile.

For Gilboa, the night, the time of inspirational flow, ironically becomes "suddenly cruel and cold." In parts two and three of *Ḥomer ha-shamayim,* poetry itself becomes "a mountain" that constantly looms over the poet. At the close of the poem, this overwhelming "mountain" has become the entire "sky." Gilboa longs to escape from its presence. Perhaps in his youth, he notes, he was able to reach out and communicate with inspirational "heights" of "fire," "power," and "tears." Now what once was a plenitude of inspiration has become—at least in this poem—a burden of emotional surfeit.[42]

After all these impassioned poetic complaints, however, the final poem, *Hishtakfut* (Reflection),[43] reaffirms Gilboa's attachment to romantic modes of expression. In the opening scene the poet-speaker is entranced.

בְּלַיְלָה שֶׁל יָרֵחַ עַז בְּטַבּוּרוֹ שֶׁל כְּפָר
עָמַדְתִּי לְטוּף אוּרִים.
רְצוּדִים הִתְרַפְּקוּ הֵם עַל גּוּפִי
וְלֹא קָם בִּי הַכֹּחַ לָצֵאת מִן הַקּוּרִים.

On a night of strong moon in the center of a village
I stood caressed by lights.
Prancing they leaned on my body
and I could not muster the strength to leave the web.

Here Gilboa's oft-displayed sense of enthrallment takes on the palpably physical dimension of being caught in a web. "Caressed by lights," lights "prancing," being entangled almost willingly—all these are romantic images (in some contexts, Gothic ones) par excellence.[44] The theme of physicality intensifies, even to the point of sensuality, in the second stanza. When the rooster crows at dawn, the speaker notes that "it awakened the sleepers of desire *(nirdemei ha-yetsarim).*" The lights' embrace also grows in intensity, an intensity expressed in ecstatic repetitions of visionary images.

וְעַל גּוּפִי הָאוֹרוֹת מְשַׂחֲקִים בְּכָל צֶבַע
אוֹרֵי אוֹרוֹת וּבְנֵי אוֹרוֹת, הִשְׁתַּקְּפוּת הָרִים בֶּהָרִים
כַּאֲשֶׁר עֵינֵי אוֹהֲבָה.

And on my body in every color play
lights of lights and children of lights, a reflection of mountains in

mountains
precisely what my eye loves.

The work presents a grand euphoric vision of the poet's sensual involvement with night and the natural landscape and is a fitting end to this section. The play of darkness via-à-vis the intense effulgences of light affirm Gilboa's penchant for contrast. The layered images provide an unending source of inspiration. Here Gilboa offers no complaint at the plethora of—or his entrapment in—these visionary delights. He remains the romantic nature poet, even at the risk of being overwhelmed by his own enchantment.

"Shirim she-ka-ele" (Poems the Likes of These)

Gilboa's title for this grouping seems to express ambivalence toward its contents. It might be understood as "[Who could care about] poems the likes of these?" Indeed, one may question whether some of these are poems at all—or merely insubstantial jingles. On the other hand, many find the lighter works precisely to their liking. Such has been the case with *Lu me'a kova'im* (If Only a Hundred Hats),[45] a long-standing favorite which has even been set to music as a popular folk tune. Whichever the perspective, most of the *"Shirim she-ka-ele"* poems are quite different from Gilboa's "typical" works. Though not monolithic, the poems share a number of characteristics. Speakers and situations are childlike, and the experiences described mostly mundane. Although at times there is a serious theme, an ambiguous happiness predominates. Most significant, the works allow us to see some of the simpler, more personal aspects of Gilboa's character: his strong temperament, his gentleness, his love of family, his playful sense of humor.

The first two poems, *Simḥa* (Happiness) and *Gevul* (Border or Limit),[46] present scenes and images reminiscent of both Kafka and Alterman. In *Simḥa* the speaker, while taking a walk, is repeatedly confronted by passersby who ask him " . . . why are you happy." Each time, the somewhat bizarre response is, "And I didn't hear because I was happy." Maybe he does not want his happiness disrupted in order to answer the question. Or perhaps the very state of happiness keeps him from noticing the usual sorrows of the world. Certainly there are several other ways to understand the passage, but that is precisely what Gilboa is portraying here—a playful yet engaging game of ambiguity and absurdity. Gilboa develops both with growing intensity throughout the poem.

In the first stanza the speaker arrives "almost at the end of the streets." There he meets a small boy playing in the sand and extends to him an apparently well-meaning invitation.

אָמַרְתִּי לוֹ בּוֹא הֱיֵה גַּם אַתָּה שָׂמֵחַ
אָמַר לִי אַתָּה נִמְצָא בְּסוֹף הָרְחוֹבוֹת.

I said to him Come be happy too
He said to me You're at the end of the streets.

The nonsequitur is complicated by the addition of a metaphorical dimension in the second stanza, where the speaker finds himself arriving "at the end of happiness" and finds a young boy "who has not come to the end of happiness."

אָמַרְתִּי לִי אַתָּה עוֹד וְעוֹד תִּהְיֶה שָׂמֵחַ
וּלְעוֹלָם לֹא תָבוֹא עַד סוֹף הַשִּׂמְחָה.

I said to myself More and more you'll be happy
and you'll never come to the end of happiness.

The final stanza, however, dashes this assertion. The anticlimax is intensely ironic because at the outset the speaker assertively repeats his claim that he cannot hear "at a time of happiness." Then, in place of the boy, he finds "a long day when I was not happy."

וְתָמַהְתִּי עַל כָּל אֶחָד שֶׁ אָ ז שָׁאַל לַשִּׂמְחָה
וְתוּגָה אָכְלָה בַּלֵּב גְּדוֹלָה כַּשִּׂמְחָה.

And I wondered about everyone who *then* asked about happiness
And sorrow ate at my heart [a sorrow] as great as happiness.

The "plot" of this poem, then, is about a person who is very happy, who does not hear when others ask him about it, who feels that his happiness is readily contagious, but finds it is not. He tries to reassure himself that his happiness will last forever, but, alas, inevitably feels sad. It is perhaps then—the ambiguity remains—that he begins to understand all the questions about happiness. His closing statement, that his sorrow was "as great as happiness," is an Alterman-like example of metaphorical double-speak.

Gevul, the poem which follows, provides the same sort of philosophical mini-drama. Here the speaker is quite agitated. The central phrase is "I was almost at my wits' end" *(kimat avarti kol gevul*—literally, "I almost crossed every border" or "I almost went beyond all limit"). In this emotional state, he is suddenly stopped on the street by an unfamiliar person who claims to be a friend, reminisces about common acquaintances, and wants to hear the speaker say his name. The perturbed speaker bizarrely asks himself, "And what if the house I've stopped by falls down, and I haven't yet received my reward" *(va-ani terem bati al gemul).* Increasingly agitated, he begins to shout at the stranger, who responds, "My friend, my good friend, alas, you have come to the end [of your wits]." This seems to jolt the speaker back to a relatively calm state of mind.

וַאֲנִי שָׂמַחְתִּי אֶל גְּמוּל
כִּי לֹא עָבַרְתִּי גְּבוּל.

And I was happy to [the point of] reward
for I did not go beyond the limit.

The playful rhyme of *gemul* (reward) and *gevul* (border or limit) highlights the poem's meaning. In a situation not unlike the one presented in *Simḥa,* once again the speaker cannot listen to the passerby—this time not because he is so happy but because he is so frantic about the possibility of dying without receiving his due. Instead of the hoped-for reward, he settles for the simple realization that he has calmed down—because of the intervention of the man on the street. Though farcical in its confrontative dramatization of the speaker's absurd paranoia, *Gevul* might well be expressing the fragility of Gilboa's own emotional state.

Although Gilboa has depicted street scenes and volatile speaker-personae in earlier works, these poems contain new poetic and rhetorical elements—

word-play substitutions, an overriding ambiguity, a general atmosphere of absurdity, and the complete absence of a mythical framework or traditional vocabulary. The language is highly colloquial, though some euphuistic phrases (such as *terem bati al gemul)* are used. Although the larger themes are familiar, here Gilboa focuses on the inner workings of the mind in everyday situations.

The poems which follow *Simḥa* and *Gevul* evince an unsubtle, childlike quality and a genuine exuberance for the homey experiences of family, pets, and the simple joys of life. In rhythmically structured couplets, *Liora ve-Lior* (Liora and Lior)[47] touchingly portrays the summer adventure of a loving father and his two children. With much charm the father idealizes the looks and laughs of his children to the point of imagining their voices in nightly conversation as those of heavenly cherubs. At the beach the children write identical messages in the sand, "Beloved Daddy. You are loved. I'll always love you." But the summer idyll soon ends and the poem closes with a non-idealized statement about the real world.

כָּךְ קַיִץ עָבַר וּסְתָו עָבַר וּבָא הַחֹרֶף.
כִּי קַיִץ עָבַר וּסְתָו עָבַר בָּא הַחֹרֶף.

And so summer passed and fall passed and then came winter.
For summer passed and fall passed and then came winter.

Be-veiteinu haya ḥatul (In Our House There Was a Cat)[48] is quite simply a reminiscent paean to Gilboa's cat.

בְּבֵיתֵנוּ הָיָה חָתוּל. הָתוּל עֲנָק.
הָיִינוּ יְדִידִים.
הוּא, מוּבָן, הָיָה חָתוּל. וּמְאוּם.
הֲבִינוֹתִי זֹאת כְּבָר אָז.
הָיִיתִי מְחַלֵּק עִמּוֹ הַכֹּל.

In our house there was a cat. A giant cat.

We were friends.
Of course, it was a cat. Nothing more.
I understood that even then.
I shared everything with it.

In each of the poem's episodes, Gilboa repeats the refrains "In our house there was a cat" and "We were friends." The relationship, obviously, was uncommon. It survived even a terrible scratching episode, when Gilboa was teasing the cat with its favorite colored marble. Gilboa sullenly divulges that after the incident "a whole mountain separated us." But the poem ends with the confirmation that this was indeed a close, loving relationship.

הָיִינוּ יְדִידִים.
צָרִיךְ הָיִיתִי לְשָׁכְחוֹ מִזְּמַן.
מִשּׁוּם־מָה אֵינֶנִּי שׁוֹכֵחַ יְדִידִים.

בְּבֵיתֵנוּ הָיָה חָתוּל. חָתוּל עֲנָק.

We were friends.
I should have forgotten it long ago.
For some reason I don't forget friends.

In our house there was a cat. A giant cat.

Lu me'a kova'im (If Only a Hundred Hats)[49]

The popularity of this poem among Israeli readers is probably due to its madcap, exuberant quality—the speaker, an impulsive happy celebrant, reaches for a way to express his overflowing glee. There is no ambivalence or ambiguity here, only abundance. Not only does the speaker fantasize about wearing one hundred hats, which he would toss "on high out of joy." The hats themselves would feature a hundred different colors, each of which would have a hundred "shadings of color." In other words, their variety would be infinite. At the marketplace, all those gathered would make way for him, waiting for the hats to be thrown. He would be the star, the center of attention, and even the sun would salute him.

לוּ מֵאָה כּוֹבָעִים

לוּ מֵאָה כּוֹבָעִים לְרֹאשִׁי
מֵאָה כּוֹבָעִים מֵאָה צְבָעִים
מֵאָה כּוֹבָעִים מֵאָה צְבָעִים וּבְנֵי צֶבַע
מֵאָה כּוֹבָעִים מְטַר צְבָעִים

לוּ מֵאָה כּוֹבָעִים לְרֹאשִׁי
הָיִיתִי יוֹצֵא אֶל כִּכַּר הַשּׁוּק
מְפַנֶּה לִי דֶּרֶךְ בְּכִכַּר הַשּׁוּק
וְזוֹרְקָם עָל מִשִּׂמְחָה

לוּ מֵאָה כּוֹבָעִים לְרֹאשִׁי
הָיִיתִי יוֹצֵא אֶל כִּכַּר הַשּׁוּק
וְכָל הָאֲנָשִׁים מְפַנִּים לִי הַדֶּרֶךְ
מְצַפִּים לְרֶגַע נִפְנוּף הַכּוֹבָעִים

לוּ מֵאָה כּוֹבָעִים לְרֹאשִׁי
מֵאָה כּוֹבָעִים מֵאָה צְבָעִים וּבְנֵי צֶבַע
לוּ מֵאָה כּוֹבָעִים וְשֶׁמֶשׁ גְּבֹהָה
יָשָׁר אֶל רֹאשִׁי יָשָׁר אֶל צְבָעַי

הוֹ הָעָם קְרִיאוֹת הִתְפַּעֲלוּת בִּגְרוֹנוֹ נָכוֹנוּ
וּמִתְפָּעֵם לִבּוֹ הַכַּבִּיר בַּכִּכָּר
לֵב הָעָם הַמְצַפֶּה

לְנִפְנוּף מֵאָה כּוֹבָעִים מֵאָה צְבָעִים וּבְנֵי צֶבַע

If Only a Hundred Hats

If only [there were] a hundred hats on my head
A hundred hats   a hundred colors
A hundred hats   a hundred colors and hues
A hundred hats   a rainfall of colors

If only a hundred hats on my head
I'd go out to the marketplace square
make a pathway in the marketplace square
and toss them upward out of joy

If only a hundred hats on my head
I'd go out to the marketplace square
and all the people would make me a pathway
waiting for the moment to wave their hats

If only a hundred hats on my head
A hundred hats   a hundred colors and hues
If only a hundred hats   and a high sun
right at my head   right at my colors

Oh the populace   cries of excitement readied in its throat
and its mighty heart pounds in the square
the heart of the populace waiting

for the waving of a hundred hats   a hundred colors and hues

The poem may be a whimsical version of Theodor (Dr. Seuss) Geisel's well-known *Bartholomew Cubbins and the 500 Hats.* In Eli Mohar's interview, Gilboa recalls that the poem was a *ketiva shel capriza* (a capricious work) whose idea came to him while he was riding a Tel Aviv bus one day and imagining a boy throwing hats into the air. The image, he notes, was based on street performers who used to appear from time to time in his home town of Radzivil. He thought he had written the entire poem "spontaneously," but years later found the original sheet and noticed he had crossed out most of the opening line.[50]

On another level, *Lu me'a kova'im* may be read as a commentary on the relationship between the poet and his audience, a relationship which is, in part, one of expectation and aesthetic gratification. To wear a hundred hats in a hundred-plus colors might refer to the romantic poet's ability to produce a constant stream of poetic images of infinite variety. Here, however, perhaps Gilboa is indulging in wishful thinking, imagining his readers gathering to applaud and celebrate his poetic feats. Based on this playful, legend-like scenario, *Lu me'a kova'im* might be considered a happy alternative to the poet-king's lonely and unappreciated existence in *Ḥomer ha-shamayim.*

In *Halkha Simḥa ba-shuk* (Happiness Walked in the Marketplace),[51] Gilboa creates a personification, a woman called Simḥa, and sets her in a dramatic situation of rejection. He also uses a new poetic structure consisting of verses broken by internal lines of demarcation.

הָלְכָה שִׂמְחַה בַּשּׁוּק / הָלְכָה בָּרְחוֹבוֹת, בַּגַּנִּים / וְלֹא שָׂמוּ בָּהּ
עַיִן / וְלֹא הִטּוּ לָהּ הַלֵּב.

וּמִמּוּל / לֵב אָדָם הָלַךְ / לֵב אָדָם עָצֵב.

Happiness walked in the marketplace/walked in the streets, in the gardens/and no one
looked at her/or paid attention to her.

And across the way/the heart of a man walked/the heart of a sad man.

The figure of Happiness here evokes two biblical images: the beloved woman of the Song of Songs and the destroyed city of Jerusalem, personified as a defiled woman in the book of Lamentations.[52] Beyond these proof-texts, the allegorical characterization, the archaic style, and the pausal structures of the verses further the illusion of biblical parallelism. Moreover, Happiness herself takes on the image of the Fallen Woman. Rejected and derided by her enemies and "The Sorrows" *(ha-yegonot),* she begs for attention and sadly awaits "her day." Only "Wonderment" *(timahon)* seems to notice her, albeit only passively. As a result, Happiness, like the personification of Jerusalem in Lamentations, falls to the lowest level of degradation.

> פָּשְׁטָה שִׂמְחָה בִּגְדֵי יָמֶיהָ / וְלָבְשָׁה סוּדָרֵי לֵילוֹתֶיהָ / מְצַפָּה כִּי מִן
> לַיְלָה / יָבוֹאוּ קְרוּאֶיהָ.

Happiness removed her daytime clothes/and donned her nighttime veils/waiting for the
night/to bring her callers.

The first stanza ("Happiness walked in the marketplace . . . ") is repeated at the close of the poem and emphasizes the poet-observer's brokenheartedness at this derision and downfall. The *"Shirim she-ka'ele"* poems stress the importance of the simple joys in life. Too many people are at their wits' end in pursuit of their just reward on earth. Too many see only "the end of streets" or "the end of happiness." Too many lack spontaneous exuberance—playing with a cat or with one's children. For most, Happiness is neglected; Sorrow and Wonderment get in the way. Certainly both the medium and the message of these works evince some measure of recovery from the unmitigated sorrow conveyed in so many of Gilboa's earlier poems.

Eineinu ha-ne'etsamot (Our Closing Eyes),[53] the last poem in this section, seems to depict a traditional nature scene. However, Gilboa cleverly utilizes the framework of the idyll to create another poem of romantic ambivalence.

עֵינֵינוּ הַנֶּעֱצָמוֹת

זְהָרִים בַּבֹּקֶר. כְּחֻלִּים בַּשֹּׁקֶת.
וְנִים מוֹשֵׁחַ פְּנֵי מַיִם שֶׁכִּסּוּ יְרֹקֶת.
יְרֹקֶת. וְעֹקֶץ. בְּלִי עֹקֶץ. וּבָא קֵץ.
וְטוֹב כָּךְ לָנוּחַ עַל סַפְסָל פָּשׁוּט מֵעֵץ
בְּקֶרֶן שֶׁל גַּן שָׁכוּחַ וְזָנוּחַ.
וְלִדֹּם. וְלִדֹּם. וְלִשְׁמֹעַ סִפּוּרָיו שֶׁל הָרוּחַ

אֲשֶׁר נָשָׂא הָרוּחַ וְהֶאֱבִיר מֵעַל לְרָאשֵׁינוּ
וְאַךְ הָאֵפֶר אַךְ הָאֵפֶר נִזְרָה לְתוֹךְ עֵינֵינוּ.
עֵינֵינוּ. עֵינֵינוּ. וּכְבָר כָּל זֹאת אֵינֶנּוּ.
אֵינֶנּוּ. וְהָלַךְ. וְאֶפְשָׁר סָט לָנוּחַ. לָנוּחַ
מוּל עֵינֵינוּ הַנֶּעֱצָמוֹת

שָׁם.
שָׁם מֵרֹאשׁ הָעֵץ
מַאְדִּים צְחוֹק צָעִיר. חִיּוּךְ בְּשִׁיר. כְּדַל חֲלוֹם בְּתִיר–
תַּפּוּחַ.

וְעוֹד הָרוּחַ

Our Closing Eyes

Morning radiances. Blue in the trough.
Slumber daubs the face of the water covered with algae.
Algae. And a sting. No sting. It's over.
It's good to rest on a simple wooden bench like this
in the corner of a forgotten, abandoned garden.
To be still. And be still. To hear the wind's tales
which the wind bore and floated over our heads
but the ashes but the ashes were strewn into our eyes.
Our eyes. Our eyes. And then it was over.
Over. It's gone. Perhaps it's just resting. Resting
in front of our closing eyes

There.
There from the treetop
reddens a young smile. A smile in a poem. A scrap of a tatter of
 dream—
An apple.

And yet the wind

As the reader readily notes as early as line 3, the idyll is disrupted semantically and syntactically. Gilboa is quite playful: he repeats the word "algae" *(yeroket)* to confirm the idyll, but the water's stillness is disturbed by a "sting" *([ve-]okets),* an approximate rhyme which semantically connects the idyllic water surface with the anti-idyllic sting. The dichotomy is followed by the phrase "no sting" *(beli okets),* a play on words which connotes that the poet is not being sardonic. The bee has flown off and left the grateful observer—and the reader—unharmed. Finally, the verse ends with another rhyme, "It's over" (a liberal translation of *u-va kets*—literally, the end came), meaning that the threat of being stung has passed and the idyll is over as well.[54]

These puns disclose a not-so-subtle ambivalence about the loveliness of nature and create a romantic interlude fraught with antiromantic resonances. Gilboa achieves a similarly anticlimactic effect in the next part of the scene as the wind whispers its tales and whisks them over the heads of the listeners. Suddenly and unexpectedly, scattered ashes spray into their eyes (line 9). Here, too, syntax plays a part in the farcical scene, this time with its elimination of stops, contrasting with the continual stops in line 3. In line 9, the repetition "Our eyes. Our eyes" conveys that the ashes are painful, but immediately thereafter, *kvar kol zot einenu* (And then it was over), rhymes playfully—twice—with *eineinu* (our eyes). Still fearful of the ashes which lurk right before their eyes, the victims protectively close them—an ironic action which also prevents them from seeing the idyllic scene. Once again, Gilboa creates a resonant binary opposition: the ashes of the Holocaust vis-à-vis the eyes, perceivers of the idyllic, which are shut to keep out the ashes.

More playful still, Gilboa points to a reddening apple peering out of the treetop. The apple takes the shape of a metonymic smile, symbolizing a return to the idyll. The smile is "young"; it promises longevity. It is "a smile in a poem," an ambiguous Mona Lisa-like expression, but also a positive romantic vision. However, the third characteristic, "a scrap of a tatter of dream," is less sanguine. If the dream has dwindled to such "a scrap of a tatter," it cannot be very idyllic.[55]

The poem's closing line provides the coup de grace. "And yet the wind" may refer to other winds which might well bring another downpour of ashes. Or it may allude to the folksong *Ru'aḥ, ru'aḥ* (Wind, Wind), with its line *min ha-ets nafal tapu'aḥ* (an apple has fallen from the tree). Like

"Rockabye Baby in the Treetop," the Hebrew tune is a lullaby with ominous portent. The connotation here is that the return to the idyll is shortlived. The smiling apple, buffeted by the wind, may soon fall.

Just as he toys with the themes of happiness and sadness in several of the earlier poems in this section, in *Eineinu ha-ne'etsamot* Gilboa plays with the notions of the idyllic and anti-idyllic, the romantic and the antiromantic. By placing the poem at the close of this grouping, Gilboa reminds us that each life scenario is fraught with conflicting and counterbalancing forces. A cat can be lovable and cantankerous. Happiness can be isolating. Time can destroy the idyllic experiences of childhood. As these works attest, the juxtaposition of opposites is clearly a cornerstone of Gilboa's poetics.

"Shirim me-erev" (Songs of Evening)[56] consists wholly of introspective, confessional poetry.[57] Once more Gilboa gives vent to a painful inner struggle, a mid-life crisis perhaps, but in any case a crisis of poetic consciousness. He is filled with remorse, anger, frustration, exasperation.

As in *Ḥomer ha-shamayim,* this section highlights Gilboa's alienation from the Israeli poetry establishment and his struggles with the very forces that make him a poet.

In *Yomam gadol od* (Their Day Is Yet Long)[58] he contrasts the light of day with his night, filled with continuous waves of both darkness and light. He wonders whether "these flashes will pursue my last memory to the end of generations." Even when he turns off the light, he feels "lights *(urim)* still inside me" *(be-ḥadarai*—which could also mean "in my rooms, i.e., my inner chambers"). The light, the bombardment of poetic images, is inescapable.

הִנֵּה אֲנִי אֶל אוֹר לַעֲשׂוֹת לֵילוֹת כְּיָמַי.

Here I am for light[59] to work both day and night.

In contrast, when he turns on the light for the third time he hears children laughing outside the window and says, "For them their day is yet long. Endlessly long." Feeling the weighty burden of poetry, he envies youth its innocence and its unbounded, unencumbered hours.

Other poems in "*Shirim me-erev*" use variations of the light motif to describe this burden. In *Ḥeshbon yashan* (Old Account),[60] Gilboa notes the hopelessness of trying to keep sunshine out of the world. Whether you want it to or not, "everything upon which the sun has shined the sun will shine upon it," says the Ecclesiastes-like speaker. In *Ketav-ha-tsohorayim she-avad* (The Afternoon-Writing That Was Lost),[61] the poet-speaker feels as if he is "trapped in white light/like an enervated butterfly in the sparkling particles of dust *(ḥereg)*." Weary of all the illumination, he becomes "a sleepwalker in the midst of the roads," ceaselessly wandering, directionless. Tormented by the uncontrolled bombardment of poetic inspiration, he also longs for proper recognition.

כָּל־כָּךְ הַרְבֵּה דְרָכִים עָבַרְתִּי
מִשְׁתּוֹמְמִים לְאֶחָד קְרוּעַ מַבָּטִים וְלוֹהֵט מֵרְגָעָיו
וְלֹא עָמַד בָּהֶם אִישׁ לִקְרֹא לִי
וַאֲפִלּוּ מֵחֹם הֲזָיוֹת.

I've traveled on so many roads
people bewildered at the wide-eyed one [literally, one torn open with looks][62] afire from his moments
but no one's risen to call out to me
not even out of the heat of visions.[63]

As a poet, Gilboa feels abandoned, alone in the world. He mourns a friend who was a confidant, one who was truthful with him and able to "shake off all [his] desolations *[mishbatai]*."[64] He misses those who knew him when he first began to write—who obviously approved and supported his work—but who are no longer around. "Where did they all go?" he cries in exasperation.[65] Then he returns to his poetic burden, railing against the very act of "inspiration." In a paroxysm of convoluted metaphors he thunders, "Who poured here the light of his flashes upon the table of my paths/and my legs cannot reach even its edges."[66] He feels like an actor with a "storming soul," "mutilated by whips of laughter and lashes."[67] He hides in a rocky fissure, a place "I myself have hewn," he admits. But he wishes with all his might to escape, "to cut myself off from myself."[68]

One senses in these works that at least part of Gilboa's writing problem is Holocaust-related. In *Ḥeshbon yashan* he posits three personality types in the world: 1) the person who has a "night vision" of how the next day will go and follows the plan "like a mathematical formula"; 2) the person who figures everything out in advance and is satisfied if "the road to his house is clear for his car"; 3) the person who strives to "build worlds [and] each and every world he builds is destroyed at the start." Perceiving himself to be in the third category, Gilboa is tormented by existential frustration.

כָּל עוֹלָם וְעוֹלָם נֶחֱרָב בְּאִבּוֹ
וְקִבְרוֹת־עוֹלָם בְּלִבּוֹ –
רִבּוֹא.

Each and every world is destroyed at the start
and [there are] eternity-graves in his heart—
tens of thousands of them.[69]

Images of tens of thousands of "eternity-graves" and the reference to "his dead [ones]" surely suggest that Gilboa's poetic inability to write freely is still linked to his implacable sorrow. The poem's closing lines support this interpretation.

וְיִירָא אֶת הָרֶגַע בּוֹ יָנִיף חַרְבּוֹ
וְינַשֵּׂא אֶת הָרֶגַע בּוֹ יָנִיף חַרְבּוֹ
לַהֲרֹס עוֹלְמוֹתָיו
וְלִבּוֹ –

וְיֵדַע חֶשְׁבּוֹן מוֹתָיו.

And he'll fear the moment he raises his sword [i.e. his pen]
and he'll extol the moment he raises his sword
to destroy his worlds
and his heart—

And he'll know the account of his dead.

These losses are alluded to in *Ketav ha-tsohorayim she-avad* as well.

לִי מֻתָּר לְהָרִים הַמִּכְסֶה וּלְהַבִּיט.
הִתְנַעֲרוּ, הִתְנַעֲרוּ כֻּלְּכֶם מֵרֶגֶשׁ תְּאֵב־רוֹאִי
וָלֵכוּ מִכָּאן.
לִי מֻתָּר לְהָרִים הַמִּכְסֶה וּלְהַבִּיט בַּפָּנִים הַקְּפוּאוֹת.
אֲנִי תָמִיד יָרֵאתִי אֶת מַסֵּכוֹת הַמָּוֶת.
אֲנִי תָמִיד תִּעַבְתִּי אֶת מַסֵּכוֹת הַמָּוֶת.

I'm allowed to lift the cover and to look.
Shake off, all of you, shake off the feeling of sight-lust
and get away from here.
I'm allowed to lift the cover and to look at the frozen faces.
I've always been afraid of death masks.
I've always despised death masks.

The poetic process, Gilboa implies, involves looking beyond the surface in order to plumb the depths of thought and feeling. But something has gone wrong. The speaker has lost this capability, even though as a poet he is "allowed" to do so. (Gilboa uses the ironic Yiddish image *kokhlefl,* one who looks into the pots to see or taste what is cooking.) Now, when he looks "deeply" into faces or objects, the sight of "frozen faces" or "death masks" limits his insight and diminishes his poetic impulse—an ironic antidote to the bombardment of images and lightning flashes of inspiration that so recently assaulted his romantic sensibility.

Ketav ha-tsohorayim she-avad closes with these lines.

זוֹ זִקִית שֶׁל חַיַּי שֶׁקָּפְאָה אֶל הַמָּוֶת.
הַלְוַאי וְעֵין אָפְרָהּ יַעֲמֹד גַּם עָלַי
לַעֲשׂוֹתֵנִי תוֹאֵם
לְסֶלַע דוֹמֵם.

This chameleon of my life which has frozen to death.
If only its eye of grey would come upon me

and make me the twin
of a mute rock.[70]

Longing to throw off his poetic burden, the speaker complains vociferously about having wasted the afternoon.[71] Yet the reality is that Gilboa is still writing. He questions aspects of his long-standing ars poetica, reviews the mechanisms of his established poetics, reassesses his role as a romantic poet. He no longer wants to be "trapped in the white light" or to wear the "flute of deception" around his neck. He wants to be free of the oppositional states of "laughter and pain" and the idyllic and heroic modes of expression. He seeks "a soft path" and "to walk in the blues *[ba-keḥulim]*." In these lines one clearly hears the self-conscious poet searching for his true voice in the content and style of his craft.

In *"Shir be-shalosh ashmurot"* (A Poem in Three Watches),[72] Gilboa presents a scornful critique of the poetry establishment. In this minicycle of three separate works, his main target seems to be editors who "steal" his poems by suggesting editorial changes unacceptable to him. Their false tone of friendship, their cajoling, "their put-on smile" and "sweeter than honey" words disgust and anger him. Gilboa offers several grotesque images to embody his dislike of this group and express his strong feeling that the boundaries of poetic expression must be determined only by the poet himself. No one may ask him to conform to externally-imposed conventions or tastes. This argument is reinforced in one sardonic poem after another.[73]

At stake here is the poet's right to control his artistic repertoire. Much of the negative criticism of Gilboa was directed not at his consistency as a romantic poet but at his efforts to create his own new poetics: innovative forms of biblical poetry; nonmythical, everyday experiences for poetic subjects; much more ambiguity, ellipsis, and jingle-like repetition; extensive experimentation with nonpunctuation, misuse of prepositions and other particles, and unconventional syntactic structures.[74] Then, as if to underscore his poetic right to do so, Gilboa closes *"Shir be-shalosh ashmurot"* with *Erev sufa* (Stormy Evening),[75] a throwback to his former identity as a romantic nature poet par excellence.

עֶרֶב סוּפָה

וְעוֹד הַשֶּׁמֶשׁ מַוְרִיד אֶת חֲזִיתוֹת הַבָּתִּים
בְּאוֹר שֶׁל חִיּוּכֵי יְלָדִים
שֶׁל דִּגְלֵי נֹעַר
שֶׁל כְּרָזוֹת חַג
בְּאוֹר שֶׁל קוֹלוֹת מְעַטִּים
בְּתוֹךְ חַשְׁרַת דְּמָמָה מְעִיקָה
טֶרֶם שׁוּב יַכֶּה הַבָּרָק.

Stormy Evening

And still the sun reddens the fronts of the houses
with the light of children's smiles
of the flags of youth
of holiday posters
with the light of a few voices
in the midst of an ominous gathering of silence
before the lightning strikes again.

Erev sufa is a beautifully resonant, impressionistic work which combines, in pure romantic fashion, the childlike innocence of evening with the blatantly frightful frame—the title and last line—of the storm. With the dissonant phrase *demama me'ika,* "oppressive silence," the poem, like a masterful haiku, turns subtly but compellingly dramatic. The soft lyric is an antidote for the harsh sardonicism of "*Shir be-shalosh ashmurot.*" The poet, Gilboa implies, has complete freedom to pen a sarcastic work, filled with grotesque images and antagonistic feelings, only to follow it with a romantic scene of nature's subtle array of moods and forces. In other words, even the editorial sequence of works, no matter how jarring, must be determined by the poet himself.

"Shirei koteret" (Headline Poems)

Continuing Gilboa's preoccupation with the poetic process, he moves beyond the tormented introspection of *"Shirim me-erev"* and the harsh anger of *Shir be-shalosh ashmurot* to focus more positively on the theme of individual creativity in *"Shirei koteret."*[76] In *She-mehalkhim be-fundak* (When One Walks in an Inn),[77] Gilboa presents an about face in his acceptance of inspiration. "When a thought comes along and there's another in [your] blood, it's a sign that all's well." Suddenly his poetic mind, even if cluttered, reflects a comfortable sense of self. It is akin to "the light of day [which is] the first and last principle [of reason and life]."

Another affirmative statement appears in *Pataḥti et ha-delet* (I Opened the Door),[78] a dream poem in which the speaker is forced to break down the walls of his room in order to accommodate the "many many" guests who have crowded inside. "My room has become the world," he notes, implying that the poet is surrounded by a superabundance of ideas, images, thoughts. Speaking now in a positive sense, he feels that his imaginative mind embodies an entire universe.

A similar message is found in *Be-kho'aḥ keri'a aḥat* (With the Power of One Rip).[79] The poet-speaker has the power to conjure up an image, to "bring down the curtain" on it, and, "with the power of one rip," to revive the image and "spread light upon it." Dealing again with poetic control, Gilboa is asserting here his poetic right to discard and then to reconsider any number of images in his mind.

At the end of *"Shirei koteret"* Gilboa presents *Al signon* (On Style),[80] which—in the apologetical tradition of *Shiri ha-paru'a* and *Signonot shonim*—more fully explores and expands the theme of authorial freedom. The first part states in circumlocutory fashion that poetic styles are so varied that "there's no end to it." Often, he implies, one's style simply appears out of nowhere, "without any signal" *(mi-bli le'otet)* and, just as often, it may be "out with the old and in with the new" *(ḥai ha-ḥai u-met ha-met).* Commenting sarcastically on critical discussions of these variations, he says, "We were so rich/and we didn't give it a name." The poet, he implies, is so immersed in the poetic process that the academic terminology for what he is doing is irrelevant. Unconcerned with delineating his stylistic changes, Gilboa sardonically concludes that he is not sure he is "right or wrong" *(tsodek o ashem)* because to his mind the whole enterprise of tracking these variations is a "pitiable" exercise *(leraḥem,* which rhymes with *ashem)* and a waste of time. In the second section Gilboa pokes fun more directly at the critical tendency to compare his style with that of other poets.

הִנֵּה עָמַדְתִּי בְּתוֹךְ הַשִּׁיר
וְנִכְלַמְתִּי בְּכֹחַ. . . .

Here I stand in the midst of the poem and I'm strongly ashamed. . . .

. . .וַאֲנִי אֵינִי צוֹחֵק לָאֲחֵרִים
אַךְ צוֹחֵק וְצוֹחֵק לַהַשְׁוָאוֹת אֶל אֲחֵרִים
וַאֲפִלּוּ נְמֵרִים
וַאֲפִלּוּ בַּעֲלֵי רְכוּשׁ וּבָתִּים

. . . And I'm not making fun of others
but I do laugh and laugh about comparisons with others
even [with] leopards
even with real estate owners[81]

In a pithy slogan at the poem's close Gilboa sums up his pejorative view of those who attempt to delineate his style: "I'm so different" *(ani aḥer kol kakh).* "True poets" *(ba'alei-ha-shir-be-emet)* are individuals who "never walk in parade" *(ba-sakh).* Hence it is impossible—and reprehensible—to group them together stylistically.

The truth is, as we have seen, Gilboa's style was indeed changing radically in the early fifties, and both the poet and his critics are reflecting their engagement with these changes.[82] Maintaining a steady, watchful eye on the "professional" aspects of his career, Gilboa periodically registers his sensitivity to critical opinion, even in early works which explain and defend his poetics. Now he is rattling his professional sabres even more resolutely. No longer the vulnerable, youthful author of the self-published *La-ot,* by the early fifties Gilboa is more confident, ready to challenge both the conventions of his craft and the evaluations of his critical readers. He abandons the apologetic tone of *Shiri ha-paru'a* and the notion of instinctual style in

Signonot shonim.[83] On the one hand, he is blatantly sardonic toward his "comparative" critics and, on the other, more universalistic regarding the unique aesthetic response one expects to experience with each poet. The motto "I'm so different" at once bespeaks Gilboa's right to his own individualistic creativity and promotes the general idea of varied and variable styles.

In *Al signon,* Gilboa's hostility toward recalcitrant critics or uninformed readers essentially reflects the negative side of his general optimism about his new identity. The first issue he poses in *"Shirei koteret"* is the change he wishes to establish in his thematics.[84] At least six of the works in this grouping refer to laughter replacing sadness, liberation from the feeling of tragedy and mournfulness, setting goals of "blessing" rather than "cursing" one's days, and "banishing fear."[85]

Even the form of these "headline" works reflects a commitment to new modes of expression. Gilboa's preferred genre here is a view from a man-on-the-street. The speaker is a wanderer who takes as his topics objects, persons, or incidents he finds along his way. The poems emerge as poignant vignettes based on everyday experiences and lessons: a young mother responding with tears to her infant's cries; two shadows approaching the lonely observer and planting a kiss on his face; a highly charged scene of youthful lovers strolling under a lamplight.[86] In each of these poems Gilboa dramatizes a passing event whose ordinariness is emblematic of his newfound freedom of expression. It is a freedom which Gilboa clearly relishes. He will be not the wanderer in the throes of war and despair, but the creative observer of normal life in all its vicissitudes. He can be playful, surreal, down-to-earth, comic, moralistic, romantic, and antiromantic. The new Gilboa can be any kind of poet he wants to be.

"Shirim ba-boker ba-boker" (Early Morning Songs)

As if demonstrating his newly considered independence, Gilboa opens this section by exploring a completely new theme: response to the reality of the State of Israel. In some of these poems Gilboa blends a mythical framework with contemporary images of victory and celebration. At the same time, he continues his poetic contemplations of the expressibility of joy within the context of painful remembrance.

From its outset the language of the motto poem, *Hayinu ke-ḥozrim* (We Were As Returnees),[87] takes on an ancient resonance.[88] The title phrase is reminiscent of the opening of Psalm 126: *hayinu ke-ḥolmim,* "We [the Jews who hoped to return from Babylonian exile to the land of Israel in the sixth century B.C.E.] were like dreamers."[89] Gilboa's use of *el ḥalom* (to a dream) connects the two episodes. The mythical aura is bolstered by the returnees' goal of "joining the rifts into a whole *[shalem].*"

Two images dominate the poem. The sunrise over Jerusalem is described as "a young sun/[which] rose again gleaming over the roofs of Jerusalem" — a romantic depiction which gives the city a palpable sense of vibrancy. The second image is Jacob's mythical ladder: "a standing ladder, which a whole nation strove to mount" — a sacred vision of angels joining the entire populace to build the new state together. Continuing the juxtaposition of the ancient with the contemporary, the rhyming of *shalem, ḥolem,* and the archaic name *Yerushlem* (whole, dreaming, and Jerusalem) suggests a merging of the people with their capital city.

"Shirei adanim" (Trestle Poems)

The first of the four "Trestle Poems," *Bokrei temunot* (Picture Mornings),[90] bears a thematic resemblance to the motto poem by contrasting "our ancestors [who] walked to the end of days holding in their hands golden frames[91] for the picture of the vision [of return] in their heart" with "we [of the current generation who] walk in picture mornings and our heart is full of them."[92] The ancestors' mornings were filled with sad songs and hopeful prayer, whereas the young men of today are heroes, even gods *(asherim),* to the "virgin-daughters-of-Zion," who choose them over the somber ancestors of old. On one level, the poem may be viewed as an arrogant, anti-Diaspora statement by a chauvinistic young lion of Israel. Published in the 1951 edition of *Orlogin,* the four works may well have been written in 1950, only a year or so after the end of the War of Independence. Considered in that context, the triumphalist view of Jewish history is quite understandable. But Gilboa soon moves on to other themes. Struggling again to liberate himself from a reputation of mournfulness, he wrestles with mixed emotions: how to achieve a sense of gladness when one's heart is burdened with pain and loss. With deliberate effort, he forces himself to write about and convince others of the joy of Israeli statehood and the everyday delights of life.

In *Serefot ha-or* (Fires of Light)[93] the speaker is a visionary who witnesses "upon my nights a wave of light like a train upon trestles." At the same time "an arrow flies from a bow to announce a celebration in my streets." But no one seems to believe these wondrous signs. There are many doubters who still sit in their basements, "extinguished of sight *[kevuyei mabat]* and discussing whether my word is true or false." The poet affirms his vision and urges all to "see in my face the fires of light [and to] see the celebration in all my streets in my face." In this context, the motifs of light, eyes, faces, lanterns, frames, mornings, days and nights all become dualistic, referring both to life's fullness and to its sorrow. Vacillating from one side of the equation to the other, Gilboa is caught in the transition from Holocaust to statehood and in the poetic dilemma of breaking new ground in theme and style while still rooted in earlier patterns of writing and feeling. In *Bati lamilim ha-peshutot* (I've Come to the Simplest Words),[94] the last poem of *"Shirei adanim,"* he considers a solution to his dilemma.

בָּאתִי לַמִּלִּים הַפְּשׁוּטוֹת

וּמַה כִּי יָבוֹא מִי וְיֹאמַר: הִנֵּה הַנֵּבֶל. נַגֵּן לִי בְּזֶה הַנֵּבֶל.
הֶבֶל נֵבֶל. חוּטִים וָחֶבֶל. יֵשׁ גָּבֹהַּ מִשִּׂמְחָה. יֵשׁ עָמֹק מֵאֵבֶל.
אַל תִּתְּנִינִי לָלֶכֶת. אֲנִי כָּל כָּךְ שִׁכּוֹר מִמִּלּוֹתַיִךְ־בָּר.
מִלּוֹת הַבָּר. מְלִילוֹת הַבָּר. רְאִינִי נָא אֵיךְ יָשְׁרוּ דְבָרַיִךְ עַל אֲדָנַי.

בָּאתִי לַמִּלִּים הַפְּשׁוּטוֹת בְּיוֹתֵר. בְּרוּכִים אַתֶּם, אֲדָנַי!

I've Come to the Simplest Words

And what if someone comes and says: Here's the harp. Play for me on this harp.
Fool harp. Strings and rope. There's something higher than happiness. Something deeper than grief.
Don't let me go. I'm so drunk with your wild words.
Wild words. Wild speech. Look at me I pray how straight are your words on my trestles.

I've come to the simplest words. Blessed be you, my trestles![95]

The imagery here expresses the poet's need to "straighten," mitigate, or control his outpourings of poetic inspiration or emotion. The resolution of his problem, Gilboa suggests, is to "come to the simplest words." Immersed in ambiguity, he seeks a figurative but pragmatic control factor in his "trestles," a figure which from the outset has loomed equivocally over *"Shirei adanim."* Addressed even sacrally in the poem's last line, the trestles appear to be a counterbalance to the "wild words" and "wild speech" which emanate from the female addressee, an image of the poet's muse.

The speaker-poet is asked to take hold of a harp and to play on it. Upset, he posits that the harp is a mere instrument—only "strings and rope," whereas it takes feelings like "happiness" and "grief" to make a poem. Clearly, he fears that the act of control may destroy all possibility of inspiration. "Don't let me go," he says to his muse in line 3. The struggle between an "intoxicated" effusiveness and a controlled verbiage comes to a head in line 4. The "wild words" and speech are finally constrained by the speaker's "trestles," the control device which, to his relief, will now shape his poetic vocabulary.

The notion of "the simplest words" is quite ambiguous. In his review of *Keḥulim va-adumim,* Eliezer Schweid understands the notion of "simplicity" *(pashtut)* as Gilboa's affecting in style and context "a childlike way of thinking." By reflecting the "primal reaction of a child," says Schweid, Gilboa brings the reader to respond in kind—that is, with unfiltered emotion. Schweid echoes Ḥamutal Bar-Yosef, who finds "a childlike logic" *(higayon-shel-yeled)* in the playfulness, puns, and irony in *Shirim ba-boker ba-boker.* Shimon Sandbank also notes a newness and a "rough simplicity" *(pashtut meḥuspeset)* in this collection. He describes Gilboa's method as getting down to "the primary, concrete meaning of words," especially through the use of tautology.[96]

Perhaps the key to understanding the notion of the trestles is found in line 2: "There's something higher than happiness. Something deeper than grief." Gilboa is saying that these emotions in themselves—they are not just a thematic dichotomy—are impossible to express verbally to the fullest. The temptation is always a problematic superfluity, a "wildness" of words which needs restraining, and restraint implies a limiting of emotion. "The simplest words," therefore, is a metaphor for the poet's most serious dilemma: defining the bounds of his verbal expression.

The style and structure of *Bati la-milim ha-peshutot* are especially significant: long verse lines broken into short elliptical phrases; sarcastic alliterativeness and playful rhyme; a general ambiguity in imagery and theme. These elements anticipate the similarly constructed poems—to be written fifteen to twenty years later—of *Ratsiti likhtov siftei yeshenim* and *Ayala eshlaḥ otakh.*

The Poetics of Ideological Lyricism

True to his idiosyncratic, contrary ways, Gilboa reverts to an unbounded rhetoric of enthrallment in the next group of nature poems. *Ha-shir al ha-or* (The Poem on Light)[97] is a paean to the sunrise, whose light causes "the shards [to fall] from the eyes of the dreamers and the dying."[98] At the end of *Shir emuna* (A Song of Faith),[99] the dark night on the waters turns into "fertile, warm-bosomed, steaming, new earth [which] rises again." In the fable-like *Shir shaket ve-talul* (A Quiet Dewy Poem),[100] the speaker wanders "quiet and cleansed" in the forest, whose trees nod to him "the heads of their wisdom." And in *Shir ba-boker ba-boker* (Early Morning Song),[101] the beautiful spring morning makes the speaker feel larger than life, a part of nature itself: "like an icy stream./A shepherd's song./A branch." Nature is both the premise and the tool for Gilboa's poetic expression. As such, he offers two messages: he is still an unabashed romantic nature poet; and his poetry of joy and enthrallment is life-giving and revitalizing in its force. The speaker in *Ha-shir al ha-or* feels the full effect of this force: "A Poem on Light! . . . I could no longer control myself," he cries. The light here is the very essence, symbolically, of an emotive awakening inherent in the poetry itself. In this sense, Gilboa proclaims not only a romantic aesthetic but a romantic *ethic* as well.

That ethic becomes clearer in *Shir emuna,* where the speaker is less enthralled than he is bold. His act of tearing open windows[102] is a radical means of enlightenment whose tool, in this case, is an axe described as "shining and aflame" *(zahur ve-lohet),* two of Gilboa's favorite romantic terms. But the axe is formidable, deadly.

הוּא נִתֵּץ אֶת שְׁעוּת הַמְּלִיצָה. אֶת כָּל הַפְּסִילִים הוּא נִתֵּץ,
עֲרֵמִים נֶעֶרְמוּ עַל כָּל דֶּרֶךְ.

> It smashed the hours of flowery language. It smashed all the idols piled up naked on every path.

In smashing the "flowery language," Gilboa is denouncing poetry that features clever verbiage or sacred-cow structures and themes. What he seeks is not fancy intellectualized images but human experience and emotion, earthiness and warmth—lyrical poetry that is strong and all-encompassing.

Such poetry is exemplified in the work entitled *Shir ba-boker ba-boker,* where Gilboa employs hyperbole—specifically, exaggerated size and numbers of surrealistic images—to engender a sense of overstated grandness-in-nature. As the speaker walks down the street, "cornstalks" *(deganim)* instead of bits of grass or weeds loom up from the cracks in the sidewalk. The mountains have "ten thousand" rays of light which "will give birth to a canopy of light for his wedding." When the person-people figure laughs, "he laughs the courage of the generations [sic] from the mountains." This causes "the wars" to bow down prostrate "to the magnificence of a thousand years flowing in mystery." Before him are another "thousand young years"; and all this while he will endure in the forms of "a cold stream," "a shepherd's song," and "a branch."

שִׁיר בַּבֹּקֶר בַּבֹּקֶר

פִּתְאֹם קָם אָדָם בַּבֹּקֶר וּמַרְגִּישׁ כִּי הוּא עַם וּמַתְחִיל לָלֶכֶת
וּלְכָל הַנִּפְגָּשׁ בְּדַרְכּוֹ קוֹרֵא הוּא שָׁלוֹם.
דְּגָנִים עוֹלִים מוּל פָּנָיו מִבֵּין חֲרִיצֵי הַמִּדְרֶכֶת
וְנִיחוֹחוֹת לְרֹאשׁוֹ מַדִּיפִים עֲצֵי אִזְדָּרֶכֶת.

הַטְּלָלִים רוֹסְסִים וְהָרִים רִבּוֹא קַרְנַיִם – הֵם יוֹלִידוּ חֻפַּת־שֶׁמֶשׁ לִכְלוּלוֹתָיו.
וְהוּא צוֹחֵק גְּבוּרַת דּוֹרוֹת מִן הֶהָרִים
וְנִכְלָמוֹת מִשְׁתַּחֲווֹת הַמִּלְחָמוֹת אַפַּיִם
לְהוֹד אֶלֶף שָׁנִים מְפַכּוֹת בַּמִּסְתָּרִים.
אֶלֶף שָׁנִים צְעִירוֹת לְפָנָיו –
כְּפֶלֶג צוֹנֵן.

כְּשִׁיר רוֹעִים.
כְּעָנָף.

פִּתְאֹם קָם אָדָם בַּבֹּקֶר וּמַרְגִּישׁ כִּי הוּא עַם וּמַתְחִיל לָלֶכֶת
וְרוֹאֶה כִּי חָזַר הָאָבִיב כְּמוֹ הוֹרִיק שׁוּב אִילָן מִן הַשַּׁלֶּכֶת.

Early Morning Song

Suddenly a person gets up in the morning and feels he's a people and
begins to walk
and calls out "shalom" to everyone he meets on his way.
Cornstalks rise before him between the sidewalk cracks
and the margosa trees waft sweet aromas about his head.

Dew drops sprinkle and mountains, ten thousand sunbeams — they
bring forth a canopy of sun for his betrothed.
And he laughs the courage of generations from the mountains
and, ashamed, all wars bow down
to the glory of a thousand years mysteriously flowing.
A thousand young years are before him —
like a cool stream.
Like a shepherd's song.
Like a limb of a tree.

Suddenly a person gets up in the morning and feels he's a people and
begins to walk
and he sees that spring has returned like a tree turning green again
after the leaf fall.

The poem is a rapturous expression of enchantment with the very idea of a new spring. With the exuberance of romantic overstatement, the idea of "feeling like a nation" projects an all-embracing togetherness in the joy of greeting a lovely spring morning.[103] Like *Lu me'a kova'im,* the work has become a favorite of Israeli readers and has been set to music (by Ben-Tsiyon Orgad). Its popularity is linked to its interpretation as a vision of the nascent state of Israel: rebirth, an individual becoming a nation, beginning to walk, the "courage of generations," the vision of a messianic time, a dream of a pastoral existence of a thousand years' duration. The poem should not be regarded, however, as a work with two mutually exclusive interpretations: natural vs. national rebirth. Instead, it works simultaneously on two levels to imply that both notions — writing poetry and living as Israelis — are impelled by an exuberant, idealized impulse. Gilboa's vision develops a syllogistic equation here: Zionism is romantically infused with poetry, and his poetry is romantically infused with Zionism — an aesthetic symbiosis of ideology and art into a mode which might be called "ideological lyricism." The poetics of this mode might very well represent the direction Gilboa was seeking in the early fifties as he forged his own individualistic path.

"Shirim ba-tal" (Poems in the Dew)[104]

In *"Shirim ba-tal"* Gilboa continues to experiment with this poetics. In *Shir asher-ḥalamti* (A Poem That-I-Dreamed), he evokes images of the *ḥalutz* experience, building the land.

וַהֲקִימוֹתִי מַחֲנוֹת־עֲבוֹדָה.
וְסָלַלְתִּי כְּבִישִׁים.
וּמָתַחְתִּי קַוֵּי חַשְׁמַל.
וְהִנַּחְתִּי צִנּוֹרוֹת –
כְּפָר. עִיר. אֵזוֹר. חֶבֶל אָרֶץ. עוֹלָם וּמְלוֹאוֹ בָּנִיתִי.
וְהָיוּ הֵם שִׁיר. וְהַשִּׁיר מְהַלֵּךְ בֵּינוֹתָם.

I erected work encampments.
And paved roads.
And lined electric wires.
And laid pipes —
A village. City. Region. District. I built an entire world.
And they became a poem. And the poem walks among them.

In effect, these activities are metonyms for Gilboa's blend of poetry with the Israeli experience. Seeing his work as inextricably bound to the history and biography of his generation, he also sees the linkage increasingly penetrating the readers' perceptions of his works. Through the common memory of the poet and the reader, the poem communicates the experience of the age as a cultural model or value system.[105]

Shir ha-toda'a ba-mitsad (A Poem of Consciousness at the Parade)[106] continues the lyrical approach to the expression of national issues. The dramatic situation is an Israeli Independence Day military parade, probably in the spring of 1951. The opening stanza graphically describes the angle of bayonets held high and the rhythmic rows of marching feet. Immediately the speaker cries out in prayer to the Shekhinah or another goddess of peace, "Let my son be, let my only son be, let him live." Gilboa's thoughts turn from pride and fervor to the horrors of war, the death of innocents, the hope for a peaceful future.

A series of metaphors expresses the poet's feelings about the New Israeli. At their center is a fictive child whose delineation as the "only" son reminds us of the Binding of Isaac. The series opens with a second plea to a female divinity to let the son "walk with the banks of his rivers," an idyllic, myth-like image that sets the tone for the son's normal activities, were he to be allowed to live in peace. The boy is larger than life, a Herculean figure whose fire columns—symbols of his future deeds—rise higher than those of the Burning Bush. They last up to fifty years—perhaps even to messianic times. He has the strength to forge steel, yet he is a gentle, simple person at heart. Although the hero evinces a vast potential, however, his future is not bright. In place of the dream vision of *Shir asher-ḥalamti,* Gilboa foresees here only the anti-idyllic in the years to come, when the hero's children will inevitably have to fight again.

Much of *Shir ha-toda'a bamitsad* is static in its envisionings of the sacrificial son. The blocks of equivalent (or "simultaneous")[107] deeds and physical characteristics suspend the poem's successive structure until the rhetorically climactic ending.[108] The effect is an abrupt turning from the imaginary world of lyrical visions to the actual parade setting—especially with the word *tseriḥim,* tank turrets. The strong anticlimax suddenly evokes all the poet's "awarenesses," which are "bared unto weeping."

Now using the poetics of ideological lyricism, Gilboa once again responds to the Holocaust. In the first line of *Shir seliḥa min ha-ko'aḥ* (A Poem of

Forgiveness From Strength),[109] Gilboa describes a new dawn—the favorite time of day in his poetry.

הַלַּיְלָה נוֹטֶה לְקִצּוֹ. וּכְמוֹ שָׁכַחְתִּי אֶת הַבֹּקֶר הַקּוֹדֵם

Night approaches its end. It's as if I've forgotten the morning before

Line 2, however, discloses the real reason the speaker has forgotten, perhaps repressed, yesterday.

שֶׁקָּרְדְּמֻהוּ מְגֻלְּחֵי הַצַּמּוֹת

which was chopped by the ones with shaven braids.

The abrupt sequence evokes a chilling image of the archetypical executioners, who have "chopped" away the past from the speaker's memory. A similar anticlimax appears in the middle of the poem.

הַבֹּקֶר בָּא. יְחִידִי הָלַךְ הַלַּיְלָה. יְחִידִי הָלַךְ הָלוֹךְ וּבָכֹה.

Morning is here. Night has gone off alone. Gone off, off, alone and weeping.

The preceding lines described the coming morning as "smiling," "forgiving," and "rageless" *(lo nizam)*, and this line begins in a neutral lyrical mood. However, the final word *u-vakho,* "and weeping," at once attributes sorrow and loneliness to both the night and the speaker who has come through it. A similar pattern occurs in lines 4–5, where a lyrical, positive description is followed by an anticlimactic reversal.

יַחְזְרוּ הָעֵצִים הַכְּרוּתִים מִמִּצְעַד הַיָּגוֹן וְהַכְּאֵב לְלַבְלֵב מֵחָדָשׁ עַל כֵּן גִּזְעָם.
אֵין סוֹף שֶׁל סוֹף.

They will come back, the felled trees of the march of sorrow and pain,
    to blossom anew on the base of their trunk.
The endlessness of ending.[110]

The aphoristic comment on *sof,* the end, flies in the face of new blossoms after the tragedy. This structural irony is evident in all of the anticlimactic reversals which appear in the poem—even at the end, where Gilboa switches the sides of the equation and goes from a lyrical but ambiguous description to a climactic, positive close.

מִן הָאֵפֶר, מִן הָאֵפֶר דּוֹלֵק בְּכָל אוֹרוֹתָיו –
הַפְּאֵר.

From the ashes, from the ashes burning with all its lights—
the wonder.

The image reproduces the vision of the cut-down trees returning to life. By reversing the structure from negative to positive, Gilboa emphasizes the incredulous speaker's sense of wonderment and his willingness to move on, leave pain behind, and see the possibilities of rebirth.

The matrix of the poem is embodied in the phrase, "the endlessness of ending." By continually reverting to horror or sorrow after the lyrical passages, the structural anticlimaxes demonstrate the speaker's ambivalence. The final image, seeing wonder in the "lights" of the ashes, might also be dualistic. But Gilboa's oft-used symbols of light, burning, and wonder convince the reader that the miracle of new growth is indeed possible and might have even come to pass.

That possibility is reinforced by a secondary motif which supports and goes beyond the theme of regrowth. In the description of the rising new day, the morning is portrayed as "smiling," "forgiving" *(salaḥ),* and "rageless." The poet accentuates these descriptive words by setting them graphically in three separate, one-word lines. As the lonely weeping night of the past, the night of Holocaust sorrow, is slowly replaced by the new day, the speaker describes his own feelings. "All night," he says "I did not cry. All night powers were with me *[pekaduni koḥot].*"

A climactic ending of wonder emerges in the form of a generational dialogue.

כַּסֵּה, בְּנִי, בְּכַפֶּיךָ עַל פָּנֶיךָ וְכַפֵּר.
כַּפֵּר.
כַּפֵּר.
כַּפֵּר.

Cover, my son, your face with your hands and forgive.
Forgive.
Forgive.
Forgive.

As in *Shir toda'a ba-mitsad,* the image of the fictive son[111] appears, here to listen to his father's exhortation. Like the new morning, the son's generation should be "rageless," so that it might experience a true rebirth, unburdened by the pain of the past. In the context of the agonized Holocaust images of Gilboa's earlier works, the father's position is a shocking about face. How can one forgive the perpetrators of horrendous acts? Should the next generation be encouraged to forget? Should children be coddled into a blind innocence? Perhaps Gilboa is saying that rage is deleterious, that some accommodation with the past must take place so that the young may look to the future without the painful bonds to the Holocaust with which his generation was burdened.

But another interpretation is possible in the context of the reparation payments from West Germany which began in 1953.[112] Line 3 of the poem reads: "In a poem give us the property and take the persons for yourselves." The reverse of the statement made by the King of Sodom to Abram in Genesis 14:21, the expression is intriguing in its ambiguity. Could Gilboa be saying that in "chopping" off or forgetting the past we are virtually saying to the murderers: "We will take your money, and you can keep the lives that you took from us"? Is this, then, a sardonic poem which ironically tells us that the new generation should certainly not forget? That the new morning is false and not forgiving? That the "wonder" seen in the ashes is anathema? That the son covers his face in a rite of shame and mourning? That the "endlessness of ending" is a position that Gilboa wishes to uphold?

A deconstructive reading might indeed lead to such conclusions, since the rhetoric of the text, as we have shown, reverses itself several times. On the other hand, it is difficult to interpret this poem as a sarcastic work. A more nuanced resolution is possible. Each set of images, though rhetorically dualistic, points to the image of a new day and the idea of new growth. Although the new day predominates, the presence of a very difficult night still looms. Despite the claim that the speaker was attended by "powers" and did not cry, there is a sense of crisis here. He is able to tell his son to forgive only after he has emerged from the night of trauma—and resolved his own conflict of rage versus pardon.

The process of resolution is complex, and an entire rite of forgiveness ensues. The father tells his son to cover his eyes, much like one does to light the Sabbath candles—a moment of prayer. Then the father intones, *"kaper"* (forgive), in three separate lines. With its aura of authentic supplication, the ritualistic image conveys a good measure of ambiguity. The same is true when the father-speaker notes that he hadn't cried all night, that "all night powers were with me." But the connotation in both instances is that forgiveness is a sacred act; it serves more to heal the soul of the victims than to patronize the perpetrators. In Gilboa's case, at least, what will be retained "from the ashes" of the Holocaust is "the wonder." Perhaps it is a redolent remembrance of dear ones consumed. Perhaps it is the painful but inevitable uprooting of the hatred embedded in one's heart. Perhaps it is the miracle of forgiveness itself.

Other works in *"Shirim ba-tal"* also focus on Gilboa's poetic response to issues of remembrance and pardon. To be sure, the poems bear similarities to responses evinced in his earlier works: his attempts in the late 1940s to move on to other topics, his unwillingness to follow the conventional path of other poets or the advice of critics, and his personal need for a different kind of poetry. Beyond these thematic focal points, however, the works in *"Shirim ba-tal"* express once again Gilboa's renewed commitment to lyricism. When he writes in *Shir barzel ha-nefesh* (A Poem of the Soul's Iron),[113] that he wishes to return to his "smelting furnace" *(kur)*, his point of origin or original shaping, he conveys that his "iron" responses to the Holocaust must give way to a revival of his original poetic impulses. Although it is obvious that Gilboa never abandoned his romantic vision, his wish for lyrical renewal is nonetheless emphatic.

In the groups of poems which follow *"Shirim ba-tal,"*[114] the major themes are creativity and politics. Gilboa chides himself about his responsibilities as a poet.[115] He is committed to the positive role poetry plays in the universe. He is concerned about the world's apathy towards art, its indifference to the artist's need for freedom to innovate.

Allegedly afflicted with writer's block, Gilboa maintains a regimen of walking the streets, observing details of everyday life. On these jaunts he feels he is "like an entire people," virtually at the center of the human and cosmic universe.[116] Once again his imagination flourishes; it makes him feel "radiant" and "earthy," not ethereal. But it is this very power that makes poets—and poetry—different, magical, and timeless.[117]

He embraces political issues in the early 1950s. In *Shir navo ḥeshbon* (Let's Do an Accounting Poem)[118] he pointedly protests his government's policy regarding reparations; his redolent memories cannot abide the idea of making a deal with Germany.

אֵיךְ נָבוֹא עִמָּם חֶשְׁבּוֹן
אִם עַל יָדֵינוּ יִשְׁקְלוּ שְׁלֹשִׁים שֶׁקֶל.
אֵיךְ נִשְׁמֹר לָהֶם שִׂנְאָה
אִם נִמְכְּרֶנָּה
וּלְבָנֵינוּ נוֹרִישׁ אֶת הַשֶּׁקֶר.

פָּנֵינוּ לְטוּפִים עוֹד בִּשְׂפָתַיִם שֶׁהוּצַנּוּ.
זְרוֹעוֹתֵינוּ חַמּוֹת עוֹד מֵחִבּוּק מְשֻׁלָּב.
וְחוֹלְמִים עוֹד יוֹשְׁבִים לְצִדּוֹ שֶׁל הָאָב.
וְאֵי פֶּתַע בָּרְחוֹב בִּשְׁמוֹתֵינוּ שֶׁלָּנוּ
הֵם קוֹרְאִים עוֹד
א וֹ תָ נ וּ
א וֹ תָ נ וּ
א וֹ תָ נ וּ.

How can we do an accounting with them
if they hand out thirty shekels to us.[119]
How can we continue to hate them

if we sell it
and bequeath the lie to our children.

Our faces are still touched by their lips grown cold.
Our arms are still warm from a mutual embrace.
We still dream that we sit by our father.
And suddenly at times they call us by name in the street
They still call
us
us
us.

Specters of war and nuclear disaster mercilessly haunt Gilboa. He writes of "a nation of mothers" left behind after all the young men have been called to battle. Ghostly images of dead riders stare into the faces of their terrified horses.[120] Nuclear armaments will eventually bring the end of the world, he writes—and, most pertinently, the destruction of nature and the death of poetry.

וְכָל הַסִּפּוּרִים הַיָּפִים
וְכָל הַשִּׁירִים הַמְכֻנָּפִים
כַּסּוֹד שֶׁמִּתְּהוֹמָיו נִמְשָׁה
וְגָלוּי מוּל יוֹם אַכְזָר
הוּא אוֹפֵר וְאוֹפֵר.

And all the beautiful stories
and all the poems hidden
like a secret drawn out of its depths
laid bare before the cruel day
it turns to ashes, to ashes.[121]

The destruction of poetry is paralleled by the death of legend in Gilboa's beautifully lyrical, almost ballad-like *Si'aḥ le-Yitsḥak* (A Prayer for Isaac).[122]

שִׂיחַ לְיִצְחָק

א

פְּעָמִים הַרְבֵּה
הוּא בָּא בְּדִמְיוֹנַי
בְּהִתְהַלְּכוֹ פֹּה
בֵּין מְתִים.

וִידַעְתִּיו מִשִּׁיר אֶחָד
וּמִשֵּׁנִי
וּמִשְּׁלִישִׁי
שֶׁלֹּא כְּתַבְתִּים.

וְתָמִיד עָלָה בָּהֶם
חַי בֵּין הַחַיִּים
וּמֵעוֹלָם לֹא בֵּין הַמֵּתִים.

ב

הוּא בָּא תָמִיד פָּשׁוּט. אֱנוֹשִׁי.
וַאֲנִי רְאִיתִיו בָּא מִלְמַעְלָה
גָּדוֹל
גּוּשִׁי
מְחַיֵּךְ
וְחַי בִּמְלֹא־הַחוּשִׁים.

הוּא בָּא תָמִיד כֹּה פָּשׁוּט
וְהָיָה כַּחַשְׁמַל הַמַּכֶּה לְפִתְאֹם
בְּאוֹר
הַנֵּרוֹת שֶׁבַּבַּיִת

שֶׁבִּצְלִיף עָלוּ עִמּוֹ
לְאֵין־חַיִץ.

ג
אֲנִי אֲהַבְתִּיו כָּל כָּךְ
כִּי לִמְּדַנִי אָבִי לֶאֱהֹב
הַטּוֹבִים וְהַיְשָׁרִים
הַמְהַלְּכִים עַל פְּנֵי אֶרֶץ
בְּצֶלֶם וּבִדְמוּת.

וְהֵם בַּשָּׁמַיִם
נְשָׁרִים.
וְשׂוֹנְאִים לָמוּת.

ד
מֵעוֹלָם לֹא דִבַּרְנוּ עַל כָּךְ
אַךְ בֵּינֵינוּ קַיָּם הָיָה
קֶשֶׁר־סוֹד
שֶׁל הַמַּפְלִיגִים בַּיַּמִּים
הָרְחוֹקִים מְאֹד
לְמַמֵּשׁ אַגָּדוֹת
לְקַשֵּׁט בָּן אֶת חֲדָרֵינוּ.

עַכְשָׁו הוּא אֵינֶנּוּ
כִּי הָיָה לְאַגָּדָה שֶׁכָּזֹאת.

A Prayer for Isaac

1
Many times
he came into my imagination

as he walked here
among the people.

And I knew him from one poem
and from a second
and from a third
I hadn't written.

And he always rose in them
alive among the living
and was never among the dead.

2

He always came simple. Human.
And I saw him come from above
big
dense
smiling
and alive with all the senses.

He always came simple as that
and was like lightning that struck suddenly
at the light
of the Sabbath candles at home
which *went up* with him undivided.

3

I loved him so much
because my father taught me to love
the good and righteous
who walk upon the earth
in God's image.

And they in heaven
are eagles.
And hate to die.

4
We never spoke about this
but between us there was
a secret bond
of travelers on the very
distant seas
to make legends real
to decorate *our rooms* with.

Now he is gone
because he became such a legend.

For Gilboa, Isaac has always been a vital figure. In *Si'aḥ le-Yitsḥak,* the patriarch is simple, humane, and sensuous. But he can also be forceful and surprisingly incandescent, "like lightning that strikes suddenly/in the light/of the Sabbath candles." A looming presence in the poet's artistic imagination, Isaac, it is implied, is beloved because of the gentle teachings of Gilboa's father. Stories of Isaac, probably in the form of biblical myths, seem to have been a part of Gilboa's childhood and thus contributed the force of legend and the love of the righteous of the earth to his literary and ethical heritage.

The romance collapses, however, with the reversal of this gentle, moral universe at the poem's closing. In the final section, two key antecedents are ambiguous. In the first line it is not clear whether Gilboa is referring to his father or to Isaac. A more sequential reading would have the pronoun refer to Gilboa's father. (I refer to the father as the central topic in part 3 and its contiguity with the opening verse of part 4, i.e., "we never spoke about it.") However, it seems fairly clear that the "he" in the next-to-last line of part 4 refers to Isaac, who "always came simple" into the poet's imaginings. The ambiguity suggests that Isaac may be the one with whom Gilboa has had a secret bond. The closing line, too, surely refers to Isaac, who "became such a legend," like the ones drawn and hung by school children to decorate the walls of their rooms. If so, Gilboa implies that Isaac has been transformed from a mythical personage into a trifling, insubstantial being who by now has completely disappeared from the Jewish heroic cosmogony. Either way, the poem conveys the ironic death of legend by dint of the subject himself becoming a legend. Gilboa's father, slaughtered in the Holocaust, becomes part of the history of Jewish martyrology. Isaac, nearly slaughtered by Abraham, was also a victim, so the connection between the two is based on improbable deaths, whether storied or actual.[123]

In this poem of father-Isaac symmetry, Gilboa is suggesting that what once had the potential to be legendary, mythical, filled with possibilities of meaning and emulation, is now dead—concretized, in fact, in actual tragedy. The same fate, he posits, has befallen legendary ideas such as the earth being transversed by "good and righteous" beings who are formed "in God's image." Such notions are dead; they have become remote, unattainable untruths. As in *Zekhor!* (Remember),[124] which is placed immediately before it, *Si'aḥ le-Yitsḥak* abjures naive piety and predilection. With the loss of legend comes the loss of innocence. In setting its future course, says Gilboa, Israel must never forget the realities of the past.

Malkhut demama (Kingdom of Silence)[125]

Although Gilboa has demurred on the subject,[126] many readers and critics feel that *Malkhut demama* is one of his most engaging works. Gilboa has mentioned that this poem was written in response to the American nuclear bomb tests in the early 1950s.[127] Several interpretations of it are available.[128] A relatively long poem of 49 lines, it consists of a vision of the aftermath of a devastating battle in ancient times.[129] The chronological distancing, the antique war descriptives, and certain archaic usages lend the work an air of classical historicity. The vision of aftermath suggests a combined forgetfulness and recurring trauma. One day the battlefield will return to normalcy and the cycle of seasons will be reinstated. Lovers will embrace on the nearby shore. But then a "blazing summer" will recur and bring with it new calls to battle. The cycle of violence will continue and the ultimate result will be a "kingdom of silence," a world of complete quietude, of death, with every thing and every person "at rest" in a devastated world.

In consonance with other works of this period, the poetic mode here is ideological lyricism—lyricism incorporated in romantic and antiromantic fashion both for the scenes of devastation and death and for the intervening vision of normalcy.

דְּמָמָה יוֹרְדָה. בַּדִּמְדּוּמִים
קוֹלוֹת הֶהָמוֹן עוֹמְמִים.
דְּמָמָה. עָלִים נוֹשְׁרִים
נוֹשְׁרִים. כִּי יִסְתַּו.

Silence settles. The throng's sounds
dim in the dusk.
Silence. The leaves are falling
falling. Soon it will be fall.

The alliterative description of the battlefield bridges the post-battle scene and the subsequent return to a flourishing, peaceful time. However, all resurrective possibilities are undermined by the paradoxical insertion of an ominous unlyrical image—anachronistic and all too familiar.

יִרְחַק. יִרְחַק הַכֹּל. עַל פְּנֵי הַשֶּׁטַח
הַכֹּל יִשְׁלַו. שׁוּב יִפֹּל הַגֶּשֶׁם
בַּאֲרֻבּוֹת פּוֹלְטוֹת עָשָׁן. וּלְפֶתַע
סְעָרָה בַּנְּחָלִים תְּהִי רוֹגֶשֶׁת.

Distant. All will be distant. The ground will
all be at peace again. The rain will fall again
on chimneys belching smoke. And suddenly
a storm will surge through the streams.

In the subsequent "normalcy" section all seems beautiful and lyrical, as "the willow bows its branches" and "young eyes . . . rouse love on the shore." But immediately, as if part of the lovers' torrid passsion, the summer begins to "clamor with heat" and, suddenly, "it [calls] to battle." The forces of innocence and love which grow naturally out of peace self-destruct in an almost instinctive cycle of violence.

The same blend of lyrical and antilyrical components are evident in the section describing the recurrence of war.

לֶעֱנוּת קוֹלוֹת הֲדֵי גְבוּרָה
יַעֲנוּ. לַדּוֹקְרִים וְלַמְדֻקָּרִים.
הָרִים גֵּאִים יִהְיוּ דוֹקְרִים
בָּעֵינַיִם־מִן־הֶעָפָר. מְדוּרָה
תְּלַחֵךְ. תִּשְׁלַח לְשׁוֹנוֹת. תְּלַחֵךְ
לְשׁוֹנוֹת לוֹקְקוֹת עָפָר. מְדוּרָה
תְּהִי לְאֵפֶר. גְּוִילֵי סֵפֶר
בֵּין הָעַמּוּדִים הָעֲשֵׁנִים
יַשְׂגִּיאוּ מַלְכוּת דְּמָמָה. יְשֵׁנִים
יַשְׂגִּיאוּ מַלְכוּת דְּמָמָה. . . .

Valiant echoes will answer the affliction
of voices. The butchers and the butchered.
Majestic mountains will pierce through
eyes from the dust. A fire
will flicker. Give off flame tongues. Flicker
tongues licking dust. A fire will
turn to ashes. Parchment scrolls
among smoking pages
will sing praises to a kingdom of silence. The sleepers
will sing praises to a kingdom of silence. . . .

The violence of the battlefield is offset by the image of the fire—itself a metonymy of the battle in that it flickers, spreads, and then turns to ashes. Its ending brings with it songs of praise. The "kingdom of silence," much like the post-battle scene at the beginning of the poem, now can be expected to revert to a blossoming, idyllic, normal world. But this does not happen. The "kingdom of silence" is the end of the world.

וְאֵין עוֹד אִישׁ לָבוֹא. וְאֵין עוֹד
אִישׁ לְהִמָּלֵט. וְאֵין עוֹד קוֹל
הוֹרִישׁ הַמֵּת. וְאֶחָד נוֹתָר עוֹמֵד.

And there's no one else to come. No one
else to flee. No voice for the
dead to bequeath their will. And one alone is left, standing still.

The ending is reminiscent of one of Gilboa's earliest poems, *Ba-emek,*[130] in which "one [person] alone" stands in the fields, enthralled by the landscape, singing praises to the beauty surrounding him.[131] In *Malkhut de-mama* Gilboa combines the abject lyricism of that earlier work with the antilyrical vision of world devastation. The result is the poetics of protest, the mode of ideological lyricism which, in this work, highlights issues of nuclear responsibility and disarmament.

The motif of myth or legend is also common to these early-fifties poems. Here, the motif is altered and becomes history, the written record of events. At the outset, Gilboa uses two images which attest to the battle. The first is a conventional, realistic one, despite the use of personification: "Piles of ashes/bear the news: the bloody summer is consumed." The second is more metaphorical: "Its [i.e., summer's] firebrands fume now in words" (or more literally, "Its firebrands already smolder in books.") The battle has been entered into recorded history.

The theme of the book or history reappears later with the "parchment scrolls [singing] praises to a kingdom of silence."[132] Although scrolls may refer more to holy books or to the Torah itself, Gilboa uses the image to refer to Jewish tradition and, by extension, to ancestral Jewish life. Here it is the history of a long-lived human civilization which has been reduced to ashes in the nuclear age. Later he expands the image of devastation to include "all things bound in books."

יַשִׁיר יַשִׁיר הַסְּתָו
אֶל הַשָּׂדוֹת. אֶל הַדְּרָכִים. כָּל הַדְּבָרִים
נִצְרְרוּ בַּסְּפָרִים יָנוּחוּ. סֶלָה. כָּל הַדּוֹרוֹת
יָנוּחוּ. סֶלָה....

Fall will cast down cast down
upon the fields. Upon the roads. All things
bound in books will be at rest. Selah. All the generations
will be at rest. Selah. . . .

By presenting a trifold blend of an ancient battle, written history, and the end of history, Gilboa gives the lie to those who see either progress or a source of security in nuclear weapons. His vision of a destroyed world at once focuses on the death of nature and the death of poetic possibilities.

"Shirim min ha-lu'aḥ ha-yafe" (Poems From the Beautiful Tablet)[133]

Gilboa's preoccupation with the Holocaust continues in the closing section of *Shirim ba-boker ba-boker.* The first words of the untitled poem which opens this section, *Kol ha-devarim ha-peshutim* (All the Simple Things), refer to things that offer comfort to those "who have walked all their days in the burning storm." The "simple things" are also personified as "patient" things. These include "the twilight that falls . . . at the feet of the lone wanderer in the desolate expanse," or things of beauty which bring on "complete oblivion" or things that are "trusting and dreamy . . . like flocks of sheep [and] ancient wells at the forks of ancient roads."

Written in prose-poem style and structure, *Kol ha-devarim ha-peshutim* continues to denote the lyrical aspects of nature and the divinely illumined artifacts of the ancient past—all of which comfort the survivor's soul. Within these objects of nature and history a "hidden hand" touches and comforts "the eyes and the brow and the face" of the one who "returns and comes to them from the whirlwind of the storm." Dated "24 Sivan [June], 1952," the poem shows Gilboa still immersed in memory and sorrow.[134] Much as he has turned to "the simple words" in *Bati la-milim ha-peshutot,* he still draws upon a profuse lyricism and the love of nature for emotional support.

Included in this section are several beautiful love poems, written in the early days of Gilboa's marriage to Gabriela (Gabi). Each poem has the sound of the Song of Songs: "[All my friends] see how you blossom [like a] lilac/in the gardens/and our head is dew," reads a line from *Ani goref be-yad aḥat* (I Gather with One Hand).[135] His feelings of love are also expressed by a lyrical imaging of nature, which in turn creates a sense of renewal and wholeness of being.

עַל שֶׁנָּטַעַתְּ בִּי שׁוּב עֵצִים יְרֻקִּים
וּמְפַכָּה תּוֹכִי מַעְיָנוֹת
וְשָׁרָשַׁי בְּשָׁרָשַׁיִךְ דְּבוּקִים

For you've planted green trees in me again
and send springs streaming within me
and my roots cling to your roots[136]

A ballad-like piece, *Alei zikaron* (On Memory),[137] is written as a letter from a soldier to the beloved he has left behind. Here, too, the soldier uses the words and images of the Song of Songs. "The guards have caught me, my love/the guards walking about in the city/silently have brought me to the field." They bring him not to the field of lovers, however, but to the battlefield. The poet-speaker and his comrades have loaves of bread in their hands, but when they are given rifles, they plunge them into the bread—and convert the conventional soldier-to-sweetheart poem into an antiwar protest.

Tov ki yesh mi (It's Good That There's Someone)[138] continues the mode of ideological lyricism by combining the lovers' words of ardor with their reflections on the Holocaust. More an exploration of individual feelings than a fullblown philosophical exchange, the poem reflects Gilboa's reticence—a common response of survivors—and his relief in being able to share his visions of horror with an intimate auditor.

טוֹב כִּי יֵשׁ מִי שׁוֹאֲלֵנִי שְׁאֵלוֹת....
וְכַאֲשֶׁר מַרְאוֹת הַזְּוָעָה לְעֵינַי עוֹלוֹת
אֲנִי חָשׁ אֶת דָּמֵךְ עִם דָּמִי זוֹעֵק.

It's good that there's someone to ask me questions. . . .
And when the horror visions rise up into my eyes
I feel your blood scream along with mine.

Shir ke-ḥolem (A Poem Like a Dreamer),[139] the volume's closing poem, takes poetry itself as its subject. As we have seen in *La-ot* and *Sheva reshuyot,* Gilboa often closes volumes or major sections with self-reflective poems about his art. Here Gilboa purports to tell us just how he writes.

שִׁיר כְּחוֹלֵם

שִׁירַי כָּךְ נִכְתָּבוּ:

הֵם בָּאוּ עַמִּים עַמִּים.
אֲגָלִים אֲגָלִים נִקְווּ.

בַּבֹּקֶר בַּבֹּקֶר הִתְאַהֲבוּ.

וְרוֹחֲצִים בְּיַמִּי הַדָּמִים
תַּחַת קִמְרוֹנַי הַקְּרִירִים
הִתְבַּהֵק גּוֹנָם הֶחָמִים.

וְאִמְרָתִי כַּטַּל
רוֹחֲצָה כָּל פָּנִים.

A Poem Like a Dreamer

My poems are written like this:

They come [like waves of] many peoples.
And they're gathered drop by drop.

In early morning they fall in love.

And they bathe in my silent sea
under my cool arches
their warm hue sparkles.

And my word like dew
washes each face.

Gilboa's explication is a pithy, lyrical, imagistic depiction of the process of inspiration, production, and intent. As he has often acknowledged, a recurrent problem has been controlling the flow of visions which often bombard him. Here, however, he speaks also of the need to shape each word laboriously. Gathering the words "drop by drop" may be Gilboa's response to those critics who have called him emotional or impulsive, implying that he simply flings words and images onto the page. At the least, Gilboa wants to be regarded as a careful craftsman.

While he confirms our suspicion that he prefers to work in the morning—perhaps the very early morning hours *(ba-boker ba-boker)*—Gilboa also shows how consistent he is in his use of imagery. He lists his favorites here—water, coolness and warmth, light, and color. His works are transmitted to the reader in love and purity—like dew, they are meant to gently cleanse the reader's face. For Gilboa, the process of writing is impelled by tenderness and devotion. The title "A Poem Like a Dreamer," however, may be ironic. Playing the cat-and-mouse game of the sometimes antiromantic romantic poet, it is very likely that the view here is overly idealized. Indeed, from his other poems about poetry, we know that the process is far more complex and tortuous than Gilboa admits here.

Chapter V

The Poet Redux: Towards a Modernist Style

Shelosha she'arim ḥozrim/ Three Recurring Gates,[1] *1963*

With the exception of a few works which appeared in 1956 and one in 1961,[2] Gilboa published no poetry from April 1953 to April 1963. During these years he worked as an editor at the Masada Publishing Company and, with his wife Gabi, raised two daughters, Avital and Tagil. When he began to write again, he published several biblical-theme poems which eventually formed the frame of the first section of *Shelosha she'arim ḥozrim.*[3] In these works two familar themes emerge: the Holocaust and the poetic process. Here, however, the old themes are presented in inventive and even surprising new ways.

Penei Yehoshua (Joshua's Face)[4] is a dream poem in which the poet is deliberately ambiguous about the Joshua persona. Gilboa offers details which identify him as the Joshua of the Bible—and at the same time makes it explicitly clear that he is speaking about his brother.[5]

פְּנֵי יְהוֹשֻׁעַ

וִיהוֹשֻׁעַ מֵעָל אֶל פָּנַי מַבִּיט. וּפָנָיו זָהָב
שָׁחוּט. חֲלוֹם קַר. חֲלוֹם חָנוּט.
וּלְרַגְלַי הַיָּם מַכֶּה נְצָחִים אֶל הַחוֹף.
אֲנִי חוֹלֶה נְהִיָּתוֹ. דּוֹמֶה, אֲנִי עוֹמֵד לָמוּת.
אַךְ מַכְרַחֲנִי, מַכְרַחֲנִי לְחַכּוֹת חַי
אֶל־תָּמִיד.
אָחִי מֵעָל פָּנָיו עוֹלִים בָּעָב
לְהַגִּיד עִקְּבוֹתַי בַּחוֹל הַנִּשְׁטָף.

הַיָּם מַכֶּה וְנָסוֹג. מַכֶּה וְנָסוֹג.
מִלְחֲמוֹת אֵיתָנִים מַתְנוֹת בַּחֹק.

אֲנִי. בָּרוּחַ. אַחֵר. בּוֹרֵחַ. רָחוֹק.
גַּם יְהוֹשֻׁעַ עַכְשָׁיו נָח מִמִּלְחָמוֹת.
שֶׁהִנְחִיל נַחֲלָה לְעַמּוֹ,
אֲבָל קֶבֶר לֹא חָצַב לוֹ
בְּהָרֵי אֶפְרָיִם.
עַל כֵּן לַיְלָה לַיְלָה הוּא יוֹצֵא
לָשׂוּחַ בַּשָּׁמַיִם.
וַאֲנִי חוֹלֶה, דּוֹמֶה עוֹמֵד לָמוּת
מְיַחֵף בְּחוֹל יָרֵחַ קַר
בְּשׁוּלֵי הַמָּיִם
וְהוֹמֶה בִּי, הוֹמֶה בִּי סוֹף
הַמַּכֶּה לְרַגְלַי אֶת מוֹתִי
גַּל אַחַר גָּל–

עַל פְּנֵי חַיִּים רַבִּים
יִתְרוֹמֵם וְיִתְגַּדֵּל.

Joshua's Face

And Joshua from above looks at my face. And his face is gold leaf.[6]
A cold dream. An embalmed dream.
And at my feet the sea strokes eternities at the shore.
I am sick with his sobbing. It seems I'm about to die.
But I really must, really must wait alive
for-ever.
My brother above, his face rising in a cloud
to tell of my footsteps in the washed-away sand.

The sea strikes and recedes. Strikes and recedes.
Wars of the mighty are controlled by law.
I. In the wind. Other. Fleeing. Distant.
Joshua too rests now from wars.
He who bequeathed an inheritance to his people,

but hewed himself no grave in the
hills of Ephraim.
And so night after night he goes out
to take a walk in the sky.
And I am sick, it seems I'm about to die
walking barefoot in the sand of a cold moon
at the water's edge
and it resounds in me, the end resounds in me
and strokes my death at my feet
wave after wave—

Upon much life[7]
may God be exalted and glorified.

The main themes here are continuing anguish and unabated mourning. Joshua's ghost still haunts Gilboa—and his brother's death makes him think of his own. At the same time, the convergence of the biblical Joshua with Gilboa's brother creates both classical and contemporary resonances of war and the loss of revered figures. Like the biblical persona, the contemporary Joshua "bequeathed an inheritance *[hinḥil naḥala,* lit., portions of land, but generally a 'heritage'] to his people." Gilboa may be referring here to the literary and ideological influence his brother had on him. Unlike the ancient Joshua, however, his brother did not live to make aliyah and "hewed himself no grave in the hills of Ephraim." The vision of Joshua in "gold leaf" and the image of "an embalmed dream" also add an antique touch. The main idea, however, is that even after twenty years Gilboa still bears a fresh memory of his brother's death.

The poem also evinces the theme of survivor's guilt. In line 11 Gilboa describes his unwitting escape from Europe, his fateful departure from the family home (because he was "other," different) while Joshua remained behind to help with the family's tailoring work.[8] The ghostly presence of Joshua and the rhythmic sound of the waves are constant reminders of unmitigated grief. The poem closes poignantly with a mini-Kaddish.

As in the *Shirim ba-boker ba-boker* collection, another major theme in these opening poems of *"Shelosha she'arim ḥozrim"* is the image and labor of the poet—a motif to which Gilboa returns most explicitly in *Shibolet mitehilim 69* (A Wave from Psalm 69).[9] Written in an archaized, Psalm-like style, the work again presents the poet-speaker as dizzied and overwhelmed by the "flood" (or "wave" *[shibolet])* of images which constantly come over him.[10] As with many earlier poems, Gilboa prays for the control required to keep him from drowning in the images. On the other hand, he notes that often "[his] throat is dry" just when he wishes "to sing for [you, i.e., the wave]."

אֲנִי עָנִי וְכוֹאֵב,
יוֹדֵעַ אִוַּלְתִּי וְאַשְׁמוֹתַי,
אַךְ שִׂיחֵךְ בִּי כָּל הַיּוֹם
עִם יוֹשְׁבֵי שָׁעַר
מְכַסֶּה כְּלִמָּה פָּנַי
כְּמוֹ נְגִינוֹתַיִךְ לָיְלָה
עִם שׁוֹתֵי שֵׁכָר.

אֲנִי שִׁכּוֹר אוֹתָךְ, שִׁבֹּלֶת.

I am poor and in pain,
I know my foolishness and sins,
but your word is with me each day
with those who sit at the gate
I cover the shame my face
like your songs at night
with those who are drunk.

I am drunk with you, O wave.

Once again the poet faces a familiar dilemma. He is filled, even flooded, with words of inspiration, yet cannot articulate them. Gilboa still fears the paralysis of writers' block—and perhaps provides one explanation for his ten-year hiatus from poetry.

Azariah min-ha-adumim (literally, Azariah of the Red), which refers more obliquely to the poet and his self image, casts further light on his decade of silence. Azariah de Rossi (ca. 1511–1570) lived in Mantua during the period of the Italian Renaissance. A cultured Hebrew scholar, he was nevertheless considered an apostate because of his interest in mysticism, classical philosophy, and the works of the Church Fathers. As a result of his major work, *Me'or einayim* (The Enlightener), both the man and his writings were placed under a ban of excommunication by rabbinic authorities in Venice and elsewhere.

As the poem opens, a sympathetic speaker notes how de Rossi was taunted by the pejorative epithet *goy goy* (gentile gentile) in the Jewish neighborhoods of Mantua. He was especially vilified—at least in the context of the poem—for his suggestion that the universe was much older than Jewish tradition purported it to be.[11] Gilboa depicts the alleged sin quite majestically.

וּמָשַׁךְ אֶת חֻפַּת הַיְצִירָה אֶל מַעֲמַקֵּי זְמַנִּים
אֵי הַרְחֵק הַרְחֵק
מֵעֵבֶר לִגְבוּלוֹת הַתְּנָ"ךְ
לְמַעַן כְּבוֹדוֹ מְלֹא עוֹלָם
שֶׁאֵינוֹ רַק בֶּן כָּךְ וְכָךְ.

He spread the canopy of creation to the depths of time
distant so distant
beyond the borders of the Bible
to the glory of the One who fills the world
which is not x number of years old.

Here Gilboa turns away from de Rossi and focuses on himself.

הוֹ, כַּמָּה טוֹב שֶׁפַּרְעוֹת רֹאשִׁי מִתַּלְתְּלִים בָּרוּחַ
וַחֲלוֹמוֹתַי מְרַחֲפִים הַרְחֵק
בְּחֵיק אַלְזְמַן לְהִתְרַפֵּק.

Oh, how good it is that my wild hair wafts in the wind
and my dreams hover in the distance
lying in the bosom of timelessness.

As with de Rossi's view of the universe, the speaker claims that his own poetic image, even his poetic being, was formed eons ago. He views himself as having been buffeted through time, now hidden by curtains, now rising to the lights; here cast into the pit, there raised up "to play all the games/which He created/for me." For Gilboa, the life of the poet, like de Rossi's, has been a privileged, inspired, yet often painful experience. He has often expressed his feelings about the indifference or hostility of critics and readers. Recognizing in de Rossi a soul brother—a man of talent, cultured beyond his time, yet denounced by those who found his work lacking—Gilboa may have excommunicated himself from the poetic community for ten years in order to come to terms with this lack of public approval.

The first section of *"Shelosha she'arim ḥozrim"* closes with *Shimshon ha-gibor* (Samson the Hero, or Samson the Mighty),[12] in which the life of the biblical figure obliquely suggests Gilboa's own experiences. The poem presents a revisionist view of Samson by altering the facts of the biblical narrative and by interpolating characteristics elsewhere ascribed to other biblical figures. Samson, it notes at the start, "lived to a ripe old age." But according to the story in Judges, he died a heroic suicidal death at Dagon soon after the Delilah episode, apparently still a young man. The opening lines report that Samson had trouble sleeping at night—a malady usually ascribed to King Saul. Moreover, they add, when Samson was a small child "he lifted the world on its axis with one hand," a feat usually attributed to the legendary Atlas and totally absent in the Samson story. These purposeful interpolations of erroneous detail loosen the fetters of convention and inform the reader that the poem is playful—and that even its connotations are to extend beyond the "factual" biblical account.[13]

Still another revision of the biblical story is Gilboa's poetic claim that "when [Samson] grew up and became a young man he wanted to die on the night of his seventeenth birthday."

לֹא רָצָה לָמוּת זָקֵן: בֶּן שְׁבַע עֶשְׂרֵה וְיוֹם.
עַל כֵּן קָשַׁר לַפִּידִים בְּזַנְבוֹת שְׁלֹשׁ־מֵאוֹת הַשּׁוּעָלִים
כְּדֵי לִשְׂרֹף הַכֹּל.

He did not want to die old: seventeen and one day.
That's why he tied torches to the tails of three hundred foxes
so as to set fire to everything.

The narrator goes on to say that in his twenties Samson aimed to do wondrous feats "until his death at thirty-three," the purported age of Jesus at the time of his death. According to Gilboa's version, he eschewed living to old age because he wanted to live as the heroic "Samson the Mighty" and go out as a legend—which is what he actually did, adds the reader. Suddenly, however, there is a change in Samson's thinking.

בַּיָּמִים שֶׁנִּקְּרוּ אֶת עֵינָיו
הִתְפַּלֵּל לַחֲזוֹת בַּחֲתֻנַּת בְּנוֹתָיו.

In the days that they put out his eyes
he prayed [to live] to see his daughters' weddings.

There is no biblical evidence that Samson had any children, but by now the reader has no expectation of Gilboa's faithfulness to the original story. In wanting to see his daughters married, Samson becomes a middle-class burgher, desirous of living a staid and steady patriarchal family life. He is no longer the biblical hero or even the revised Gilboan hero who wishes to live hard and die young, and the poem closes with a vision of Samson in old age.

בֶּן שְׁמוֹנִים לֹא בָּגַר עוֹד
וּבְשִׁכְחַת שְׁעוֹתָיו הָזָה כְּתִינוֹק בֶּן־יוֹמוֹ.

וַעֲדַיִן שַׁעֲרֵי עָזָּתוֹ רוֹדְמִים בַּבֶּצֶר.

וּדְלִילָה

At eighty he grew [or matured] no more.
And in the forgetting of his hours he had dreams like a new-born babe.

And still the gates of his Gaza slumber in the [primal] ore.

And Delilah

When he grows old, Samson becomes a dreamy child again. Both his great feat, carrying off the gates of the city of Gaza, and his great fall, his death at Gath, loom as potential events.

Much as he does in *Sha'ul* and *Yitsḥak,* Gilboa uses *Shimshon ha-gibor* as a source of self-reflective dramatization. In the earlier works, resonances from the biblical framework help to convey a sense of the poet's helplessness regarding the Holocaust in general and the slaughter of his family in particular. In *Shimshon ha-gibor* Gilboa reflects on the career of the poet or artist who feels in youth that he or she can conquer the world. The youthful impulse is to create exceptional works, to be a revered celebrity, then to go out like a star. But then one settles into a career and raises a family. And in old age, like a dreamy child, one can only envision his distant, treasured—or foolish—feats of love and art.

The second section of *"Shelosha she'arim ḥozrim"* demonstrates a full measure of Gilboa's playfulness and love of experimentation. Several of the poems consist of doggerel verse, with close, repetitive rhyme, jingle-like sequences, word plays, a surfeit of alliterations, and witty double-talk. After ten years of silence Gilboa apparently sought to return to the poetic scene with yet another change in image and style.

While the dominant mode is playful and conundrum-like, some of these poems are moralistic or based on observations of social behavior. In *Asher yagi'a rishon* (The One Who Comes In First),[14] the poet satirizes the categorization of successful and unsuccessful people. Using pithy aphorisms, he describes the success quotient of three types of individuals as they strive, or eschew striving, toward goals.

What one does with one's life is also the topic of *Ve-khol ha-hirhur ha-ze* (All This Pondering).[15] While the verbal structure is very playful, the message is that one may strive throughout one's life and still be found "guilty," presumably of not having striven enough. There is a basic unfairness in the system, says Gilboa, using the same anticonventional moralistic pose here as in *Asher yagi'a rishon.*

In comic, even farcical ways, the speaker records domestic arguments and casual events he witnesses as he is walking down the street. At times the situation becomes serious. In *Yom yom midei ovri* (Every Day As I Pass By),[16] the speaker is accosted daily by someone peering at him through the shrubs. The speaker adamantly refuses to acknowledge this person, perhaps a neighborhood child, who increasingly demands to be recognized. One day a "soon-to-be-bloodied axe is raised from the thicket fence," and the hidden person bursts out crying. The axe is imaginary, but the speaker realizes that both sides are wrong to be so distanced and hopes that the two will now reconcile.

Although this sort of moral or social message emerges in some of these works, the predominant mode is a more basic, quasi-anthropological observation of human behavior. In *Halah she-bi-meromei ha-mirpeset* (The One Up High on the Balcony)[17] the speaker-observer notes that a man standing on his apartment balcony is all smiles as he watches a woman walking down the street. Once his glance meets the speaker's, however, the apartment dweller's visage turns angry and hostile. "Oh, how weary [of this] am I," says the speaker, "how weary." Though there may be some moralizing here, the poem seems to be just a slice of life, a simple glimpse of a common everyday occurrence.

Though these works are thematically quite distant from those that deal with nature, Holocaust memories, and the challenges of being a poet, in this section the overriding tone is sad frustration and the atmosphere often Kafkaesque or absurd. While Gilboa records his astute observations of the behavior of others, he also displays—consciously, I would say—a willingness to observe and record his own social and psychological characteristics. In *Kol ha-zeman* (All the Time)[18] the dismayed poet-observer wonders why he lets others speak and does not respond to what they have to say. The image here is of a schlemiel, a dejected, inept antihero who sits on the periphery of action and events, too disheartened to act.

In sum, in these works of the early sixties, Gilboa strives to write in a new poetic milieu. Alhough he displays his sense of fun through playful verbiage and structures, Gilboa also presents a portrait of an artist in transition, a poet who combines the perception of others with concomitant observations about himself.

The poem which best captures this duality of self and style is *Adam be-emet eino tsarikh* (A Person Really Needs Only).[19]

אָדָם בֶּאֱמֶת אֵינוֹ צָרִיךְ

אָדָם בֶּאֱמֶת אֵינוֹ צָרִיךְ אֶלָּא לְסֵפֶר אֶחָד בְּחַיָּיו
כַּאֲשֶׁר כָּל חַיָּיו נִקְבָּצִים לְעֵינָיו בַּסֵּפֶר הַפָּתוּחַ לְעֵינָיו
כַּאֲשֶׁר הוּא קוֹרֵא בּוֹ דַּף אַחַר דַּף וְרוֹאֶה לְעֵינָיו
אֵיךְ יוֹם אַחַר יוֹם רָדַף כְּמוֹ דַּף אַחַר דַּף
בַּסֵּפֶר הַפָּתוּחַ לְעֵינָיו.
וְאַף לֹא אֶחָד נֶעֱזָב וּבְרַחֲמִים רַבִּים נֶאֱסָף
דַּף אַחַר דַּף
בַּסֵּפֶר הַפָּתוּחַ לְעֵינָיו
כִּי רוֹאֶה לְעֵינָיו
פָּתוּחַ סֵפֶר חַיָּיו
בְּרַחֲמִים רַבִּים נֶעֱזָב.

A Person Really Needs Only

A person really needs only one book in his life
when all his life is gathered to his eyes in the book open to his eyes
when he reads in it page after page and sees with his eyes
how one day chased another like page after page
in the book open to his eyes.
And not even one was abandoned and with great mercy gathered up
page after page
in the book open to his eyes
for he sees before his eyes
the book of his life is open
with great mercy abandoned.[20]

The central metaphor here is the dual image of the mythical "Book of Life" and "the book of [the poet's] life," which, because of its nature as artifice, may also be deemed mythical or fictive. The poet's works are equivalent to the poet's life, at least insofar as the poet can read through his works and "see" his life passing before him.

The book-as-life image, however, is only the premise for the poem's message, which is conveyed with great ambiguity. The ambiguity is visibly evident in two places, lines 6 and 11. In line 6, the subject modified by the adjective "abandoned" *(ne'ezav)* is not clear; it may be either "day" or "page," both of which appear in line 4. The ambiguity is moot, however, since the predominant dual image of "book" and "life" suggests that "day" and "page" are equivalent.

In line 11, the ambiguity is more opaque. Again it is the subject of "abandoned" that is unclear. The adjective seems to modify "book," which is repeatedly noted as being open and clearly visible to the eyes of the one who sees or reads it (most likely the poet). But if the book is so plainly open, visible, and readable—and if, as noted in the entire second half of the poem, the pages of the book have been gathered together with such "great mercy"—why then would the book be said to be "abandoned," and why with "great mercy"?

The meaning, it seems, is dualistic. It is merciful and good that his book (of poetry, assumedly) is gathered together and offers a portrait of his life. It is also merciful and good that the book, as a portrait of his life, may also be "abandoned," that is, set aside, not considered the only source of his life and his being. One's professional "product," he implies, is not the complete record or measure of a person's life.

The poem, however, might have emerged from a more specific context. These works were written and published late in 1963, during the time when Gilboa was also preparing for publication the manuscript of *Keḥulim va-adumim,* his first volume of collected works.[21] Certainly he spent many months selecting, revising, and ordering the poems which would constitute that major effort. Reviewing all his published and as yet uncollected works, Gilboa, for an extended period of time, was literally confronting his life in art, and *Adam be'emet eino tsarikh* is a statement about that confrontation. The poem embodies both an acknowledgment of the life in art and the need to move away from the conception that art itself is life.

As is his habit at points of closure, Gilboa ends this section of *"Shelosha she'arim ḥozrim"* with a poem on poetry. Titled *Murgeshet tekhuna, kefi she-omrim* (One Feels Anticipation, As They Say),[22] the poem addresses Gilboa's relentless bugaboos: a runaway imagination and imagistic overload. The prolific visionariness, including its anticipation, is presented in three increasingly intensifying stanzas, each beginning with the ecstatic refrain: "One feels [the] anticipation, as they say, it's beginning to move *[ze matḥil lazuz].*"

Gilboa first notes his obsession with statues of horses, which he prefers to envision not on pedestals, but at gallop in a storm. Then his imagination "moves." He sees his entire neighborhood suddenly flocking into the street, a quiet place where there are usually "only a couple of insects." The whole street is lit up. In the final stanza, he sees himself jumping onto a horse which proceeds to gallop across the illumined street. It "runs all about and creates a storm."

Although the poem could be read as a delusion of grandeur, more likely Gilboa is simply giving his creativity full rein. In contrast with earlier poems about the poetic process, the reader notes the absence of complaints about uncontrollability or defensive justifications of his stylistic innovativeness. Instead, we are presented with Gilboa's runaway imagination itself, which he seems to savor.

This new freewheeling attitude is evident throughout this section. Alhough there are some serious, introspective moments, Gilboa displays a more casual, playful style in this potpourri of farcical observational poems of everyday life. Much like the exuberant, often comical poems of *Shirim ba-boker ba-boker,* these works broaden our view both of Gilboa's creativity and of his sense of humor.

As if acting upon a new freedom from topical strictures, in the third section of *"Shelosha she'arim ḥozrim"* Gilboa reverts to a more serious, plaintive mode. His life-long romance with nature predominates, often with an aura of myth. He also ponders his own place in the world, both as a poet blessed with creative powers and as a person burdened by memory. The poems are suffused with emotion. Some, however, reflect a restraint which often belies a surfeit of uncontrollable feeling. An awareness of aging and growing closer to death emerge as recurring motifs. Several of the poems might be considered *pensées*—short personal reflections on aspects of life and the art of poetry. Others are ambiguous symbolic works which embody the poet's feelings toward unnamed political events or mythical dimensions of experience.

The poems display a wide array of structures. Some contain long effusive verse lines; others have very short ones. Still others range from conventional stanzas with regular rhyme to free-verse styles in various line configurations.

Some poems appear ungrammatical; others are playful in their use of syntax or repetitive rhyme. The overall aesthetic effect of the twenty-odd works in this section is one of creative variation and innovative experimentation.

The prevailing tone is plaintive; the poet is haunted by the specters of loss and death. Simultaneously, however, he is immersed in the delights of nature—the rain, the wind, the seashore, the early morning. Parallel to the dualistic thematics, the speaker's self-image is both vulnerable and heroic. Though clouded by sorrowful remembrance, his poetic vision is bolstered by a sense of uniqueness and strength. "I have come from my self *[ani me-atsmi bati],"* the voice proclaims.[23] Like Atlas he props up the world's foundations, but he also muses on the whereabouts of his grave and daydreams about his "sleepers," his beloved dead whose memory shimmers in gold and flame.[24]

As noted throughout this study, the voice and the image in Gilboa's poetry are those of the poet himself. As before, in each of these works he appears in the combined guise of a real and poetic persona, an intense emotional entity. His actual and poetic countenances are multiple: proud father, befuddled house-husband, lover, angry protester, doleful rememberer, enthralled nature lover, witty punster, troubled existentialist, dreamer, sojourner in mythic worlds. With few exceptions, Gilboa places himself and his various faces and concerns at the dramatic center of these works.

In the nature poems, for example, the poet-intertwined-with-nature replaces nature itself as the focus. *Ha-boker ha-ze* (This Morning)[25] opens with "So [it is] to enter into this morning/With the sound of a flute that comes to me from above." Not simply an observer, the speaker is involved in a symbiotic and epiphanic relationship with morning, which he "enters into" as a constituent part of the experience. He hears its celestial voice and then "greets [the face of] the sun." The "clear and blue" morning follows suit and works its magic on him by removing "the evil things that had covered the face of the sun on all sides."

Similarly, in *Ke-she-ba'a ha-se'ara ha-zot* (When This Storm Comes)[26] a sandstorm *(se'ara)* suddenly comes up, and at that very moment the speaker says that his "soul is storming" *(niseret).* Once again nature and the poet are one. As if to demonstrate this unity, the speaker is lifted and carried off by the storm. This, he says, is precisely "what I've always yearned/to do to fly with the sand and dust and with them to roam/in the wind. . . ." The dramatic scene is similar to that in Bialik's *Zohar.* However, unlike Bialik's idyll, here Gilboa's vicious sandstorm "beats upon the shutters of [his] eyes dessicated by fire." Ironically—perhaps romantically—despite the storm's ferocity, the speaker expresses his extreme pleasure with the ride.

The poem ends with the storm's passing and the speaker's return to earth. When the city dwellers reopen their shutters, he is embarrassed—not wanting them to think that it was he who "worked [his] magic *(she-asiti ba-lehatim)*/and my face was all blushes" *(lehatim lehatim)*. It is as if the enthralled poet actually brought on the sandstorm for his own pleasure.

This affective affinity with nature evinces the essential difference between Gilboa's earlier nature poetry and the works in *"Shelosha she'arim ḥozrim."* The theme is expressed most cogently in *Ohav kara shimshit zo* (I Love This Sunlight Cold).[27]

אֹהַב קָרָה שִׁמְשִׁית זוֹ

אֹהַב קָרָה שִׁמְשִׁית זוֹ בַּחֲלָלִים שֶׁל שְׁקִיפוּת מִתְכַּחְלֶלֶת.
כְּמוֹ שָׁקַט כֹּל שֶׁבְּתוֹכִי וְהִתְקַדֵּשׁ לִקְרַאת חַג בַּגְּבָהִים.
אֵין דְּבָרִים. לֹא מִשּׁוּם צִפִּיָּה לַהֲוָיָה שֶׁבְּמִסְתּוֹר.
זוֹ הֲוָיָה לְעַצְמָהּ. דַּקָּה בְּרַחֲבוּתָהּ. רֵיחָנִית אֵין־רֵיחַ בַּחֲרִיפוּתָהּ.
וְטִרְדָה רַק אַחַת אֵי־נֶאֱחֶזֶת כֵּיצַד לְהַלֵּךְ כָּךְ
שֶׁלְּעוֹלָם לֹא תִּמּוֹר.
אַךְ כָּל אוֹתָהּ עֵת אַחַת יְדִיעַת־רֵאשִׁית –
כְּמוֹ לִפְנֵי בְּרִיאָה שֶׁלְּאַחֲרֶיהָ שׁוּם דָּבָר לֹא צָרִיךְ לְהִבָּרֵא.
כְּמוֹ יֵשׁוּת רוֹחֲפָה הֲדֵי־עַד שֶׁל הֵיכְלֵי נֶפֶשׁ
וְהֵם הַרְרֵי הֲרָרִים אֲוִיר שֶׁלִּפְנֵי־הֱיוֹת
וְתָמִיד.

I Love this Sunlight Cold

I love this sunlight cold in spaces transparent turning blue
As if all within were calm and turning sacred for celestial celebration.
No words. Not out of expectance of hidden being.
This is being in itself. Slight in its breadth. Fragrant odorless in its
pungency.

> And only one problem to wrestle somehow to walk on so
> it will never change.
> But all that time one primal knowledge—
> As before a creation after which nothing needs creating.
> As some presence ahover with timeless echoes of soul palaces
> they're mountains of mountains of air of before becoming
> and forever.[28]

Some of the poem's components are familiar: the early morning dramatic situation, the sunrise, the enthrallment and aura of sacrality, the mythical dimensions, the archaic style, the ambiguity of certain phrases and terms, the motif of blue. Others are new: the pervasiveness of elliptical sentences which create a catalogue of features of "this sunlight cold"; the long verse lines which combine with the ellipses to accentuate both the individuality and the multiplicity of the features; and the syntactic ungrammaticalities, especially those in lines 9–10 ("ahover with timeless echoes" *[roḥafa hedei-ad]* and "mountains of mountains of air" *[harerei hararim avir]),* which force the reader to dwell on various qualities of this experience in nature.[29]

Nature also plays a key role in the more existential poems, where Gilboa ponders the meaning of the universe and of human effort in a finite world. In *Bi-veli mesim* (Unconsciously),[30] as he stands on the seashore and observes how the waves "flee to gather/strength and to return to beat at the shore/with full strength," he asks to be gathered up with the waves, "to become a sea/from now and forevermore." Though filled with a fear of the end, the speaker gains strength from the idea of being a part of the cosmic flow.

The theme of existential fear recurs in a more personal context in *Kemo she-ani holekh* (As I Go)[31] and *Odi ats el ha-reḥov* (I Still Rush Outside).[32] *Odi ats el ha-reḥov* pictures the poet trying to understand why he jumps up to go outside as the day is coming to an end. He concludes that it is a symptom of angst: although the world is "all good" *(olam she-kulo tov*—a reference to messianic days), there is still "a fear of the end/it steps before my eyes/and furtively *(basheli)* draws near."[33] *Kemo she-ani holekh* features a lighter side to the existential dilemma. As the poet goes through his daily chores, "stripping off on my way/seasons of life . . . As I go/the child [in me] goes with me." Despite life's finite limits, Gilboa's puckish personality accompanies him throughout the day.

The existential theme reaches a climax in the dream poem *Pitom ne'elam mi-meni [mekom kivri]* (Suddenly I Could Not Remember [the site of my grave]),[34] in which an Orphean nightmare reflects Gilboa's preoccupation with the thought of death. Set in the middle of the night, the poem describes his netherworld journey seeking the site of his eventual burial. The atmosphere is Gothic.

רַק כּוֹכָבִי רוֹמֵז קַר לְעֶבְרִי
הַדֶּרֶךְ בִּכְסַפְסָפִים מְרוֹסֵס
כְּמוֹ הָיוּ לִי רִבְבַת עֵינַי
בִּפְנִימַי

Only my star twinkles coldly before me
it splinters the way with silverysparks [sic]
as if I had thousands of my eyes
in my insides.

He arrives at "the threshold of the netherworld/where all falls into the abyss." At this crucial point his personal morning star comes to the rescue and returns him to "the threshold of day." In Dantesque fashion, he rises "from the pit."

Though he was only in his mid- to late forties when these poems were written, Gilboa may have been ill or apprised of some malady. It may also be that his fears were in part for all mankind, cognizant as he was of the growing arsenals of nuclear weaponry thoughout the world.[35] Whatever its impetus, the existential theme continues and predominates in Gilboa's next collection, *Ratsiti likhtov siftei yeshenim.*

The use of the Orpheus legend in *Pitom ne'elam mi-meni* demonstrates the mythical dimension in many of these poems. For example, by using the same verb for "receded" *[sh-kh-kh]* in *Ke-she-ba'a ha-se'ara hazot,* Gilboa likens the sandstorm to the biblical flood of Noah's day. Flutes and other musical sounds resonate in several other works and create a celestial backdrop for the poetic action. *Bikashti la'atsor et ha-peleg* (I Tried to Hold Back the Stream)[36] presents a Gilboan version of the boy who saves Holland by plugging the hole in the dike with his finger. *Ohav kara shimshit zo* also evinces mythical dimensions in its references to "a creation after which nothing needs creating" and "some presence ahover with timeless echoes of soul palaces" *[heikhlei nefesh]*.

Sofei devarim lo nishme'u od (The Ends of Things Were No Longer Heard),[37] a poem about the end of time, is perhaps the most mythically resonant. In the poem's narrative, everything has fallen to earth and turned to dust. All things are "ashen" and "cleansed," a dualistic image which enhances both the frightfulness and the sacredness of the earth's final moment. "Only the Burning Bush shone guarding/our clenched fists," Gilboa writes. But the protest does no good. The world is destroyed as the day begins to lighten; "and now we are speechless." The poem continues Gilboa's recurrent warnings regarding the earth's fragility and the threat of nuclear catastrophe.

In the midst of these existential poems, Gilboa inserts *Dimit asher dama [ha-ma'ayan]* (You've Imagined What [the Spring, i.e., font] Has Wept),[38] an imagistic work which combines the motifs of love, the passage of time, and the poetic process.

דִּמִּית אֲשֶׁר דָּמַע

דִּמִּית אֲשֶׁר דָּמַע הַמַּעְיָן
מִזְּמַן מִזְּמַן נִדְמָה.
אַךְ בְּתֵבָתֵךְ מְשֻׁבֶּצֶת הַצְּדָפִים
מִלּוֹת הַשִּׁיר
יָבְשׁוּ
הָיוּ דַר
נוֹצֵץ
מַבְהִיק
וָקָר
כַּתְּרָפִים
קָפְאוּ בְּלַחַשׁ עַתִּיק
שֶׁכַּמַּעְיָן

לָעַד יָקִיר
מִלּוֹתָיו
הַשִּׁיר.

You've Imagined

You've imagined what the spring has wept
from time to time it seems.
But in your box decorated with shells
the words of the poem
    have dried up
    turned to marble
    sparkling
    shiny
    and cold
like teraphim
they've frozen in an ancient incantation
which like the spring
the poem
            will ever express
its words.

Poetry, not love, is the central subject here. The speaker-to-lover, man-to-woman format is used more for the intimacy of tone than for an expression of feeling.[39] The woman figure seems predisposed to poetry, in that she often seems to have thought of "what the spring [i.e., font] has wept." The metaphor connotes a sensitive consciousness, the proclivity to understand the world by listening to nature and its pain. By virtue of the fact that it comprises the box's contents, Gilboa implies that nature's most valuable treasure is a sad romantic poem.

But Gilboa's view of the treasure is negative here. Turning to the woman's jewelry box, "decorated with shells," the speaker finds "the words of the poem" have "dried up" *(yavshu)* and turned to "marble [or mother-of-pearl]/sparkling/shiny/and cold." Like teraphim, though valuable, they have become mere household objects; once fluid and vibrant, they have become lifeless and distant, frozen "in an ancient incantation."

Once a poem moves from the mysterious experience of its creative formation into the concrete shape of its final words, suggests Gilboa, there is a measure of loss. The very gathering up and writing down of images creates something of lasting value, but at that point a poem is far removed from the primal inspiration by which it was conceived. The woman, then, is the image of the muse, the spirit within the poet that first "imagined what the spring has wept." The subject of the poem is poetic inspiration and its ironic disappearance as the work is shaped into a polished jewel.

The last four lines, however, reverse the idea of loss. No predicate follows the phrase "which like the spring." Instead, a new subject and predicate, "the poem . . . will ever express," replaces the prior phrase. The ungrammaticality accentuates the return to the image of the spring and joins it with a more informal, instinctive connecting device to the work's initial idea—namely, that despite its alleged petrifaction, romantic poetry indeed has the power to capture the primal force of its own inspiration.

The metaphors and other figurative images in *"Shelosha she'arim ḥozrim"* do not differ significantly from those in earlier collections. One still sees a penchant toward oxymoron ("sunlight cold," "slender in its breadth," "fragrant odorless").[40] Dualities persist (the colts of youth are first of "gold and fire" and later are "flowing with blood"; snow is "fiery in its frost").[41] Eyes, springs, and effulgences abound in a variety of figurative modes, as do allusive language and a predominance of phrases from the liturgy, the Bible, and Bialik.[42]

The volume's innovations consist mainly of Gilboa's creative uses of syntax and structure.[43] In several instances it is his ungrammaticalities, some of which we have seen above, that cause the reader to pause and reflect on the poet's intended meaning. The middle section of *Geshem yored ve-shotef* (Rain Falls and Floods)[44] is a good example.

גֶּשֶׁם יוֹרֵד וְשׁוֹטֵף

גֶּשֶׁם יוֹרֵד וְשׁוֹטֵף, אוֹמֵר הַלֵּב
וּמְטַפְטֵף בּוֹ רָחוֹק רָחוֹק
נְהִי קָדוּם, אָזֵב
יָרֹק בְּשׁוּלָיו

צְלִיל עַתִּיק שֶׁל זָהָב
שֶׁתִּעְתַּע בּוֹ
שֶׁתָּעָה וְשָׁאַר
שֶׁגַּיְא שֶׁהַר
שֶׁשֶּׁמֶשׁ
בְּתוֹכוֹ שָׁמַר
שֶׁאֵלָיו חָזַר
כַּאֲשֶׁר גֶּשֶׁם יָרַד וְשָׁטַף
וְרָחוֹק נִגֵּן בּוֹ עוּגָב.

Rain Falls and Floods

Rain falls and floods, say the heart
and distantly distantly there drips in it
an ancient lament, moss so
green at its edges,
an ancient sound of gold
that deceived it [i.e. the heart]
that was lost and remained
that a valley that a mountain
that the sun
kept within it
that returned to it
when rain fell and flooded
and distantly in it a pipe sang.[45]

Lines 1–7 contain two instances of ambiguity: the rain-engendered lament becomes a "sound of gold," and the lament/sound is both "lost" and "remained" — it attracts and repels simultaneously, plays wantonly on his emotions, and becomes a source of consternation. Gilboa is apparently referring here to the memory of his losses in the Holocaust. Though it grows more distant with time, it always remains part of his consciousness.

In lines 8–11, the speaker's bewilderment at the persistent presence of the dualistic sound takes the shape of an uncertain syntax. First, Gilboa switches the subject of the relative pronoun "that" (the prefix *she-)* from "sound" to a triple subject—"That a valley that a mountain/That the sun"—which is coupled with the predicate "kept" (or held, *shamar).* The use of a multiple subject with a singular verb in itself is confusing; added to this are the lack of punctuation and the ironically playful rhyming of *sha'ar* (remained), *she-har* (that a mountain), *shamar* (kept), and *ḥazar* (returned).

In much of Gilboa's poetry, the rain and other images of nature evoke mixed emotions of love, devotion, happiness, loss, and sadness. In *Geshem yored ve-shotef,* the effectiveness of the uneven syntax lies in the metonymic idea that for him all parts of nature are sources of both gladness and sorrow. The ungrammatical listing of natural phenomena mirrors the intensity of his feeling of loss.

Cultivated here and further refined in *Ratsiti likhtov siftei yeshenim,* disjointed syntax becomes Gilboa's predominant stylistic method.[46] It may be said, in fact, that the earlier Gilboa would have become unrecognizable in his later works were it not for the experimental efforts evident in *"Shelosha she'arim ḥozrim."* These structural changes of the early sixties anticipate the even larger innovations in Gilboa's next two collections.

Ani lo (I'll Not),[47] the short closing poem of *"Shelosha she'arim ḥozrim"* reflects these innovations.

אֲנִי לֹא

אֲנִי לֹא אֹמַר לָךְ אֲשֶׁר בְּלִבִּי שׁוֹכֵחַ
אֲנִי לֹא אֹמַר לָךְ אֲשֶׁר בְּלִבִּי פּוֹלֵחַ
אֲנִי לֹא אֹמַר לָךְ אֲשֶׁר בְּלִבִּי פּוֹתֵחַ
וְאֵין סוֹגֵר

I'll Not

I'll not say to you what I forget in my heart
I'll not say to you what pierces my heart
I'll not say to you what opens my heart
And no one to close

Shaped mainly by repetition and ellipsis, the poem uses an ironically intimate tone to say that certain feelings will not be explicitly expressed. The final line, however, belies the cover-up by stating that the heart does not close. The dualistic theme of hidden-yet-open emotions is familiar to Gilboa's readers, but his experimental uses of ellipses, graphic innovation, enjambment, and a variety of ungrammatical structures constitute a preview of his new modernist style.

Chapter VI

Poetry as Consciousness

Ratsiti likhtov siftei yeshenim/ I Wanted to Write the Lips of Sleepers, 1968

Published five years after the appearance of the *Keḥulim va-adumim* collection, *Ratsiti likhtov siftei yeshenim* (henceforth, *Ratsiti)* signals a radical and frequently astounding change in Gilboa's poetic work. Although he more and more frequently incorporated certain innovations in *"Shelosha she'arim ḥozrim"*—a playful conundrum-like rhetoric, a confusing double-talk repetition of words and phrases, a plethora of word associations and numberless puns—in *Ratsiti* these tested devices become the focus of individual works and not just their embellishments. In addition, the poems in the *Ratsiti* collection display a nearly ubiquitous, overriding ambiguity; a constant use of ungrammaticalities; a confusing use of run-on verses (enjambment); a purposely disorienting lack of punctuation; and a variety of ellipses which often leave the reader to complete unfinished thoughts and sentences.[1]

Added to these devices of apparent obfuscation—their purposes are explored at length below—are speaker figures, some of whom often seem befuddled, ambivalent, struggling for articulation, and others who speak solely in abstract metaphors and images; subjects and moral or social concerns which are heatedly argued but not spelled out with any recognizable clarity; and an abiding sense of duality which permeates both the narrative and the emotive aspects of the poems.

Most of all, an ambiguous syntax—words and phrases placed so as to allow for dual readings—engenders in the reader a feeling of wandering in a maze of words with no clear path to reasonable comprehension.[2] The reader struggles for understanding, much as the speaker—perhaps the poet as well—struggles for expressibility. Indeed, this mirroring of articulation and comprehension becomes in itself the subject of many of these poems. In trying to make sense of the works, the reader is engaged both intellectually, solving the poetic puzzle, and emotionally, sharing the speaker's intense encounter with feelings and words.[3] Although most of Gilboa's poems tend to be puzzles of sorts, the puzzle-poems of *Ratsiti* are far more daunting than anything he has written before; they signal his belated but unambivalent entry into the realm of modernistic poetry.[4]

A relatively small number of the seventy-six poems in this collection—perhaps a half dozen—relate directly to the appreciation of nature. Several other works are concerned with social, philosophical, or psychological issues. There are also a few dream poems and poems of protest, the latter directed at critics whom Gilboa sees as trying to limit freedom of expression or style. The poems in the fourth formal section of the volume relate to the 1967 Six-Day War. But by far the largest thematic groupings are poems on poetry and poems with existential themes, which together constitute more than half the collection: the poems on poetry contribute about one third and the existential poems about one fourth of the total contents. Thus *Ratsiti* is devoted mostly to the personal *Weltanschauung* of the poet in the late sixties and to the perennial exploration of his manifestly arduous task as a writer.[5]

The collection's ambiguous, figurative title, "I Wanted to Write the Lips of Sleepers," itself attests to Gilboa's main interest here—somehow to articulate the visionary world of the "dream," to capture the elusive moment of insight, so difficult to retain or transmit once the dreamer awakens. The poet is the dreamer, the one asleep. He is caught in a kind of thought-limbo between ignorance and knowing, fear and wonderment, confusion and awareness, negation and affirmation. These oppositional emotions, in turn, delineate the poems' seemingly inarticulate structures. Often, too, the poet interjects phrases pertaining to the very effort of articulation. These interjections constitute a *metalingual commentary*—Roman Jakobson's term referring to a text's "speaking about language"[6]—which accentuates the conflicting forces sensed by the poet in his quest for the right word, the effective phrase.

Already complex in connoting the act of poetic composition, the "lips of sleepers" metaphor is also multilayered. In the volume's introductory poem, *Be-kho'aḥ oḥaz bedal ḥalom* (I'll Grab Hold of a Butt of Dream),[7] Gilboa sets the poet-dreamer in an oppositional context of memory and forgetfulness.

בְּכֹחַ אֹחַז בְּדַל חֲלוֹם.
וְאָסוּר לְהַעֲלוֹתוֹ דַל שְׂפָתַיִם.
וְאַף אֵין לְהַרְבּוֹת וְלִזְכֹּר

כִּי אֶפְשָׁר עוֹד לַחֲלוֹת.
הוֹ, בַּת יְרוּשָׁלַיִם.

שָׁכַחְתִּי נֵצַח מִי לֹא יְשַׁקֵּר
בִּסְבַךְ הַשִּׂיחִים שֶׁבְּשֵׁנָה.
תָּמִיד יָדַעְתִּי זֹאת. כְּמִכְוַת הֶכֵּר.
עַד שֶׁקַּמְתִּי יוֹם כִּלְאַחַר שִׁבְעִים שָׁנָה.

וְאֵין לְדוֹבֵב עוֹד שִׂפְתֵי יְשֵׁנִים.
שָׁנִים מְאֵרָה כָּל סַף תְּמַלְּאֶנָּה.
עַל שֻׁלְחָן כּוֹס חֲלוֹמוֹת עֲשֵׁנִים
עוֹד מְעַט וַי לְעֵינַי לֹא
אֶרְאֶנָּה.

I'll grab hold of a butt of dream.
I mustn't let it touch my lips.
Mustn't even remember so much
For I might still fall ill.
Alas, daughter of Jerusalem.

I've forgotten whose glory would not fail
In the tangle of shrubs asleep.
I've always known this. Like a telltale scar.
Until one day I revived as if after seventy years.

And no more may one gently move the sleepers' lips.
The years fill each doorstep with malediction.
On the table a glass of smoking dreams
just a bit longer my poor eyes I'll not
see it.

The poet-speaker holds onto the dream forcefully *(be-kho'aḥ)* and yet maintains that he "mustn't let it touch [his] lips." The taboo seems to derive from an ironic unwillingness to remember, justified by the plaint that he "might still fall ill." In other words, some foreboding is connected with the dream-memory, a foreboding which engenders in the poet a debilitating ambivalence. The first stanza closes with the hortatory biblical phrase "Alas, daughter of Jerusalem," itself an ominous allusion to the ancient heretical rebelliousness of Israel and its tragic destruction.[8]

The second stanza continues the motif of ominousness by alluding successively to several familiar phrases: "the Glory of Israel [shall never lie],"[9] "the thicket of bushes,"[10] "a telltale [or "burn"] scar,"[11] and "after seventy years,"[12] which, in many biblical and rabbinic sources, including the Passover Haggadah, denotes the passing of one's entire lifetime. Taken together, these allusions connote dilemma, sacrifice, divine testing, uncleanness, ostracization, and a feeling of impending death. The foreboding grows stronger with Gilboa's negation of the opening phrase, which he changes to "[I've forgotten] whose glory would not fail." The substitution of "whose glory" for "Israel's glory" *(netsaḥ Yisra'el)* simmers with anger and bitterness toward the Divine, whose "glory," for Gilboa, has been exceedingly tarnished.

The convergence of these allusions and images suggests that Gilboa is referring again to the Holocaust, the tragedy that is often dreamt, that demands simultaneous remembering and forgetting, that reminds us of God's testing, that remains a festering scar in the flesh of humanity. The last line of the stanza supports this interpretation by implying that the poet has succeeded, after nearly an entire lifetime, in bringing a sense of daylight back into his life.

Despite the hopeful thought, the third and final stanza opens with a mournful, desperate tone. "And no more may one gently move [or rouse] the sleepers' lips" *(ledovev siftei yeshenim)*—that is to say, even though the poet-speaker has made a life for himself, it is impossible for him to rouse the dead. All that's left is "each doorstep [filled] with malediction" and before him "on the table a glass of smoking dreams." The closing sentence seems to offer some solace, that before long the horrible dream will disappear. However, this conflicts with the poem's opening line, which has the speaker tenaciously holding onto the dream. The fear, then, is two-fold: that the dream-memory may be lost—and that it may endure. This is the irony of time and forgetfulness. The dilemma is to persevere, to remember, even though the memory itself is an abiding curse.[13]

Be-khoaḥ oḥaz bedal ḥalom was written separately from other works later collected in the main body of *Ratsiti.*[14] Unlike the existential poems in the volume, it refers more particularly to the Holocaust trauma and not to the abstract idea of death. Its motif of writing and memory, however, relates directly to the large group of poems on poetry, which constitutes the volume's central genre.

Existential Poems

Entitled *"Bi-teshuva le-mikhtavkha"* (In Response to Your Letter), the entire first section of *Ratsiti* is devoted to fairly conventional existential subjects: a nihilistic view of the universe, the awareness and fear of death, the impossibility of knowing when it will come, and the consequent weakness and vulnerability of the individual.[15]

To these themes Gilboa adds his own nuances. He describes himself as a clown, a Pagliacci who possesses no outer mirth but only an abiding inner pain. Calling that pain an "ancient fear," he often attributes to the death theme a mythical quality. At times his speaker is the perennial loner of his earlier works, here given the especially gloomy mien of a person confronting the ultimate end. Elsewhere he is a reluctant doomsayer who sees only black but wishes his vision were otherwise. Feeling weak, sick, and naked, one speaker is likened to an old siddur whose margins are completely frayed and whose words fly about, seeking a resting place. The image replicates a talmudic depiction of the Hadrianic persecutions in the second century C.E.: the burning of Rabbi Hanina ben Tradyon enwrapped in a Torah scroll, its Hebrew letters flying up to the heavens. The battered siddur image also parallels the worn Gemara in Bialik's poetry.

One particularly Gilboan theme is the idea of the end of nature—indicating the poet's continued attachment to romantic modes of thought, even in this later existentialist poetry.[16] *She-yoredet ha-ḥashra* (That the Gloom Descends) is a good example.

שֶׁיּוֹרֶדֶת הַחַשְׁרָה וְהַכֹּל מַחְשִׁיךְ בְּאֶמְצַע יוֹם וַאֲנִי אַךְ
דַּקּוֹת מְעָטוֹת לִפְנֵי כֵן חָלַצְתִּי נְעָלַי אֲנִי
חָשׁ יָחֵף לְהִסָּחֵף עִם הַנַּחְשׁוֹלִים שֶׁוַּדַּאי עוֹד
מְעַט יִגְרְפוּ כֹּל וְסוֹף הָעוֹלָם מְנַסֶּה אֲנִי לְהַרְגִּיעַ

עַצְמִי וּלְנַחֵם כְּבָר הָיָה לְעוֹלָמִים וּלְעוֹלָמִים כְּבָר
נִגְרְפוּ עוֹלָמִים וּמִי יוֹדֵעַ מֶה הָיָה מַה שֶׁהָיָה הוּא
שֶׁיִּהְיֶה וְאִם לֹא יִהְיֶה כְּשֶׁלֹּא אֶהְיֶה מַה
מִנִּי יַהֲלֹךְ הַפַּחַד הָעַתִּיק הוּא שֶׁקּוֹשֵׁר לְכָל
הָעוֹלָמִים וְהוּא שֶׁמַּפְרִיד מִכָּל הָעוֹלָמִים
כִּי לְרָעָתִי מוֹתַר הַפַּחַד.

That the gloom descends and all grows dark in midday and I just
a few moments ago took off my shoes I
rush barefoot to be swept away with the waves which surely in a
moment will wash away everything and the end of the world I try to calm
myself and to comfort it's been forever and forever worlds have
been washed away and who knows what was what was is
what will be and if it will not be when I will not be what
of me will go on the ancient fear is what binds to all
the worlds and that is what separates from all the worlds
for to my misfortune fear has dominion.

The opening adverbial prefix *she-* immediately impels the reader into grammatical confusion. It is unclear whether Gilboa means literally to say "that," or whether he is using a shortened but nonlexical version of *ke-she-* (when), which would make more sense. Amid the confusion several dramatic details are fairly transparent. The speaker appears to be walking on the beach on a cloudy day after having removed his shoes. He feels the pull of the waves, and this makes him think of how the world (or time, or life) is being steadily eroded. He comforts himself with the thought that this is how it has always been and how it will always be. He perceives steady movement toward the end as an "ancient fear" which has a powerful hold on human thought and being. The central theme of the poem, then, is the long-standing dominion of existential angst.

Several other aspects of the work, however, demand clarification. At the outset, *ḥashra* (gloom) seems semantically overstated but may be understood as a hyperbolic backdrop accentuating the turgid, doleful nature of the main theme. Toward the end, however, the poem itself, and not just its setting, becomes murky. The power or role of the "ancient fear" is that it "binds to all the worlds and . . . separates from all the worlds" (lines 8–9), but the object of these verbs is ambiguous. One may conclude that it is the individual, the human being throughout history. But the process of binding to and separating from "all the worlds" is more problematic.

A complicating factor in comprehending the wording about "the worlds" lies in the particular phrasing Gilboa uses in two different places in the poem. In line 5 the Hebrew word for "forever" is *[le-]olamim.* The same word is used in line 9 for "the worlds," *[ha-]olamim.* Thus, in the Hebrew, time and experience have an identical delineation. The reference to "the end of the world," *sof ha-olam* (line 4), connects the two other uses of *olam* (world) to the poem's existential theme, and the associative wordplay becomes a recurring motif which unifies the theme. Thus the poetic exposition is dualistic: it is both bifurcated and unified by the repetitive use of *olam/olamim.*

Once the unified existential vision of time and experience is grasped, the reader perceives the poem's central idea: in every generation people have feared death. And since death is our common fate, the existential fear "binds" us all to past generations. At the same time, in every generation each individual must confront the same experience and the same fear. Thus the fear of death both unites us with and "separates" us from the experience of those who have gone before us. "All the worlds" denotes all past lives to which we are existentially and humanly bound and from which we are experientially separate.

These semantic complexities are only the tip of the iceberg. The central difficulty is the predominant (and often complete) lack of punctuation. The result is a stream-of-consciousness flow of words which must be semantically reshaped. In comparison with many other poems in the volume, the task here is not so daunting. After two or three readings of *Ke-she-yoredet ha-ḥashra,* one catches on to the technique and can readily identify at least the basic stops: after "shoes" in line 2; after "worlds" in line 5; after "go on" in line 8.

There are, however, further complications. For example, the phraseology in lines 3–4 does not present a clear sense of ending. Where should the period be placed in the flow of " . . . the waves which surely in a/moment will wash away everything and the end of the world"? Actually it is not so much the end of the sentence which is troubling; it is more the elliptical nature of the phrase "and the end of the world." Since the phrase is appended to an already completed sentence, it seems syntactically detached. The conjunction "and" exacerbates rather than resolves the sense of its being an ungrammatical appendage.

Another syntactic confusion appears in lines 6–7. Here the linguistic ploy is the use of double-talk, a patter of words which is repetitive, ambiguous, and usually syntactically obtuse.

> . . . and who knows what was what was is
> what will be and if it will not be when will I not be what
> do I care . . . [17]

The undefined syntax, lack of punctuation, run-on lines, and various repetitions of "what," "was," "will," "not," and "be" create a kind of stuttering diction, whose sense is initially difficult to understand. With another glance or two, however, most readers can grasp the meaning of these jumbled lines. The poetic ploy, therefore, is not simply obfuscation, but the creation of a verbal situation in which the reader struggles not with metaphors or images, themes, or allusions, but with Gilboa's reproduction of the act of expression itself.[18]

This is Gilboa's radical move into modernistic verse. Though his critics have accused him of aping his younger contemporaries, some concede that he has added much originality and surpassed the others in virtuosity[19] — and that the poems of *Ratsiti* are a logical outgrowth of his stylistic development in the fifties and sixties.

Af lo aḥat meḥaka (Not Even One is Waiting),[20] the opening work in the first section of *Ratsiti*'s existential poems, begins with a sentence whose subject is entirely ambiguous. This is immediately followed by a statement of abject uncertainty which is coupled, in turn, with a dualistic explication by the speaker.

> אַף לֹא אַחַת מְחַכָּה. וּמִי וּמַה שֶּׁמְּחַכֶּה
> לְפִי הֶגְיוֹן נַפְשִׁי מֵאָז כְּבָר נִזְרָה
> בֶּחָלָל נִזְרַע בֶּחָלָל וְלֹא אֲנִי
> אֶקְצֹר וּלְפִי הִגָּיוֹן הַנַּ"ל מֵאָז

אֲבֹרָךְ אִם בְּתוֹךְ אֵלֶּה אֶקָּצֵר גַּם אֲנִי. אֲנִי
עַתָּה אַךְ מְהַתֵּל וּבְכָךְ מַרְוִיחַ
יוֹמִי. כְּדֶרֶךְ הַלֵּצָן. אַךְ שֶׁלֹּא
כָּמֹהוּ לֹא צוֹחֵק מִבַּחוּץ וְרַק כָּמֹהוּ
בּוֹכֶה מִבִּפְנִים. אָמַרְתִּי בּוֹכֶה. לֹא
בְּדִיּוּק. בְּדִיּוּק בּוֹכֶה בְּלִי

Not even one is waiting. And whoever and whatever is waiting
according to my soul's thinking has long since been strewn
in space sown in space and it will not be I who
will reap and according to the above-mentioned logic I will have long since
been blessed if among these I might also be reaped. Now
I'm only joking and that's how I earn
my pay. Like the clown. But unlike
him not crying on the outside and only like him
crying on the inside. I said crying. Not
exactly. Exactly crying without

The subjects "whoever" and "whatever" in the second sentence of line 1 deepen the ambiguity of the subjectless opening statement. The oppositional phrases which follow—"strewn in space" and "sown in space"—engender an even denser illucidity. The speaking voice appears at once befuddled and confused. It is Gilboa's obvious intent to present a complex set of poetic problems to which the reader must seek multiple solutions with every successive piece of the poem.

An interpretation of the opening lines is helpful. As noted above, the first section of *Ratsiti* is entitled *"Bi-teshuva le-mikhtavkha."* Though the method is metatextual, it seems logical to understand the poem's title and its first line as a response to the sectional title. That is, "In response to your letter," says the speaker, I can tell you, that "not even one is waiting." In other words, there is no simple answer to the letter writer's query (presumably about the grim nature of the world). While Gilboa has no clear answer, his thoughts on the matter shape the thematic contents of the work as well as its stylistics.[21]

The speaker offers his own attitudes about the existential dilemma. No matter "whoever" or "whatever" has the answer, it has long ago been "strewn in space sown in space." Of course, there is a great difference between having the ultimate answer to existence "strewn" as opposed to "sown" in the universe. "Strewn" seems chancy, hit-or-miss, even destructive. "Sown" is more deliberate and more promising. Gilboa attaches his exposition to the latter phrase, but only after he syntactically informs the inquirer and the reader that he is keenly uncertain as to whether the answer has been "strewn" and lost or "sown" and possibly available. The ironic juxtaposition of the two phrases conveys unmitigated uncertainty.

When Gilboa resumes the poetic exposition, he proceeds along the lines of word association (lines 3–5). The reference to "reaping" follows the earlier reference to "sown," but the general sense of "it will not be I who will reap" is that the poet will not be privy to the answer to the question. The rest of the thought purports that he would feel blessed were he himself to be "reaped"—that is, considered part of the group of thinkers or poets whose works will constitute the answer that has been "sown." What follows is an ungrammatical phrase: "and according to thinking noted above" *[u-lefi higayon ha-na"l]*. At the very least, the wording here should read "and according to the [or my] thinking above *[u-lefi HA-higayon ha-na"l]."* If not a sign of uncertainty, the ungrammaticality may be a manifestation of a telescopic sort of writing by which the poet abbreviates (as in the case of *ha-na"l,* Hebrew shorthand for "mentioned above") or jots down his thoughts quickly. In this case, the reader might be led—led astray, is more likely—to consider the thought a trifling *pensée.*

While the reader ponders these possibilities, the poem moves on to an intriguing metalingual section. Although Gilboa does not directly discuss the language of his poetry here, he does offer an explanation of sorts for the obscure nature of the first five lines. Whether a response to the entire passage or part of it, the expository flow stops at this point, so that Gilboa may apologize for the lack of clarity.

Of course, the apology—Gilboa says, "I was only joking"—in itself may also be a joke, another instance of ambiguity about his sincerity or confidence. It is also possible that he is explaining his function: by fooling with the reader he is playing the role or game that he, as a poet, is expected to play. This is the way I earn my keep, he says. I play with words. The reader is asked to play along, even though the point or goal may seem unclear. In either case, Gilboa presents here another metalingual comment on his poetic style.

From here he moves on associatively to the clown image, returning to the mode of contiguity he had used up to the point of his digression, the confessed "joke," in line 5. Through line 9 the subject is a Pagliacci-like figure, even sadder than Pagliacci, bereft even of external laughter—either because of his not knowing the answer, or because of not knowing whether he will be part of the "reaping" which might supply the answer. Dramatically and structurally, a tone of hopelessness sets in, and the poet once again interjects a metalingual comment, a pathetic, halting explication of his use of the word "crying" (lines 9–10).

The poem stops with *without,* and the reader must "fill in the blank." Is it without tears? Without hope? Without solace? Whatever the choice of words—Gilboa has already chosen no wording at all—the ending confirms the uncertainty conveyed throughout the poem. One may conclude that there is no answer, that the mystery is impossible to fathom, that no one can be sure of the worthwhileness of life. Having run out of words, Gilboa cannot express how "exactly" terrible his crying might be. The abrupt silence resonates in the reader. The ambiguity of the opening comes full circle. The answer is left unexpressed, but it is deeply felt.

Although his existential thoughts seem to have been tossed onto the page in helter-skelter fashion, what Gilboa does here is to open his mind and heart to the reader through verbal jaggedness and poetic unneatness. The new style is wrought precisely and purposefully to express exactly his "soul's thinking," what he calls *hegyon nafshi* in the second line of the poem. Difficult though it is to comprehend, the new style brings to the surface the poet's inner flow of thoughts and feelings, chaotic though they may be.

It is perhaps useful to perceive the manifest illucidity of these works through the prism of Roman Jakobson's views on aphasia and its effect on language. Aphasia, he suggests, disrupts language usage in two different ways: the aphasiac has difficulty either with selection and substitution or with word combination and contexture. He identifies selection with semantic similarity, hence, metaphor—saying one thing in terms of another, and he identifies contexture with semantic contiguity, hence, metonymy—the expansion of an image (a place or character, say) through synecdochic details. In literature, he notes, "the interaction of these two elements is especially pronounced."[22]

Throughout the *Ratsiti* volume, Gilboa's new style reflects both patterns. For example, in the first five lines of *Af lo aḥat meḥaka* he presents the subject of the elliptical and ambiguous answer—a metaphor for the meaning of life or death—and develops a variety of images that the answer may take ("strewn" or "sown") and how he might relate to the answer ("reap" or "be reaped"). He then breaks away from this set of metaphors and moves on to the "joke" and the clown image. In doing so, he creates a new "semantic contiguity" in the poem and, as Jakobson puts it, thereby "manipulates these two kinds of connections (similarity and contiguity) [and thereby] exhibits his personal style, his verbal predilections and preferences."[23]

Subtle as it is in this poem, the switch from a metaphoric to a metonymic context is in itself emblematic of the vast stylistic change Gilboa demonstrates in this volume. Jakobson suggests that the metaphorical mode was very popular with the romantics, while the realists showed a propensity for metonymic usage. Indeed, we have seen that the great majority of Gilboa's poems through and including *"Shelosha she'arim ḥozrim"* are filled with semantic doubling, used extensively by the romantics for heightening the emotive or other contextual aspects of a work. In *Ratsiti,* however, by both creating and abrogating semantic contiguities, Gilboa signals his fundamental shift from a metaphor-based romanticism to a syntax and structure-based modernism.[24]

Without exception, each poem in the *Ratsiti* collection is "spoken" by the poet's "I." Gilboa seems especially driven to divulge his innermost feelings on existence and recreate the experience of shaping his art. Of course, one cannot be sure that all the personal "facts" in the poetry are factual. Even after the image is identified as Gilboa, the speaker is, after all, a mythopoetic figure whose existence requires creative artifice to be credible. Gilboa is not the garbled, cluttered, disjointed voice of the poems' respective speakers. The poet has created them to represent a mimetic, verbal rendition of his heightened, agitated feelings. But it is this combination of autobiographical authenticity and mythopoetic expressivity which broadens the poems into universal statements and impresses the reader with their forcefulness—especially in the existential works, with their desperate message of unalleviated angst.

Beyond the modernistic style, the language of these poems evinces a blend of romantic resonances, neologisms, and colloquialisms. There are archaic or traditional usages, many of which are allusions to biblical or Age of

Bialik texts: *higayon* for "thought," *tushiya* for "wisdom," *novlot* for "fallen fruit" (or "leaves"), *ḥashra* for "gloom," *nitnapets* for "shattered," *tikhla* for "end," *shalmu* for "were completed," and the familiar Bialikian phrase *u-mi yode'a,* "who knows," a frequently-appearing thematic motif which expresses the fragility of the very idea of knowing.[25]

Alongside the traditional and allusive terms, one finds neologisms such as *azel* for "weak" or "empty" *(Ani mitpalel mi-tokh ha-lev,* [I Pray from the Heart])[26] and the juxtaposition of archaic and modern words such as *tikhla,* "measure" or "end," and *tekhula,* "contents" *(Ve-kha'asher et kol ha-kisim* [When All the Pockets]).[27]

There are poems composed wholly of colloquial language with no archaic usages at all. *Eineni rotse lirot shaḥor aval* (I Don't Want to See Black But),[28] the last work in *Ratsiti*'s first section, is a good example.

אֵינֶנִּי רוֹצֶה לִרְאוֹת שָׁחוֹר אֲבָל
אָפֹר בָּא מִכָּל עֵבֶר וַאֲנִי יוֹדֵעַ מַה
שֶׁאֵינִי רוֹצֶה לָדַעַת וַאֲפִלּוּ כְּבָר לֹא
טוֹמֵן רֹאשִׁי בַּחוֹל כָּאן עָלַי
לְהַפְסִיק אִם אֵינִי רוֹצֶה לֹאמַר אֶת
הַדְּבָרִים הָאֲחֵרִים אֲבָל מַה שֶּׁבּוֹכֶה בִּי
הוּא

I don't want to see black but
grey comes from all sides and I know what
I don't want to know and already I don't even
bury my head in the sand here I must
stop if I don't want to say the
other things but what's crying in me
is

This poem is linguistically uncomplicated and thematically transparent, and its only metaphors are "black" and "grey"—both merely stock symbols of a psychologically negative or semi-negative view of life and the world. The double-talk phrase "And I know what/I don't want to know" conveys the sense of an abiding dread—the existential angst, a theme repeated often via the motifs of "knowing" and "not knowing" throughout the volume. The use of the definite article in "the other things" creates a measure of ambiguity, since it refers to an unstated list of scary or depressing items in the mind of the speaker. Ironically, the elliptical ending is not ambiguous. All the same, in a dually ironic combination with the absent list, the nonending intensifies the emotive nature of the speaker's plaint.

Without the trappings of linguistic layers and esoteric allusions, the poem lays bare the simple outline of Gilboa's new style: a thematic emotiveness, based on ambiguity and ellipsis, set in a stream of consciousness-like structure of run-on verses and ungrammaticalities, "improper" syntax, and the lack of punctuation. Throughout the *Ratsiti* volume, the speaking voice remains disdainful, pained, confessional, full of foreboding. With its varied but overlapping, often interchangeable components, each poem becomes a metonymy for Gilboa's pessimistic perspective.

Poems On Poetry

Occupying nearly one third of its space, poems on the subject of poetry and the poet constitute the largest individual genre in the *Ratsiti* volume. The majority of these works are placed in the volume's second section, which is entitled *"Ha-shura ha-rishona"* (The First Line), although they comprise only half of it (the remainder consisting of poems on nature and existential themes). In editing the collection, Gilboa did not segregate the poems by theme. Thus all of *"Ha-shura ha-rishona"* emerges as a unified conception of the poet's life and art.

As he has often done before—but now with far more intensity and duration—Gilboa attempts to convey to the reader aspects, both emotive and philosophical, of the writing process. He does all this in the same convoluted, disjointed style he uses in the existential poems—further proof of his attempt to unify and not to differentiate between his worldview and his view of poetry.[29]

U-ve-khol zot ze lo kakh (And Even So It's Not Like That)[30] is one of the many works, all untitled, in which Gilboa expresses the feeling of being at the very center of the moment of setting down the poetic word or phrase.

וּבְכָל זֹאת זֶה לֹא כָּךְ כִּי
כָּךְ הָיָה מַעֲשֶׂה וְהַמַּעֲשֶׂה אֵינֶנּוּ כְּלָל
פָּשׁוּט שָׁכַחְתִּי לֹא מַה שֶּׁבִּקַּשְׁתִּי לֹאמַר אֶלָּא
כֵּיצַד לְאָמְרוֹ כְּלוֹמַר כֵּיצַד הָיָה לִי
לֹאמַר כְּפִי שֶׁעָלָה בִּי מִן הַמְּצוּלָה וּמִן
הַמַּעְיָן בְּרֶגַע זֶה נִסְתַּם הָאֶחָד וְהָאֶחָד
נֶעְכַּר לֹא לֹאמַר כְּפִי שֶׁעָלָה בִּי בְּרֶגַע זֶה עַד
אֲשֶׁר דִּמִּיתִי כִּי כָּל זֶה אֵינוֹ אֶלָּא מִשְׂחָק סְתָם
וְאוּלַי כָּל הָאֹשֶׁר שֶׁיָּכוֹל הָאָדָם לְהָכִיל לִבְלִי הָכִיל.

וּבַחֲלֹף הָרֶגַע הַזֶּה בְּלֹא לֹאמַר יָדַעְתִּי שֶׁנִּגְנַבְתִּי.

And even so it's not like that because
this is how it happened and how it happened is not so
simple I've forgotten not what I was seeking to say but
how to say it that is to say how I should have
said it as it rose up in me from the depths and from
the font at that moment the one was stopped up and the other
became murky not to say as it rose up in me at that moment until
I imagined that all this is nothing but simply a game
and perhaps all the happiness that a person can contain
uncontainedly.

And as that moment passed without saying I knew that I'd been
stolen.[31]

The varied repetition of "to say" accentuates the notion of capturing the desired word as it rises into consciousness. But the word escapes as the poet objectifies or distances himself from the experience of "inspiration." The metalingual moment, which Gilboa finds tremendously enjoyable, ironically cuts him off from the experiential flow. And since the moment of poetry turns into a moment of nonpoetry—"without saying," in Gilboa's terms—the poet feels at a loss, robbed by the very experience of poetic production.

More generally, Gilboa is frank in these works about the difficulties and vicissitudes of writing poetry. He wonders why he does it and whether his work will survive and be of any value to the world. He admits to despair as he ponders the first line and the remaining unfilled space on the page. He confronts his bouts of writer's block, lapses into confusion, worries how he will survive the night, admits to an abject, cosmic loneliness, confesses the need to flee the house, to escape the confrontation with art, its workplace and its frustrations. As in previous volumes, he is once again out of control, overwhelmed by visions and images, and longs for self-definition separate from the poetry he creates. He is fearful, vulnerable, agitated, frustrated and, as in *U-vekhol zot ze lo kakh,* deceived.

But Gilboa also alludes to the joy of writing. He sees poetry as discovery. His creative life is filled with overflowing possibilities. Often he is able to set aside the imagistic flow and come back to it later. He deeply cares about perpetuating the tradition of poetry. Ultimately, he notes, he has found himself in poetry—perhaps in this new modernist style, which apparently allows him to be the most creative and expressive he has ever been. In *Kol pa'am ani megale Amerika ḥadasha* (Each Time I Discover a New America),[32] Gilboa wittily and, it seems, happily offers a view of the delights of continual inspiration.

כָּל פַּעַם אֲנִי מְגַלֶּה אֲמֶרִיקָה חֲדָשָׁה
וְנוֹסֵעַ בָּהּ וְרוֹאֶה. וְטוֹב שֶׁאֵינִי תּוֹלֶה
אוֹתָהּ עַל קִיר. לָרֹב. לָרֹב מְאֹד. כִּי לְאַחַר
זְמָן אֲנִי רוֹאֶה אוֹתָהּ שֶׁכְּבָר קַיֶּמֶת. שֶׁכְּבָר
נִתְקַיְּמָה. שֶׁתִּתְקַיֵּם.

אֲבָל מַזָּלִי רָב. גַּם אֶת אֲמֶרִיקָה
שֶׁעֲדַיִן אַף לֹא אֶחָד גִּלָּה וְהִיא
מוֹפִיעָה אֶצְלִי מִפַּעַם לְפַעַם אַחֶרֶת. גַּם
אֲמֶרִיקָה זוֹ. הָרַבּוֹת. אֲמֶרִיקָה
רַבּוֹת. אֵינֶנִּי מְגַלֶּה אַף לְעַצְמִי. לֹא
שׁוֹמְרָהּ אַף לְעַצְמִי. נוֹתֵן לָהּ לָלֶכֶת.

וְעִמָּהּ גַּם אֲנִי.

Each time I discover a new America
and travel in it and see. And it's good that I don't hang
it on a wall. So many. So very many. For after
a time I see it already existing. That it's
come into existence. That it will exist.

But my luck is great. Even the America
that no one has yet discovered and it
appears to me different from one time to another. This
America as well. The many ones. Many
America [sic]. I don't discover [it] even for myself. Don't
save it even for myself. [I] let it go.

And with it I too.

The repetition of "many" *(larov, rav,* and *rabot)* emphasizes a constant flow of newly discovered poetic objects which remain living entities in his mind and not hung on the wall like an inert map. The ungrammatical phrase "many America" *(Amerika rabot)* stresses Gilboa's sense of the endless variety in his visionary repertoire. There are so many poetic objects, in fact, that he feels free to "let go" of some of them. The closing line, which connotes that Gilboa can freely separate himself from the poetic endeavor, is here a positive view of artistic control—a theme often expressed in less sanguine terms in these and many of his earlier poems.

As the above examples demonstrate, an implacable ambivalence shapes the thematic content of these poems. On the one hand discovery, control, the heroic, the beautiful, the flow, and the self; on the other, an overwhelming tide of images, nakedness, aloneness, the abyss, thoughts of escape and death—these also beset Gilboa each night at his writing desk. Dualistic leitmotifs—echoes from his romantic past—fill these works with a host of contrary dimensions: quiet and raucousness, sunrise and night, "for myself" and "not for myself," to know and not to know, the eternal and the fleeting, "within me" and "above me." Above all these motifs hovers Gilboa's ultimate existential quest for meaning and worth in his poetry and in the world.

The ambiguity which is a central motif in these poems is mitigated only by faint appeals—more romantic echoes—to mythical beings and places: "beyond the mountain," "the great eternal forest," "a children's story," the "mother of poetry." Perhaps one of these mythical entities will come to rescue poetry, to perpetuate its survival. Though figurative language has been downplayed in these works, some personification still lingers: the poems' first lines "shock" the poet; other looming lines "stare" at him; visions and images are said to have fathers and mothers; a street is too "clever." Some additional romantic imagery remains as well: falling leaves signify aging; poetry is variously symbolized by fiery waves, a singing river, the great forest, and a "revolving terror," alluding to the "revolving" sword at the entrance to the Garden of Eden after the banishment.

In dramatizing the writing process, many poems portray the poet talking things out to himself as he goes along. The poet *in flagrante delicto,* so to speak, is at the center of each poem and, acting as the speaker throughout, the figure of the poet himself becomes a grand metonymy of the imagination. He is the target of flailing visions; his mind flows endlessly with images; either he has lost control over the flow of poetry or he can set "himself" aside, as it were, and regain control. He describes his self as "a great night of nights"; this is the inner essence of the poet, the grand, symbolic configuration of his inner being. The night spent in writing becomes the poet, and the poet becomes the night. *Ha-shura ha-rishona she-maka ba-rosh* (The First Line that Strikes Your Head)[33] attempts to describe the process.

הַשּׁוּרָה הָרִאשׁוֹנָה שֶׁמַּכָּה בָּרֹאשׁ
וּמְהַמֶּמֶת אֶפְשָׁר לִכְתֹּב בְּכֹחַ
מְהַמֶּמֶת לֹא לִזְכֹּר עוֹד כֹּל וְלָרוּץ
שְׁלוּחַ רֶסֶן פְּרוּעַ שֵׂעָר וּלְבוּשׁ עַל
פְּנֵי כָּל הַשּׁוּרוֹת בֵּין כָּל
הַשּׁוּרוֹת הַצּוֹפוֹת בְּךָ נִדְהָם אִישׁ
שֶׁלֹּא מִן הָאֲנָשִׁים וּלְהַגִּיעַ אֵיכְשֶׁהוּ
שׁוֹבֵר רֶגֶל וּמַפְרֶקֶת עַל פְּנֵי
מַהֲמוּרוֹת מַרְאוֹת חַיִּים שְׁלֵמִים
נִשְׁבָּרִים לִמְכִתּוֹת אֶל סַף שֶׁל
תֹּהוּ בֹּהוּ בְּרֵאשִׁיתִי

וְכָל שֶׁלֹּא אָמוּר אָמוּר בֵּין הַשִּׁיטִין.

The first line that strikes your head
and shocks its possible to write with force
shocks not to remember anything anymore and to run
unbridled unkempt in hair and clothes over
all the lines between all
the lines that stare at you shaken a person
not of people and to arrive somehow
breaking a leg and spine on
pits visions of an entire life
broken into pieces at the threshold of
primeval chaos

And everything that's not said is said between the lines.

Gilboa's view of the act of beginning a poem is graphic. The force of having a first line in hand is so shocking that he feels as if he has forgotten everything. (This is reminiscent of the midrash which has an angel strike the mouth of the infant being born, causing the child to forget the entire body of Jewish learning he has absorbed in the womb.)[34] The *tabula rasa* image prompts the harried poet to lurch forward heedlessly through the rest of the poem. The disjuncted style and lack of punctuation mirror the mindless jaunt. Throughout the process he is in a state of shock *(nidham),* physically broken, haunted by the lines that stare at him, bedeviled by a host of images from his entire life which splinter into a chaotic mess.

Both the opening and closing lines are ironic: the poet is shocked to the core, yet claims he is able to write the opening line "with force." Then again, the "force" he refers to may simply be the strength of the opening line itself, as compared to the emotive, uncontrolled rush of the rest of the poem. The closing line is a wry, metalingual comment on the way this poem—in Gilboa's mind, perhaps every poem—is written. Even though he tries to divulge the inner stratagems involved, his attempt to describe the poetic process is marred. He gropes for phrases, dismantles the syntax, borrows well-worn clichés *(shelu'aḥ resen, peru'a se'ar u-levush,* "unbridled unkempt"), opts for mythological verbiage such as *mahamurot,* ("pits" or "graves," from Psalms 140:11), *mikhtot,* ("shattered pieces," referring to the destruction of the Temple, from Isaiah 40:13), and *tohu bohu bereshiti* ("primeval chaos," from the opening verses of Genesis).

Photographs courtesy of the Genazim Literary Archives, Tel Aviv, unless otherwise noted

Gilboa ca. 1933

Gilboa with unidentified companions on his day of embarkation to Erets Israel, December 1937

With the British Eighth Army
in Malta, 1943

Amir and Gabriela Gilboa, 1952
Photographer: Benno Rothenberg; courtesy of Gabriela Gilboa

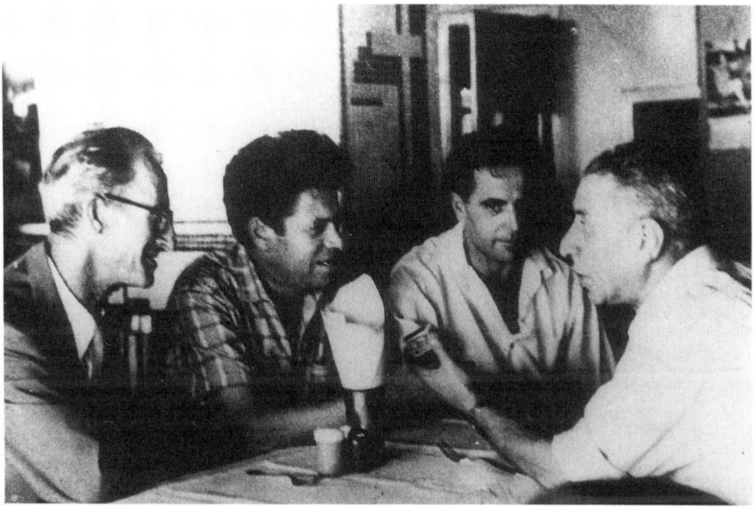

Gilboa at the Café Kasit in Tel Aviv, ca. October 1953, with (*left to right*) Uri Zvi Greenberg, Ḥaim Gouri, and Nathan Alterman

Gilboa in his back yard, 1964

Gilboa with daughters Avital (*left*) and Tagil, 1970

Gilboa in his study, December 19, 1971
Photographer: Boris Carmi; courtesy of Gabriela Gilboa

The poet realizes that these measures do not adequately capture the essence of the experience. Read "between the lines," he advises, for a more palpable feeling of the process. The advice, however, may be doubly ironic. Should the reader not be able to grasp the poet's feelings by absorbing the poem as written, how will it be possible to look further into the implied text? Gilboa seems to be saying: this is it. If, with all the efforts I have made, I cannot impress you with a feeling for the poetic process, then you, dear reader, are on your own.

In *Eikh ani yakhol shuv ve-shuv* (How Can I Again and Again)[35] he tries to delve into the process of the imagination itself, employing the oppositional motif of "remembering" and "forgetting."

אֵיךְ אֲנִי יָכוֹל שׁוּב וְשׁוּב לִשְׁכֹּחַ הַכֹּל כְּדֵי לִזְכֹּר מַה
שֶׁלְּמַעֲשֶׂה לֹא הָיָה וַאֲפִלּוּ הָיָה הָיָה עָלַי לִשְׁכֹּחַ. מַשֶּׁהוּ
לֹא נָכוֹן בָּרֶגַע הַנָּכוֹן מְכַוֵּן כָּל שֶׁהוּא לֹא לְרָצוֹן,
שֶׁל מִי, לְהַעֲלוֹת מַה שֶּׁאֵין לְהַעֲלוֹת וְשֶׁלְּאַחַר כִּכְלוֹת
אֵין בִּי הַכֹּחַ לְשַׁלְּחוֹ כְּבֵן אֲשֶׁר יֻלַּד מֵרֶגַע שֶׁהֻלְהַט
כַּאֲשֶׁר הֻלְהַט וְהָיָה נִשְׁכָּח אִלְמָלֵא

How can I again and again forget everything in order to remember what
in fact never was and even if it was it was incumbent on me to forget. Something
not right at the right moment directs everything that's unwilled,
by whom, bringing up what should not be brought up and which in the end
I have no strength to banish it like a son who was born in a moment that was heated
when it was heated and would have been forgotten if it were not

The poet appears to be concerned about memory overload. Before or even as he writes he feels it necessary to "forget," perhaps to empty out whatever is there—a computer with limited memory function comes to mind—so as to have room for new material. However, since in Gilboa's view the poet's memory is really a depository of fictional images or ideas generally called "imagination," he is puzzled by the very need to empty out the old to make room for the new. This is true, he maintains, even if the material is indeed factual.

Ma she-ḥashavti ḥaser (What I Thought Missing),[36] the volume's closing work, demonstrates most cogently that the "self" of the poet is the main topic and central metonymy of this volume of poetry. In it Gilboa poetically sums up his own view of his new stylistics and divulges the *je ne sais quoi* which he feels was missing in his earlier works.

מַה שֶּׁחָשַׁבְתִּי חָסֵר בְּהֶכְרָח וּבִלְעֲדֵי זֶה לֹא יִתָּכֵן
דּוֹמֶה כְּבָר הָיָה לְאַוַּת חֵן.
שֶׁחָשַׁבְתִּי שִׂפְתֵי יְשֵׁנִים בַּחַיִּים בְּקֶבֶר אֵין שָׁם אֲדוֹבֵב
יָדַעְתִּי אַךְ בְּאֵין קוֹל הַחַיִּים בַּקֶּבֶר אֲדוֹבֵב
וְקוֹלִי לֹא יִשָּׁמַע.
שֶׁחָשַׁבְתִּי הַפְּחָדִים שֶׁלֹּא יְתֹאַר שֶׁאַף בָּרוּחַ עִם הָרוּחַ חָלְפוּ
וְאַף כִּי שָׁלְחוּ מַעְגָּלִים הַמַּעְגָּלִים הֵם מִמֶּנִּי וְאֵלַי
עַל כֵּן בִּי פַּחַד גָּר.
שֶׁחָשַׁבְתִּי אֵימָה כְּמַהְפֶּכֶת תְּלוּיָה, לַהַט הַחֶרֶב מִשַּׁל יְלָדִים,
וּגְזָר שֶׁבֶּעָתִיד טָמוּן
הוּא הֹוֶה נָכוֹן רֶגַע רֶגַע לְהַטּוֹת כָּל נִבְרָא עַל מִשְׁקַל עָבָר
וְיָדִי קְצָרָה.
שֶׁחָשַׁבְתִּי שִׁפְעַת חֲצוֹצְרוֹת הַכֶּסֶף בַּלֵּב וְתוֹרְעִים בִּי אָבוֹת
שׁוּרָה אֲרֻכָּה אֲרֻכָּה
וּמֵעָלַי שָׁמַיִם גְּבוֹהִים וְאֶרֶץ גְּדוֹלָה לְרַגְלַי
לָמָּה יָדִי רוֹעֲדָה מִלְּהַגִּיעַ הַשּׁוֹפָר אֶל שְׂפָתַי.
שֶׁחָשַׁבְתִּי קוֹסְמַי בַּמֶּרְחָק שֶׁעִרְסְלוּ גוּפָם בֵּין בַּדֵּי הָאַלּוֹן
וְאַף רַגְלֵיהֶם רָאִיתִי מִטַּלְטְלוֹת בָּאֲוִיר טֶרֶם הִצְמַחְתִּי בָּעֵט
סִימָן רַגְלֵיהֶם עוֹד מִטַּלְטְלוֹת בָּאֲוִיר.
שֶׁחָשַׁבְתִּי אֲפִלּוּ אֲנִי מֵת עֵינַי רְעֵבוֹת, אוֹמְרִים חוֹמְדוֹת,
נִמְנָע מִלְּהַעֲלוֹת עַל הַדַּעַת יָכוֹל אֲנִי נִלְעָג

אַאֲרִיךְ לְהַבִּיט בְּעִקְּבֵי הַיָּפוֹת.
שֶׁחָשַׁבְתִּי כָּל זֹאת, וְרַב מִזֹּאת, לֹא שְׁקוּלוֹת גַּם טוֹבוֹת, אֶפְשָׁר
פָּסַקְתִּי, לֹא פָּסַקְתִּי, מֵחֲשֹׁב
אַךְ נוֹתֵן לַיָּמִים נוֹתֵן לַלֵּילוֹת לִשְׁטֹף מֵעָלַי
גַּלִּים בַּנָּהָר שֶׁמֵּעוֹלָם לֹא יָדַעְתִּי לִשְׂחוֹת בּוֹ.

מַה שֶּׁחָשַׁבְתִּי אָהַבְתִּי הַנָּהָר הַזֶּה. וַדַּאי לִי אֹהַב עוֹד.

וּמַה שֶּׁחָשַׁבְתִּי חָסֵר בְּהֶכְרָח חָסֵר.
מַשְׁמָע אֲנִי הָסֵר.

What I thought was perforce missing and without which it's impossible
already seems to be but a whimsical desire.
That I thought I'd stir the lips of sleepers in life in a nameless grave
I knew only that voiceless I'd stir the living in the grave
and my voice would not be heard.
That I thought the fears that are indescribable which only in the wind with the wind had passed
and even though they emanated circles the circles are from me
and to me
and so fear dwelt in me.
That I thought terror suspended like a revolving [sword], the sword's flame a children's parable
and a [divine] decree that's hidden in the future
it exists prepared any moment to turn every created thing to the pattern of the past
and I am incapable.
That I thought the plenitude of silver trumpets in my heart and they blare in me patriarchs
in a long long row
and above me were high heavens and a great earth at my feet
why does my hand tremble from putting the shofar to my lips.
That I thought my entrancers in the distance who entwined their body among the limbs of the oak

and I saw only their feet still dangling in the air before I destroyed with
 a pen
any sign of their feet still dangling in the air.
What I thought even if I were dead my eyes are hungry, they say
 lusting,[37]
I avoid bringing [them] to mind I might be scorned
I'd look long at the footsteps of the beautiful [women].
That I thought all this, and much more than this, unconsidered things
also good ones, perhaps
 I stopped, didn't stop, thinking
just letting the days letting the nights flow above me
waves in the river which I never knew how to swim in.

What I thought I loved that river. I'm certain I'll love still.

And what I thought missing [was] perforce missing.
That is: I [was] missing.

This "confessional poetics" poem is a blend of both the existential and the poetic-process genres with added psychological and emotional dimensions. Its quasi-unarticulated style, its long list of unrelated images, and the ungrammatical anaphoric refrains *ma she-ḥashavti* ("what I thought") and *she-ḥashavti* (lit., "that I thought") make the poem quite a challenge.

Gilboa opens with a statement about something missing in his poetry, something without which his poetry cannot exist. This lack, of course, is very serious. Yet in line 2, he notes that the missing component—or his search for it—has become merely a "whimsical desire," *(avat ḥen)* and not a "soulful desideratum" *(avat nefesh,* the usual expression). Thus whatever it is that has been missing is so desirable but so unattainable that he has nearly given up looking for it.

Gilboa then proceeds to list a number of larger poetic subjects and responses with which he has been engaged or about which he has written, negating each one *in seriatim.* The first is the idea of stirring (or moving, *ledovev)* "the lips of sleepers." The phrase is used earlier in the volume in *Be-khoaḥ oḥaz bedal ḥalom* as well as in *Ratsiti likhtov siftei yeshenim,* the work which closes the *"Ha-shura ha-rishona"* section. In the latter Gilboa also describes his frustrated attempt "to write the lips of sleepers." When he finds that "they're all really asleep" and that they will not "hear my heart's awake,"[38] he panics.

רָצִיתִי לִכְתֹּב שִׂפְתֵי יְשֵׁנִים
וְרָאִיתִי בֶּאֱמֶת כֻּלָּם יְשֵׁנִים
וְלֹא יְהִי שׁוֹמֵעַ לִבִּי עֵר
וְנִבְהַלְתִּי מְאֹד
וְרָפוּ יָדַי

I wanted to write the lips of sleepers
and I saw they're really all asleep
and there won't be anyone to hear my heart's awake
and I was terrified
and my hands went limp[39]

The now-familiar "lips of sleepers" line is based on Song of Songs 7:10: *ve-ḥikekh ke-yayin ha-tov . . . dovev siftei yeshenim,* "And the roof of thy mouth is like the best wine [which] gently [moves] the lips of sleepers." Gilboa imbues the phrase with at least three levels of meaning: In a more literal sense, it expresses both his wish to poetically bring back to life his beloved Holocaust dead[40] and his wish to rouse his audience, to make them respond to his poetry. In a metalingual sense (as discussed above, p.224), he wishes to articulate the visionary world of the "dream"—to control and express the conflicting poetic forces that impel and detract him in his search for the right word.

In *Ma she-ḥashavti ḥaser,* Gilboa once again expresses frustration in his attempt to "stir the lips of sleepers," but here he tries to "stir the living in the grave" through voicelessness. The very image of "the living in the grave" and his admission that his "voice would not be heard" preclude any possibility of success. However, much as two negatives make a positive, the syllogism of "voiceless" and the unheard voice connotes that until the *Ratsiti* volume, Gilboa's poetic voice had no power. Becoming "voiceless" *(be-ein kol,* literally, "with no voice"), therefore, may be a more successful alternative. With a new voice, perhaps he can fully express his feelings about the "sleepers in a nameless grave," reach his unresponsive audience, the "sleepers" who are alive, and articulate his elusive poetic self.

The second item in Gilboa's list refers to his fears, many of which have been noted in the broad range of his poetry but particularly in the latter sections of *Keḥulim va-adumim* and in *Ratsiti*: fear of dreams, of forgetting or remembering, of uncontrolled poetic images or the absence of them, of being a social outcast, of the death of nature, of a cosmic sadness in the world, of being unable to continue writing. Although lines 6–7 connote that at times there has been some mitigation of these fears, that "winds" have come along and have carried some of them off, he notes in line 8 that fear constantly dwells inside him. The fears have been intense *(she-lo yeto'ar,* "it's indescribable"), and their "circles" (or ripples) have radiated from Gilboa (have moved "from me and toward me," *mimeni ve-elai)* like echoes which return to the source of the sound. Thus all the poetic expression of these fears has not assuaged them.

The third item combines the fear motif with mythological themes. Though very palpable, here Gilboa states it in mythical terms: It looms overhead like the revolving sword which God, after the banishment, placed at the entrance to Eden "to protect the path to the Tree of Life" (Genesis 3:24). Although he seems to toss off the fiery sword image as "a children's parable" or metaphor, he apparently takes seriously the implication of a divine "decree that's hidden in the future" (line 9) and is ever present. This "decree" (or harsh divine judgment) sounds like the inevitability of death, which threatens at "any moment to turn every created thing to the pattern of the past" (line 10).

Gilboa's use of language is very clever here. He employs the technical language of Hebrew verb conjugations, so that the phrase *lehatot kol nivra al mishkal avar* might read: "[The decree is prepared at any moment] to conjugate every created thing in the pattern of the past tense" *(nivra* is the present form of the passive mode, *nifal).* This dual reading suggests that even though *Ratsiti* contains a large proportion of existential poems, it is not simply the thought of death which looms over the poet. The subtext of switching the present to the past makes reference to Gilboa's poetry, which he is striving to write in the present. Although his goals are to modernize and capture the essence of the ongoing experience, there always seems to be some obstacle, a "decree," an external control, perhaps a curse, which causes him to inject mythological images or archaic language into his poetry. The final phrase here, "and I am incapable" *(yadi ketsara),* implies that he lacks the strength to ward off this "curse"—that he, in midlife, is incapable of completely setting aside these "old-fashioned" usages as he tries to forge a new experimental style. Gilboa's awareness of the lateness of his modernism is obvious in this passage.

The fourth item is mythological as well, but it posits the other side of the coin. Instead of mythical images which induce fear, the poet conjures up images of "the plenitude of silver trumpets [blaring] patriarchs" and the "high heavens [above him] and a great earth at [his] feet." These are ecstatic, triumphant figures, which should have led the poet to great heights of creativity. Yet the opposite is the case: despite the magnificent images of a glorious God, ancestry, and Land, he is blocked, unable to raise the shofar to his lips.

The fifth image is of Gilboa's "entrancers in the distance," a somewhat ambiguous image but probably a reference once again to his family and other Holocaust victims. Gilboa uses the plural possessive form *kosmai,* "my entrancers," the same grammatical form he has previously used to refer to his beloved dead, e.g., "my sleepers" *(yeshenai)* and "my dead" *(metai).* Obsessed with these specters from the past, Gilboa depicts them as those "who entwined their body among the limbs of the oak." The picture that follows replicates a hide-and-seek game, with the speaker seeing the dangling legs of those hiding in the oak's limbs above. The entire scene appears to be an innocent sort of play.

What follows at the end of line 16 and in line 17, however, turns the scene on its head. Gilboa suddenly—and unexpectedly, perhaps, even to the poet himself—"destroys *(hitsmati)* with a pen/any sign of their feet dangling in the air." It becomes clear here that this depiction presents the very opposite of a game, and that the situation that Gilboa has conjured up is redolent with danger, survival, and death. Those who have climbed into the branches are trying to hide, but their legs dangle from the tree and give them away. They are vulnerable victims to those who are seeking—perhaps hunting—them. Once the poet realizes that he has imagined an ignominious, traumatic event—manifestly a group hanging—he quickly blots out the image "with a pen." (The verb *ts-m-t,* used here in the *hifil* form, is usually found in contexts of struggling and overcoming an enemy.)[41]

This interpretation derives some support from the lines (18–22) that follow. The basic idea here—it comes close to a confession—is that Gilboa, as he recaps the main themes of his recent poetry, cannot help but conjure up these kinds of scenes. He seems to "lust" after them, in the sense of being obsessed, throughout his poetry, with the horror of the Holocaust. And in lines 18–19 he seems to say something contrary; namely that he wishes he could "avoid bringing them to mind." He would rather look at beautiful women or let the days and "the nights flow above [him]" in a kind of peaceful reverie, instead of bringing to mind fearsome dreams of legs dangling in the air.

Gilboa's final thought is that he has completely lost his sensibility, that he is emotionally, perhaps aesthetically, "dead." Although he still has "hungry" or "lusting" eyes,[42] for some reason he is "prevented from bringing [anything] to mind," unable to express any feeling. A symbolic voyeurism takes the place of writing. The poet looks longingly at beauty but is scorned.

From this point on Gilboa seeks to express precisely what it was that has been missing from his poetry—and indeed, might have even been the cause of his ten-year sabbatical from writing.[43] As we might expect, Gilboa's pondering of the question is fairly ambiguous and seems to have been an intermittent activity over a long period of time—the image is of days and nights flowing above him. There is also a dimension of nostalgia: the days and nights are depicted as "waves in the river which [he] never knew how to swim in." The image may have originated in the river in which he and his friend swam in their youth.[44] That is to say, the innocence of childhood and the experience of nature are an inherent part of Gilboa's soul and of his poetic sensibility, as are the death of memory, the demise of the things that shaped him as a poet. The river may also be a symbol of Gilboa's romantic imagination, a flow of myriads of images, the way he has written in the past. Though he appears to reflect on feelings of loss and uncertainty here, Gilboa notes affirmatively in line 24 that the beloved river is no sine qua non for his life as a poet. "I'm certain I'll love still," he says, despite his abiding feelings of sorrow and inadequacy. He finds the "missing link"—his "self," at the very end of the poem.

וּמַה שֶּׁחָשַׁבְתִּי חָסֵר בְּהֶכְרֵחַ חָסֵר.
מַשְׁמָע אֲנִי חָסֵר.

And what I thought missing [was] perforce missing.
That is: I [was] missing.

In placing his "self" into his new poetics, Gilboa seems to be referring to his entire effort to capture poetically the actual experience of the creative process. Every work in *Ratsiti* is engaged in that expressive goal: to place himself and the very moment of poetic production at the dramatic center of the poetry in order to create a live recording, so to speak, of the poet at work.

Next to the existential poems and the poems on poetry, the most representative genre in *Ratsiti* is Gilboa's poetic expression of his love for the Land. Of the ten works with that theme, three seem to have been written during the terrifying days of the blockade of Eilat and the Straits of Tiran by Egypt in April and May of 1967. The others, most of which are found in the section entitled *"Likhtov ha-tikva"* (To Write "Hope," the title of Israel's national anthem), apparently were written shortly after the ensuing Six-Day War.[45]

The general idea in the prewar poems is the fear of impending tragedy as well as the imminent death of the messianic vision of the end of all war. In *Oto yom ra'iti* (On That Day I Saw)[46] Gilboa counterposes the loss of the vision and its resurrection. While the vision is blurred and fading from sight, a mythical "fire of happiness" on the mountaintops arises to drive off the dark cloud of threat and fear. In a pragmatic sense, however, these myths are too weak to be effective. As Gilboa puts it, these are legends "which still linger after their listeners were murdered." Real events, he seems to say, will overwhelm the most cherished myths.

Gilboa touches on another universal but doggedly Israeli theme in these mid-1967 works. In *Ani ḥash bahem* (I Sense Them),[47] he says quite plainly that he feels "the streams of destruction" approaching. Imagistically he sees the Medusa-like hair of a "distant head of lust . . . kindling all the tongues of flame of my nights with blood to destroy." In this situation of impending battle he confronts himself.

וְאַף כִּי אֶפְשָׁר וְלֹא כַּצָּרִיךְ שׁוּב לֹא אִכָּוֶה בָּאֵשׁ

And even though it's possible but not essential I'll not be scorched
again by fire

Fifty years old at the time and too old to be called to fight again, Gilboa is certain, nevertheless, that he will be "swallowed up" by the war, consumed by its horror and rage. This ambivalence is a recurring theme in Israeli fiction and poetry, but it was particularly pronounced in the wake of the 1967 conflict.[48] Instead of going to battle, Gilboa pledges an eternal covenant with the Land. In *Ratsiti lehishava kol od* (I Wanted to Vow as Long as [*kol od* are the first two words of the Hatikva anthem]),[49] he envisions himself in the guise of Abraham, walking throughout the Land in all directions and prostrating himself, priest-like, on the ground.

...וְנָפַלְתִּי מְלוֹא
קוֹמָתִי עַל פָּנַי עַל צִלִּי וּמָחַקְתִּי צִלִּי
וּבָאוּ הַמַּיִם וְלִחֲכוּ כַּפּוֹת רַגְלַי וִירֵכַי
וְיָדַעְתִּי בְּרִית עוֹלָם בֵּינִי הֶעָפָר לְבֵין
יְמוֹת עוֹלָם שֶׁבַּיַּמּוֹת מֵעוֹלָם

. . . and I'll fall to my whole
length on my face on my shadow and I'll erase my shadow
and the waters will rise and lick at the souls of my feet and my
thighs
and I'll know there's an eternal covenant between me the dust and
eternity in the waters forever

The epiphanic imagery here is reminiscent of Gilboa's nature poems and fervid Holocaust works. The style is more flowing than in the existential works or the poems on poetry. The articulation is smoother, the tone and mode of expression more romantic, the structure more linear.

Such were the feelings of love and fear Gilboa expressed in the face of expected disaster in 1967, when the specter of the Holocaust was rampant in the Israeli and international Jewish consciousness. The remainder of these Jerusalem and love-of-the-Land poems appear to have been written after the hostilities were over. As did many other writers and poets, when the war turned out to be a triumph and not a disaster, Gilboa responded with poems of praise, thanksgiving, and celebration. Jerusalem is the beloved, the eternal, the locus of existence. "I am in my place, which is my place,"[50]

Gilboa emotes, hearing the mythical echoes of thousands of years. After this miraculous deliverance, the world—and his poetry—seem ripe for becoming whole. Ecstatic, his capacity for vision and language is increased several fold.

...בְּכָל הַמִּלִּים שֶׁיָּדַעְתִּי וְלֹא,
מֵעֵבֶר לְכָל הַשָּׂפוֹת שֶׁרָאִיתִי בַּמַּרְאָה מִשֹּׁרֶשׁ וְעַד רוֹם בְּצִבְעֵי קְשָׁתוֹת
וְעוֹד

. . . with all the words I've known and don't,
beyond all tongues that I've seen in a vision from root to on high with
the colors of rainbows
and more[51]

In a personal epiphany, the "King"—an image of the Godhead itself—appears in Gilboa's imagination, confirming that he has indeed witnessed a divine miracle. He is joined by masses of "dreamers" (or "sleepers"), who number in the tens of thousands. Like Bialik's speaker in *Zohar* who confronts the entrancing splendor of the forest, Gilboa "is opened" to the enthrallment of the experience. In *Yadati ba-ḥalom* (I Knew in the Dream)[52] he waxes still more effusive in declaring that "the dream will not fade like a dream." It will be endless; the resurrection of Jerusalem will become *yom ha-tamid,* the "day of forever."[53]

Gilboa's romantic echoes blend with his new stylistics in these poems of the Six-Day War. In *She-ha-kol kvar halakh* (That All has Already Gone),[54] he again borrows Bialik's description in *Metei midbar* of the "desert dead": "days upon days and times have passed" *(yamim al yamim u-zmanim yinkofu).*[55] The allusion accentuates the fervor of the long-awaited resurrection of Jerusalem. In *Yadati ba-ḥalom* he alludes to the miraculous "midnight" *(ba-ḥatsi ha-layla)* of the Exodus and to Joshua's vistory at Gibeon, where "the sun [stood] still." He also uses the language of the prophet Elisha, who saw in the destruction of Shomron a miraculous sign of God: *He-haya ka-davar ha-ze* (Has there ever been such an event?). Surely this is a miracle.[56]

To these allusions Gilboa adds a continuous flow of puns, conundrums, facile rhymes, and associative language to create a babble of effusiveness.

Line 4 in *Yadati ba-ḥalom* reads: *ve-shemesh omed dom ba-ḥalon ba-ḥalom ke-va-yom ha-hu be-Givon* (and the sun stands still in the window in the dream as that day at Gibeon). The verse plays on the assonance and rhymes of *dom-ba-ḥalom, ba-ḥalon-ba-ḥalom-ke-va-yom,* and *ba-ḥalon-ba-ḥalom-be-Givon.* The opening lines of the poem repeat the word for "dream" or "dreaming" so often that it virtually becomes a mantra.

יָדַעְתִּי בַּחֲלוֹם הַחֲלוֹם לֹא כַחֲלוֹם יָעוּף.
יָדַעְתִּי בַּחֲלוֹם הַחֲלוֹם חוֹלְמִים בִּי רִבּוֹאוֹת.

I knew in *the dream the dream like a dream* will not fade.
I knew in *the dream the dream* tens of thousands *dream* in me.

The closing lines again repeat "dream" three times and end with a flourish of motifs familiar from Gilboa's earliest poems.

יְרוּשָׁלַיִם.
וַאֲנִי רוֹאָהּ אֲנִי רוֹאֶהָ בְּרִבּוֹאוֹת עֵינַיִם.

הֶהָיָה כַּדָּבָר הַזֶּה מֵעוֹלָם
חֲלוֹם נֶחֱלָם בְּאַחַת
בְּעֵינֵי רִבּוֹאוֹת בְּחָלְמָם.

. . . Jerusalem.
And I see her I see her with ten thousand eyes.

Has there ever been such an event
a dream dreamed at once
in the eyes of tens of thousands as they dream.

The cumulative effect of these allusions, repetitions, and semantic and stylistic usages is to engender an epiphany—a visionary experience of a grand historic event which may be likened to mythic victories and to the Exodus itself. This combination of classical and modernistic ingredients may be regarded as the shaping force of Gilboa's eclectic, idiosyncratic new poetics.

Two poems in *Ratsiti* graphically demonstrate Gilboa's efforts to replicate the experience of poetic production. The first, *Ad ha-laila ha-me'uḥar* (Till the Late Night),[57] depicts the poet's time and space for writing and his synergistic relationship with the night. By showing the physical and spiritual symbiosis of the poet with his familiar, secure work place, it presents the framework for the action of the imagination.

עַד הַלַּיְלָה הַמְאֻחָר. עַד סוֹפוֹ. לֹא
לִשְׁכַּב לִישֹׁן. לִשְׁמֹר. שְׁמֹר עַל עַצְמְךָ בְּלַיְלָה
זֶה. שְׁמֹר יַחַד עִמּוֹ. אַל תִּתֵּן לוֹ לִשְׁמֹר
עָלֶיךָ לַעֲטֹף אוֹתְךָ. עֲטֹף אוֹתוֹ. לֹא, חֲטֹף
אוֹתוֹ מִמֶּנּוּ אֶת תּוֹכוֹ. תּוֹכוֹ בְּךָ תִּמְלָא
הָאָרֶץ בָּכֶם אֶחָד. שׁוּב לֹא יִרְדֹּף
אוֹתְךָ תִּרְדֹּף עִמּוֹ. אוֹר בַּלַּיְלָה דָּבָר
יָפֶה. לַיְלָה שֶׁל אוֹר בְּתוֹכְךָ וְאַתָּה
אוֹר בּוֹ. דּוֹמֶה אֵין יָפֶה מִזֶּה
דָּבָר שֶׁלֹּא נִגְמָר שֶׁלֹּא יִגָּמֵר לְעוֹלָם אֵין
לוֹ סוֹף. וְכָכָה טוֹב. וְשׁוּב אֶפְשָׁר
לִשְׁאֹף כַּאֲשֶׁר הַכֹּל כְּבָר בָּרוּר שֶׁאֵין
לְפָנֶיךָ גְּבוּל גָּדוּר. כָּךְ אֶפְשָׁר
לִשְׁאֹף רַק כַּאֲשֶׁר הַכֹּל וַדַּאי
מֵרֹאשׁ. בָּטוּחַ. לִשְׁאֹף בְּלִי כָךְ זֶה
בְּכִי וְלַיְלָה סְבִיבְךָ. וְאֵין מוֹצָא. וְסוֹף.

Till the late night. Till its end. Don't
go to sleep. Be on guard. Guard yourself this
night. Guard together with it. Don't let it guard you
envelop you. Envelop it. No, snatch
it from it its essence. Its essence is in you fill

the earth with you as one. It won't pursue you
again pursue with it. Light at night is a beautiful
thing. A night of light within you and you
are light in it. Nothing it seems is more beautiful than this
an unended thing that will be endless forever without
end. And that's good. And you can breathe [or wish]
again when all is already clear that there's no
fenced border before you. So you can
breathe only when all is certain
from the start. Safe. To breathe without this it's
tears and night is all around you. And no way out. And end.

The poet is bound to the night in an adversarial relationship. He is on guard, lest it envelop him, but instead of guarding against it, he envelops it, grasps its essence, fills the world with himself-as-night. The light of night and the light of the poet are one in an endless unity which will never be torn apart. The synergism of the poet and the night provides the poet with the certainty of an unfenced border, the open-ended power to "breathe," wish, imagine, dream.

The second poem, *U-va-yom, u-va-ḥalomi* (And In Daytime, and In My Dream),[58] portrays the poet in the midst of the poetic experience.

וּבַיּוֹם, וּבַחֲלוֹמִי, כֵּן, וּבַחֲלוֹמִי, כְּמוֹ בַּיָּמִים הַטּוֹבִים וְהָרָעִים
אֲנִי שׁוּב עַל מַיִם רַבִּים, שׁוּב לֹא אֵדַע אִם בֶּאֱמֶת בִּתְחוּשַׁת
עַד אַחֲרוֹן הַנִּימִים וְאִם בְּהֶחְזֵר מַרְאֶה מִמַּה שֶׁקָּרָאתִי פַּעַם בַּסְּפָרִים.
וַאֲנִי רוֹאֶה אֶת הַזְּרָמִים וַעֲדַיִן אֲנִי רוֹגֵעַ אַךְ בְּעוֹד רֶגַע
וַאֲנִי חָרֵד לְמַרְאֵה הַזֶּרֶם הַמַּכֶּה דַּרְכּוֹ אֶל הַבַּיִת שֶׁבְּמוֹרַד הָרְחוֹב
אַךְ עֲדַיִן אֲנִי מְעַט רוֹגֵעַ אַף כִּי כְּבָר מִתְמַלֵּא חֶמְלָה עַצְמִית עַד
אַרְגִּיעָה בָּאָה הָאֵימָה גְּדוֹלָה מִדַּי בִּשְׁבִיל הֶקֵּף רְאִיָּתִי כִּי
הִנֵּה רָאִיתִי הַזֶּרֶם מַכֶּה בַּחֲזָרָה וְשׁוֹטֵף עַז וְנִמְרָץ חֲזָרָה בְּמַעֲלֵה
הָרְחוֹב שׁוֹטֵף וְאוֹכֵל גְּדוֹת עֲפָרוֹ סוֹחֵף עִמּוֹ הָאֲבָנִים וְהַמִּדְרָכוֹת
וְהוֹלֵךְ וּמִתְרַחֵב הַיְשֵׁר אֵלַי לַחְתֹּר מִתַּחַת לְקִירוֹת הַבַּיִת בֵּיתִי וְעוֹד מְעַט
וְיִמּוֹט תַּחְתָּיו וְיִגָּרֵף וַאֲנִי שָׁעוּן אֶל מַעֲקֵה הַבַּיִת וּבַחֲלוֹמִי אֵינִי

יוֹדֵעַ כִּי אֲנִי בַּחֲלוֹמִי כִּי אֵיךְ אֵדַע שֶׁאֲנִי בַּחֲלוֹמִי כַּאֲשֶׁר הַכֹּל כֹּה
מוּחָשׁ וּמְצִיאוּתִי וַחֲלוֹמִי אֵינִי יוֹדֵעַ שֶׁהוּא חֲלוֹמִי אַף אֵינִי יוֹדֵעַ
אִם נִרְגַּעְתִּי וְאִם חָשַׁבְתִּי אַחַר כָּךְ שֶׁהָיִיתִי בַּחֲלוֹמִי

And in daytime, and in my dream, yes, and in my dream, as in the
  good and the bad days
again I'm upon many waters, again I don't know if it's really the
  feeling of
to the very last threads [of thought] or if it's the return of a vision from
what I once read in books.
And I see the flows and still I'm calm but in a moment
I'll tremble at the sight of the flow beating its path to the house at the
  bottom of the street
but still I'm somewhat calm even though I'm already filled with
  self-pity as
I grow calm the terror comes too great for my range of vision for
here I see the flow striking back and flowing strong and bold back to
  the top
of the street surging and devouring the edges of dust sweeping with it
  the stones and sidewalks
ever widening directly toward me tunneling under the walls of the
  house my house and soon
it will topple and be swept away and I'm leaning on the [balcony]
  fence of my house and in my dream I don't
know that I'm in my dream for how can I know that I'm in my dream
  when all is so
tangible and real and my dream I don't know that it's my dream I don't
  even know
if I've calmed down or if I thought afterwards that I was in my dream

Despite its disjointed, stream-of-consciousness style, *U-va-yom, u-va-ḥalomi* is one of the more narrative poems in this collection. After a few musings on past writing days and on the possible sources of images that have come to mind (lines 1–3), the poet launches into a long description of a disconcerting dream. In the closing lines (11–14) he wonders if he was really dreaming—indeed, if it is possible to know if one is dreaming or not. Perhaps he was only daydreaming, musing, or remembering.[59] Thinking about it, he recalls that the "dream" was too true-to-life to be a dream at all.

The poem presents a forceful oppositional structure in the narrative. On the one hand, the dream is vivid and unambiguous. On the other, the opening and closing sections are blurred and fraught with uncertainty. In the dream itself, the vulnerable speaker fluctuates between calm and terror. Ironically, the dream also appears far more concrete and perceptible than the ambivalent speaker, who is not sure he has dreamt at all. Moreover, at the point of highest drama and threat (lines 10–11), he suddenly awakens and speaks theoretically about the whole enterprise of dreaming. Thus the dream is framed by the talk of dreams; the poet as dreamer is enveloped by the poet as denier of the dream; and the concreteness of the dream is denied because of its very concreteness.

Gilboa is depicting a struggle between the speaker's two personae, the poet and the dreamer. The poet, terrified by his dream, casts it aside—denying its existence, ironically, because it seems so real. He is immersed in the reverie which provides his work with its essential tenor of disquietude. At the same time, however, his wakefulness denies the uncontrollable power of his imagination and manifests itself in his poetic tone of rejection. Wanting to be in control, Gilboa portrays himself as the victim of his own penchant for the visionary. In this poem's depiction of the poetic experience, Gilboa offers yet another glimpse of his conflicted conception of himself and his art. The struggle, in sum, is between Gilboa the romantic, who has strived to distill the emotive essences of nature and the cosmos, and Gilboa the belated modernist, who attempts in *Ratsiti likhtov siftei yeshenim* to capture the very moment of poetic creation.

The Romantic Modernist

Ayala eshlaḥ otakh/ Gazelle I Send You, 1972

The last collection Gilboa was to publish in his lifetime, *Ayala eshlaḥ otakh*[1] (henceforth, *Ayala)*, opens with Gilboa's poetic responses to the Six-Day War. Most of the volume, however, reverts to familiar themes—nature, memory, the writing process, and the loneliness of the poet.

There is no joy in the title poem, as the despondent speaker sends off the gazelle, the Song-of-Songs symbol of the beloved, "to the wolves."[2]

אַיָּלָה אֶשְׁלַח אוֹתָךְ אֶל הַזְּאֵבִים לֹא בַּיַּעַר הֵם
גַּם בָּעִיר עַל מִדְרָכוֹת תָּנוּסִי מִפְּנֵיהֶם בְּהוּלַת
עֵינַיִךְ יָפוֹת יְקַנְאוּ בִּי לִרְאוֹתֵךְ אֵיךְ
אַתְּ פּוֹרַחַת נִפְחֶדֶת וְנִשְׁמָתֵךְ

אֲנִי אוֹתָךְ אֶל מוּל פְּנֵי הַחֲזָקָה אֶשְׁלַח
הַמִּלְחָמָה לֹא בִּשְׁבִילִי עוֹד

לִבִּי אַיָּלָה לְמַרְאֵךְ פְּצוּעַת דָּם בַּשַּׁחַר שׁוֹטֶטֶת

gazelle I send you to the wolves not in the wood they're
in the city too on sidewalks run from them the panic
in your lovely eyes they envy me watching how
you leap up in fright and your breath

I send you into the thick of the battle[3]
the war's no more for me

my heart gazelle at the look of you wandering bloodstained in the
dawn[4]

The speaker, aware of the wolves' envy, finds it unbearable to see his beloved in a panic, "wandering bloodstained in the dawn." The message is fairly transparent. The gazelle, of course, is Israel; the wolves are the enemy; the gazelle, sent into battle, is wounded. But beyond the sad message, "Here we go to war again—and death will visit us once more," the poem expresses other themes. The wolves being "not [only] in the wood they're in the city too" bespeaks political protest. The gazelle is threatened not just by the enemy in the field but also by the jingoistic attitudes of politicians and the Israeli populace. Relatedly, the middle stanza points to the aging of Israel's former warriors. Gilboa states it outright: "the war's no more for me"—a common theme in the literature produced after the 1967 war, when the soldiers of 1948 were well into their forties and fifties and did not believe that war was the only course of action.[5]

Much as in *Ratsiti likhtov siftei yeshenim,* Gilboa purposefully incorporates elliptical phrases, ambiguous syntax, enjambments, and a complete lack of punctuation. The ellipses *ve-nishmatekh* (your breath [or soul]) and *libi* (my heart) make the phrases stand out in their ungrammaticality and figuratively connect the gazelle's plight with the speaker's sorrow. The elliptical form of the word *behulat* is similarly suspended but even more complicated. It leaves the reader hanging in unfulfilled expectation of the construct's second half: panicked by? with? at what? As the last word in the verse, *behulat* also creates the impression of an ensuing enjambment, but again the expectation is thwarted. The reader may opt for "panicked" alone, matching it later with *petsu'at dam* (bloodstained; lit., wounded with blood) in the poem's last line.

Alternatively, one may view *behulat* as a true construct, with *einayikh* or *einayikh yafot* as its second half. If so, the phrase might read: "panicked of [or in, or by] your eyes," which is still strongly ungrammatical. *Yafot* further complicates the passage, either by creating an ellipsis ("panicked of your eyes which are lovely") or by turning the reader back to the first possibility, namely, that *behulat* stands by itself as an emphatic, and *einayikh yafot* ("your eyes are beautiful") is an independent phrase in which the speaker soliloquizes as he praises the beloved and mourns her vulnerability.

Another possibility is that the phrase "your eyes are beautiful" constitutes the second half of the *behulat* construct: "panicked by your eyes are lovely." In this reading, it is the very fragility of the gazelle's beauty which causes the animal (and the poet) to be so frightened.[6]

As he has done in *Ratsiti,* Gilboa engages again in purposeful obfuscation — not with the intent to confuse but rather to immerse the reader in the poetic articulation itself. The ellipses scattered throughout the poem — *behulat, ve-nishmatekh, libi . . . le-marekh* — create a network of emotive utterances. The speaker has no trouble expressing himself in cogent, declarative ways. Indeed, the poem is constructed on a framework of "action"-oriented narrative: "I send you," "run from them," "they envy me," "you leap up in fright," "the war's no more for me." By manipulating the syntax and structure, however, Gilboa creates a semantic countertext of impassioned outbursts. The complete lack of punctuation — there is no period even at the end — provides additional irony by creating the illusion of a long uninterrupted flow disrupted only by ungrammaticalities. From a semiotic point of view, the poem projects at once a clash between and a complement to the act of going to war and Gilboa's underlying feelings about the act.

The poems which follow *Ayala eshlaḥ otakh* mirror the feelings of all Jews who in 1967 feared another Holocaust, mourned the dead, celebrated the victory, and exulted in the rebirth of a united Jerusalem.[7]

In *Semoli ki-le'aḥar shevu'a* (My Left Hand's Like After a Vow),[8] the bewildered speaker suddenly feels helpless and old. His left arm is "like after a vow" and "it hurts." He is not sure "if it's where it should be." He seeks his tefillin (phylacteries) as if they might be "the reins of long life." He wants to use the straps to make his arm "outstretched *[netuya]* for me again." The imagery is biblical, and the scene is reminiscent of the closing section of *Yitsḥak,*[9] when the dreamy child wakes from the nightmare of his father's self-sacrifice and finds his "bloodless" arm completely numb. Here, however, the speaker is awakening in the morning and "trying to dream again" — to fall back asleep. He wants his arm to be strong, in order "to bring a dream once again against this heart rebelling to slow down/at dawn."

The poem's structure contrasts sharply with that of *Ayala eshlaḥ otakh.* The effect is similar in both poems — a blurting out of deeply-felt statements by an agitated speaker. Instead of the complete lack of punctuation in the earlier work, however, the first section here is over-punctuated. There are ten periods in the space of six verses, with six periods in the first two lines alone. The result is a multiplicity of short phrases, most of which are elliptical.

The second section is composed of one free-flowing run-on sentence, framed by a shorter one and an elliptical phrase. Attempting to recapture some control over his life, the speaker tries to conjure up or increase the number of his remaining years by counting all the hairs on his arm.

קְרִירָה מַחְוֶרֶת תְּסַמֵּר שְׂעַר זְרוֹעִי. וּמוֹלִיךְ שׁוֹלָל עַצְמִי
בְּכַוָּנָה עֲמֻקָּה אֲנַסֶּה אַחַת לְאַחַת לִמְנוֹת שַׂעֲרָה לְשַׂעֲרָה בָּהֶן
כְּמוֹ תְלוּיִים מִנֶּגֶד חַיַּי הַמְעֻתָּדִים לִי עַד לְבַסּוֹף
אֹבַד צוֹחֵק בְּחֶשְׁבּוֹן חַיִּים שֶׁאֶפְשָׁר יָקוּמוּ לִי בֵּין לַיְלָה
לְיוֹם שׁוּב אֶקְרָא לוֹ שֶׁלִּי. אִם אֲנִי בִּמְקוֹמִי.

Grown pale and cold, the hair on my arm stiffens. And I deceive myself
with deep intent I'll try to count each and every hair, one by one
as if my future life is suspended until at last
I'm lost, laughing at life's reckoning, life that should it rise for me between night
and day I'll call it my own once more. If I'm where I should be.

Numbed by the war, the poet-speaker wishes for the strength to dream on and to live without aging. He knows, however, that this is chimerical. As the closing phrase implies, he is very unsure of where he is in the world—if he is "where [he] should be."

The war-response poems which follow continue to explore mixed feelings, romantic themes (the gazelle, the tefillin reins), and modernistic structural and syntactic usages. *Li kol ha-arets ha-zot* (This Whole Land Belongs to Me)[10] is not a political statement[11] but a paean to Jewish survival, victory over defeat, and the reunification of Jerusalem.

סִיעוֹת סְנוּנִיּוֹת בִּסְעִפֵּי הָעֵץ סוֹרֵג הַחַלּוֹן
וְעַצְמוֹתַי וּבְשָׂרִי בְּרוּחַ סְחַרְחֶרֶת עַל אֶרֶץ רַבָּה
שֶׁכֻּלָּהּ שֶׁלִּי.

flocks of swallows on the tree boughs and the window screen
and my flesh and bones in a dizzying wind upon a mighty land
that is all mine.

The poet, at one with nature, speaks as a visionary, "sleeping and awake" at the same time. Like a prophet, he sees "one long electric flash of a dream" *(ani ro'e ḥalom eḥad arokh ḥashrat ḥashmalim)*, which brings together in a whirlwind the swallow, the tree boughs, the window, and the flesh and bones of the speaker. With its unpunctuated, run-on structure, the short poem itself embodies the whirlwind.

Iri li (My City Mine)[12] captures the poet's palpable feeling of unity with Jerusalem.

עִירִי לִי. שׁוּב לֹא אוּכַל
לָבוֹא בִּשְׁעָרַיִךְ עִירִי
בְּלִי עִירִי לִי עִמִּי בָּךְ.
סָחוּף, וּמְבֻיָּשׁ, אַשְׁפִּיל מַבָּט
אִם אֶעֱשֶׂה צַעַד בָּךְ
וְלוּ אֶחָד עִירִי וְלֹא אֶל עִירִי
לָדַעַת כִּי עִמִּי בָּךְ
עִירִי לִי תְהִי.
כִּי מִמֶּנִּי תִלָּקְחִי עִירִי
בְּאֵין עִירִי לִי עִמִּי בָּךְ, עִירִי
אִם מִמֶּנִּי תִלָּקַח.

My city mine. No more can I
enter your gates my city
without *my city mine*[13] with me in you.
Worn, ashamed, I'll lower my eyes
if I take a step in you,
be it one my city and not toward my city
to know that with me in you
you'd be *my city mine.*

For you'll be taken from me my city
without *my city mine* with me in you, my city
if it were taken from me.

By repeatedly juxtaposing the title phrase "my city mine" with confusing prepositional and possessive references to both the city and the speaker, Gilboa creates an affective double-talk. Combining the double-talk with untrammeled syntax, the poem becomes a graphic representation of physical intertwinement.[14]

Two poems in the group deal specifically with the war's many casualties. *Le-eini gilu sofam* (To My Eye They Revealed Their End)[15] conveys a haunting vision of the dead, who appear in the poet's imagination both as a fading, speechless eye pupil *(bava)* and as a tangible looming whiteness that ironically effaces any source of light.

וּכְבָבָתָם גַּם שֶׁלִּי
רָחֲקָה רָחֲקָה שׁוֹתֶקֶת
וּבְחֶדְרִי נִשְׂתָּרְעָה לְבָנָה
לְאֵין קֵץ אַדְמַת חַצְרוֹתָם
בִּדְמָמָה מְיָרְאָה מִתְקָרֶשֶׁת
עַד בְּלִי יָרֵחַ

and like their eye [pupil] mine too
growing distant distant silent
and in my room spread white
without end the earth of their graveyard
in a frightening gelid silence
unto the absence of moon

A blend of various elements creates an effective Edgar Allen Poe-like illusion of the presence of death: the eerie, quasi-Gothic scene; the short, unpunctuated, *piyut*-like lines; the confusing syntax (lines 7–8); the double entendre at the end of line 7 (*levana* may be either "white" or "moon"); and an abundance of internal and end rhymes throughout the poem.

In *Kulam yakumu* (They'll All Get Up),[16] the poet poignantly envisions a dream-like scene of resurrection. "They'll all get up. I know I see them/getting up turning homeward each one,"[17] says the visionary speaker. A fantasized family reunion is described in flowing, unpunctuated lines.

כְּבָר צוֹחֲקָה הָאִשָּׁה מִבַּעַד לַדְּמָעוֹת וִילָדָיו
מְחַכְּכִים לֶחָיָם בְּלֶחְיוֹ וּמְסַפְּרִים סִפּוּרָם
שֶׁצִּפָּה לְשָׁמְעוֹ בַּשֵּׁנִית לְאַחַר שֶׁסּוֹדַד עַל אָזְנוֹ
בְּפִיּוֹת שָׁרְשֵׁי הַצְּמָחִים

the woman's already laughing through her tears and his children are
rubbing cheeks with him and telling him their tale
which he expected to hear once more after it was whispered in his ear
by the mouths of gaping roots[18]

But reality replaces fantasy in the poem's anticlimactic ending. In their graves, the soldiers listen to their families' voices only through the undergrowth.

In nearly all of these postwar poems, sadness and mournfulness coexist with wonderment and exultation, an enthralled dream-like mood with blatant inarticulation. The quasi-expressionistic usages reflect both a passionate poetic response and a genuinely harmonious synthesis of romantic and modernistic styles.

At this point, Gilboa seems again to have taken stock of himself and of his poetry. Returning to existential themes, he ponders the ways of the world and his relationship to it. The last work in the war series (and segregated in its own section entitled *"Eḥad"* [One]), *Ve-im halakhti me'az* (And If I Walked Since Then)[19] depicts the poet "still standing there"—that is, still contemplating the trauma of the 1967 war and seeing himself as one of the "innocents . . . who asked no questions."

וּבְיָמִים שֶׁל שֶׁמֶשׁ הָלְכוּ כְּסוּמִים בַּחֲשֵׁכָה
וְעָבְדוּ הָאֱלֹהִים בְּאַהֲבָה וּבְיִרְאָה
וַאֲנִי עֲדַיִן עוֹמֵד שָׁמָּה

And in the sunny days they walked like the blind in the dark
and worshiped God with love and awe
And I'm still standing there

Although there is no specific reference in the poem, the setting appears to be the Western Wall, where Gilboa had been before but now "still stands," trying to understand "the ways of Providence." His puzzlement about war and peace, self and others, life and death reappears in the works that follow.

In *Ke-she-ani le-atsmi eineni yode'a* (When I Am By [or For] Myself I Don't Know),[20] Gilboa expresses his uncertainty fairly directly. He feels as if he is "cast upon the many [i.e., troubled] waters"—a recurrent phrase throughout his poetry. Although there are many paths to follow, he has no idea which he has taken or whether he has even departed. Should anyone be looking for him, "he will not know [whether] to search among the living or among the dead." He calls himself "an exceedingly wealthy man" *(ashir mu-flag)*—but his wealth is measured only by his innumerable paths to being lost. In philosophical and emotional limbo, he feels "dead," overwhelmed, bewildered. The dilemma is presented with a plethora of negatives: "don't know," "not to be confused," "not because of that," "won't know." In a structural ploy, the phrases beginning with "but" and "perhaps" repeatedly qualify each proposal of action to the point of inertia.

Beyond the main themes of ambivalence, helplessness, and puzzlement, the poems in this section also voice protest and moral reproof. *Ze ka-nire yavo ke-ḥetef* (I Guess It Will Come Suddenly)[21] is a harsh admonition expressed through the idea of memory or its opposite, oblivion. The "it" of the opening line, which the speaker notes "will come suddenly," refers to an eventual recognition of the negative and even tragic side of 1967 events. Using the grim phrase *ketev meriri* (bitter destruction or plague, Deuteronomy 32:24), he notes that it all turned out well this time—but next time the outcome could be the opposite.[22] If only, says the speaker, there would be "one rememberer" *(eḥad zokher)*, one who could recall the "midday terrors," one who would tell the other side of the "shining" story of these times.

The speaker, of course, is the *eḥad zokher*. (The phrase is unambiguously reminiscent of Gilboa's fervent Holocaust works.) The rememberer must counter the "story retold later," the anecdotes of victory and achievement that omit a full recounting of the war. At the same time, the "real" story may be retold often, but it is powerless, blown away by the wind. Indeed, the speaker is completely unclear about which account will prevail. At the poem's close even his version is a jumble of rambling, disjointed phrases.

יִהְיֶה סִפּוּרְךָ־לְאַחַר
יָפֶה כְּפִי רְצוֹנְךָ אֵי תָמִיד. כַּאֲשֶׁר כָּל תַּחֲנָה אַךְ
שֶׁלֶט הָיָה וְשֵׁם בָּדוּי, שֶׁעַכְשָׁיו, אַךְ עַכְשָׁיו יִהְיֶה לוֹ
קִיּוּם יִהְיֶה לוֹ כִּסּוּי כַּאֲשֶׁר הַכֹּל כְּבָר גָּלוּי לְכָל
עַיִן וְלִרְאוֹת אֵין דָּבָר עוֹד
אֶחָד מַה יִזְכֹּר

Your story retold later will be
all right, just as you always wanted. When each stop [at a station]
was only a sign, a phony name, which now, even now, will still
exist, will have a cover when everything's perfectly visible
but there's nothing more to see,
one person, what will he remember

The tone is one of despair. Certainly the story will prevail—the wrong story, most likely, the story with a "phony name." Even when the whole truth becomes visible, it surely will not be absorbed. The Six-Day War will be recalled only as a grand heroic victory, and its realities will evoke a raging, barely articulate response from those who are sensitive to more than the outer dimensions of events.

The ambiguous work *Laruts merḥak laila* (To Run a Night's Distance)[23] may be a comment on the war and/or an existential statement about a night of writing.

לָרוּץ מֶרְחַק לַיְלָה, מֶרחַקִּים בַּלַּיְלָה, אֵין קַל מִלַּעֲבֹר מֶרְחַקִּים
בַּלַּיְלָה אֵין קַל מִזֶּה, שֶׁאֵין כָּל מַחְסוֹם נִרְאֶה לְפָנֶיךָ בַּלַּיְלָה,
שֶׁכָּל אֲשֶׁר לְפָנֶיךָ מֵאֲחוֹרֶיךָ כַּר דָּחוּס
לֹא מַעֲלוֹת לֹא מוֹרָדוֹת בַּלַּיְלָה סַכִּין חוֹתֵךְ

הַמַּאֲפֵלָה כַּדּוּר פּוֹלֵחַ הָעֵץ הָעִוֵּר חֲפַרְפֶּרֶת
בְּלֵב הֲוָיָה שְׁחוֹרָה חוֹתֶרֶת לִקְרֹעַ
מָסָךְ שֶׁעָבְיוֹ עַל אַף הַכֹּל אֶל
גְּבוּל אוֹר יוֹם נִמְשָׁךְ
וַאֲפִלּוּ לֹא יִגָּלֶה לְעֵינֵי מִי
עוֹלָמוֹ חָשַׁךְ עָלָיו.

To run a night's distance, distances by night, nothing's easier than
traveling distances
by night nothing's easier, for no obstacle appears before you at night,
for whatever's before you is behind you a dense meadow
no ups no downs at night a knife cuts
the murk a bullet pierces the blind tree a mole
at the heart of black being burrows to tear
a screen whose thickness despite everything
extends to the edge of daylight
and won't be revealed to the eyes of one
whose world has gone dark.[24]

The poem opens as an axiomatic ode to running at night. Because of the absence of obstacles, because in the dark everything looks the same in front as well as behind, because there are "no ups [and] no downs," says the speaker, "nothing's easier than traveling distances/by night." Further along in the poem, however, deterring images appear: a knife which "cuts the murk"; a bullet which "slices the blind tree"; a mole which "at the heart of black being burrows to tear/a screen whose thickness . . . extends to the edge of daylight."[25] The experience becomes two-sided: night gives the runner a feeling of access and boundlessness, but it is also fearsome and unrevealing in its opacity.

The last two lines in particular create a sense of ambiguity. Although the screen's thickness "despite everything" seems to be making its way "to the edge of daylight," the speaker still maintains that "it won't be revealed to the eyes of one/whose world has gone dark." Though they have embraced the night and survived its threats, the sorrowful find neither revelation nor comfort in the light.

Are the night-runners heroic soldiers who brashly move through unchallenged areas and survive the hazards of war? Are the sorrowful those whose sons have died, those whose lives have been darkened despite the return of the light of day? Or is this a work about the poet himself—one who begins the long night without obstacles but who soon encounters deadly hazards, the greatest of them an existential "black being" which even at daybreak leaves him bereft of light?

In the context of earlier poems such as *Ke-she-ani le-atsmi eineni yode'a*, *Bein ze la-ze* and *Ze ka-nire yavo ke-ḥetef*, all of these interpretations are possible. The existential persona questions the value of poetry in a world which continually bears the dark news of conflict and death. And the dual dilemmas of consciousness and conscience reflect subtle political protest and moral objection.[26]

After these poetic responses to the war, Gilboa reverts to the mixed repertoire of his previous collections: existential poems, poems on the imagination and the poetic process, nature poems, and a few poems of whimsy, social criticism, and love. At the same time, his style remains as ungrammatical, rhythmically varied, disjunctive, and ambiguous as it was in the *Ratsiti* volume.

In *Litlosh kokhavim* (Plucking Stars)[27] he borrows star images from earlier nature poems[28] and creates an idyllic moment of nocturnal quietude.

לִתְלֹשׁ כּוֹכָבִים, פְּטָלִים מְשִׂיחַ בַּלַּיְלָה
מִתּוֹךְ הָאֲפֵלָה, הַקְּטִיפָה, זְמַן הַיָּחִיד
נוֹשֵׂם נֹעַם, עוֹטֵף חֲמִימוּת בְּתוֹךְ
בְּדִידוּת רַחוּמָה, שְׂכוּחַת הֲמֻלּוֹת,
דְּבוּבַת שֶׁקֶט, הוֹרָה סוֹד מִתְהַוֶּה,
וּלְהַלֵּךְ הָלְאָה כְּעַל כַּפּוֹת הֶחָתוּל
יוֹדֵעַ רְוָחָה אַלְמוֹתִית שֶׁגּוֹנֵב מְנָת חַיִּים
לֹא נֶחְלֶקֶת, מְנַת בַּרְזֶל אֱלֹהִית
שֶׁבֵּין יֵשׁ וְיֵשׁ, שֶׁבֵּין אַיִן וְאַיִן,
וְלִשְׁכַּב מִתְכַּרְבֵּל עַל הָאָרֶץ, מֵרִיחַ עָפָר,

קְרוּם הַלֶּחֶם הַטּוֹב, גָּדֵל וְגָדֵל
עֻבָּר בְּחֵיק רַחֲמִים גְּדוֹלִים.

Plucking stars, berries from a bush at night
out of the dark, the plucking, private time
breathing bliss, enveloping warmth within
merciful solitude, oblivious to tumult,
resonant with silence, pregnant with a growing secret
and walking on as on cat's paws
knowing an eternal calm that purloins a slice
of life, a divine K ration between
being and being, between nothing and nothing,
and to lie curling up on the ground, smelling the earth,
a crust of good bread, a fetus steadily growing
in the bosom of great mercies.

Heaven and earth intersect here to create a sense of "in-between"—a romantic interlude of a unified universe filled with secret solitariness and the sense of new beginnings. Beyond these oft-used motifs,[29] the poem projects a dual thematics: stars and berries, momentariness and "eternal calm," something and nothing, a "divine portion" and a good crust of bread. The duality is fortified by the syntax—brief, sequential phrases and continuous pauses—and by the simultaneous flow of thoughts which build in intensity until the closing, fetus-like image.

Ḥelkat yam (A Stretch of Sea)[30] expresses a similar sense of enthrallment but ends with a less joyous message.

חֶלְקַת יָם, בְּשָׂרָהּ לִשְׂחוֹת בָּהּ
בַּשַּׁיִשׁ, בַּבַּהַט, שֶׁיֵּחַם וּלְסוֹפוֹ יִמַּס,
גַּם הָעֵינַיִם, תְּחִלָּה תַכְחֵלְנָה, שׁוּב תֵּעוֹרְנָה
אֶל חֶלְקַת יָם, לְדַמּוֹת כְּחוֹל לִכְחוֹל
בְּתֵבַת יָם, סוֹדוֹת יָמִים רְחוֹקִים
שֶׁתָּפֵז שֶׁמֶשׁ, קַרְנַיִם אַחֲרוֹנוֹת מִגְּנִיזַת צַעַר,
יֹפִי שָׁמוּר לְעֵינַיִם שֶׁכְּבָר אֵינָן
רוֹאוֹת אֶלָּא לְמַעֲרָב

A stretch of sea, its flesh, to swim in it
in its marble, its alabaster, which grows warm and eventually melts
the eyes as well, at first they turn blue, awake again
to the stretch of sea, to liken blue to blue
in the sea-chest, secrets of distant days
that the sun turns to gold, last rays of sorrow's treasure,
beauty saved for eyes which now look only
toward the west

Beyond nature's enduring mystique, the "last rays" of sun bring to Gilboa's mind a sense of finality. At the very moment of enthrallment — the eye motif punctuates the poet's sensitivity — the poet acknowledges feelings of mortality (he was in his mid to late fifties when *Ayala* was published in 1972). The sea holds in its mythical treasure chest the "secrets of distant days" — Gilboa's sorrowful memories. Again the joy of immersion in nature, here in the very "flesh" of the sea — a sexual image, rare in Gilboa's works[31] — is mitigated by the poet's abiding mournfulness.

Gilboa uses the central motifs of being "between" and being "distant" in more than one fourth of the volume's works. Because of the Holocaust, his "secret [which] comes from afar,"[32] he is *bein ha-zemanim,* "between the times," living simultaneously in the past and the present. The motifs also delineate figuratively the deaths of soldiers in the Six-Day War or express the artistic dilemma of being between poems — or between periods of creativity and blockage. In the main, however, they reflect a general existential angst. In *Raḥok raḥok baḥuts* (So Far Off Outside),[33] nature beckons romantically, but the poet feels an accompanying sense of unease and threat that causes him to bring the poem to a prayerful, open end.

In *Zemanim mitorerim bi* (Times Stir in Me),[34] he lives in a state of undefined chaos.

זְמַנִּים מִתְעוֹרְרִים בִּי לֹא לְפִי לוּחַ הַזְּמַנִּים, בִּמְעֻרְבָּב,
מִישֶׁהוּ לוֹבֵשׁ בִּי וּפוֹשֵׁט בִּי לְבוּשַׁי, הַאִם, בְּלִי נִשְׁאָל אֲנִי,
הַתְּשׁוּבָה תָּמִיד בְּפִיו
לְבוּשֶׁיךָ אֵלֶּה לְבוּשֶׁיךָ אֵלֶּה

שֶׁלְּךָ כֻּלָּהֶם
נוֹלַדְתָּ בְּלִי הֶרֶף נוֹלָד

גַּם בְּבֹקֶר כְּגוֹן זֶה שֶׁלְּךָ אָפֹר

Times stir in me uncalendrically, chaotically,
someone in me dresses and undresses, is, without my being asked,
the answer is always in his mouth
these clothes of yours these clothes of yours
all yours they are
you were born unceasingly are born

Even on a morning like this yours is gray[35]

The speaker mechanically goes through the motions of his daily routine devoid of feeling or connection with his surroundings—even devoid of the structure of time. His repeated identification with the image of clothing accentuates his lack of self-motivation, and the two closing lines describe even his origin and development as undefined and unshaped. The last line qualifies the notion of new life with the ironic idea that every birth each morning is dark and unpropitious.

Ve-kha'asher ani al ha-mayim ha-rabim (And When I Am Upon the Many Waters),[36] adds a dream-like, mythological aura[37] to the existential theme.

וְכַאֲשֶׁר אֲנִי עַל הַמַּיִם הָרַבִּים
כְּמוֹ פָּתַחְתִּי, וְאוּלַי נִפְתְּחוּ, הַסְּכָרִים וְנִגְּרוּ הַמַּיִם
וְאָזְלוּ הַמַּיִם וְעֹרְתָה אֶרֶץ טִין מְקֹעֶרֶת שֶׁל רִיק,
עֶרֶשׂ רִיק, לְאֵין שָׁעֵר וּלְאֵין הָכִיל כָּל הַקַּדְמוּת הַהִיּוּלִית הַזֹּאת
שֶׁאֱלֹהִים בִּלְבַדּוֹ מֵטִיל בָּהּ אֶת צִלּוֹ
וְקֹר עַז
וּפִתְאֹם כְּלָבִים מְרַדְּפִים כְּלָבִים

וְחַיִּים נוֹבְחִים
בְּעֶרֶשׂ רִיק אֲנִי חוֹלֵם

And when I am upon the many waters
as if I had opened the dams, or perhaps they were opened, and the
  waters poured out
and the waters drained and the earth, concave, was mixed with
  empty silt,
a cradle of emptiness, measureless, unable to contain the primal
  antiquity
upon which God alone casts his shadow
and a mighty cold
and suddenly dogs chasing dogs

and alive they bark[38]
in a cradle of emptiness I dream

Gilboa has often used "on many waters" *(al mayim rabim)* to denote, as in numerous Psalms, the troubles and burdens of life. Here, however, the addition of the definite article sharpens the expression of frustration. The abstract "waters" become concrete, and once they mix with silt they can no longer contain God's "primal antiquity" (a euphemism, perhaps, for divine holiness).[39] Any possibility of renewal is lost in this diluvial description. The "cradle," the concave crux of creation, becomes a "cradle of emptiness" *(eres rik).* In a Lurianic-like cosmological scene, cold winds and siccing dogs fill the void, and life seems to Gilboa a long, nightmarish howl.

Parallel to this cosmogony gone awry, the ghostly dream of Holocaust dead haunts him[40] with irrepressible force in *Zeman hakima min ha-mavet* (The Time of Rising from the Dead).[41]

זְמַן הַקִּימָה מִן הַמָּוֶת מִן הַחֲלוֹם
אֶל מֵחוּשׁ מֵצִיק, תּוֹקְפָנִי, מְדַכֵּא
אַךְ עוֹבֵר בְּסוֹפוֹ שֶׁל דָּבָר כְּדֵי לַחֲזֹר
וְלִפְקֹד, כְּעוֹנוֹת הַשָּׁנָה, כְּעוֹנוֹת הַשָּׁנָה
צָפוּי, וּכְאֶצְבַּע מְאַיֶּמֶת תָּלוּי לְעֵינַיִם בְּבֵין הַזְּמַנִּים,
בַּהֲפוּגוֹת, לֹא נִשְׁכָּח. אַךְ זְמַן הַקִּימָה מִן הַמָּוֶת
מִן הַחֲלוֹם כְּמוֹ שׁוֹכֵחַ כֹּל אַךְ לִרְגָעִים מְעַטִּים
כַּאֲשֶׁר לְפִתְאֹם, כַּאֲשֶׁר רוֹחֵץ פָּנִים, וְגוּף, גַּם כְּמוֹ מִטַּהֶרֶת

הַנֶּפֶשׁ, לְפִתְאֹם זוֹכֵר פָּנִים מֻכָּרִים, זָרִים לְךָ
אַךְ מֻכָּרִים לְעֵינֶיךָ, מִמֶּרְחָק, שֶׁלְּעֵינֶיךָ בַּחֲלוֹם
שָׁתְתוּ דָם מִפְּצָעִים כְּבָר מֵתִים, בּוֹסְסוּ בִּסְחִי הַמָּק
וְחִוְרוֹן בְּשָׂרָם הִדְהָה אֶת הֶעָפָר

The time of rising from the dead from a dream
to a troubling, assaulting, depressing pain,
but it passes finally only to return
and recur like the seasons, like the seasons
expectant, and like a threatening finger it looms in the eyes in
in-between times,
intermittently, unforgotten. But the time of rising from the dead
from a dream as if forgetting everything only for a few moments
when suddenly, when I wash my face, and body, it's also like cleansing
my soul, suddenly I remember familiar faces, strange to you
but familiar to your eyes, from a distance, which to your eyes in a
dream
they bled from wounds already dead, trampled in rotting decay
and the pallor of their flesh darkened the earth

When the speaker awakens (he calls it rising "from the dead," literally, "from death," *min ha-mavet)*, he tells how his pain soon dissipates but does not disappear. It becomes a cyclical phenomenon, "like the seasons." In the next sequence (lines 5–6), however, the pain is more than seasonal: it becomes a "threatening finger" which is felt first "in in-between times," then comes "intermittently," and finally is "unforgotten." Paralleling the pain, the poem's structure is one of growing intensity, accentuated by the placing of the only full stop after "unforgotten."

When the speaker begins to repeat the recitation of his feelings (lines 6–7), he claims to have forgotten his dream. Suddenly, however, everyday acts—washing his face or his body—jog his memory, and in lines 9–12 he graphically reexperiences its horrid images. The structure is circular: the poem moves linearly toward the images, but they in turn lead the reader back into the dream from which he wakes. In this way, the death dream is continuously replayed and recalled, reinforcing Gilboa's notion that forgetting is fragile and passing, and only remembering is permanent.

For Gilboa, poetry is a fickle mistress. In *Et she-ahava nafshi* (What My Soul Desired)[42] he depicts it as a lover constantly sought by the poet-paramour. Despite his best efforts, he languishes "each night upon my bed," held fast in poetry's thrall. In *Im od yavo'u li tsohorayim ele* (Should This Noontime Again Come to Me),[43] however, poetry is soulfully gratifying. He tells of one particular afternoon as "a flow of song in an hour of grace, a flow whose process is imperceptible." More often, though, he experiences emptiness, frustration, and defeat. In *Pitom be-kho'aḥ ba ḥoser ha-ko'aḥ* (Suddenly With Strength Comes the Lack of Strength),[44] poetry is "like the first rains" which then bring the drought. A frightful feeling, a kind of abandonment, "it comes,/doesn't come, nothing comes not [sic], there is/nothing."

Gilboa often addresses the problem of writer's block, but never more poignantly than in *Mahu she-ani shokhe'aḥ, ha-milim* (What Is It I Forget, the Words).[45]

מַהוּ שֶׁאֲנִי שׁוֹכֵחַ, הַמִּלִּים, עֶצֶם טִבְעָן?
אִם טִבְעָן הוּא שֶׁרָחַק מֶנִּי וְנִזַּר, וְלֹא שֶׁלִּי עוֹד?
אֵי בֵּיתִי עַכְשָׁיו עוֹמֵד, וְאִם לַהֲקִימוֹ
מַה הֶחֳמָרִים נֶאֶסְפוּ לִי, וְהֵיכָן.
אֵחַרְתִּי קוּם, אֵיזֶה קוֹרִים הָיוּ לֹא הָיוּ
סִבְּכוּנִי בַּחֲלוֹם, הֲמֵעַצְלוּת מְתוּקָה
לֹא אָבִיתִי עַצְמִי מֵהֶם לְהַתִּיר?
לֹא, כָּל הֶחֳמָרִים, לְשֶׁם שְׁבוֹ וְאַחְלָמָה,
הִתְחַנְּנוּ לְיָדִי כִּי אֲשִׂימֵם בַּמַּסָּד וּבַטְּפָחוֹת,
וּכְבָר כֶּתֶר נוֹצֵץ בִּטְוַח הַיָּד לְהַנִּיחוֹ
בְּרֹאשׁ הַגָּג, בִּנְיָן לְתִפְאֶרֶת, וְזֶה
חִשּׁוּב לֹא נָכוֹן שֶׁל זִיעַ פָּעוּט
מוֹטֵט הַכֹּל וּמְצָאַנִי עֵר
שָׂרוּעַ בֵּין חֳרָבוֹת.
מַהוּ שֶׁשָּׁכַחְתִּי, קִסְמָן שֶׁל מִלִּים, עֶצֶם טִבְעָן
לַהֲרֹס וַאֲנִי, הֲלֹא, אַךְ בַּחֲלוֹם עָמַדְתִּי,
לֹא עָמַדְתִּי, לִבְנוֹת.

What is it I forget, the words, their very nature?
Is their nature such that it has parted from me, is it no longer mine?
Where does my house now stand, and if I would raise it
what materials were assembled for me, and where.
I've risen late, there were some cobwebs, some were not
they entangled me in a dream, is it out of sweet languor
that I had no desire to cut myself free?
No, all the materials, amethyst, agate and topaz,
begged me to set them in the rafters and the floor,
and already a crown sparkled within reach to set it
in the rooftop, a wondrous structure, a
faulty calculation of a slight tremor that
brought it all down and found me awake
scattered among the ruins.
What is it that I've forgotten, the magic of words, their very nature
to destroy and I, it seems, only stood in a dream,
I did not stand, to build.

The poem posits several possible explanations for his poetic failures. Perhaps they were not his fault: Words are, after all, fickle and unreliable; sometimes they come and and other times they are off somewhere in the distance. Another possibility is that he has been lazily—and happily—languishing in an unproductive dream-like state.[46] In still another explanation he blames his overly grandiose plans—the "materials" with which he will build his "house" are much too precious. Like the sun and moon in biblical lore, the gemstones of the High Priest's breastplate (i.e., the best words) plead for the most honorable places in the poet's "house" (*bayit* means both "house" and "stanza"). He complies. He reaches the point of perfection with the placement of the "sparkling crown" in the rooftop, only to find his work and himself in ruins, the result of his own hubris and the unstable nature of language. The "very nature" of words is to destroy, after all. And he has only himself to blame for having forgotten this truism.

This is a somewhat different approach from the one Gilboa presents in other poems about his writing problems. Whereas in the earlier works a barrage of "inspired" images flooded his mind, here the culprits are gems of words and diction. The poetic problem, however, is the same—namely, that in his experience too much of a good thing has been detrimental to the process of poetic composition. Much like a house of cards, one too many destroys the entire structure. A relaxed attitude or idyllic mood is more likely to lead to artistic success, he infers in *Hazer lefazer peraḥav* (Scatter the Bouquet Its Flowers).[47]

הַזֵּר לְפַזֵּר פְּרָחָיו עַל פְּנֵי רִצְפָּה וְשֻׁלְחָן
לֹא בְּאֶגֶד מְהֻדָּק וְתָקוּעַ בַּכַּד כְּאֶצְבַּע שֶׁל יִפְעָה מְאַיֶּמֶת,
גַּנּוֹת וּפַרְדֵּסִים לְהַעֲלוֹת בֵּין קִירוֹת תּוֹחֲמִים,
וּלְהִתְהַלֵּךְ אָדָם בַּגָּן בְּטֶרֶם שֻׁלַּח
וְלִשְׁמֹעַ בְּקוֹל אֱלֹהִים הַמְהַלֵּךְ מַנְגִּינָה מְלַוָּה
וְלֹא קְרִיאַת תְּגָר. וְיוֹסִיף וְיִקְרָא אֱלֹהִים
לְלֹא הֶרֶף. קוֹל מְהַלֵּךְ
שֶׁיְּהַלֵּךְ

Scatter the bouquet its flowers upon the table and floor
not in a tight bunch stuck into a vase like a finger of threatening
beauty,
growing gardens and orchards between limiting walls,
and strolling Adam in the garden before banishment
and listening to the voice of God strolling a tuneful accompaniment
not a call to strife. And God will continue to call
without end. A voice strolling
let it stroll

This is a metaphorical ode to romantic poetry. A poem, Gilboa suggests, is not a bunch of words clumped together and displayed, sculpture-like, as a finished piece of art. Like single, strewn flowers, each element — the words, phrases, images, and lines — are to be relished, for from these components the poet creates an entity redolent with the spirit of the poem. The infinitives *lefazer, leha'alot, lehithalekh, lishmo'a* (scattering, growing, strolling, listening) evoke an ongoing, continuous present of creative activity in which poetic inspiration is equated with an easy-going listening to God speaking melodiously and without end in the Garden of Eden.

Gilboa takes on the role of a gadfly, a social critic, in several poems in the *Ayala* volume. In some works, he is critical of the rat race he finds increasingly prevalent in Israeli society and in the world at large.[48] In others he voices his long-standing complaints about the poetry establishment's failure to recognize and appreciate his art.[49] In *Yashav panav el ha-kahal* (He Sat Facing the Crowd),[50] noteworthy for its candor and its unvocalized text, Gilboa dramatizes a trial in which he, the accused, turns the tables and confronts his audience on these grounds of *ad hominem* evaluation. He is nervous, confused; the jury seems to relent, though he is not sure whether it is "out of affection or out of denigration." There is a has-been feeling: "in their eyes he's not someone who's worth the trouble." In the closing lines, however—here the vocalization returns—the poet counterposes his shame *(kelima)* with his inner voice *(penima)*, saying, in effect, that his integrity and creativity are more important to him than the audience's response. He values the power of his imagination far more than his reception in the world.

וּפָנָיו פְּנִימָה כְּבָר שׁוֹמְעִים אֶת הַקּוֹלוֹת
וּנְהָרָה עַל פָּנָיו

and his face inside already hears the voices
and there's radiance in his face

Typical of his endings of volumes and sections of poems, Gilboa closes *Ayala* with a manifesto-like confirmation of his ars poetica, *Be-Kitso le-mereshito* (At Its Conclusion to the Beginning).[51]

בְּקִצּוֹ לְמֵרֵאשִׁיתוֹ. וְכָל הַמַּרְאָה הַזֹּאת
מִתְרַחֶשֶׁת עִמּוֹ לְעֵינָיו
בְּשׁוּלָיו שֶׁל כַּר חָשׂוּף,
בְּצֵל עֲנָפָיו הַקְּטַנִּים שֶׁל שִׂיחַ
תְּמוּרָה אֱלֹהִית
וְחַג וַחֲרָדָה
כַּאֲשֶׁר שְׁמֵי צָהֳרַיִם שֶׁנִּתְאַחֲרוּ

נוֹשְׁקִים שִׂיחַ סָחוּף, דַּל עָלִים
וּכְמוֹ הַשֶּׁמֶשׁ כְּבָר בָּא
הַמַּלְאָךְ הַגּוֹאֵל
אִם יִירָא רָע

At its conclusion to the beginning. And all this vision
happens to him before his very eyes
at the edge of a bare meadow,
in the shade of a shrub's small branches
a divine exchange
and joy and trembling
when the noon skies which have tarried
kiss an abused, bare-leafed shrub,
and like the sun there comes
the redeeming angel
should he fear evil

The poem summarizes both aspects of Gilboa's poetic production: his conception of how poetry is created and his relationship to his art. On the one hand, inspiration is described as "a divine exchange" similar to a holy annunciation or heavenly illumination. By intimating in the first line that here, at the end of his work, he feels a return to the beginning, Gilboa seems to be affirming the inspirational spark that kindled his poetic spirit in varying degrees ever since his youth. In this sense, then, the poem is a paean to the romantic foundations of his poetic enterprise.

But the other aspect of the process is poetry's self-referentiality. The creative process, as we have noted in so many of Gilboa's poems about poetry, elicits both a sense of celebration and an antithetical fearsomeness.[52] Reflected in the closing lines here, the poet's nervousness takes the form of the fear of "evil." Its timing is ironic, since the climactic moment of nature's kiss creates the impression of a romantic fulfillment. The scene is subtly ambiguous: the phrase *ha-shemesh kvar ba* may be understood as "the sun is setting," while the context seems to refer to the "redeeming angel" as coming on or arriving on the scene "like the sun."[53] The context includes an allusion to the Twenty-third Psalm: "I will fear no evil *[lo ira ra]*,"[54] but the poet is more tenuous than the psalmist; he welcomes the angel "should he fear evil."

In looking toward the beginning just as he reaches the ending, Gilboa is not only recalling his poetic origins. He is also contemplating his next bout with a new beginning, perhaps the opening line of his next poem, perhaps the opening poem of the next volume. Poetically speaking, at the closing/opening of the day the romantic realist summons a guardian angel to help him through the next travail of composition.

Chapter VIII

Posthumous Poems

Ha-kol holekh/
Everything is Going, 1987

Published a year or so after the poet's death (September 2, 1984), the poems of *Ha-kol holekh*[1] were written after Gilboa's bypass surgery in early spring, 1983. In much of the volume he ponders aspects of mortality: what one might feel at the very moment of death, the difference between that moment and the moment after, the idea of an afterlife, what an individual leaves behind, projected postmortem "experiences," and his views on the fate of the spirit or soul.

Though the subject may be morbid, the poems are not overwhelmed by melancholy, but are informed instead by a somewhat distanced probing into death's mysteries, expressed imagistically, linguistically, and aesthetically. Much as in the structurally and semantically ambiguous *Ratsiti* and *Ayala* collections, *Ha-kol holekh* displays Gilboa's attempt to highlight the poet's groping for words to articulate complex feelings. *Alai lehasig mashma'ut ha-rega* (I Must Grasp the Meaning of the Moment)[2] aptly demonstrates his already familiar poetics of inarticulation.

עָלַי לְהַשִּׂיג מַשְׁמָעוּת הָרֶגַע הַכֹּל־
יָכוֹל לַחְדֹּל
הָרֶגַע הַקּוֹבֵעַ נֵצַח לִכְלוֹת
הַנֶּפֶשׁ כְּלוֹמַר חַיִּים אוֹ כְּלוֹת
הַכֹּל כְּלוֹמַר קֵץ שֶׁאֵין עִמּוֹ קוֹל
עוֹד זוּלַת רַחַשׁ מְסוֹס וְרָקָב
עַד מִתּוֹלָע אַחֲרוֹן נֶעֱזָב כִּי
אֵין עוֹד שְׁיָר בּוֹ לְהָזִין
כָּל זֹאת עָלַי סוֹ״ס לְהַשִּׂיג
כְּלוֹמַר לְהָבִין
כָּל עוֹד קוֹרְאִים לִי
בִּשְׁמִי

וַאֲנִי עוֹנֶה
(בְּקוֹלִי שֶׁלִּי)

I must grasp the meaning of the moment the omni-
potent moment of ceasing
the moment that marks infinity ending
the soul that is life the ending of it
all that is the end that has a voice
no longer beyond the rustle of rot and decay[3]
till left alone by the last worm for
there's no longer a nourishing scrap
all this I must finally grasp
that is to understand
as long as I'm called
by my name

and I answer
(with my own voice)

The opening statement in line 1 lucidly presents the poem's premise: "I must grasp the meaning of the moment." The statement, however, continues with a second thought ("the omni-/potent moment of ceasing"), which not only defines the "moment" as the time when all ceases but also sardonically broadens the sense of "the omni-potent [sic: *ha-kol-yakhol]*." Here Gilboa alludes to the human foible of feeling omnipotent until one confronts death's imminent reality. The only other possibly complete sentences are found in lines 8 and 9, which offer an image of the body in the grave and the speaker's repeated thought that he "must finally grasp" the final truth of the end.

With the exception of the toned-down rhetoric of the ending (lines 11–14), the poem is a jumble of undifferentiated phrases, parenthetical remarks, and motif-oriented individual words. These include "the end that has a voice/no longer" (lines 5–6), which is broken by the awkward enjambment; the thrice-repeated remark "that is" *(kelomar,* lit., "that is to say"; lines 4, 5 and 10); and the infinitive or stative form of the verb "destroy" or "end" *(likhlot* and *kelot,* lines 3 and 4). Of course, part of the problem — or effect —

is the complete lack of punctuation. However, even if punctuation were included, it would merely delineate more graphically the purposely inarticulate style. Indeed, by making readers supply the phrasing for themselves, Gilboa involves them more intimately in the painful confrontation of his sense of imminent demise.

Beyond the end of life and the fearsome images of the grave, the poem's main motif is the concept of the voice. Speaking for himself, as usual, Gilboa suggests that he is still alive "as long as I'm called/by my name" and as long as I can answer "with my own voice." The notion is ironic, however, since the moment of death is mythically linked to the heavenly pronouncement of one's name. The irony is intensified in the last line of the poem, when he encloses "his own voice" in parentheses and implies that his aliveness is weakened, tenuous. The next time he uses his voice to respond may be the last.

Aspects of the poem's rhyming and the semantics of its homophonic wording also accentuate the fine line—"the moment"—Gilboa draws between life and death. Despite different spellings, *kol* for "voice" rhymes with *kol* for "all" and *hakol* for "everything," and all three words appear frequently in various forms in the poem. In lines 1–2 *hakol-lyakhol* has been translated literally as "the omni-potent." In line 4 *hakol* ("everything") is paired through enjambment with the last word in line 3, *kelot* ("ending"), to form the familiar phrase *kelot* [usually *kikhlot] hakol,* meaning literally the completion or destruction of everything, or, in the common usage, "in the end," or "ultimately." *Kol* ("voice") is the last word in this line and the opening word in line 9. It also opens line 11, but here it is part of the phrase *kol od* (as long as) with the continuation alluding to the pronouncement of Gilboa's name. To the homophones *kol* and *hakol,* we can add *yakhol* (able), used here in the idiom *hakol-yakhol* (omnipotent), and the approximate rhymes *likhlot* and *kelot* and *kelomar,* all of which use the consonants *k* and *l* and the vowel *o* of *kol.*

Semantically, then, the poem highlights the convergence of "all," "end," "omni-potent," "voice," "that is to say" and "as long as," which unites and thus thematically accentuates the dual concept of the "voice" and the "end." One might say that the very phrase *kikhlot hakol* could homophonically represent both "the end of it all" and "the end of the voice," thus joining the theme of death with its metaphorical representation.

Gilboa offers a variety of imagistic depictions—some mythological, others of his own invention—of the process of death and the experience in the grave and the afterworld. The passing from life to death is described as "the purifying cold/sweeping toward a distant no-border [sic]." The speaker says he will not rise (physically) again but adds "I am silent rising/for I/already I am other."[4] In *Dome, vadai* (It Seems, Surely)[5] an image of the grave emphasizes the motif of coldness: cold earth pressing against the cold body "embracing/choking the human soul till there is no breath." The soul is likened to a bird seeking freedom and life in a landscape of desolation. The image is conventionally mythical and romantic, but Gilboa's convoluted language evokes the dual agony of finality (death) and ambiguity (judgment).

...הַשֵּׁם
יְרַחֵם גּוּף נֶעֱזָב וְגוּף צוֹרֵחַ חַיָּיו
וְזֶה וְכֵן זֶה אִם זַכַּאי אִם
חַיָּב יִקָּרֵא לוֹ שֵׁם מִן הַבּוֹר מִתַּחַת
לְשִׂיחַ מִקֹּר אֳרִיחַ גָּבְהֵי רָקִיעַ
אִם יְרוֹמֵם וְלֹא
יְהִי נוֹקֵם
אָמֵן וְאָמֵן

. . . may God
have mercy on a forlorn body and a body screaming its life
and this yes this whether innocent or
guilty it will be given a name from the pit from under
a shrub from the cold of the floor of heavenly heights
whether it rises or not
let there be vengeance
Amen Amen

The motif of vengeance for the "forlorn body" broadens Gilboa's use of the theme of individual death to include the Holocaust dead, buried in desolate, unknown graves. In contemplating his own death, he evokes the memory of his departed family (which has always been "a gnawing pain limitless/timeless") as "a mass passing before my eyes . . . [so] distant/distant from the waters of terrors of days of oppression."[6] In another poem he tells his dear ones that he is coming to join them and "will be silent" with them.[7]

Ha-kerira ha-zot ba-zikaron (This Coldness in my Memory)[8] is another Holocaust response poem in *Ha-kol holekh.*

הַקְּרִירָה הַזֹּאת בַּזִּכָּרוֹן
רַעֲנַנָּה וּמְלַטֶּפֶת
כָּךְ בְּקַשְׁתִּי גַּם הַבֹּקֶר
שֶׁתְּהִי אוֹתִי עוֹטֶפֶת
וּבְעוֹד בָּהּ אֶתְכַּרְבֵּלָה
מְדַמֶּה לִי שְׁעַת חֶסֶד
רַחוּמָה וּמְעַלֶּפֶת
עֲדַנְדַּנּוֹת כָּךְ אֲטַיֵּלָה
וְרַקֶּפֶת מִתְיַפְיֶפֶת
אֶחֱרֹז לִי בְּלִי כָּל רֶתַע
וְהִנֵּה פִּתְאֹם לְפֶתַע
רַגְלִי שְׁלוּחָה כְּאַיֶּלֶת
חָבְטָה בְּכֹחַ בְּחֹד בַּדֶּלֶת
אָז בֶּן־רֶגַע בְּמַהֲלוֹם שֶׁל פֶּגַע
נָפְלוּ נָשְׁרוּ פֶּגֶר פֶּגֶר
יֶלֶד פֶּלֶא חֲרִיק שֶׁל דֶּלֶת
מִגְדָּל פֶּלֶד קִיר שֶׁל מֶלֶט
לֹבֶן שֶׁלֶד עֵין הַתְּכֵלֶת
וְחוֹרֶקֶת שֵׁן מִתְחַלְחֶלֶת
הִתְפָּרְקָה לָהּ הַשַּׁלְשֶׁלֶת
חֲלִיָה חֲלְיָה לְנַפְשָׁהּ
קְפוּאָה קְרוּעָה

מָה אָמַרְתִּי לְנַפְשָׁהּ

מִמַּה נַּפְשָׁהּ

בְּנַפְשִׁי

הַקְּרִירָה הַזֹּאת
חַכִּי חַכִּי
עוֹד מְעַט
אַפְּ שִׁיר

This coldness in my memory
fresh and touching
this is what I've asked for this morning too
that it envelop me
and let me curl up in it
forming for me a time of grace
merciful and enchanting
gently I amble
a lovely cyclamen
I'll poetize [or rhyme] without inhibition
and suddenly
my leg extends like a gazelle's
struck with force the basalt tip
then in a flash with a mortal blow
they fell down corpse after corpse
a wondrous child the squeak of a door
a steel tower a concrete wall
a skeleton's whiteness the color of blue
the grinding of a trembling tooth
the chain broke apart
link by link by itself
frozen torn

what do I say to it

whatever the case

upon my soul [9]

this coldness
wait wait
a bit
I'll melt [or: even a poem][10]

The poem embodies various aspects of Gilboa's poetic subjects. In the first ten lines he describes walking in the chill of the morning, a favorite activity—"a moment of grace" *(she'at ḥesed)*—which inspires him to write (line 10). Suddenly, the mood changes; the scene is fraught with images of violence, rage, and death (lines 13–19). The beloved victim, the gazelle, the basalt rock, the tumbling corpses, the steel tower, the cement wall, the white skeleton—all create a montage of Holocaust horrors. The chilling effect is intensified by the images of coldness and the frozen chain, an allusion to Yitsḥak Lamdan's famous poem *Shalshelet ha-meḥolot* (The Chain of Dances), whose refrain, "The chain is not broken/the chain is still sustained,"[11] links Zionism and Israel as the repaired link in the chain of Jewish civilization.

Beyond these works and a few specific references in other poems, Gilboa does not dwell on the Holocaust in this volume.[12] Indeed, most of its death imagery is romantic, not historical. Borrowing one of his early nature images, Gilboa pictures himself at death in "an empty field and I/sober and empty alone/staring into nothingness distant."[13] Elsewhere he imagines himself standing "face to face with/the coldlight [sic] of this morning walking strong/freed from a thousand and one woes/and stresses which have destroyed the soul,"[14] which brings to mind Gilboa's early nature poems[15] and his penchant for hyperbole.

There are other mythological resonances. In *Kol she-yavo efshar lomar* (All That Will Happen One Could Say)[16] Gilboa alludes to an Ezekiel image of "water flowing . . . in the Euphrates/our bones whitening before our very eyes." In the same work he interpolates an image of Moses "seeing the Land/from a mountaintop." *Ani yode'a ani yode'a* (I Know I Know)[17] pictures the speaker sprouting wings as if to escape death but ultimately "falling into the darkness." The poem's opening lines recall the poems in *Ratsiti* which feature a tenaciously aware speaker who "knows" but finds himself continually in situations of complete ambiguity.[18] In *Pa'am be-leil geshem bi-*

rushalayim (Once On a Rainy Evening in Jerusalem)[19] Gilboa combines mythical and romantic entities in a vision of "the man in the sky/tall/far off/in front/in the gold of morning extending beyond the horizon/moving moving in the blue of sky."

Beyond these depictions of death, the poems evince landscapes, locales, aspects of nature, and personal experiences that the poet will long for when he is no longer alive. These include Jerusalem as both endangered and flowering, rain on the pavement, a budding plum tree, the beautiful symmetry of apples, walking in a field, and eating various foods (a bit of humor here: for many years Gilboa suffered from an ulcer and had a restricted diet).

Like Raḥel Bluvstein in the late twenties, Gilboa, knowing that his days were numbered, contemplated the fate of his poetry. Indeed, for both writers, their last works serve as poetic wills. In most of *Ha-kol holekh* the subjects of death and poetry are intertwined. In *Lo, lo akhale* (No, I'll Not Finish)[20] Gilboa writes that he knows he will not be able to complete "what has not been granted me to begin and create." Though preoccupied with everyday survival, he adds in the last third of the poem that he prays for "a blessed rain" which will fructify the barren land and provide "an hour of comfort and light." Then, he says, he will feel comfortable, even happy, at the moment of death. His hope is for the actualization of the optimistic vision of a land of milk and honey, an image probably very close to his youthful vision of a renascent Zion.

In *Lo, lo medubar be-ikarei devarim* (No, I'm Not Talking About Central Issues),[21] Gilboa adds a long list of items *(devarim tserikhim)* that to his mind poetry cannot do without: shrubs, blossoms, the sparkling of mist, light bursting forth, buds of new growth, new creation, and "thousands of thousands of more things" which God, preoccupied with the creation of humanity, forgot to create. Adding a mythical touch to his desiderata, Gilboa clearly promotes the romantic spirit as the very essence of poetry.

Ze rak ḥalomot (It is Only Dreams)[22] expresses Gilboa's ultimate despair about the end of his creativity.

זֶה רָק חֲלוֹמוֹת. מִפַּעַם לְפַעַם. אֶת הַשִּׁיר.
כְּבָר לֹא אֶכְתֹּב.
רַק הָרוּחַ. מִפַּעַם לְפַעַם. כַּאֲשֶׁר תֵּעוֹר.
בְּעַלְעוֹל. הָעַלְעָלִים. אִם אָמְנָם. תֶּאֱסֹף.

וּבְכֹחַ. וּבְלִי דַעַת. בִּכְנָפֶיהָ. תְּצָרְרֵם.
וְאֶל גְּבָהִים. תָּרִים. תַּנְסִיק.
וּבְכֹחַ. וּבַחֲמַת זַעַם. הֲמִדַּעַת. אֶל חוֹר.
שֶׁל רִיק. שָׁחוֹר. אֵין שֵׁם.
תִּשָּׂאֵם.

נְקֻדָּה. כָּאן. רַק נְקֻדָּה. לֹא פְּסִיק.

It's only dreams. From time to time. The poem.
I'll write no more.
Only the spirit. From time to time. When it arises.
In the rush of the wind. The little leaves. If indeed. It gathers.
And forcefully. And unknowingly. With its wings. It will bind them.
And to heights. It will raise up. Will lift.
And with force. And with great anger. Perhaps knowingly. To a hole.
Of emptiness. Black. Nothing there.
Will carry them off.

Period. Here. Only a period. Not a comma.

The poem expresses Gilboa's avowal of no more poetry. Indeed, looking at the final verse, one might conclude that this is the last poem he composed, though it is placed as the seventh last in the volume. The work, however, does not repudiate poetry, which will live on as a Platonic mode of spiritual creation even after the poet stops writing. Poetry exists in nature itself, in the leaves tossed by the storm, in the rush of the wind.

As always, there is a tone of duality in Gilboa's perception of the creative process. Though the poetic spirit "gathers" and "binds" to "heights," it does so with force and anger and both knowingly and unknowingly. But the main point is that for Gilboa poetry is ended. By having the spirit "bind" the poetic leaves and carry them off to an empty black "hole" of nothingness, Gilboa conclusively connects the death of poetry—at least of his poetry—with his own death.

Na avarekh (Let Me Bless)[23] is the collection's closing poem and Gilboa's swan song.

נָא אֲבָרֵךְ אֱלֹהֵי אֲבוֹתַי כַּאֲשֶׁר בֵּרְכוּ אֲבוֹתַי לְפָנַי
וַאֲפִלּוּ אֲנִי נוֹפֵל עַל פָּנַי וְלֹא קָם.
לְמַרְאֵה עֵץ הַשָּׁזִיף הִפְתִּיעַ כַּאֲשֶׁר אִכְזֵב אַכְזָבוֹתַי
אֵיךְ גָּבַר עַל גְּזָר נֶחֱרָץ כַּאֲשֶׁר עוֹטֶה סְחַף קְלִפָּה צוֹמֵק שָׁחוֹר
כַּאֲשֶׁר דּוֹמֶה וַדַּאי עָסִיס אַחֲרוֹן הִטִּיף שׁוּב מָלְאוּ קְצוֹת שָׂרִיגָיו
וְהֵנִיץ יָרֹק וְהִפְרִיחַ לֹבֶן שֶׁלֶג וְהֵנִיב כְּחַלְחַל וְעֵינַי הִרְהִיב עִקֵּשׁ
לָמוּת כָּלוּל כֻּלּוֹ הֲדַר אָבִיב לַהַט אָסִיף כַּאֲשֶׁר מְלַבְלֵב כַּאֲשֶׁר
אֶל פְּרִיחָה וּפְרִי לְעוֹלָם חַי אוֹ מֵת רָעֵב

Let me bless the God of my forbears as my forebears blessed before me
even if I fall on my face and do not rise.
At the sight of the plum tree surprising when it disappointed my
disappointments
how it overcame the fateful decree when it wore an eroded bark
withering black
when it seemed certain its last nectar dribbled the ends of its
branches
and it blossomed green and flowered snowy white and brought forth
blue and my eyes it stubbornly dared
to die completely all adorned with spring the heat of harvest when
it blooms when
into flowering and fruit it's ever alive or dying hungry

Na avarekh complements *Ze rak ḥalomot* by going beyond the poet's sense of the end to a vision of the perennial flowering of his plum tree.[24] Because of the tree's age or poor condition, the flowering represents a nearly miraculous scene. The ungrammatical listing of the tree's attributes creates an uninterrupted flow of romantic images which, in turn, evoke a larger-than-life scene of natural beauty, endurance, and rebirth. With typically ambiguous phrasing, the last verse may be read as the tree's "fruit [is] forever alive"—fortifying the message of nature's undying and connoting poetry's survival beyond the poet's death. Alternatively, the line may be read as "[the plum] blooms as/to *[el]* flowering and fruit"; that is to say, the one who witnesses this constancy in nature is "forever alive or dying hungry," forever filled with life and hungry for the next flowering—for the next poem.

Afterword

Two reviews which appeared after the 1987 publication of the *Collected Poems* demonstrate the opposing poles which often characterized critical response to Gilboa throughout his career.

In "Amir Gilboa u-shnei kirkhei shirav" (Gilboa and His Two Volumes of Poetry), a two-part assessment in *Ma'ariv*,[1] Ortsiyon Bartana states that Gilboa "is not an Israeli poet" and that his works should not be included in the canon of Israeli poetry. On philosophical, historical, and linguistic grounds, Bartana argues that Gilboa's oeuvre is "metaphysical poetry"—completely distinct from the "experiential-spontaneous-ironic" writing typical of his contemporaries. Referring to the poet as "a Trojan horse" and "a strange growth" *(neta zar)*, he vehemently argues that accepting him into the canon "is nothing but a fallacy *(ziyuf)*."

No doubt referring to Gilboa's extensive Holocaust work, Bartana regards his first major collection (*Sheva reshuyot,* 1949) as "basically a religious book" *(sefer dati)*. He faults Gilboa for his "Jewishness," a characteristic which caused him to write poetry which is "limited" and "flawed."

> Gilboa's problem is the incapacity to stand on his own, the incapacity to create a proud, poetic persona. [His] poetry evinces no influence of non-Jewish sources. [It also] lacks both an ideational and a rhetorical structure. . . .This is the problem of a poet who has experienced Jewish existence in a bitter, drawn-out war, in contrast with the conventional poetic trends of his time.

Bartana's argument is obviously based on a view of the "exilic" Jew as a weak vulnerable victim (in contrast to the preferable new sabra, whose image is strong, masculine, and heroic). This quasi-"Canaanite," nativistic perspective continues in Bartana's assessment of certain linguistic and poetic aspects of Gilboa's works. Gilboa, he claims, "did not create a poetics of the *tsabarit* Hebrew language" and "did not break the conventions of Russian Modernism" as did the *tsabar* Israeli poets. (Bartana uses these terms loosely. Of the poets mentioned in the article, Zach and Amichai were both born in Germany, Tanai in Silesia, Gouri in Jerusalem, and A. Hillel in Mishmar Ha-Emek.) Thus he sees Gilboa as an outsider and a non-innovator. Even his language, Bartana notes, "is full of semantic foundations which are in keeping [not with contemporary Israeli poetry but] with the Hebrew poetry of the twenties and thirties."

In the same vein, Bartana disclaims Gilboa's inclusion in Natan Zach's *Likrat* group. Referring to Zach's 1957 article "Muvanuto shel Amir Gilboa,"[2] Bartana argues that Gilboa was never the "personal" or humanistic poet that Zach claimed him to be. "If there ever was a poet in the Generation of the State [i.e., the first generation of "native" Israeli writers] who in his works contraposes the poetry of *Likrat* [i.e. Zach, et al.] with its experiential and personal connotations, it is Amir Gilboa." It was only the "mini-existentialists" of the *Likrat* group and other "deviant" writers *[ḥorgim]*, he asserts, who saw Gilboa as one of their own.

Finally, Bartana suggests that it would be a mistake to see Gilboa's poetry as

> a kind of great, wide bridge from the Erets-Israeli writing of the twenties and thirties to that of the fifties, sixties and seventies. [His poetry] is not a bridge . . . in every way it is a closing, an end. . . .Gilboa is a phenomenon, a one-time occurrence in the poetry of his generation . . . the last creator of metaphysical poetry in Hebrew.

Never "one of us" *(mi-shelanu)*, he adds, "Gilboa is a symptom [not of a new era but] of the passing of an age in Hebrew poetry."

Not surprisingly, in his *Edut kri'a* (Testimony of Reading, 1982), which focuses on Israeli poetry in the fifties, Bartana makes no mention at all of Gilboa. In contrast, Moshe Shamir's 1950 "Shoshanim noshmot" review of *Sheva reshuyot* states that "Amir Gilboa appears masculine and polished *(gavri u-megubash)* in his first book of poetry . . . and [thus] claims his place as one of the important creators of the young Erets-Israeli poetry. . . ." A similar assessment appears in the 1959 *Dor ba-arets* (A Generation in the State) anthology, edited by Azriel Ukhmani, Tanai, and Shamir. The brief biographical statement on Gilboa calls him "one of the first of the generation of the period of struggle and the [Israeli] War of Liberation in his poetry."[3]

In her 1987 response in *Davar* to Bartana's review in *Ma'ariv,* Ḥamutal Bar-Yosef echoes the positive 1950s assessments.[4] Disagreeing directly with Bartana's notion of Jewishness vs. Sabraism, she counters that Gilboa's poetry is neither weak nor flawed; it is simply individualistic and different in that it is "spiritually oriented." She points to the poetry's "tone, its emotional temperament, its poetic personality, its grasp of the role of poetry." Supporting Zach's view, Bar-Yosef argues that

> at its base, Gilboa's poetry is devoted deeply and genuinely to the empathic, committed persona, to the voice of the one who loves and hates, who is happy and in despair, who pities and rages to the end, to the point of ecstasy and self-endangerment. This is the persona which appears in works of Bialik, Greenberg, and Brenner. . . .

Bar-Yosef likes Gilboa's "spontaneity" and his conscious selection of "emotional poles," which for him, in her view, is "a project of self-restoration." She sees him as "a shy, gentle person, plagued by self-consciousness . . . his longing for love and friendship . . . restrained by a thick wall of inhibition." Citing the "Bialikian foundation" in Gilboa's poetry—namely, "the longing for purity and the aversion to impurity"—she asserts that "Gilboa [is] the most obvious heir to Bialik."

Whereas Bartana rejects Gilboa's poetic roots in the Generation of Bialik on the grounds that they are insufficiently "Israeli"—he obviously has no use for Itamar Even-Zohar's notion of a "polysystem"[5]—Bar-Yosef sees Gilboa's alleged "disconnectedness" from the canon of modern Hebrew poetry as a result of his stylistic nonconformity with the mainstream modernist poets. And because mid-century criticism focused on the works of Shlonsky, Alterman, Amichai, and Zach, Gilboa's ambivalent relationship with literary critics and editors was further exacerbated. Perhaps overgeneralizing, she asserts that as "the sense of a collective waned, Gilboa was clothed in the garb of a "National Poet," one who in assuming the Bialikian legacy was expected to write on both personal and national/mythical planes.

In *Ratsiti likhtov siftei yeshenim,* however, Gilboa attempted, through major stylistic innovation, to free himself from the "National Poet" image. Like Bartana, Bar-Yosef responds quite negatively to that attempt. Whereas Bartana accuses Gilboa of trying (but failing) to take on the guise of an insider *(mekomi),* Bar-Yosef sees the volume as embodying an apologia for Gilboa's estrangement from the spirit of his contemporaries. Echoing Hillel Barzel's 1982 view of *Ratsiti* and *Ayala* as "the tragedy of [Gilboa's] having lost his poetic path,"[6] she decries the poetry of *Ratsiti* as "completely alien to the spiritual urges that gave it birth." Here Bar-Yosef seems to bemoan the very individuality that she champions at the outset of her article.

Bartana and Bar-Yosef differ greatly in their respective views of Gilboa. Each, however, reflects a dualistic perception of the poet: rooted in the romantic era, he was stylistically varied. Intermittently and understandably a *malheureux,* Gilboa constantly sought new forms of expression, even to the point of searching for the sources and symptoms of expression itself. Though he may not have been a poetic "bridge" between the Bialikian and modernist generations, Gilboa wrote in the style of both, often blending the two. Along with other Israeli writers and poets, he was emotionally involved in two worlds: Europe and Erets Israel, the Holocaust and the establishment of the State. His focus was divided between these entities, themselves fraught with poles of despair and recovery, sorrow and exuberance. A parallel dualism is reflected also in his bouts of feverish creativity, interrupted intermittently by periods of blockage and silence. Through all the conflicting experiences of his life and art, however, one truth is evident: Amir Gilboa left his readers an astoundingly vibrant and challenging legacy of poetic expression.

Notes

Chapter I : A Cultural Biography

1. The gathering took place on May 17, 1982, at the offices of the Hakibbutz Hameuchad Publishing Co. in Tel Aviv. The tributes and reminiscences presented at the meeting are preserved in *Mi-bifnim* (October, 1982): 319–34. Ida Tsurit also relates this particular reminiscence by Gilboa in *Ha-ḥayim, ha-atsilut: Iyunim be-shirato shel Amir Gilboa* (Spheres of Life and Emanation: Studies in Amir Gilboa's Poetry) (Hakibbutz Hameuchad, 1988), 66. Hillel Barzel retells the anecdote in *Amir Gilboa: Monographia* (Monograph) (Sifriat Poalim, 1984), 13. (Unless otherwise noted, all Hebrew sources are published in Tel Aviv.)

2. Tsurit reports that about thirty of these Yiddish poems have survived in Gilboa's papers. A diary entry notes that he was still hoping to publish his Yiddish poems in a volume entitled *Ankegn haynt* (Facing Today). The entire Spivak episode is recorded in *Ha-ḥayim, ha-atsilut,* 87–89.

3. Gilboa tells Haim Gouri in an 1982 interview that he chose the name "Gilboa" while sailing on the "Poseidon" to Erets Israel. His friends on the journey added the name "Amir." See "Ha-ish ha-kotev siftei yeshenim" (The Man Who Writes the Lips of Sleepers) *Ḥotam* [the weekly magazine of *Al ha-mishmar],* Jan. 1, 1982.

4. *Ha-ḥayim, ha-atsilut,* 85.

5. Chana Kronfeld, *On the Margins of Modernism* (forthcoming, University of California Press).

6. "Al 'Shuv re'itikhem be-kotser yedkhem'" (On [Bialik's poem] "I See You Again in Your Impotence"), *Ketuvim* 6 (November, 1931): 6.

7. See the introductory chapter by Aviezer Weiss, ed., *Avraham Shlonsky: Mivḥar ma'amarim al yetsirato* (Selected Essays on Shlonsky's Works) (Am Oved, 1975), 22–30.

8. See Dan Miron, "Al ha-musag 'doro shel Bialik,'" (On the Concept "The Generation of Bialik"), *Moznayim* 13, 3–4 (Aug.-Sept., 1961): 206–13. The rubric *Dor Bialik* is also known as *Dor ha-teḥiya,* "The Generation of Revival," or the "[Hebrew] Renaissance."

9. It should be noted that Bialik died only in the summer of 1934. Also, in this period several younger poets began appearing in *Moznayim* as well. These include Avraham Broides (1907–1979), Ezra Zussman (1900–1973), Yehoshua Tan-Pai (1914–1988), Ḥayim Lenski (1905–1942/43), Shimshon Meltzer (1909–), Avraham Ḥalfi (1904–1980), David Rokeaḥ (1918–1985), Raphael Eliaz (1905–1974), Eliyahu Meitus (1892–1977), Binyamin Tennenbaum (Tenne) (1914–), and Levi Ben-Amitai (1901–1980). With few exceptions, however, these younger poets wrote much in the style of their older mentors. Shlonsky also appeared regularly in the journal. In *Amir Gilboa: Monographia,* 11–12, Barzel adds further details to this sketch of the late-1930s literary scene.

10. "Polysystem Theory," *Poetics Today* 1–2 (1979): 287–310.

11. Kronfeld, *On the Margins of Modernism,* chap. 3.

12. See Even-Zohar, "Ha-sifrut ha-Ivrit ha-Yisraelit—model histori" (Israeli Hebrew Literature—A Historical Model), *Ha-sifrut* 4, 3 (1973): 432.

13. Shlomo Sheva, "Ha-masa el ha-olam ha-gadol" (The Journey to the Big World), a review of Gilboa's *Keḥulim va-adumim* (Blues and Reds), *Devar ha-shavua,* Jan. 10, 1964.

14. In *Ha-ḥayim, ha-atsilut,* Tsurit notes that several reference works have misstated Gilboa's birthdate as 1917. Having interviewed old Radzivil friends of Gilboa, she claims that

Gilboa was born in 1914. Her argument is convincing, since several anecdotes are based on the school grades in which Gilboa and his friends were enrolled. It was also not uncommon for individuals to understate their age upon immigration. All other "official" sources retain the 1917 date; these include G. Kressel's *Lexicon ha-sifrut ha-Ivrit ba-dorot ha-aḥaronim* (Lexicon of Hebrew Literature in Recent Generations), 1965, and the biographical outline supplied by the poet's widow, Gabriela (Gabi) Gilboa, in the two-volume posthumous edition of Gilboa's collected works (Hakibbutz Hameuchad, 1987). The biographical details noted here are taken mainly from the Tsurit volume, the first part of which is a biography of the poet from childhood to 1946. Another main source is the reminiscences by Gilboa and old friends related at the May 1982 Israel Prize celebration. (See n. 1 above.)

15. For additional background about the region and the times see Warren Bargad, *Ideas in Fiction: The Works of Hayim Hazaz* (Chico, CA: Scholars Press, 1982), 2–3 and nn. 2 and 3.

16. In a 1971 interview with Eli Mohar, Gilboa attests that his desire to become a poet was kindled early in childhood by Yitsḥak Katzenelson's *Tal boker* (Morning Dew) and Fichman's *Bikurim* (First Fruits) and *Lashon va-sefer* (Language and Book) texts. See "Bi-meḥoz ha-shirim shel Amir Gilboa" (In the Realm of Gilboa's Poetry), *Devar ha-shavu'a,* December 24, 1971. In the Gouri interview Gilboa notes that the red and blue cover of the *Tal boker* textbook brought him to name his 1963 collection *Keḥulim va-adumim.* The exact chronology of Gilboa's schooling is not very clear. The sequence seems to be the *tarbut* kindergarten through second grade, then Polish public school through the age of sixteen. Reb Abba's *ḥeder* and the private tutoring with David Schneider seem to have been extracurricular, concurrent with his attendance in the Polish government school.

17. As noted, Gilboa's upbringing, culturally, ideologically and linguistically, was a blend of Yiddish and Hebrew, Socialism and Zionism. In the mid-thirties, Warsaw, about 250 miles from Radzivil, was the Hebrew and Yiddish journalistic and literary capital of Europe. Hitler in the West and Stalin in the East had for the most part silenced their Jewish presses and purged their Jewish writers and intellectuals. In the 1920s and 1930s, however, Warsaw had scores of Hebrew and Yiddish publications, including a half dozen daily Yiddish newspapers. Among these were *Haynt* (Today), *Dos Yidishe togblatt* (The Jewish Daily), and *Dos Vort* (The Word). There was also a large variety of political, mostly socialist journals, including *Frayheyt* (Freedom), *Unzer hammer* (Our Hammer), *Unzer vort* (Our Word), *Unzer frayheyt* (Our Freeedom), *Dos Naye vort* (The New Word), and *Di Fraye yugnt* (Free Youth)—all these in Yiddish; and the Hebrew journals *Ha-po'el* (The Worker) and *He-atid* (The Future).

Warsaw also boasted a number of widely-read literary publications. The Hebrew journals included the venerable *Ha-tekufa* (The Age) and *Aḥi'asaf, Ba-derekh* (On the Way, the Hebrew literary and ideological supplement to *Haynt,* and *Ha-shomer ha-tsa'ir* (The Young Guardian). The outstanding Yiddish periodicals were *Der Moment* (The Moment), edited by Hillel Zeitlin (1871–1942), and *Literarishe bleter* (Literary Pages), probably the most widely-circulated Yiddish literary journal of its day. Although one cannot be certain that Gilboa read it regularly, *He-atid,* the official magazine of the International Hechalutz Organization, can at least give us a firm idea of the literary tenor of the movement and the times. Featured in the pages of *He-atid* are articles on the Zionist-oriented *tarbut* schools, accounts of the *hakhshara* (preparatory) encampments in eastern Europe—an article on the tenth anniversary of the Klossova encampment at Lutzk, which Gilboa attended, appears in the August 15,

1934, issue—and news of the growth of the movement and *aliya* figures from around the world. Its literary pages contain a good deal of prose fiction and essays by the Zionist and *yishuv* (Erets-Israel Jewish community) leaders Berl Katznelson (1887–1944), Aharon David Gordon (1856–1922), David Maletz (1899–1981), Ever Hadani (1899–1972), Avigdor Hame'iri (1890–1970), Yehuda Burla (1886–1969), and Bialik—all revered ideologues and writers of the day. Each issue of *He-atid* features several poems, many by the journal's editor, Moshe Basok (1907–1966), and a good number by Shin Shalom, Shlonsky, Berl Pomerantz (1902–1943), Pinḥas Lander (El'ad, 1905–1987), and Binyamin Tenne. Most of the poems and works of fiction have a romantic, nationalistic tone, often relating to or reflecting the life in Erets Israel, its natural beauty, and the pains and rewards of being a part of its rebuilding. Hebrew translations of the Polish-Jewish poet Julian Tuwim (1894–1953) also appear often in this journal.

Ba-ma'ale, the journal of the "General Organization of Hebrew Laboring Youth," published in Tel Aviv in the mid-1930s and circulated all over Europe, features much the same fare. Articles focus on "the first days in the homeland," the Spanish Civil War, the *hakhshara* camps in Poland, and life in the new *kibbutzim* in Erets Israel and in the European *shtetlakh* (Jewish towns) from which the young pioneers had recently departed. Its literary pages contain works by some of the younger poets who, by then, resided in Erets Israel. These include Avraham Broides (1907–79), Levi Ben-Amitai (1901–1980), Ya'akov Orland (1914–), Alterman, and the popular kibbutz poet Zerubavel Gilead (1912–1988), who at the time was touring the youth camps of Poland and Russia as a representative of the Hechalutz movement.

In a letter to Avraham Broides dated 24 Shevat (Feb. 16), 1971, Gilboa acknowledges that in Radzivil he read his brother Joshua's copies of *Ba-ma'ale.* (The letter was originally housed in the Genazim Literary Archives in Tel Aviv; all the Gilboa materials are now housed at the Katz Institute of Tel Aviv University.) In addition, Gilboa acknowledged in his talk at the Israel Prize gathering that he also read his brother's copies of *Kuntres* and *Davar.*

18. The Gouri interview notes that Gilboa first became enamored of the idea of making aliyah when, as a young teenager, he read a book entitled *Demuyot be-ḥayei ha-arets* (Personalities in the Life of Erets Israel).

19. This number includes the *"Shelosha she'arim ḥozrim"* (Three Recurring Gates) section of *Keḥulim va-adumim, Ketaf* (Balm), 1971, and the posthumous collection *Ha-kol holekh* (Everything is Going), 1985. For further details see the Bibliography.

20. See Boaz Arpali, *Ha-peraḥim ve-ha-agartal: Shirat Amiḥai: Mivne, mashma'ut, poetika* (The Flowers and the Vase: Amichai's Poetry—Structure, Meaning, Poetics). Siman Kri'a/Hakibbutz Hameuchad, 1986, 216–19.

21. See M. H. Abrams, *The Mirror and the Lamp: Romantic Theory and the Critical Tradition* (New York: Oxford University Press, 1953), 48–56; 97–99. See also René Wellek, *Concepts of Criticism* (New Haven and London: Yale University Press, 1963), 161–217.

22. See Arpali, *Ha-peraḥim ve-ha-agartal,* 223–25, for additional characteristics of Bialik's poetry. And for Bialik's shaping influence on modern Hebrew poetry, see Yael Feldman, *Modernism and Cultural Transfer: Gabriel Preil and the Tradition of Jewish Literary Bilingualism* (Hebrew Union College Press: Cincinnati, 1986), 19ff.

23. See the chapter entitled "The Beginning of Romanticism in Hebrew Poetry at the Beginning of the Twentieth Century," in *Bo'a laila* (Come, Night) (Dvir, 1987), 11–37.

24. See *Ha-perida min ha-ani he-ani* (Taking Leave of the Impoverished Self) (Open University Press, 1986), 307–53. Miron adds a quote from Yehudit Bar-El's Ph.D. dissertation (no title noted; 1983, 311ff): "This [autobiographical] genre clearly grew out of the literary and cultural revolution brought on by European Romanticism at the end of the eighteenth and the beginning of the nineteenth centuries."

25. *Ha-shira me-ayin timatse* (Where Might Poetry Be Found) (Papyrus, 1987), 107–43 and 152ff.

26. The late Sarah Segal, a friend of Gilboa during their *hakhshara* days, notes that Gilboa always had a penchant for high diction. Gilboa claimed that he learned it from the *dayan* (Jewish religious court judge) in Radzivil. See Segal's comments in her reminiscences at the Israel Prize celebration in 1982, *Mi-bifnim,* 3–4 (October, 1982): 326–28. Chances are he also learned it from his youthful readings in the Bible and its commentaries with Reb Abba and, later, in secular sources such as Fichman, Brenner, and Karni which he studied with his tutor David Schneider. See *Ha-ḥayim, ha-atsilut,* 42.

27. See *Ha-peraḥim ve-ha-agartal* 223–25; and, for lexical preferences and the semantic fields of Gilboa's poetic language, see items 1, 2, and 6 on 250–51.

28. The idea of "residues" *(mishka'im)* is Dov Sadan's. Miron refers to the term in *Bo'a laila,* 34f.

29. See Miron, *Bodedim be-mo'adam* (Lonely in Their Own Time), 132. See also *Bo'a laila,* 34f.

30. *Bodedim be-mo'adam,* 141–50.

31. Ibid., 150.

32. See below the discussions of *Shiri ha-par'ua* (My Wild Song) and *Signonot shonim* (Different Styles).

33. See Harold Bloom's Nietzchean-Freudian (or oedipal) idea of "Poetic Influence" or "poetic misprision." *The Anxiety of Influence* (New York: Oxford University Press, 1975), 12–16, 19–45, 93–96.

34. *Postmodernist Fiction* (London and New York: Routledge, 1987), 6. In a parallel vein, Arpali points out that poets such as Shlonsky, Alterman, and Amichai display "common principles" which are variedly "romantic" or "classical." See the section entitled "Modernist No-Modernist" in *Ha-peraḥim ve-ha-agartal,* 299–304.

35. Lazar Fleishman notes that Boris Pasternak's poetry also exhibits the characteristic of being between the avant garde (or modern) and the traditional because of the "tension and dynamism" between its "'metatext' and 'text' components." See "Problems in the Poetics of Pasternak." *Poetics, Theory, Literature* 4 (1979): 44. See also the comments by Uri Margolin on various issues of literary periodization, including the role of individual styles and language layers, in "Le-va'ayat ha-ḥaluka li-tekufot ba-historia shel ha-sifrut" (On the Problem of Periodization in Literary History). *Ha-sifrut* 2, 1 (1969): 5–13.

36. The letter is dated September 4, 1933. Soon after Gilboa's death in September 1984, Sarah Segal, who saved this and other personal letters from Gilboa, gave them to the poet's widow. *Mir shpanen* appears here with the generous permission of Gabi Gilboa.

37. The last two lines are illegible.

38. Retitled in *La-ot* as *Ahava aḥat* (One Love).

39. This is the first poem which Gilboa annotated *"Mi-tokh ot"* (From Sign), later renamed *La-ot.*

40. For further information regarding the breaking of the full news of the Holocaust horror, see Bargad, *Ideas in Fiction,* 86–87.

41. With the exception of translations from *Israeli Poetry: A Contemporary Anthology* (Indiana University Press, 1986), I have purposely translated Gilboa's works in a fairly literal style throughout this volume.

42. For example, *be-hityapḥut sha'ot me'uḥarot* (in the sobbing of late hours) and *elem-re'iy-ati* (my muteness-sight).

43. The structure of the verses and the rhetorical bombast are reminiscent of Uri Zvi Greenberg's works. The overriding influence, however, is Yiddish proletarian poetry. In the 1982 Gouri interview, Gilboa states that *Ki az etsak*'s prosody is the same as the long-lined Yiddish poetry of his teen years. For a comparison of Greenberg's and Gilboa's works, see chap. 3, 74–80.

44. These, for a time, were among Gilboa's favorite images. See also Papiernikov's *Vayn un vegn* (Tears and Roads), *Literarishe bleter* 18 (May 3, 1935): 573. Papiernikov uses "red" and "blue" in describing the "distance"; the image "grabs the eye"; and, as in Gilboa's *Ba-emek,* he depicts a lone figure standing "amid the roads" with an outstretched hand.

45. See the discussion of *Shiri ha-paru'a* pp. 42–45.

46. Collected in *Iberblaybn* (Leavings) — the title parallels Bialik's *Safi'aḥ* — a volume of poems published in Israel in 1949 but originally written in Warsaw and Tel Aviv between 1918 and 1925.

47. This is especially true of the collection *In zunikn land* (In the Sunny Land) (Warsaw, 1927), which features poems on certain pioneer locales, including the Jezreel Valley, Merḥavia, and Ein-Ḥarod.

48. Collected in *Ne'urim* (Youth) (1935–1936). Similar word repetitions appear in Uri Zvi Greenberg's Hebrew works in the late twenties. Note these two examples from *Anacreon al kotev ha-itsavon* (Anacreon [a Greek writer of love poems and drinking songs, c. 570–480 B.C.E.] on the Pole of Sadness, 1928): "the man-without-a-home-on-earth/from his mother's womb alone, alone, alone *(boded, boded, boded),*" p. 5; and "this despair, lustrous, lustrous *(nahir, nahir),* p. 14.

Chapter II : La-ot

1. It should be noted at the outset that the 1942 collection *La-ot* is not the same as the *"La-ot"* section of *Sheva reshuyot.* Gilboa omitted many poems from the original *La-ot* volume and, in 1949, added a good number of new poems. References to these editorial and publication changes are made in the ensuing exposition. Toward the end of his 1984 interview with Eli Mohar, Gilboa mentions that he had had a month-long painting job and used the money he earned to have *La-ot* printed. (See chap. 1, n. 16 above.)

2. *Collected Works* I, (Hakibbutz Hameuchad, 1987), 14.

3. In the winter months the prayer asks God to "give dew and rain for a blessing" *(tal u-matar li-verakha).* The biblical source of the phrase is 1 Kings 17:1.

4. Exodus 26:1–2.

5. See, for example, Ezekiel 22:22 and Shabbat 4,5 for *kur;* Pesaḥim 4,7 and Beitza 4,5 for *grof.* Bialik uses the phrase *ligrof et ha-tanur* (to rake out the oven) in a secular, daily-chore context in *Safi'aḥ,* chap. 1.

6. Uri Zvi Greenberg's collection of lyrical Yiddish poetry, *Farnakhtngold* (Twilightgold) (Warsaw, 1921) may have been a source of the combination-word usage. In *Tefilo* (prayer), for example, he uses the images of *sod-nekht* (secret-nights) and *zekenim-velder* (old people-forests). Greenberg embellishes this usage in *Anacreon al kotev ha-itsavon* and later works.

7. Yael Feldman speculates similarly with regard to Zalman Shneour (1887–1959) in *Modernism and Cultural Transfer,* 21.

8. See his article on "Prosody, Hebrew" in the *Encyclopedia Judaica,* 1231–33.

9. Literal translation: A display window lit up in its lights/beyond it—a street./Beyond here a blind hand rhymes/for the thousandth time: sorrow. *Shirim* (Merḥavia: Sifriat Poalim, 1961), vol. 2, 53. The poem is taken from the *Avnei bohu* collection.

10. *Shirim* (Poems), 1967, 58.

11. Beyond her mention of the influence of Yiddish poetry's freer rhythms on Zalman Shneour, Yael Feldman also notes the works of Avraham Ben-Yitsḥak, who was influenced by German Modernism and "whose versification is mostly free from traditional constraints." See *Modernism and Cultural Transfer,* 21f. On the one hand, it seems improbable that Ben-Yitsḥak, who produced only eleven poems in the years 1908–1930, would have influenced Gilboa. On the other, several of Ben-Yitzḥak's motifs seem to have found their way into Gilboa's poetry; for example, *yom tsa'ir* (a young day) vs. Gilboa's *shemesh tsa'ir* (a young sun); *ha-shemesh ha-gadol* (a great sun), rendered similarly to Gilboa's *shemesh tsa'ir* in the masculine rather than the usual feminine gender; and *laila gadol* (a great night), with a similar use of *gadol* recurring often in Gilboa's works.

12. *Collected Works* I, 51.

13. In his discussion of the heroic-tragic theme in the works of the younger Israeli poets, Shraga Avneri notes that Gilboa's major poetic innovation in his World War II poetry is his "attempt aesthetically to capture the experience of sorrow" and, later, in his Holocaust poetry, to convey the idea of the unacceptibility of death. See "Shiratenu ha-tse'ira be-mivḥan ha-nose" (Our Young Poetry in the Test of the Topic), *Moznayim* 8 (Apr.-May, 1959): 420–24.

14. *Shirim,* 1961, II, 221.

15. Gilboa may have borrowed the usage from Shlonsky or possibly from Bialik, who uses the less metaphorical phrase *gavhu shemei shamayim* (the upper heavens grew high) in *Pa'amei aviv* (Harbingers of Spring). Gilboa uses the phrase doubly in the Holocaust poem *Shir ke-migdalekh ha-gavo'ah* (A Poem Like Your High Tower): "so that the heavens will be high as death," and "this is a poem on nights high unto death." *Collected Works* I, 143.

16. *Shirim,* 1967, 58.

17. Cf. *Ha-peraḥim ve-ha-agartal,* 220f, 284f, 289ff.

18. Ḥaya Shaḥam (1990) shows that in his early poems Gilboa used metalingual ars poetica comments to counter the poetics of Alterman. Although some of her evidence is convincing, my feeling is that Gilboa's comments constitute a broader oppositional voice—certainly Shlonsky should also be included—which does not approach the dialogic encounter with Alterman that Shaḥam suggests.

19. Gilboa's title may also have originated with Alterman. The poem entitled *Mazkeret la-derakhim* (A Souvenir For the Roads) [from *Kokhavim ba-ḥuts,* in *Shirim,* I, 24] contains the lines: *Od harḥek harḥek menaḥamot/harbe derakhim. . . . ha-keḥulot ve-gam ha-adumot.* (Still far far away many roads murmur . . . the *blue* and also the *red.*)

20. Judges 16:29. In Chana Kronfeld's paradigm, the allusion would come under the category of "simultaneity," i.e., "a simultaneous activation" of both the alluding and evoked texts. See "Allusion: An Israeli Perspective," *Prooftexts* 5 (1985): 137–63.

21. *Collected Works* I, 17.

22. *Va-ani mekhahen pe'er,* taken from Isaiah 61:10.

23. In *Yadati, be-onyi esha'er (Collected Works* I, 19), another poem of the same period, Gilboa also uses many archaisms, most of which are also allusions to the Song of Songs. He sensuously describes the morning sun as "a copper shovel of myrrh [which] drips its spices above my bed *[maḥtat mor neḥusha/tazlif neradeha me-'al le-mishkavi].*" Bialik's vocabulary is evident in Gilboa's use of *naḥush* (copper or hard) and *tamrurim* (bitterness or sorrows), both of which appear in *Ha-matmid* (The Yeshiva Student). The mood of despair, erotic images, and candle motifs also connect these two poems.

24. *Collected Works* I, 18. I have omitted the epilogue.

25. *Nitsnaf* and *ve-yitgal* appear in *Ba-sade* (In the Field); *yetanu* appears in the same form in Judges 5:11. In different form it opens the famous liturgical poem *U-netane tokef* (Let us proclaim the power [of the holiness of this day]), recited on the Jewish High Holy Days. *Letanot* appears as *yetanu* in Bialik's *Shiva* (Seven Days of Mourning); and *betulim* (line 7 of *Ru'aḥ erev* in *Preida* (departure). *Sho'at merḥakim* (distant destruction, line 5) is taken from Isaiah 10:3.

26. Even Shoshan quotes from three modern poets, Shin Shalom, Tenne, and Gilead, each of whom place *sa'an* in this context.

27. See Warren Bargad, "Binary Opposites in the Poetry of Amir Gilboa," *Association for Jewish Studies Review* 12 (1988): 103–27.

28. *Al ha-ra'av* (On Hunger), 36.

29. The opening stanza of *Ha-na'ar ha-meshorer* is an acrostic of the name of Chana Klieger, Gilboa's teen-aged friend.

30. See the Gouri interview, chap. 1, n. 3 above.

31. *Collected Poems* I, 31ff. The title of this poem may have been taken from Alterman's *El ha-pilim* (To the Elephants), part 3, *Shirim* I, 22: *Ein sof la-derekh ha-zot ha-ola* (There is no end to this rising road).

32. The theme of the unity of the poet and his poetry is reflected prominently in *Ma she-ḥashavti* (What I Thought), the modernistic, climactic poem of the 1968 collection *Ratsiti likhtov siftei yeshenim* (I Wanted to Write the Lips of Sleepers). See chap. 6, 242–49.

33. See Sanhedrin 98a.

34. *Collected Poems* I, 36 ff.

35. In the order given, these excerpts are from *Al ha-ra'av* (On Hunger), ibid., 36; *Al ha-tseḥok* (On Laughter), ibid., 38; *Al ha-kalon* (On Ridicule), ibid., 39; and *Al ashan ha-tseriḥot* (On the Smoke of Shrieks), ibid., 40.

36. Ibid., 17.

37. Ibid., 19.

38. Ibid., 20.

39. From the early fifties on, Gilboa was adamantly opposed to the testing and proliferation of nuclear arms. Several poems relate to this particular issue, especially *Malkhut demama* (Kingdom of Silence), ibid., 316–17. In 1982 he protested the War in Lebanon, in which Lebanese civilians in Beirut were shelled by the Israel Defense Forces. Although Gilboa did not pen many moralistic works, at times he expressed the view that poetry must also be a motivating force. In part 6 of *Shirim mi-gei ha-etsa* (Poems From the Valley of Counsel, ibid., 160), he offers a motto to this effect: lo *leshorer, lo leshorer—le'orer* (not [just] to poetize, not to poetize—to arouse).

40. In *Ha-na'ar ha-meshorer,* for example, the impulsive young poet, overcome by wine, shows that he is not yet in control of his craft.

41. For example, *roshfa* in *Bo ha-erev ba-parvar,* an archaic word and grammatical form for "flames"; *bareket,* one of the stones on the High Priest's breastplate (Exodus 28:17); and *or gadol,* the "great light" of a candle.

42. Eye motifs and eye synonyms proliferate in both the works of the Age of Bialik poets and in the early modernists. For example, Bialik's works abound with references to eyes in conjunction with light or shining *(Hirhurei laila* [Night Thoughts], *Tsafririm, Zohar),* flames or fire *(Eineha* [Her Eyes]), and unsightedness and wide-eyedness *(Lo herani Elohim* [God Has Not Shown Me], *Razei laila).* Bialik also uses related terms such as *bavot* and *risim (Zohar, Lifnei aron ha-sefarim* [Before the Bookcase], *Megilat ha-esh).* Alterman's early works also contain an abundant display of these eye motifs, though the imagery is most often figurative, usually with expressionistic, rather than realistic, overtones. For example, "My pair of pupils *[ishonim]* . . . are trapped in the thicket of rest and lust" *(Shirim* 1931–1935, 143); "Grassy earth prancing in the greenness of my eyelashes *[risim]" (Shirim,* I, 16; "[The earth] whitens the lashes of your eyes with salt" (ibid., 103). Another source is the poetry of Shin Shalom, whose early works often contain the terms *bavot* and *ishonim.*

43. In interviews later in life Gilboa often noted the difficult times he had experienced in Israel in the late 1930s. For example, see the Mohar interview (chap. 1, n. 16 above).

44. The reference is to *Gevishayikh la-helekh,* which became the second part of the *"La-ot"* section in *Sheva reshuyot.*

45. *Collected Works* I, 42.

46. See 2 Kings 2: 13–14.

47. The term *pesul-gevish* is most likely derived from the term *pesul-kehuna* (Kiddushin 66a), which refers to a person unfit, due to faulty or unclear lineage, to become a priest in the Holy Temple. The phrase implies the devalued nature of imperfect or flawed crystal, but Gilboa's phrasing is shaped to reflect also the idea of unfitness.

48. Years later, in an address in honor of Raphael Eliaz, Gilboa praised the poet's "rhythmically wild verses" *(shurotav peru'ot ha-ketsev).* See "Ḥamishim shana le-Repha'el Eli'az" (Eli'az's Fiftieth Birthday), *La-merḥav,* April 1, 1955.

49. The use of the word *nir* is significant. Its source is Avot 3:7, where the individual is warned while walking outdoors to think continually of the study of Torah and not to stop by the way to admire the trees or fields *(Ma na'e ilan ze, u-ma na'e nir ze,* "How lovely that tree is, and how lovely that field is"). The message is that such behavior is to be considered spiritually unacceptable.

50. These quotations, in order given, are taken from *Ba-ḥalomam ani melekh* (In Their Dream I'm a King), *Gevishei laila, Al ha-yofi* (On Beauty), *Ba-derekh ha-ola,* part 3, *Al ha-kalon* (On Shame), and *Yadati be-onyi esha'er. Collected Works* I, 21, 22, 27, 35, 39, 19.

51. The quotations are from *Ba-derekh ha-ola,* part 1, ibid., 32.

52. Ibid., 25, lines 1 and 12.

53. Most of the allusions are of the "simultaneity" type noted by Kronfeld in "Allusion: An Israeli Perspective," 146ff. See n. 20 above.

Chapter III : Sheva Reshuyot

1. Sources differ as to the origin of Gilboa's war poems. It is generally accepted that most were written while Gilboa was a driver in a mechanics unit of the British Army. (Later, in Italy, his unit was absorbed into the Jewish Brigade.) Gilboa's own claim is that he wrote only "a few lines." See A. B. [Yaffe], "Meshorer seva nidudim" (A Poet of Many Wanderings), *Ma'ariv,* October 9, 1953. In another interview that same year, however, Gilboa acknowledges that "most of *Sheva reshuyot* was written on cigarette packs" during the war. See the unsigned interview, which includes a review of *Shirim ba-boker ba-boker,* in *Ba-maḥane,* September 9, 1953.

2. *Collected Works* I, 44.

3. Ibid., 55.

4. See chap. 1, n. 1.

5. *Collected Works* I, 48.

6. Ibid., 49.

7. Ibid., 45.

8. Ibid., 52–53.

9. Ibid., 53.

10. Bereshit Rabba, 3. See also Bialik and Ravnitzky's *Sefer ha-Agada* (The Book of Legend), (Dvir, 1947), 8.

11. The excerpts in the order given, are taken from *Collected Works* I, 45, 48, 48, 48, 46, 46, 52, 46.

12. Chana Kronfeld differentiates between the *moderna's* "introverted" or "minimalist" poets, such as David Fogel, Avraham Ben-Yitsḥak, Yehuda Karni and Raḥel, and the "extroverted" or "maximalist" poets, such as Shlonsky and Greenberg. Certainly in these poems of figurative profusion Gilboa should be numbered among the latter. See Kronfeld's chapter 3, entitled "Beyond Language Pains: The Possibility of Modernist Hebrew Poetry."

13. Pinḥas Sadeh calls Gilboa's metaphors "daring and original" and notes that they are often difficult to interpret. He adds that Gilboa's style is "adamant, wild, incomprehensible *(bilti-muvan).*" See "Keri'at tagar al ha-metsi'ut" (A Call to Arms on Reality), *Ha-arets,* December 30, 1949. Hillel Barzel states that Gilboa has, in effect, no metaphors; instead he offers "euphuistic images" *(tsiyurim nimlatsim).* See "Alpit shel hasa'ar . . . " (One Thousandth of the Storm . . .), *Ashmoret* 6 (February 2, 1950). In "Meshorer seva nidudim" (see n. 1 above), Gilboa tries to delineate the question of his metaphorical style. Noting that he places his metaphors "close together, while one is very distant [in semantic terms] from

the other," he sees this method as the cause of his being labeled a "difficult" poet. In a review of *Shirim ba-boker ba-boker,* Moshe Shamir follows Gilboa's lead by referring to "the problem of 'the difficult poem'" in Gilboa's poetry. See "Im shirei A. Gilboa" (With the Poems of Gilboa), *Davar,* May 22, 1953. In a lecture partially published later, Shamir is emphatic: Gilboa, he states, is "one of the most extraorinarily difficult poets to read and . . . to interpret. [He is] the poet of spontaneity." See "Ha'arot le-shirat Amir Gilboa" (Insights Into Gilboa's Poetry), *La-merḥav [Masa],* May 13, 1952. Both Shamir articles are reprinted in *Amir Gilboa: Mivḥar ma'amarim al yetsirato* (A Selection of Critical Essays on Gilboa's Writings), ed. Avraham Balaban (Am Oved, 1972.) Going beyond Shamir's characterizations, Natan Goren calls *Sheva reshuyot* "wild" and "chaotic." He blames the frightful World War II experience for Gilboa's "overloaded images [and] multitude of visions." See "Sifrutenu bi-shenat 1949–50" (Our Literature in 1949–50), *Devar ha-shavua,* 39 (October 5, 1950): 12. In a similar vein, Ida Tsurit adds that Gilboa's "inner, complex world of poetry" is composed of "private images" which are created "impulsively" by the poet. Echoing a prior comment by Shamir, the term she uses is *shira hekhreḥit* (compulsive poetry). See "Shirat Amir Gilboa" (Gilboa's Poetry), *La-merḥav [Masa],* May 16, 1956. (The article is also reprinted in the Balaban volume.) The terms "difficult," "private," "impulsive," et sim., reverberate throughout the Gilboa interviews and criticism.

14. *Collected Works* I, 52.

15. Uri Carmi registers his unhappiness with this imagistic "surfeit" by calling Gilboa's writing in *Sheva reshuyot* "verbose" *(melel)* and an example of "the childhood sickness of modernism [which most modern Hebrew poets] have long ago abandoned." It is Carmi who initiates several of the descriptive terms—"impulsive," "privatistic," "imagistic surfeit," "individualistic," "opaque"—that permeate much of Gilboa criticism. By counterposing the language of the "younger" poets—Gouri, Galai, Tanai and A. Hillel—Carmi indirectly refers to Gilboa's embellished Age of Bialik style. This, in turn, demonstrates Gilboa's being caught, in a linguistic sense, between two generations of Hebrew poets. See *"Sheva reshuyot: Shirim me'et Amir Gilboa"* (Seven Domains: Poems by Amir Gilboa), *Dorot* 1, ll (December, 1949): 12–13. In a talk given at a party in honor of the publication of *Sheva reshuyot,* Tanai also notes some of his misgivings concerning Gilboa, including his "stubborn language," "incomprehensibilities" *[i-havanot]* and his writing in a "secret code" *[simanei-seter].* See "Al shirat Amir Gilboa" (On Gilboa's Poetry), *Ba-sha'ar,* November 17, 1949.

16. In "Ha'arot le-shirat Amir Gilboa," Moshe Shamir suggests that in some poems Gilboa "loses control of reality altogether." Generally he feels that despite its "great depth," Gilboa's language is much too "wild," "spontaneous" and "unpolished." (See n. 13 above.) A.B. Yaffe echoes this view by calling Gilboa's World War II poems "mood poems" *(shirei avira).* He explains the term as follows: "This is realistic poetry *[shira aktualit]* which has no need for grounding in daily events; it transmits the sense of the time which is felt instinctively." See *Metsi'ut ve-shira* (Reality and Poetry) (Sifriat Poalim, 1953) 103. Gilboa himself echoes the idea of "spontaneous" poetry in the 1953 Yaffe interview in *Ma'ariv.* (See n. 1 above.) However, in the 1971 interview with Eli Mohar, Gilboa speaks more ambivalently about the notion of "spontaneous" writing: "It seems to me that somewhere I've lied about the matter of spontaneity in my writing. Even so, there is such a thing, it's not a complete lie." Gilboa adds, however, that the essential ingredients in writing poetry are "understanding of the heart" *(bi-*

nat-lev) and "the artistry [or know-how] of things" *(ḥokhmat ha-devarim).* He adds that poetry must be written in a "condition of purity" (or devotion/*hitkadshut).* Later in the interview he also states that poetry is hard work, i.e., the opposite of spontaneity. In a letter to the critic Rivka Gurfein dated October 2, 1971, Gilboa talks about a later poem, *Im ha-geshem* (With the Rain, *Ketaf* [Balm], 34), which "is one of those that's written almost not by your own hand . . . you're only a medium controlled by a power which you're conscious of but only from forgotten distances . . . the situation is like . . . a poetic dream."

17. *Collected Works* I, 54.

18. Ibid., 55

19. See Michael Riffaterre, "Interpretation and Undecidability," *New Literary History* 12, 2 (Winter, 1981): 227–42. In his article on "Problems of Emotive Language" Edward Stankiewicz (1964) uses the term "individual deviations from the norm [which are often featured] in poetic language, in stylistics."

20. From the *"Ya'ale" piyut,* for example.

21. See especially *Ba-ritma ha-meshuleshet* (In the Threefold Harness, 1930).

22. *Collected Works* I, 55.

23. From *Ken. Kakha. Lo raḥum.* (Yes. Like that. Merciless.), ibid., 56.

24. Ibid.

25. In *Od ha-pele lo avra she'ato* (Wonder Has Not Yet Ceased) ibid., 54, written a short time before he knew of the death of his family, Gilboa writes with triumphant lyricism about "the bayonet of my sun."

26. The language and imagery in this short poem are derived from sources which relate to the theme of slaughter, both animal and human: the laws of slaughter in Ḥulin 2,1, and the famous Bialik poem *Al ha-sheḥita* (On the Slaughter), one of the poet's responses to the pogroms of 1903.

27. These examples are from *Ha-erev vadai shekhheḥani* (Surely the Night Has Forgotten Me), *Collected Works* I, 57.

28. *Bekarim bi-me'urati, Ani vekha shomer* (I Am a Guard in You), *Gam ha-laila* (Tonight Too), and *Ze tsili* (This Is My Shadow), *ibid.*, 56, 59, 62.

29. Ibid., 60.

30. Ibid., 62.

31. Ibid., 61

32. In his review of *Sheva reshuyot,* Moshe Shamir calls Gilboa's poetry "masculine" *(gavrit;* i.e., strong). The term may relate to the impassioned tone Gilboa evinces in these early Holocaust poems. It is to Shamir's credit that he, unlike several other reviewers of the volume, mentions the Holocaust directly. See "Shoshanim noshmot (Roses Breathing)" *Ba-sha'ar,* Nov. 3, 1949.

33. *Collected Works* I, 58.

34. In his article on *Sheva reshuyot,* Aryeh Anavi suggests that because of the Holocaust, Gilboa's image as a poet became "split and conflicted" *(mefutselet u-mesukhsekhet).* See *"Sheva reshuyot* le-Amir Gilboa" (Gilboa's Seven Domains), *Ashmoret* (Nov. 24, 1949): 13. *Hine va-akhabehu* was published in *La-ḥayal* [Italy], Nov. 10, 1944.

35. *Collected Works,* I, 64–65.

36. *Ru-aḥ ba-midbar* was originally published under the title *Ba-midbar* (In the Desert), *Ha-arets,* May 21, 1948.

37. The term also may mean "mist" or "vapor." (See Ezekiel 8:11.) The source of the secondary meaning, "abundance," which seems more appropriate here, may be Bialik's *Zohar (atar peraḥim ḥayim).*

38. See the comment on Gilboa's ungrammatical syntax in *Po lo she'arim,* p. 54 and n. 19 above.

39. The term is used by Reuven Tsur in his *Yesodot romantiyim ve-anti-romantiyim be-shirei Bialik, Tcherniḥovsky, Shlonsky ve-Amiḥai* (Romantic and Antiromantic Foundations in the Poems of Bialik, Tcherniḥovsky, Shlonsky and Amichai), Papyrus, 1985. Yael Feldman analyzes similar poems by Gabriel Preil. She refers to the genre as "metapoetics." See her chapter "To Imagism and Back" in *Modernism and Cultural Transfer,* 143–65.

40. The same image is featured in *Domeh, vadai* (It Seems, Certainly), a poem written close to the time of Gilboa's death in September 1984. See the posthumous collection *Ha-kol holekh,* 19.

41. *Collected Works* I, 66.

42. Ibid., 67.

43. Gilboa borrows the image from the Talmud (Yoma 20b).

44. *Collected Works* I, 70.

45. The ironic *ze ha-yom* phrase echoes *ze ha-yom asa Adonai nagila ve-nismeḥa vo* (This is the day that God has made for us to be happy and joyful upon it, Psalm 118) and its rhyme in the last line: *ani yatom. Yetom* was originally published as *Ani yatom* (I'm an Orphan) in *La-ḥayal* [Malta], May 7, 1943.

46. In medieval *piyut, Yiḥud* refers to a liturgical poem or prayer of mystical unification with the Godhead. *Yiḥud* may also refer to the custom of allowing the bride and groom a time of privacy after the wedding ceremony. (Originally, this was done in order to consummate the marriage.)

47. *Collected Works* I, 72.

48. Ibid., 73.

49. Ibid., 74.

50. The rooster is a Yom Kippur symbol of penitence in the *kapara* (atonement) ritual. A rooster (now, usually, coins to be contributed to charity) is waved about the head while one utters a prayer which asks that the rooster be slaughtered to atone for the individual's sins. *Shetum-ayin,* "wide-eyed," is a reference to Balaam, Numbers 24:3.

51. Some of the effects noted here are parallel to those produced by Alterman, especially in his *Kokhavim ba-ḥuts* (Stars Outside, 1938) and *Simḥat aniyim* (Joy of the Poor, 1941).

52. *Collected Works* I, 81.

53. Ibid., 82.

54. Published in *Ba-maḥane* 19 (Jan. 6, 1949): 12. The translation is taken from *Israeli Poetry,* 16.

55. The image is reminiscent of the ironic excessive light of day in *Ze yomi.*

56. See, for example, Exodus 38:8 and 1 Kings 2:19.

57. The precision of the rhyme retains the aura of regularity, as do (superficially) the denotations of *or, meniv, ma'alot, liftor,* and *kino.* Much like the inconclusive rhythm, the truth is hidden and complex.

58. *Collected Works* I, 83ff.

59. See Exodus 20:18, which has the Israelites "seeing the sounds" on the mountaintop.

60. In the literature of Jewish mysticism the image of the curtain serves as a *meḥitsa* or partition between God and the world. The mythical curtain *(pargod)* is also a place behind which all divine "secrets" are hidden.

61. The image of the ruined harp also appears in Yitsḥak Katznelson's Yiddish poem *Dos Lid fun oysgehargetn Yidishn folk* (The Song of the Murdered Jewish People) (New York: Ikuf Publishing) 1948.

62. In an interview with Yitsḥak Betsalel, Gilboa suggested that the only way he could write about the Holocaust was by temporarily forgetting or setting aside the reality of the trauma, "and to bring up in its place memories of a distant, past or live situation, which essentially is a dream [or vision: *ḥazaya].*" See "Shira be-emet" (Poetry in Truth)," *La-merḥav,* Mar. 27, 1964.

63. As mentioned above (n. 32), of all the early critics who responded to *Sheva reshuyot,* only Moshe Shamir refers directly to the Holocaust poetry.

64. See, for example, these poems in Shlonsky's *Shirim* (Sifriat Poalim: 2nd edition, 1961), vol. II: *Elem* (Muteness, 282), *Otot* (Signs, 289–90), *Sha'alu, serufim ba-esh* (Inquire, You Destroyed By Fire), *Neder* (Vow, 301), *Mul yom ha-akhzavot* (Facing the Day of Disappointments) and *Mi-maḥshakim* (Out of the Darkness, 307–9).

65. For an interpretation of Alterman's *Simḥat aniyim* and its relation to the Holocaust, see Boaz Arpali, *Avotot shel Ḥoshekh: Al Simḥat Aniyim le-Natan Alterman* (Bonds of Darkness: On Natan Alterman's *The Joy of the Poor)* (Hakibbutz Hameuchad, 1983), chap. 9.

66. Mendel Piekarz's (or Paikaz) bibliography lists over four hundred items through 1968 alone. See *Ha-Sho'a u-sefiḥeha be-aspaklari'at kitvei-et ivriyim: Bibliographia* (The Holocaust and Its Ramifications in the Mirror of Hebrew Journals: Bibliography) (Jerusalem: Yad Vashem, 1978), vol. 2.

67. From *Le-Eli be-Arnon/Shir hitvadut: Be-shalgei Polin* 1939 (To My God in Arnon/A Song of Acquaintance: In the Snows of Poland 1939), *Reḥovot ha-nahar* (Streets of the River, 1951; 4th ed., 1978), 18. All page references to Greenberg's poems are from this volume.

68. It should be noted that in Warsaw, Greenberg was part of the so-called "Khaliastre" (The Gang) group, which was devoted at first to proletarian-Socialist poetry and later to Expressionistic and Futuristic modes of writing. Included in this group were Avraham Liessin, Mordecai Gevirtig, Leib Kvitko, Peretz Markish, Melekh Ravitch, and Itzik Fefer. See *Ha-ḥayim, ha-atsilut,* 86, and the article, "Yiddish Literature," in the *Encyclopedia Judaica.*

69. *Shir tevel u-melo'ah ve-habayit, Reḥovot ha-nahar,* 27.

70. Ibid., 32–33.

71. *Hine ha-goy ha-magor bi-mlo'o* (Behold the Gentile Dread in Its Fullness), ibid., 169–70. See also *Le-Elohim be-Eiropa* (To God in Europe), 137–52, in which Greenberg accuses God of consorting with the gentiles and thus causing the destruction of the Jewish people.

72. *Collected Works* I, 142–44. The poem is discussed below on pp. 110–19.

73. In contrast, this is a major theme in Greenberg's works. See, for example, *Be-kets ha-derakhim omed Rabi Levi Yitsḥak mi-Berditchev ve-doresh teshuvat ram* (At the End of Roads Stands Rabbi Levi Yitsḥak of Berditchev Demanding a Response from God), *Reḥovot ha-nahar,* 261.

74. *Kinat ha-ben be-vorḥo mi-beit aviv ve-imo* (The Son's Lament As He Flees From the House of His Father and Mother), ibid., 63–64.

75. *Shir ke-migdalekh ha-gavo'ah* (A Poem of Your High Tower), *Collected Works* I, 143.

76. In his article "Temurot be-shirat Amir Gilboa" (Changes in Amir Gilboa's Poetry) *Moznayim* 40, 5–6 (April-May, 1975): 379–94, Hillel Barzel uses the term "expressionism" to refer to Gilboa's style and adds that Gilboa's poetry is "close" to Greenberg's. I disagree with this assertion, especially since Barzel provides no particular context within Gilboa's varied works to support the remark. In general Barzel uses the term too loosely. For example, toward the end of the article he also refers to the *Ratsiti* and *Ayala* collections as "expressionistic."

77. Several photographs at the Genazim Literary Archives show Gilboa at Café Kasit in Tel Aviv with Greenberg, Alterman, and Haim Gouri.

78. Compare Greenberg's *Zemer min ha-bayit* (A Tune from Home), *Reḥovot ha-nahar,* 83–86, with Gilboa's *Ke-zimrat ma'asav shel avi,* Collected Works I, 84.

79. *Al signon,* ibid., 272. The confessional statement is not directly related to Gilboa's Holocaust works. More likely, it refers to his oft-recurring bouts of writer's block.

80. *Shir tevel u-mlo'ah ve-habayit,* 27.

81. *Mi-dibur hi niset,* annotated "Livorno," was published in *Mishmar* [later *Al ha-mishmar],* Oct. 27, 1944.

82. *Dibrot,* the same term used for the Ten Commandments, connotes "principles." The imagery here is borrowed again from the biblical image of Jacob's ladder.

83. *Collected Works* I, 93.

84. Ibid., 94. *Kets ha-krav* was published in *La-ḥayal* [Italy], Feb. 9, 1945.

85. See chap. 6, n. 22.

86. A reference to the sounds heralding the arrival of the Messiah.

87. See the poem *Iri li* (My city mine), *Collected Works* II, 116.

88. Ibid., I, 95.

89. The Hebrew *bi-fra'av* is a double entendre, meaning either "in its destruction(s)" or "with its shrubs."

90. *Gan na'ul bo'er* appeared in *Yalkut ha-re'im* 2 (Summer, 1945): 56.

91. The phrase may also allude to *ein ha-ḥashmal,* Ezekiel 1:4 and 27.

92. In the order given, the three poems cited appear in *Collected Works* I, 98, 99, and 103.

93. These poems appear in ibid., 106–7 and 112–13.

94. Ibid., 110–11.

95. The same theme appears in *Rigei-ḥesed* (Moments of Grace), which opens with the verse: "We try to remember each moment of happiness,/each spurt of joy. . . ."

96. *Collected Works* I, 108–9.

97. Ibid., 104–5.

98. Published in *Ha-arets,* Aug. 8, 1947. The translation is from *Israeli Poetry,* 17.

99. The work is reminiscent of Shlonsky's ironic poem *Anaḥnu ha-gedolim* (We the Adults), *Shirim* (Sifriat Poalim: 3rd edition, 1965), vol. 2, 208–9.

100. Most of these details are taken from Tsurit's *Ha-ḥayim, ha-atsilut,* 95–96.

101. From part 2 of *Nusaḥ sheni, Collected Works* I, 115f. There are three of these *Nusaḥ* (version) poems: *Nusaḥ rishon* (first), *Nusaḥ sheni* (second) and *Nusaḥ shlishi* (third).

102. From *Zikhron devarim* (The Memory of Things), ibid., 116.

103. Even-Shoshan defines *erer* as "curse." The source of the term may be a *Hoshanot* (Hosanna) *piyut* by Eliezer Hakalir recited on the Succoth festival. The liturgical poem opens with the phrase *adama me'erer* (earth of curse). Gilboa may have added the Arabic definite article, in order to create an appropriately Middle Eastern site name and a mythical one as well.

104. *Collected Works* I, 117.

105. Ibid., 118.

106. See below the similar anaphoric structure using *ze* in *Shir ke-migdalekh ha-gavo'ah,* 118.

107. *Palmaḥ* is the acronym name *(PLugot MAḤats)* of the commando units of the nascent Israeli Defense Forces. The Palmach was founded in 1941 and absorbed into the IDF in 1948.

108. Nearly all the poems in *"Sefer ha-almog"* were published in Erets-Israeli journals and newspapers between April, 1947, and February, 1948. The only exception is the three-part poem entitled *Mi-shirei ha-yiḥud asher le-Meliselda* (From the Hymns to Meliselda), *(Collected Works* I, 138 ff.) published in December, 1946, but placed after the others in *Sheva reshuyot.*

109. The use of *eikh* (how; *kak* in Russian) in opening lines is derived from Russian folk poetry. See Roman Jakobson, "The Poetry of Grammar and the Grammar of Poetry," *Lingua* 21 (1968): 597–609.

110. *Collected Works* I, 121.

111. For example, see Bialik's poem *Levadi* (Alone), line 3: *va-ani, gozel rakh* (And I, a young chick).

112. *Collected Works* I, 121.

113. The word for destruction here is *she'iya* (Isaiah 24:12). It is close to *sho'a,* which also is an Isaiah word (10:3). *She'iya* also appears in the *piyut "Ha-adir"* in the Yom Kippur liturgy. The borrowing seems quite direct, since Gilboa uses two terms, *at* (to cover) and *noga* (light or splendor), which appear together in *Kuntres ha-piyutim II: Or at aderet noga* (Light covers [God's] garment of splendor). (See the verb *at* in the Even-Shoshan dictionary.) Here (in the last stanza, *Collected Works* I, 121) Gilboa uses *noga* and *atim* (the masculine plural form of *at)* in two successive lines: *metei gevanav ATIM,* and *ve-NOGHAN akhzar.*

114. Ibid., 131.

115. The poem is generally reminiscent of Aharon Megged's *Yad va-shem* (Memorial; usually translated as "The Name").

116. Ibid., 128.

117. The image of plunging vultures brings to mind Tcherniḥovsky's poem *Ayit! Ayit al harayikh* (Eagle [or vulture]! Eagle on your mountains). See *Shirim* (Dvir, 1966), vol. I, 408.

118. In the second stanza of *Din yamim,* Gilboa also uses water imagery to evoke an image of dreamy, liquid depth in the evening or in the cosmos. With eyes closed the speaker "plunges" into the evening, and his eyes "immerse [or bathe] in the mists." These may be the mythical heavenly waters of creation (see Rashi on Genesis 1:6) or the waters of the great Flood—or both.

119. In Jewish mystical texts prayers are imaged as rising to become a crown (or jewels in the crown) of the heavenly Sovereign.

120. *Collected Works* I, 129–30.

121. Ibid., 136–37.

122. In its use of mythological themes and "secret" motifs, this poem is similar to *Eikh ne'elmu ha-devarim* (How The Things Disappeared), part 8 of *Ke-zimrat ma'asav shel avi.* See ibid., 87.

123. The same motif is used in *Ha-erev vadai shekheḥani* (The Evening Surely Has Forgotten Me), ibid., 57, *Boker-selah,* ibid., 83ff, and *Eikh ne'elmu ha-devarim,* ibid., 87.

124. See, for example, *Gevishayikh la-helekh,* ibid., 24.

125. Ibid., 137.

126. See below, pp. 110–19.

127. Ibid., 138ff.

128. See *Sabbatai Sevi* (Princeton University Press: Princeton, 1973), 210.

129. See Scholem's article "Mitzva ha-ba'a ba-avera" (A Good Deed Via Sin) *Knesset* 2 (1937): 347–92.

130. Gilboa uses the phrase *yeven metsula,* a traditional term for tragic persecution, usually translated as "vale of tears."

131. *Collected Works* I, 139.

132. Ibid. I, 140.

133. The term is taken from the Binding of Isaac story, Genesis 22:10.

134. See 2 Samuel 1:19, David's elegy on the death of Saul and Jonathan. Gilboa returns to the gazelle figure in the title poem of his 1972 volume, *Ayala eshlaḥ otakh* (Gazelle I Send You).

135. *Collected Works* I, 142–44.

136. The discussion of *Shir ke-migdalekh ha-gavo'ah* is derived from the first section of my article "Binary Oppositions in the Poetry of Amir Gilboa." Annotated "August 1946," the poem was published in *Al ha-mishmar,* Dec. 17, 1948, under the title *Petiḥa le-sheti ha-yagon ve-erev ha-simḥa. (Petiḥa* means "opening"; it is a *piyut* term for a liturgical prayer at the outset of the service or when the synagogue ark is opened.)

137. The term and suggested procedure are Michael Riffaterre's. See "Semantic Overdetermination in Poetry," *Poetry, Theory, Literature* 2 (1977): 19.

138. This term is also Michael Riffaterre's. See *Semiotics of Poetry* (Bloomington and London: Indiana University Press, 1976), chap. 1 and passim.

139. See Nomi Tamir-Ghez, "Binary Oppositions and Thematic Decoding in E. E. Cummings and Eudora Welty," *Poetry, Theory, Literature* 3 (1978): 235–48. See also Riffaterre, "Interpretation and Decidability," *New Literary History,* 12, 2 (1981): 238f.

140. See the similar anaphoric structure of *ze* and *zo* in *Signonot shonim, Collected Works* I, 117, and above.

141. Ibid., 145–46.

142. The excerpt is taken from *Be-sakh ha-kol* (All in All), ibid., 151. This statement is parallel to Gilboa's assertion in *Ma she-ḥashavti* (What I Thought), the closing poem of the *Ratsiti likhtov siftei yeshenim* volume: "And what I thought [was] missing [was] perforce missing./That is: I [was] missing." Ibid., 145.

143. For example, in *Shir ha-mefaḥed mi-da'at,* the term *retesh guf* (body breaking) echoes the use of *retesh gev* (backbreaking) in Binyamin Tenne's *Ha-ḥoresh* (The Plowman). See

Shirim u-fo'emot (Poems and Narrative [or Long] Poems) (Sifriat Poalim, 1967) 193. In the Tenne poem the tiller works a "backbreaking" day, whereas in *Shir ha-mefaḥed mi-da'at* the poet weeps when he thinks of the "broken bodies" of Holocaust survivors. Allusions to the Balak-Balaam story are evident in Gilboa's use of *yartu* (turned aside) (Numbers 22:32) and *shur* (look) (Numbers 23:9), the latter referring to God's loyalty to and protection of the Children of Israel. Other allusions are completely unambiguous: *levarot* (for food) is from Lamentations 4:10, where it is told that women in the ancient siege of Jerusalem cooked their own children for food; and *perudot* (seeds), from the context of destruction and death in Joel 1:17. The term *levarot* also appears in *Sod she-lo nigla,* ibid., 147.

144. Ibid., 154f.

145. Ibid., 156.

146. See n. 19 above.

147. The term "estrangement" (or "making strange," *ostranenie)* is suggested by Viktor Shklovsky in the opening chapter of *Theory of Prose* (Dalkey Archive Press: Elmwood Park, IL, 1990; transl. Benjamin Sher from the 2nd Russian ed., 1929). Victor Erlich translates the term as "making strange." See his *Russian Formalism: History—Doctrine* (Moutons Publishers: The Hague, Paris, New York, 4th ed., 1980), 176.

148. Ibid., 157–60. Published in *Ha-arets,* Mar. 25, 1949.

149. Ibid., I, 160. The entire poem is enclosed in parentheses.

150. Ezra Spicehandler has shared with me another possible motive for the desired change to a simpler and happier poetry. The change, he suggests, is connected with the populism—i.e., a proletarian literature addressed to the masses—advocated by the writers of the Palmach Generation during and after the War of Independence.

151. *Collected Works* I, 161–64.

152. An alternate translation: The Book of the Day of the Daily Sacrifice *(tamid).*

153. The image recurs in the figure of the bloodied gazelle in the title poem of *Ayala eshlaḥ otakh. Collected Works* II, 109.

154. Ibid., I, 168.

155. Ibid., 171.

156. Ibid., 175.

157. See, for example, Psalms 42:2 and 126:4, and the Song of Songs 5:12.

158. *Collected Works* I, 176–77.

159. A similar example is found in part 3 of *Ba-derekh min ha-har el ha-emek: ve-aḥar—/she-alu parot rezonan lirot* (lit., "and after—/when cows their thinness in the field to graze").

160. See the discussion in Roman Jakobson's "Aphasia: The Metaphoric and Metonymic Poles" with regard to *Ratsiti likhtov siftei yeshenim,* chap. 6, 232–33 and n. 22.

Chapter IV: Shirim Ba-boker Ba-boker

1. *Collected Works* I, 198.

2. Yosef Ha'efrati finds three subjects here: the intertwining of God and the person, the person and nature, and a sense of the erotic. He sees the poem as a whole as reflecting "a connection between child's play and creation." See "Al shnei shirim shel Amir Gilboa" (On Two Poems of Amir Gilboa), *Akhshav* 7–8 (Spring, 1962): 102–12.

3. Even-Shoshan notes that the phrase *hutsad be-rishtekh* (caught in your net) is found in a Seliḥot prayer in the Siddur of Rav Saadia Gaon, 615.

4. *Collected Works* I, 200.

5. *Adama tovanit,* taken from Ta'anit 10a.

6. Ha'efrati also notes the combined child-adult perspective. He uses the term "imagistic memory" for the combination of the theme of memory and the poem's metaphorical design.

7. *Collected Works* I, 207–8. The *"Milḥama atika"* section is on ibid., 207–12.

8. Star images also appear in *Nishmat Yossi ben-aḥoti Bronia* and *Ba-kokhavim ḥatsavti.*

9. *Collected Works* I, 212.

10. In their respective poems on King Saul, Yehuda Amichai *(Ha-melekh Sha'ul va-ani* [King Saul and I], *Shirim* 1948–1968, 101–4), Natan Zach *(Te'ur meduyak shel ha-musika she-shama Sha'ul ba-Tanakh* [A Precise Description of the Music That Saul Heard in the Bible], *Shirim shonim* [Different Poems], 33), and Meir Wieseltier *(Sha'ul momlakh ba-sheniya* [Saul Re-enthroned], *Perek alef perek bet* [Chapter 1 Chapter 2], 45) also provide this anachronistic blend. In "Poems of Saul: A Semiotic Approach," *Prooftexts* 10 (1990): 315–18 (see also n. 19 below), I discuss the curious fact that all these Saul poems, including Gilboa's, were published between 1950 and the mid-1960s.

11. *Collected Works* I, 213.

12. The poem is reminiscent of the first part of Shlonsky's *Ḥulin* (Secularities), *Shirim* (1965), vol. 2, 248.

13. See, for example, the interpretation given by Arieh Sachs in S. Burnshaw, T. Carmi, E. Spicehandler, eds., *The Modern Hebrew Poem Itself* (Schocken Books: 1966), 136–38. In an article entitled "Nose ha-akeda be-sifrutenu ha-ḥadasha" *(Davar,* Oct. 2, 1959), Baruch Kurzweil refers to *Yitsḥak* as "only a child's nightmare." He adds that "the poem shows the noncoordination between modern forms of life and the biblical motif which is thrust upon the child."

14. The motif of surrogate death also appears in *Hu nofel. Mat (Collected Works* I, 44), in which Gilboa first wrote of his fear for the life of his brother. It occurs again in *Ze tsili* (This Is My Shadow), ibid., 62, in which Gilboa expresses directly his response to the news of his family's slaughter. In both these instances Gilboa says either that he feels as if he himself had died along with them, or that he wishes he had died before knowing of their awful deaths. Thematically, at least, the images are parallel.

15. *Yitsḥak, Moshe,* and *Sha'ul* were published together in *Al ha-mishmar,* April 12, 1950. *Raḥav,* the fourth biblical poem in this series, appeared separately in *Al ha-mishmar,* September 1, 1950.

16. *Collected Works* I, 214.

17. The line echoes Judges 8:20 and 2 Chronicles 34:3.

18. It is possible that Gilboa is referring to Gabriela (Gabi), his girlfriend at the time, whom he married in June 1952. Speculatively speaking, the poet may have been referring to the consonants G-L-B which appear in both names.

19. *Collected Works* I, 216. First published in *Al ha-mishmar,* May 12, 1950. The discussion of *Sha'ul* combines a close reading with the perspective of cultural semiotics. See my article, "Poems of Saul: A Semiotic Approach." The article is informed by Yuri Lotman's views in

Alexander D. and Alice C. Nakhimovsky, eds., *The Semiotics of Russian Cultural History* (Ithaca and London: Cornell University Press, 1985).

20. In this sense the poem falls into the semiotic category described by Lotman (ibid., 30) as a cultural statement which "reveals a dependence upon the cultural model that existed earlier." For the Tcherniḥovsky poem, see *Shirim* (Dvir, 1966), vol. 1, 341–42.

21. As noted above (chap. 3, n. 137), the term is Michael Riffaterre's.

22. The textual references are I Samuel 31:4 and I Chronicles 10:4.

23. My use here of Ferdinand de Saussure's notion of *parole* indicates that the poem itself is a "speech act" which expresses Gilboa's personal anguish. The survivor's *langue,* also a Saussurean term, connotes the system or form of language—oppositional, ungrammatical, etc.—which provides the base for the individual speech act. For discussions of *langue* and *parole,* see Jonathan Culler's *Ferdinand de Saussure,* (Penguin Books: New York, 1977), 22–28, 42–49, 85–89; and his *The Pursuit of Signs: Semiotics, Literature, Deconstruction* (Cornell University Press: Ithaca, 1981), 22–25.

In his article "Ḥamisha shirim al ha-melekh Sha'ul" (Five Poems on King Saul), *La-merḥav,* May 16 and 23, 1958, Gershon Shaked states that Gilboa's *Shaul* represents "a formal break [with] collective literary forms." He bases his assessment mainly on the colloquial language used in the poem and on the quasi-personal relationship with the King that is engendered by the speaker. However, toward the end of his discussion, Shaked also notes that the poem reflects the "heroic, collective image" typical of the 1948 War-of-Independence generation of writers. For a close reading parallel to mine, see Rivka Gurfein, *Im shir* (Eked: 1967), 38–43.

24. Jerusalem, the capital of Judea, was captured by the Babylonians in 586 B.C.E., and the Jewish population of Judea was exiled to Babylon. The scene is depicted in Psalm 137.

25. Gilboa published *Al naharot Bavel* in *Al ha-mishmar,* Feb. 27, 1953, nearly three years after the publication of *Yitsḥak, Moshe,* and *Raḥav.* The poem appeared with three other works which Gilboa placed elsewhere in *Shirim ba-boker ba-boker: Be-derekh zekhura* (On a Remembered Path), *Hayinu ke-ḥozrim* (We Were Like Returnees), and *Shir am* (Folk Song). The common theme in these poems, especially in *Be-derekh zekhura* and *Hayinu ke-ḥolmim,* is mournful memory of friends and family lost in the Holocaust.

26. *Collected Works* I, 220. Israel Baal Shem Tov, also known by the acronym, the "Besht" (ca. 1700–1760), was the founder of Hasidism. Ida Tsurit points out that the poem is based on a tale of the Besht which pictures him as making a living as a dirt digger. See "Shirat Amir Gilboa," *La-merḥav,* May 18, 1956. The same comment appears in *Ha-ḥayim, ha-atsilut,* 224. Gilboa has used the image of the clay pits in *Bi-sedei ha-ḥemar* (Collected Works I, 200) and in decidedly more hopeful poems.

27. *Shoshanim* can also mean "embellishments," such as those which a scribe might use in lettering, or "ornaments," such as those used in the metalwork of ritual objects (Torah crowns, etc.).

28. See Gittin 57b.

29. The phrase *ein-ḥomer* is a pun on *ḥemar* (clay). It refers to the Hasidic notion of *hitpashtut,* transcendence. Joy is also a Hasidic ideal.

30. The phrase *ota ka-talit* alludes to the well-known image in Psalms 104:2, which refers to God as "wearing [or wrapped in] light like a coat" *(ota or ka-salma).*

31. See *El rishon ha-orot,* chap. 3, p. 95 and n. 111 above, for prior allusions to *Levadi.*

32. *Rabi Yisrael Ba'al Shem Tov al borot ha-ḥemar* is reminiscent also of Greenberg's prose-poem, *El geviyat ha-geviyot ba-sheleg* (To the Mound of Bodies in the Snow). In this poem the spirit of another Hasidic Rebbe (Master) comes down from heaven to witness the torture and murder of the speaker's father.

33. *Collected Works* I, 223.

34. The theme of poetic instinctiveness is familiar from Gilboa's Holocaust poems of the mid-forties. See, for example, *She-etsei mi-ma'avai* and *Mi-dibur hi niset* (ibid., 81 and 90). Gilboa uses the *ever min ha-ḥai* again in *Bein ze la-ze. Ki-ve-nadneda* (Between this and that. As in a swing), *Collected Works* II, 123. See my discussion of this image in "Binary Oppositions in the Poetry of Amir Gilboa."

35. *Collected Works* I, 224.

36. In "Muvanuto shel Amir Gilboa," *Davar,* Oct. 25, 1957, Natan Zach counters the notions of "difficulty," stating that Gilboa is among the most "comprehensible" *(muvanim)* of Hebrew poets. (His comments are directed mainly to the contents of *Shirim ba-boker ba-boker.*) He praises the works in that they lack a "stylized metrical uniformity," they avoid "conventionality" *(matkonet),* they contain much musicality and varied rhythms, and they are sensitive without being sentimental. Zach's opinions are challenged by Dan Miron in the latter's review of the *Keḥulim va-adumim* volume. He states that Gilboa does not succeed in concretizing his inner, visionary world in "language and image." He finds the poetry vague, repetitious, and verbose, and the poet nonselective and "exaggeratedly involved with the fervor of the creative process" *(pe'ilut mugzemet [be-]kadḥanut ha-yetsira).* He also sees Gilboa's unconventional meter as detrimental and a sign of the poet's "pathos and enthrallment" *(ecstaza).* Miron rejects precisely what Zach finds appealing in Gilboa's works. Zach finds in Gilboa the opposite of what he dislikes in Alterman: the impersonal symbolism, the "mechanical rhythm," the lack of a human "I." Miron vitriolically rejects the essence of Gilboa's romanticism: his hyperbolic imagery, emotionalism, "the megalomanic conception of the dimensions of the poet's 'I.'" See "Hirhurim al shirat Gilboa" (Thoughts on Gilboa's Poetry), *Ha-arets,* Apr. 2, 1964, and "Bi-teḥum u-miḥuts la-teḥum: Hirhurim nosafim al shirat Gilboa" (Within and Without the Pale: Additional Thoughts on Gilboa's Poetry), *Ha-arets,* Apr. 24, 1964.

37. *Collected Works* I, 225–31.

38. Ibid., 226–27.

39. Numbers 17:23.

40. I Kings 6:18.

41. The theme of uncontrollability appears in Gilboa's poetry as far back as the mid-1940s. For example, see the discussions of *Zikhron ha-tov* and *Tefilat azkara* in chap. 3.

42. The issue of the pains of excessive imagination and the wish for its diminution or demise is raised by Bialik in *Mi ani u-ma ani.*

43. *Collected Works* I, 234.

44. The terms *retsudim* (prancing) and *hitparku* (leaned) and spider-web images are often used by Bialik, and Bialik's language and general poetic presence is felt in several of these *"Shirim bodedim."*

45. *Collected Works* I, 240.

46. Respectively, ibid., 235 and 236.

47. Ibid., 237.

48. Ibid., 238–39.

49. Ibid., 240.

50. See chap. 1, n. 16. See also Arieh Sachs, *The Modern Hebrew Poem Itself,* 144.

51. *Collected Works* I, 242.

52. The textual allusions are skimpy but confirming. In Song of Songs 3:2, for example, the beloved is said to wander "in the marketplaces and the streets" seeking her lover. In Lamentations 1:2, the hapless female figure of Jerusalem is betrayed by her turncoat friends. In verse 7 they laugh "at her desolations *(mishbateha),*" as do the enemies of Happiness in Gilboa's poem. Natan Alterman's *Simḥat aniyim* also comes to mind in this context. His ambiguous allegorical persona—also named *Simḥa*—experiences some of the same sorrow and rejection depicted in this poem.

53. *Collected Works* I, 242.

54. There are some semantic similarities here to Bialik's *Zariti la-ru'aḥ anḥati* (I've Strewn My Sighs to the Wind), especially in Gilboa's use of *zara, efer,* and *ru'aḥ.* A later poem, *U-vekhen, tafasti et ha-parpar* (Yes, I caught the butterfly), ibid., II, 88 also bears some resemblance to *Eineinu ha-ne'etsamot* because of the "now you see it, now you don't" sort of dramatic structure utilized here. A translation of *U-vekhen, tafasti et ha-parpar* appears in *Israeli Poetry,* 26. For a discussion of the poem see Bargad, "Binary Opposites in the Poetry of Amir Gilboa."

55. See the use of the same term, *bedal ḥalom,* in the poem *Be-kho'aḥ oḥaz bedal ḥalom* (I'll Grab Hold of a Butt of a Dream), which opens the *Ratsiti* volume. A translation appears in *Israeli Poetry,* 23.

56. It bears repeating that the contents of this section, written in the early 1950s, serve as background to the general contents of the 1968 collection, *Ratsiti likhtov siftei yeshenim.*

57. The very title, "Songs of Evening," reflects a mood of confessionalism or at least a modality of plea or prayer. *Me-erev* (of evening) is probably taken from the liturgical, penitential hymn *Ya'ale [taḥanunenu me-erev]* (May our prayer of evening rise up), recited at the Kol Nidrei service.

58. *Collected Works* I, 244.

59. In these confessional and poems-on-poetry works of the early fifties, Gilboa increasingly uses the ungrammatical *el* ("to," "for" or "toward").

60. Ibid., 246.

61. Ibid., 249, part 4.

62. Referring to himself as *keru'a mabatim,* Gilboa uses his familiar eye imagery to describe the poet as a visionary. The phrase is used also in *Al ha-kalon* (On Disgrace), ibid., 39.

63. Ibid., 248.

64. *Ad dalto* (At His Door), ibid., 245.

65. *Ketav-ha-tsohorayim she-avad,* ibid., 248, part 3.

66. Ibid., 249, part 4.

67. *She'elat beinayim* (An Interim Question), ibid., 250.

68. *Bemo ani* (By Myself), ibid., 250.

69. Ibid., 246.

70. The strong rhythm and rhyme of these verses are more powerful in the Hebrew: *la'asoTEni to'EM/le-SEla doMEM,* ibid., 247.

71. Part 5 of *Ketav-ha-tsohorayim she-avad* presents a "stream-of-consciousness" diatribe against wasting time and "turning forever and ever into stone *[lehistale'a].*" In the interview with A. B. Yaffe after the publication of *Shirim ba-boker ba-boker,* Gilboa states that he is not "a real writer." He goes on to say that "a writer is someone who works and is occupied with this always. But for me there are weeks and months when I don't even pick up a pencil or pen. And then in one night I burst forth and write a poem of many lines. Writers of poetry of my type—I really don't know what they are." See "Meshorer seva nedudim" (A Poet of Many Wanderings), *Ma'ariv,* Oct. 9, 1953. For a similar self-assessment twenty years later, see Bina Barzel, "Ha-ketiva hi tsorekh—kemo le'ehov ve-le'ekhol" (Writing is a Need—Like Loving and Eating), *Yedi'ot aharonot,* June 1, 1973.

72. *Collected Works* I, 252 ff.

73. See especially *Huledet ha-ru'aḥ* (The Birth of the Wind) and *Derekh ha-ru'aḥ* (The Way of the Wind), ibid., 254–55 and 256–57.

74. Examples include the following: (1) Ungrammatical usage: See *Huledet ha-ru'aḥ,* line 13: *Mashal ani yeled shovav IM rats be-taḥarut le-ra'ava* (lit., "As if I [were] a mischievous boy IF running in a contest for-display); (2) Non-punctuation proliferates in the first stanza of the same poem, though the effect is to create a rapid flow and development of events; (3) *Derekh ha-ru'aḥ* displays much verse repetition. See lines 1–2 and 7, 3 and 8, and 10, 12, and 14.

75. *Collected Works* I, 258.

76. Six of these *"Shirei koteret"* were published with a number of other works in *Yevul,* Avraham Shlonsky's Fiftieth Jubilee volume, which appeared in 1954.

77. *Collected Works* I, 261.

78. Ibid., 265.

79. Ibid., 262.

80. Ibid., 271–72.

81. These are probably references to the verbiage used by various critics, to the effect that Gilboa has "changed his spots" or "moved into a new house"—i.e., radically changed his style.

82. In an unsigned interview published in *Ba-maḥane* 44 (July 9, 1953), Gilboa views himself as one of the younger modern poets on the Israeli scene. He castigates the older "post-Bialik" poets and critics, who, in his view, "try their best to block the way of modern poetry in Israel." Just two weeks later there appeared a negative review of *Shirim ba-boker ba-boker* by Gideon Katzenelson, who saw in it an infelicitous combination of "excessive ambiguity and unrealized metaphors" with an "overdone simplicity" in its colloquial language. See "Shirei Amir Gilboa" (Gilboa's Poems), *Ha-arets,* July 24, 1953. Natan Zach came to Gilboa's defense against Katzenelson in "ha-ḥotem hitatesh" (The Nose Sneezed), *Ma'avak* 69, July 31, 1953, in which he calls Gilboa "our poet" *(meshorerenu)*—i.e., the younger poets' mentor.

83. Zach may well have shaped the title of his seminal collection *Shirim shonim* after this Gilboa title.

84. Gilboa has done this before in poems such as *Simḥa, Lu me'a kova'im* and *Liora ve-Lior.*

85. See, for example, *Im tseḥok im paḥad* (Whether Laughter or Fear), *Hayom o'el shir halel* (Today I Begin with a Song of Praise), *Ani levarekh bati* (I Have Come To Bless), *Meshal ha-reḥovot, Shelaḥ tseḥokkha* (Send Forth Your Laugh), and *Tseḥokam me-avarim* (Their Laughter From All Sides), *Collected Works* I, 260 and 264–67.

86. See *Segor ha-bekhi* (The End of Weeping) and *Al panai* (On My Face), ibid., 263, and *Im tseḥok im paḥad,* ibid., 264.

87. Ibid., 174.

88. Two years separate the motto poem from the four *"Shirei adanim"* (Trestle Poems) which follow. The former was published in *Al ha-mishmar,* Feb. 27, 1953, along with *Al naharot bavel, Be-derekh zekhura,* and *Shir am.* See n. 25 above. The four "Trestle Poems" appeared together in the Shlonsky-edited journal *Orlogin* (1951, 81).

89. A parallel image of the Babylonian exile appears in *Al naharot Bavel, Collected Works* I, 218.

90. Ibid., 275.

91. The image of "frames of gold" is reminiscent of Amichai's image of "a frame of golden rage" in the last section of his *Ha-melekh Sha'ul va-ani (Shirim 1948–1962,* 103).

92. The language here—*karei ha-tefila* and *ma'ayenei ha-yehav*—is reminiscent of similar phrases in the works of Bialik and Shlonsky.

93. *Collected Works* I, 275.

94. Ibid., 277.

95. The translation is taken from *Israeli Poetry,* 18.

96. See Eliezer Schweid, "El ha-milim ha-peshutot" (Toward the Simple Words), *La-merḥav [Masa],* December 12, 1963. Hamutal Bar-Yosef, "Meshorer she-hifsik shtikato le-aḥar 10 shanim" (A Poet Who Has Ended His Silence After 10 Years), *Yedi'ot aḥaronot,* March 15, 1963. Shimon Sandbank, "'Le-aḥar she-hayiti har, le-aḥar she-hayiti yam': Al shirat Amir Gilboa" (After I Was a Mountain, After I Was a Sea), *Amot* II, 3 (Dec. 1963): 102–4.

97. *Collected Works* I, 278.

98. The image of the shards covering the eyes refers to a traditional custom of placing pieces of clay or clods of earth on the dead before burial.

99. Ibid., 279.

100. Ibid., 280.

101. Ibid., 281.

102. The phrase appears at the end of Bialik's *Al saf beit ha-midrash* (On the Studyhouse Threshold).

103. The theme is reminiscent of one of Gilboa's earliest poems, *Halelu am* (Praise the People).

104. *Orlogin* IV, 195–98.

105. See *The Semiotics of Russian Cultural History,* 30.

106. *Collected Works* I, 283.

107. See Edward Stankiewicz, "Poetics and Verbal Art," in T. Sebeok, ed., *A Perfusion of Signs* (Bloomington: Indiana University Press), 66.

108. The closing lines are intensified by an effusive repetition of rhymes: *merḥav-devarav-banav-banav* and *tseriḥim-noflim-kamim-hasheliḥim.*

109. *Collected Works* I, 286.

110. *Ein sof shel sof,* which may also be translated as "There is no end to end." The use of "endlessness" has a resonance of the mystical term *Ein* (or *Eyn) Sof,* which in Jewish mysticism refers to an aspect of the Godhead. My understanding is less theologically oriented.

111. The figure also appears in *Shir dam be-kaḥol* (A Poem of Blood in Blue), which is placed immediately before *Shir seliḥa min ha-ko'aḥ* in the *"Shirim ba-tal"* grouping.

112. See H. M. Sachar, *A History of Israel,* vol. 1 (New York: Knopf, 1976), 468.

113. *Collected Works* I, 288.

114. *Shirim ba-reḥov ha-gadol* (Songs of the Big Street), *Collected Works* I, 290–96; *Shirim be-anan u-va-shemesh* (Songs in the Cloud and in the Sun), 297–301; *Shirim be-khol lashon* (Songs in Every Tongue), 302–8.

115. *Huledet ha-shir* (Birth of the Poem), ibid., 290.

116. *Ani holekh ba-reḥov* (I Walk in the Street), ibid., 293.

117. *Zaru'aḥ* (radiant) and *artsi* (earthy) are found in *Shir ketovto* (A Poem of His Address), ibid., 299. The idea of the timelessness of the imagination is also expressed in this poem.

118. Ibid., 306. See also *Shir kol ha-yom* (A Poem All Day Long), 308.

119. Thirty shekels was Judas Iscariot's payment. See Matthew 26:14–15.

120. *Ani ekra lakh* (I'll Call for You), ibid., 320.

121. *Be-yamim ra'im* (On Bad Days), ibid., 319.

122. Ibid., 312–13.

123. The affinity between Isaac and the father image in this poem is reminiscent of Gilboa's poem *Yitsḥak,* in which father and son walk innocently together, and, in the end, the father shouts that he, not the child, has been slaughtered. (See above, p. 138)

124. *Collected Works* I, 311.

125. Ibid., 316–17.

126. In a conversation at his home, December, 1982.

127. Gilboa noted this response to Stanley Chyet and me in the same conversation noted above. Lili Ratok also notes this in her "Malkhut demama" article in *Shedemot* 58 (1976): 82–85. She adds that the work may also refer to the Holocaust. In *Im arba'a meshorerim* (1979, 62f), Lev Hakak states that the poem reflects Gilboa's feelings toward war "as a part of history" and that the poem has "an apocalyptic tone." The hydrogen bomb tests began at Eniwetok November, 1952. See R. B. Morris, ed., *Encyclopedia of American History* (New York: Harper, 1953). *Malkhut demama* was published in *Ha-arets,* April 3, 1953. The nuclear threat was an abiding source of concern for Gilboa. In the 1982 Gouri interview Gilboa notes that his later poem, *Ba-ra'a* (In Evil), *Collected Works* I, 386, was a response to the Cuban missile crisis. (See chap. 1, n. 3).

128. Notably, *Im arba'a meshorerim,* 59–101.

129. An English translation appears in *Israeli Poetry,* 18–19.

130. *Collected Works* I, 16.

131. The poem is also reminiscent of another early work, *Ba-sheki'a,* ibid. 17, which depicts a priestly ritual as the sun sets into the sea. At the opening of *Malkhut demama,* Gilboa injects an image of the High Priest, who, while "cries still linger on the battlefield," already "gives thanks for the victory."

132. As we have seen, the image of scrolls *(gevilim)* is used often in Gilboa's earlier writings.

133. Immediately before this closing section of *Shirim ba-boker ba-boker,* Gilboa inserts in the *Keḥulim va-adumim* collection (pp. 322–25) a group of poems which were written and published in 1956, three years after the appearance of the *Ba-boker* volume. Entitled *"Shirim mi-laila kaved"* (Poems of a Heavy Night), the grouping expresses a vehement protest against "the wicked ones *[nevalim],*" most likely literary editors who may have not been kind to the poet. In the Mohar interview Gilboa calls them "the ugly ones" and refers to them as "[literary] bureaucrats." See chap. 1, n. 16. Gilboa may have been especially angered, because, as he notes to Mohar, at the time he was just coming out of a bout of writer's block. The four poems were published by Shlonsky in *Orlogin* XI (1956).

134. In the poem to follow, *Gedolim ma'asei Eloheinu* (Great Are the Deeds of Our Lord) Gilboa prayerfully thanks God for giving him happiness. However, the voice still echoes with abiding sadness.

135. *Collected Works* I, 330.

136. The stanza is taken from *Al she-natata bi* (Because You Planted in Me), ibid., 331.

137. Ibid., 334–35.

138. Ibid., 337.

139. Ibid., 340.

Chapter V : Shelosha She'arim Ḥozrim

1. The title is ambiguous: *she'arim* could be translated as "gates" or "chapters"; *ḥozrim* could be translated as "returning."

2. *Shirim mi-laila kaved* (Poems of a Heavy Night), *Orlogin,* 12 (1956), 117 *(Collected Works* I, 322–325); and *Shir ke-ḥolem, La-merḥav,* Jan. 27, 1961 (Collected Works I, 340).

3. A number of copies of *Shelosha she'arim ḥozrim* were published (by *Hotsa'a Lididim*—For Friends' Publication) in a special volume for private distribution.

4. *Collected Works* I, 344.

5. Other poems about Gilboa's brother include *Hu nofel. Mat* (ibid., 70), *Igrot-edut le-aḥi* (ibid., 132–33), *Shir holekh-sovev* (ibid., 134–35), and *Milḥama atika* (ibid., 207–8). The ambiguity of Joshua as "brother" is also evident in *Ve-aḥi shotek* (ibid., 212.)

6. *Zahav shaḥut* is idiomatic: "gold leaf"; but the phrase is also a double entendre: lit., "slaughtered gold."

7. *Ḥayim rabim,* a parody of "many waters," *mayim rabim.*

8. See *Ha-ḥayim, ha-atsilut,* 30ff.

9. *Collected Works* I, 352–53.

10. The phrase in Psalms 69:3 is *shibolet shetafani,* "a wave [or whirlpool] has inundated me." Line 15 is taken from the same source, verse 6.

11. The story parallels the experiences later faced by Galileo (1564–1642). In the 1982 Gouri interview, Gilboa expresses his admiration for De Rossi's scientific devotion and straight-talking rebelliousness.

12. *Collected Works* I, 356.

13. In similar fashion, Gilboa gives somewhat erroneous versions of the facts in *Sha'ul.* See chap. 4, pp 142–43.

14. *Collected Works* I, 359.
15. Ibid., 360.
16. Ibid., 367.
17. Ibid., 368.
18. Ibid., 365.
19. Ibid., 366.
20. The translation here is done as literally as possible, so that the reader may fully experience the repetitions. For example, *patu'aḥ le-einav* might be translated as "open in his sight," but I have kept the phrase "to his eyes." The repetitions are also accentuated by the constant recurrence of the final "___av" (or "___af") syllables in *ḥayav, einav, daf, ne'esaf,* and *ne'ezav.*
21. *Adam be-emet eino tsarikh* was published in *Davar,* November 22, 1963. The publication date of the first edition of *Keḥulim va-adumim* is noted as November, 1963.
22. *Collected Works* I, 370.
23. From *Kol ha-devarim she-yadati* (All the Things That I Knew), ibid., 381.
24. See n. 35 below.
25. Ibid. 372.
26. Ibid. 374.
27. Ibid. 373.
28. The translation, with minor changes, is taken from *Israeli Poetry,* 20.
29. The Hebrew does not express certain particles of speech in these lines. The translation of line 9 reads "ahover with," but the original uses only "ahover" *(roḥefa).* Also, in line 10 the translation reads "mountains of mountains of air," but the original is ungrammatical: lit., "mountains of mountains air."
30. *Collected Works* I, 377.
31. Ibid., 379.
32. Ibid., 380.
33. See II Samuel 3:27.
34. *Collected Works* I, 390.
35. There may have been a medical basis for Gilboa's preoccupation with mortality. For many years he suffered severe stomach ulcer attacks and at one point had to be hospitalized. However, the existential dilemma seems to have been more psychological. In response to my query, Gabi Gilboa wrote (in a letter dated Sept. 19, 1991) that Gilboa "often pondered death and was convinced that he would die young. . . .It seems to me that the fear of death accompanied him always." These comments are all the more relevant when one considers the many existential poems in the *Ratsiti* collection.
36. Ibid., 376.
37. Ibid., 387.
38. Ibid., 382.
39. The same format is used by Yehuda Amichai in many of his poems.
40. These phrases are taken from *Ohav kara shimshit zo,* ibid., 373.
41. Taken from *Ha-sheleg yored* (Snow Is Falling), ibid., 384 and *Ani omed ba-ḥalon* (I Stand in the Window), ibid., 393.

42. For example, the phrase *yaḥil ve-dumam* is found both in Lamentations 3:26 and in Bialik's *Hem mitna'arim me-afar* (They Arise From the Dust). *Mosdei olam* appears in Bialik's *Be'ir ha-harega.*

43. These usages are manifest throughout the *Ratsiti* volume.

44. *Collected Works* I, 375.

45. The translation, with minor changes, is taken from *Israeli Poetry,* 20.

46. Purposeful lapses of grammar or syntax appear in several other poems in this group of works. These include *Ha-boker ha-ze (Collected Works* I, 372), which contains several elliptical clauses, unpunctuated run-on sentences, and ambiguous enjambments, all within a ten-line poem which, in its entirety, is one long elliptical sentence. Similarly, *Bi-veli mesim* contains the elliptical, run-on central line: "[to stand on the shore] facing waves till I'm at rest they fled to gather/strength. . . ." Moreover, as noted in the text above, *Ohav kara shimshit zo* features an effective use of a series of pausal, elliptical, ungrammatical sentences, in order to emphasize the evocative quality of the cold, sunny morning he is describing.

47. Ibid., 394.

Chapter VI : Ratsiti Likhtov Siftei Yeshenim

1. In his review of the *Ratsiti* volume *(Davar,* Dec. 12, 1971), Boaz Arpali lists similar characteristics.

2. In *Ha-shir ha-nakhon* (The Correct Poem) (Sifriat Poalim, 1982), 70–75, Shimon Sandbank notes that throughout the volume there is a tension between the line and the syntax. In his *Amir Gilboa: Monographia,* Hillel Barzel describes the style as one of "flow and diffusion *(hitpashtut).*" He also refers to the difficulty in comprehension due to the lack of punctuation and confusing verse endings. See *Monographia,* 33.

3. Arpali puts it somewhat differently. He states that Gilboa is attempting "a breaking down of the aesthetic process." He adds that Gilboa himself admitted to abrogating his usual poetic guidelines and "left [the poems] just as they were written in the first draft." The source of this remark is a second Yitsḥak Betsalel interview in which Gilboa states: "I did not make any changes in [the poems] because I did not intend at all to publish them." See "Shira be'emet" (the same title Betsalel used for his first interview with Gilboa in 1964), *La-merḥav,* January 1, 1969. Both interviews are collected in Betsalel's *Ha-kol katuv ba-sefer: Im sofrim ha-kotvim be-Yisrael kayom* (Everything is Written in the Book: With Authors Writing in Israel Today) (Hakibbutz Hameuchad: 1969), 183–91. Arpali, however, disagrees with this suggestion—I side with Arpali—and states that these works are "the result of a considered, well wrought textual reality, rich in ploys and filled with literariness *[ashira be-taḥbulot u-gedusha sifrutiyut].*" Rivka Gurfein also concurs with Arpali's evaluation. "Each poem," she writes, "is well wrought *[melekhet maḥshevet]* with a spark of all the phonetic and semantic possibilities concealed in the individual words." She calls the poetry "intellectual" rather than "emotional" and characterizes the volume generally as "an inner dialogue [of Gilboa] with himself." See "Sifro he-ḥadash shel Amir Gilboa" (Amir Gilboa's New Book), *Moznayim* 27, 3–4 (Aug.-Sept., 1968): 248–51. In contrast, Hillel Barzel sees the works of *Ratsiti* (and *Ayala eshlah otakh)* as evidence of "the tragicalness of [Gilboa's] loss of his poetic way *[ovdan ha-derekh*

ha-piyutit]." See "Min ha-kolel el ha-mesuyam: Al yesodot ha-poetika shel Amir Gilboa" (From the General To the Particular: On the Foundations of Gilboa's Poetics), *Moznayim* 54, 6 (May, 1982): 5–9. The article is partially collected in *Meshorerei besora* (Yahdav, 1983), 38–43. See also vol. 2 of his *Meshorerim bi-gedulatam* (Poets in Their Greatness), 293–317.

4. Sandbank defines the modernism in the *Ratsiti* volume mainly in terms of Gilboa's use of "elliptical syntax." See n. 2 above.

5. Sandbank's view is that in this volume Gilboa is taking a look at himself and his prior poetry in an effort to move away from the possibility of "self-mannerism *[lehistalek me-atsmo].*" See the section below on the "Poems on Poetry."

6. See "Linguistics and Poetics," in Thomas A. Sebeok, *Style in Language* (Cambridge, MA: M.I.T. Press, 1960), 356.

7. *Collected Works* II, 7. The translation is taken from *Israeli Poetry,* 23.

8. See, for example, Isaiah 37:22 and Lamentations 2:15.

9. *Netsaḥ Yisrael lo yeshaker* (I Samuel 15:29).

10. *Sevakh ha-siḥim,* reminiscent of the thicket in the Binding of Isaac (Genesis 22:13).

11. *Mikhvat ḥeker,* a sore examined for leprosy (Leviticus 13:24).

12. *[Ki]le-aḥar shivim shana.*

13. Arpali also sees the "sleepers" as Gilboa's remembered dead. In support of the Holocaust connotation here, see *Ani omed ba-ḥalon (Collected Works* I, 393), where Gilboa uses the term *yeshenai* (my sleepers) in the context of bloodshed and weeping. Here, too, the term alludes to his murdered family or to all Holocaust victims. See the similar use of *motav* (his dead) in *Ḥeshbon yashan, Collected Works* II, 246. The term *siftei yeshenim* is ironic, since the biblical source of *ledovev siftei yeshenim* is the Song of Songs 7:10, where it denotes the beloved's erotic power to arouse her lover's lips even from sleep. See also pp. 244–46 below.

14. It appeared in *Ha-arets,* July 1, 1966, while the eight poems constituting the opening section of *Ratsiti* were published in *Yokhani* a year later. It is possible to accommodate the time lapse, since publication in a journal takes much longer than in a daily newspaper. However, most of the other *Ratsiti* works published before the volume appeared were offered as prepublication excerpts only in the spring of 1968.

15. Perhaps because of the more existential and self-conscious nature of the *Ratsiti* poems, Sandbank states that "the great tone *[ha-ton ha-gadol,* i.e., the emotive or bombastic rhetoric]" of Gilboa's earlier works is gone and in its place are works that are more "intimate." My view is that the rhetoric may have changed, but because of the complex syntactic structures the poems are certainly not less intense. See n. 2 above.

16. The existential nature poems I refer to are *She-yoredet ha-ḥashra* (That the Gloom Descends), which follows here, and *Hine ze ba* (Here it Comes), both in this first section of *Ratsiti (Collected Works* II, 15 and 16), and *Ve-kha'asher yagorti* (And as I Feared), 21.

17. The meaning of *ma mini yahalokh* (Job 16:6) is ambiguous. Literally, it may mean "What of me will go on [i.e., after my death]." Gilboa may indeed be using the phrase in this literal sense. However, the phrase generally has come to mean, "What do I care?" similar to *ma ikhpat li.*

18. Semadar Shiffman notes that the metaphorical language in *Ratsiti* is "more moderate" *(tsenuma yoter)* and that the reader is forced instead "to confront sentences . . . as if they were linguistic figures." See "Me-ḥatsiva ba-kokhavim li-nesi'a ba-otobus: Al kav eḥad be-hit-

patḥut ha-poetika shel Amir Gilboa" (From Stonecutting in the Stars to Riding in a Bus: One Line of Development in Amir Gilboa's Poetics), *Siman kri'a* 16–17 (April 1983): 58–63.

19. This is the view of Boaz Arpali. Shimon Sandbank suggests that Gilboa's use of repetitive words within the poems is a result of Natan Zach's influence. (See *Ha-shir ha-nakhon,* n. 2 above.) My opinion is that the word repetition is used in most cases to highlight the ambiguity of the particular repetition. The method is parallel to Gilboa's earlier use of pathos-engendering repetitions, such as "I remember and remember."

20. *Collected Works* II, 10.

21. In the 1982 Gouri interview Gilboa notes that he "pushed" to write these poems in the winter of 1967 "because the whole country was depressed." He is probably referring to a feeling of letdown or unresolved direction in the post-1967 War period. (See chap. 1, n. 3.) In the 1969 interview with Yitsḥak Betsalel, Gilboa calls the period "a time of cynicism and anarchy *[sheliḥut-resen]* in Israel." He also says that he began writing the poems in response to an actual letter which asked the poet how hope for the future might be revived; hence, the title of the first section of *Ratsiti: "Bi-teshuva le-mikhtavkha."* See n. 3 above.

22. See "Aphasia: The Metaphoric and Metonymic Poles," in J. V. Cunningham, ed., *The Problem of Style* (Greenwich, CN: Fawcett, 1966), 260–65. For a comparable discussion of "discontinuity and incoherence" in Rimbaud's *Illuminations,* see Tzvetan Todorov, *Symbolism and Interpretation* (Ithaca: Cornell University Press, 1982), 80–91.

23. Ibid., 261.

24. In the 1969 Betsalel interview Gilboa admits to a sort of escapism in his new, disjointed style. He also confesses—or claims—that he wrote these poems almost in an associative mode, with "nearly each line beginning a new poem and moving on to the next." The reason he gives for this process is the post-1967 trauma which engendered in him a "disbelief in the power of poetry to enchant . . . since it is unable to offer life, to help, to defend." Similar statements are made by Gilboa in an interview with "Nira": "Pan el pan im Amir Gilboa" (Face to Face With Amir Gilboa), *Ba-mivḥan,* October, 1973.

25. The sources are as follows: *higayon* in *Af lo aḥat meḥaka*—Bialik: *Megilat ha-esh; tushiya* in *Ad le-et aḥarona*—Job, Proverbs, Isaiah; *novlot* in *Ad le-et aḥarona*—Bialik: *Shiratenu ha-tse'ira* (also in Fichman); *ḥashra* in *She-yoredet ha-ḥashra*—Bialik: *Ha-berekha; nitnapets* in *Ve-khol ze*—Bialik: *Zohar; tikhla* in *Ve-kha'asher et kol hakisim* (And When All the Pockets)—Bialik: *Gamadei laila; shalmu* in *Bein kakh lekhakh* (Between This and That)—Bialik: *Yona ha-ḥayat; u-mi yode'a*—*Ha-berekha* and other Bialik poems.

26. *Collected Works* II, 13.

27. Ibid., 31.

28. Ibid., 17.

29. Echoing Arpali (see n. 3 above), Ḥayim Shoḥam describes Gilboa's effort here as "trying to understand the inner experiential tension *[ha-metaḥ ha-ḥavayati]* of writing poetry [and] to arrive at a disclosure of poetic expression *[pishut ha-haba'a ha-shirit]*." See his review of *Ratsiti* in *Ha-arets,* July 26, 1968.

30. *Collected Works* II, 35.

31. The last word in the poem is *nignavti,* lit., "stolen," as translated. The sense of it may be "deceived," as in the colloquial phrase "I was robbed." My colleague, Prof. Avraham Balaban, has pointed out that in the Hebrew original Gilboa repeatedly uses the morpheme

lo ("no" or "not") and couples it with the phoneme *lo*-specifically in the word *lomar,* to say. The effect is the recurring negation of speech, which is a central theme of the poem.

32. *Collected Works* II, 22. In Israeli slang the phrase connotes the idea of "reinventing the wheel." Gilboa uses it here in both its ironic and its literal sense.

33. *Collected Works* II, 28.

34. Nidah 30b.

35. *Collected Works* II, 44.

36. Ibid., 91–92. Gilboa opens the poem with the phrase *ma she-ḥashavti,* "what I thought" (lit., "what that I thought," or "that which I thought"). In the rest of the poem, however, he truncates the phrase and uses as an anaphoric refrain only the word *she-ḥashavti* (lit., "that [or which] I thought"). (See lines 3, 6, 9, 12, 15, 18, 21 and 24. He returns to *ma she-ḥashavti* in line 25.) In order to reflect the recurring ungrammaticality, I have translated *she-ḥashavti* awkwardly (i.e. literally) each time it appears as "that I thought."

37. An allusion to the Bialik poem *Ha-einayim ha-re'evot* (Lusting Eyes).

38. Another allusion to Song of Songs 5:2 is *ani yeshena ve-libi er,* "I am asleep but my heart is awake."

39. *Collected Works* II, 51. The translation is taken from *Israeli Poetry,* 25.

40. The poem's ending is reminiscent of the ending of *Yitsḥak (Collected Works* I, 213). Both speakers are in a dream-like state, and both feel a weakness or numbness (i.e., a sense of helplessness) in their hands or arms. These images connect the two works as Holocaust poems. See above, pp. 138–39.

41. See Samuel 22:41 and Psalms 143:12.

42. Bialik's *Ha-einayim ha-re'evot* depicts a young innocent who gives in to lust and pays the spiritual price.

43. Gilboa published less than a dozen poems between the publication of *Keḥulim va-adumim* (1963) and *Ratsiti* (1968). Some of these were collected in *Ketaf* (Balm, 1971).

44. See *Almog adom, Collected Works* I, 129.

45. In the 1969 Betsalel interview (see n. 3 above), Gilboa mentions that the first three sections of the volume *("Bi-teshuva le-miktavkha"* [In Answer to Your Letter], *"Ha-shura ha-rishona"* [The First Line], and *"U-va-yom, u-va-ḥalomi"* [And In Daytime, and In My Dream] were written between November 1966 and May 1967. The last two sections *("Likhtov ha-tikva"* [To Write Hope] and *"Kemo she-ani holekh"* [As I Go]) were composed between November 1967 and May 1968.

46. *Collected Works* II, 67.

47. Ibid., 68.

48. See, for example, Ḥaim Gouri's *Shimshonai* (My Samsons) in *Tenu'a le-maga* (Movement to Touch, 1968), 13. A translation appears in Israeli Poetry, 64–65.

49. *Collected Works* II, 69.

50. From *Le-aḥar elef shanim* (After a Thousand Years), ibid., 72.

51. From *Litpos et kol kitei ha-kur* (To Grasp all the Parts of the Web), ibid., 82. Note the similar testimonies of writers such as Ḥaim Gouri, Moshe Shamir, and Ḥayim Hazaz at the 1967 Writers Convocation in Jerusalem, October, 1967. See *Moznayim* 25 (Aug. 1967): 169–88.

52. *Collected Works* II, 83.

53. As previously noted, *tamid* may mean either "forever" or "endless," but it is also a reference to the daily sacrifices in the Temple. Gilboa also uses the double entendre in *Shirim be-yom ha-tamid,* ibid., I, 178–80.

54. *Collected Works* II, 81. The title of Gilboa's last, posthumously published collection is *Ha-kol holekh* (Everything is Going, 1985), ibid., 179–251.

55. The reference is to the Israelites who left Egypt but who were doomed to die in the desert before reaching Canaan. See the discussion on *Ru'aḥ ba-midbar,* in which Gilboa also borrows images from Bialik's *Metei midbar,* chap. 3 pp. 60–63.

56. See II Kings 7:19.

57. *Collected Works* II, 42.

58. Ibid., 55.

59. See Freud's article on "The Relation of the Poet to Day-Dreaming," *On Creativity and the Unconscious: Papers on the Psychology of Art, Literature, Love, and Religion,* selected and with introduction and annotations by Benjamin Nelson (New York: Harper & Row, 1958), 44–54. In his review of *Ratsiti* (see n. 29 above) Ḥayim Shoḥam characterizes the volume's poems as "dream monologues." Specifically, he calls *U-va-yom, u-va-ḥalomi* "entirely dream-based" and reflective of "a supernal reality" *[metsi'ut ila'it].* See also Gilboa's description of his experience in writing an early seventies poem as a "poetic dream" (chap. 3 n. 16).

Chapter VII : Ayala Eshlaḥ Otakh

1. *Collected Works* II, 109–76.

2. The gazelle is a common figure in medieval Hebrew poetry. See Raymond Scheindlin, *The Gazelle: Medieval Hebrew Poems On God, Israel, and the Soul* (Philadelphia: Jewish Publication Society, 1991).

3. The allusion here is to David's betrayal of Uriah in II Samuel 11:15.

4. *Collected Works* II, 109.

5. In addition to Gouri's *Shimshonai,* the general theme of antiwar sentiment is echoed by Yehuda Amichai. See especially his *Mu'ar migdal David,* part 3 of *Yerushalayim 1967,* in *Akhshav ba-ra'ash* (Now in the Storm), 9–10. (A translation is included in *Israeli Poetry,* 86).

6. See the discussion of the phrase *iri li* (my city mine) in the poem by the same name below, p. 261.

7. See chap. 7, n. 51, regarding the various responses of several eminent writers and poets to the 1967 war.

8. *Collected Works* II, 112.

9. Ibid., I, 213.

10. Ibid., II, 113.

11. See the cautionary poem, *Ze ka-nireh yavo ke-ḥetef* (I Guess It Will Come Suddenly), ibid., 124 (a translation appears in *Israeli Poetry,* 33); and *Lo ani ekba [gevulot ha-mamlekhet]* (I'll Not Be the One to Fix [the Kingdom's Borders], ibid., 128), a sardonic, anti-expansionist poem, aimed at the right-wing "Greater Land of Israel" *(Erets Yisrael ha-shlema)* group which formed after the war. In a letter to the poet Reuven Ben-Yosef, dated 1 Kislev (November 27), 1981, Gilboa offers his frank, hostile view of that group, which he calls "persons who have fos-

tered cynicism, moral corruption, self-centeredness, bourgeois snobbism, obsequiousness toward robber oppressive nations, and [they are] hypocrites and self-haters."

12. *Collected Works* II, 116.

13. My emphasis, here and below—WB.

14. The Hebrew is more effective than the English translation *(Israeli Poetry*, 31), since Gilboa takes advantage of the relentless sing-songy internal rhyming of the final long vowel ___*i* (pronounced "ee"). Lines 2–3 read: *iri/beli iri li imi bakh;* and lines 8–11 read: *iri li tehi./Ki mimeni tilakaḥ iri/be-ein iri li imi bakh, iri/im mimeni tilakaḥ.*

15. *Collected Works* II, 114.

16. Ibid., 115.

17. Gilboa uses the archaic phrase *ish le-veito ish le-veito* to give the scene a biblical, quasi-mythological tone.

18. A full translation is included in *Israeli Poetry*, 31.

19. *Collected Works* II, 120.

20. Ibid., 122.

21. Ibid., 124.

22. The phrase is taken from the section of the *Ha'azinu* portion, which spells out the curse for Israelites who turn away from God.

23. Ibid., 125.

24. The translation, with two emendations, is taken from *Israeli Poetry*, 34.

25. At least two of these images recall figures found in poems by Alterman: a knife in the dark appears in *Leil kayits* (Summer night) in *Kokhavim baḥuts;* a burrowing mole and blindness appear in *Ha-ḥoled* (The Mole) in *Simḥat aniyim.*

26. Two poems which follow *Laruts merḥak laila* corroborate its political nature. *Tire, im she-kamohu be-meitav* (Look, If Someone Like Him at Best) features the image of a moral gadfly who challenges society's behavior. The not-so-subtle message is that the poet, otherwise unvalued, must play this role. *Lo ani ekba et gevulot ha-mamlekhet* (I Shall Not Fix the Borders of the Kingdom), is also less subtle in conveying his disdain toward the idea of a Greater Israel.

27. *Collected Works* II, 135.

28. For example, *Nishmat Yossi ben-aḥoti Bronia, Ba-kokhavim ḥatsavti* and *Zera'im shel oferet (Collected Works* I, 131, 206, 207–08).

29. Especially noteworthy in the volume are the motifs of being in-between, nighttime, and the image of the child. See, for example, *Bein ze laze* (ibid., II, 123), *Zeman hakima min ha-mavet* (The Time of Rising From the Dead, ibid., II, 136), *Semoli ki-le'aḥar shevu'a* (ibid., II, 112), *Laruts merḥak laila* (ibid., II, 125), *Me'ei sham ma'aglei rokdim* (From Somewhere Circles of Dancers, ibid., II, 152), *Kulam yakumu* (They All Will Rise, ibid., II, 115), and *Mitokh ha-ovekh* (From Amid the Haze, ibid., II, 138).

30. Ibid., II, 137.

31. See also *Ba-sade ha-tsahov* (In the Yellow Field, ibid., II, 167), in which the sexual imagery is more pronounced.

32. See *Zeman hakima min ha-mavet,* below.

33. Ibid., II, 134.

34. Ibid., II, 144.

35. The translation is taken from *Israeli Poetry*, 34.

36. *Collected Works* II, 148.

37. Yosef Ha'efrati characterizes the entire *Ayala* volume as embodying Gilboa's "personal myth, [his] closed individual world." See "Al motiv be-*Ayala Eshlaḥ Otakh* le-Amir Gilboa," *Siman kri'a* 6 (May 1976): 311–12. Gilboa's comments in the Gouri interview (see chap. 1, n. 3) confirms Ha'efrati's view of the personal nature of these works.

38. An alternate translation of *ve-ḥayim novḥim* (alive they bark) is "and life barks."

39. Gilboa uses the term *orta* for "mix" or "in contact with." The term is primarily a talmudic one, referring to the taboo of mixing or allowing contact between certain items. For example, if eggs are allowed to touch the fowl's flesh, the eggs cannot then be eaten as part of a dairy meal. (Beitsa 7a.)

40. In her letter to me of Sept. 19, 1991, Gabi Gilboa writes that " . . . the death of his parents and his whole household killed in the Holocaust—this accompanied him all the time and he was never able to free himself from it, and it constantly permeated the mood at home—even when it wasn't mentioned—and our daily life." Similarly, in the Gouri interview *(Al ha-mishmar,* Jan. 1, 1982) Gilboa states that "the Holocaust is always with us." Chana Ya'oz quotes this citation at the end of her chapter on Gilboa in *Ha-sho'a be-shirat dor ha-medina* (Eked, 1984), 90–101.

41. *Collected Works* II, 136.

42. Ibid., 132.

43. Ibid., 158.

44. Ibid., 161.

45. Ibid., 168.

46. See the reference to Freud's "The Poet and His Relation to Day-Dreaming," chap. 6, n. 59.

47. *Collected Works* II, 162.

48. See, for example, *Tire, im she-kamohu be-meitav,* ibid., 126, and *Eikh hem ratsim* (How They Run), ibid., 156.

49. See *Eikh e'emod az* (How Will I Stand Up Then), ibid., 150.

50. Ibid., 174.

51. Ibid., 176.

52. This sort of combined response to the inspirational moment is reminiscent of *U-vekhol zot ze lo kakh* (ibid., 35), which posits the antithetical notion that once the poem is born (i.e., set down on paper) it is lost. (See chap. 6, p. 236)

53. See the phrases using *shemesh* and *bo* in Joshua 23:4, Isaiah 60:20, and Jeremiah 15:9.

54. The translation is from *The Holy Scriptures: A New Translation* (Philadelphia: Jewish Publication Society, 1945).

Chapter VIII: Ha-kol Holekh

1. The collection's title echoes the phrase in Ecclesiastes 3:20, *ha-kol holekh el makom eḥad,* ("everything goes to one place," i.e. to the grave.)

2. *Collected Works* II, 180.

3. The phrase "rot and decay" *(mesos ve-rakav)* is used by Bialik in *Ḥoze lekh beraḥ* (Prophet, Go and Flee).

4. *Ha-ru'aḥ she-be-lev ha-kor ha-metaher* (The Spirit in the Heart of the Purifying Cold), *Collected Works* II, 190.

5. Ibid., 191.

6. *Hineh kan me-ever la-ḥalon* (Look, Here Beyond the Window), ibid., 182.

7. *Shevu ahuvai* (Sit Down My Beloved Ones), ibid., 183.

8. Ibid., 205–6.

9. The Hebrew here is idiomatic and playful. In lines 20–22 Gilboa speaks about the chain of memory which has been broken and is now "by itself" *(le-nafshah)*, i.e., forlorn. He then continues to use the term *nefesh* (lit., soul) in different ways: In line 23 the speaker repeats the phrase *le-nafshah* (by itself). In line 24 Gilboa uses a rabbinic expression, *mima nafshah,* which usually means "What do you [here: does it] think" or "Whatever the case (you have no control over the result)." In line 25 *be-nafshi* may be "upon my soul," an oath that shows that the speaker is just as forlorn as the broken chain of memory. Literally, it is "in my soul."

10. The last line is a play on the words *af shir.* Gilboa separates the two syllables of the verb *afshir,* meaning "I will melt" or "thaw." He does so without the final form of the letter *fay.* The second meaning of *af shir* is "even a poem."

11. *Masada* (Dvir La'am edition, 1960, 39–40). Originally published in 1927.

12. Besides these few Holocaust images, Gilboa includes in *Ha-kol holekh* a poignant memory of his youth in Radzivil. Reminiscent of *Almog adom (Collected Works* I, 129 30), *Al ha-ye'or ze haya* (It Was at the River, ibid., II, 215) depicts a childhood swimming scene and a tag game of sorts from which Gilboa had to be rescued by his older brothers.

13. See, for example, *Ba-emek,* ibid., I, 16. The excerpt is from *Pa'am yatsa'ti el ha-kikar* (Once I Went Out to the Square), ibid., II, 185. A similar image of being alone in a field appears in *Lalekhet lalekhet milin* (To Walk and Walk for Miles), ibid., 216.

14. *Eizo ge'ut niskha bi,* (What Pride Flowed in Me), ibid., 196.

15. For example, *Ohav kara shimshit zo,* ibid., I, 373.

16. Ibid., II, 192.

17. Ibid., 193.

18. In *Ani yode'a ani yode'a* Gilboa also uses the phrase *oḥez be-kho'aḥ,* "grabbing hold" or "holding on," from the poem *Be-kho'aḥ oḥaz bedal ḥalom* (ibid., II, 7).

19. Ibid., II, 197.

20. Ibid., 212.

21. Ibid., 232.

22. Ibid., 245.

23. Ibid., 251.

24. Gilboa has written before about the plum tree in his backyard in the Ramat Aviv section of Tel Aviv. See *Shazif ba-or* (Plum Tree in the Light, ibid., I, 199) and *Be-ḥatserenu ha-shazif pore'aḥ* (In Our Yard the Plum Tree is Blossoming), ibid., II, 103.

Afterword

1. *Ma'ariv,* June 19 and 26, 1987.
2. *Davar,* Oct. 25, 1957.
3. Shamir, *Ba-sha'ar* 43 (1950): 13. *Dor ba-arets,* Merḥavia: Sifriat Poalim, 1959.
4. "Sus esh baishan" (A Shy, Fiery Horse), *Davar,* Aug. 28, 1987.
5. See chap. 1, p. 3 and n. 12.
6. Hillel Barzel, "Min ha-kolel el ha-mesuyam: Al yesodot ha-poetika shel Amir Gilboa," *Moznayim* 54, 6 (May, 1982), 5–9.

Appendix

A Selected List of Lexical Items Common to Gilboa and Bialik

ITEM	GILBOA POEM	BIALIK POEM
*yetanu**/** (proclaim)	*Ru'aḥ erev*	*Megilat ha'esh* (etc.)
*ve-yitgal** (reveals)	*Ru'aḥ erev*	*Pa'amei aviv*
nitsnaf (flow)	*Ru'aḥ erev*	*Ba-sade*
ulpe (weak)	*Ha-na'ar ha-meshorer (3)*	*Shirat Yisrael*
me'ura (cubicle)	*El ha-even*	*Ha-matmid*
mabu'a (spring)	*Ahava aḥat*	*Yesh li gan*
ḥelkha (wretched)	*Shiri ha-paru'a*	*Hirhurei laila*
*nigar** (pour)	*Zikhron ha-tov*	*Yehi ḥelki imakhem*
ratsim (strands)	*El kadmon* (etc.)	*Tsafririm*
*eghar** (sit)	*Tefilat azkara*	*Hetsits va-met*
shibolet (sheaf/flood)	*Tefilat azkara*	*Ba-sade*
liput (grasp)	*Tefilat azkara*	*Be-ir ha-harega*
*metamer** (coil)	*Ken. Kakha.*	*Bein nehar Prat . . .*
*zilfi** (flow)	*Ru'aḥ ba-midbar (1)*	*Gamadei laila*
tif (drop)	*Ru'aḥ ba-midbar*	*Yesh li gan*
garger (seed)	*Ru'aḥ ba-midbar*	*Yehi ḥelki imakhem*
atar/ateret (plenty)	*Ru'aḥ ba-midbar* (etc.)	*Zohar* (etc.)
miksam (magic)	*Miksam*	*Mikhtav katan li khatava*
i (ruin)	*Ir zokheret*	*Hirhurei laila*
kilon (well pail)	*Im benei dami*	*Safi'aḥ*
zog (bell)	*El ganayikh ki paraḥu*	*Mi-shirei ha-ḥoref*
enut (suffering)	*Mi-dibur hi niset*	*Be-yom kayits, yom ḥom*
she'at (scorn)	*Rigei ḥesed*	*Lo herani Elohim*
melilot (strips)	*Ne'um ha-govim*	*Mi-shirei ha-ḥoref (3)*
masad (base)	*Benei beli shem*	*Birkat am*
ritspat esh (ember)	*Laila be-karaḥat ha-ya'ar*	*Davar*
korḥa (clearing)	*Laila be-karaḥat ha-ya'ar*	*Shira yetoma*
mardut (punishment)	*Almog adom*	*Aryeh ba'al guf*
beḥir (chosen)	*Nishmat Yossi*	*Bein nehar Prat*
yeven (abyss)	*Mi-shire ha-yiḥud . . . (1)*	*Tikkun ḥatsot*

chart continues

*These verbal and nominal forms may vary in the respective works of each poet.

**These items are especially significant, since they appear in exactly or almost exactly in the same form in the works of both poets.

ITEM	GILBOA POEM	BIALIK POEM
go'e (increase)	*Mi-shirei ha-yiḥud . . . (2)*	*Mi-shirei ha-ḥoref*
*gavhu** (grew tall)	*Shir ke-migdalekh* (etc.)	*Pa'amei aviv*
geyonim (arrogant)	*Sod she-lo nigla (1)*	*Arye ba'al guf*
nohim (longing)	*Shir shel me'aḥer yomo*	*Mi-shirei ha-kayits*
talul (steep)	*Shir shel me'aḥer yomo*	*Megilat ha-esh (7)*
lehaki'a (penetrate)	*Ata ha-mehalekh ba-derakhim*	*Safi'aḥ*
*mahgot*** (coo)	*Shirim mi-gei ha-etsa (6)*	*Megilat ha-esh (6)*
lehatslif (shower)	*Shirim mi-gei ha-etsa*	*Tsafririm*
remets (coals)	*Le-aḥar she-yakumu me-evlam*	*Safi'aḥ*
yaḥil ve-dumam (silent and expectant)	*Yaḥil ve-dumam****	*Hem mitna'arim me-afar*
siftei yashen/yeshenim (the lips of sleeper[s])	*Ratsiti likhtov siftei yeshenim*	*Razei laila*

***This is a later, 1963 poem, collected in the *"Shlosha she'arim ḥozrim"* section of *Keḥulim va-adumim.*

Bibliography

1. Amir Gilboa's Works
(All items published in Tel Aviv unless noted otherwise.)

POETRY

1942. *La-ot* (For the Sign). Orḥa.
1949. *Sheva reshuyot* (Seven Domains). Merḥavia: Sifriat Poalim.
1953. *Shirim ba-boker ba-boker* (Early Morning Songs). Hakibbutz Hameuchad.
1963. *Keḥulim va-adumim* (Blues and Reds). Am Oved. (A collection of all three of the above items, with the addition of the section entitled "*Shelosha she'arim ḥozrim*" [Three Recurring Gates]. See the following entry.)
1963. *Shelosha she'arim ḥozrim* (Three Recurring Gates). Hotsa'a Lididim (Publication for Friends). (A number of copies of this group of forty-nine poems were published privately for distribution to friends.)
1968. *Ratsiti likhtov siftei yeshenim* (I Wanted to Write the Lips of Sleepers). Am Oved.
1971. *Ketaf* (Balm). Hakibbutz Hameuchad. (A small-format anthology of previously published poems, with the addition of about a dozen published for the first time.)
1972. *Ayala eshlaḥ otakh* (Gazelle I Send You). Hakibbutz Hameuchad.
1985. *Ha-kol holekh* (Everything is Going). Hakibbutz Hameuchad. (A posthumous volume edited by T. Carmi, with the assistance of Gabriela Gilboa, from Gilboa's manuscript. The poems were written between August 5, 1983 and August 8, 1984, less than a month before Gilboa's death on September 2, 1984.)
1987. *Collected Works* [in 2 volumes]. Hakibbutz Hameuchad. (Volume I is a reproduction of the 1963 *Keḥulim va-adumim* collection. Volume II contains all the other items listed above, including the new, so-called "Twelve Poems" first published in *Ketaf*.)

SELECTED PROSE

1954. "'Mahu Bialik bishvili?': Hu nasa esel u-shnei delayim" (What is Bialik To Me? He Was Carrying a Yoke and Two Pails). *Devar ha-shavu'a,* July 22.

1955. "Ḥamishim shana le-Rephael Eli'az" (Rephael Eli'az at Fifty). *Lamerḥav,* April, 1.
1961. "Ha-shir ve-inyano" (The Poem and Its Goal). *Al ha-mishmar,* Feb. 10.
1969. "Retson ha-hisha'arut" (The Desire for Constancy). *Ha-arets,* May 22.
1971. "Shelosha Brenner sheli" (My Three Brenners). *Moznayim* 32, 1: 330–34.
1982. "Ha-devarim mitkashrim, ha-ma'agal nisgar" (The Things Interconnect, the Circle Is Closed). *Mi-bifnim* 44, 3–4: 319–20.

WORKS IN TRANSLATION

Israeli Poetry: A Contemporary Anthology. Edited and translated by Warren Bargad and Stanley F. Chyet. Bloomington: Indiana University Press, 1986, 13–56.
The Light of Lost Suns. Translated by Shirley Kaufman with Shlomith Rimmon. New York: Persea Books, 1979.
The Modern Hebrew Poem Itself. Edited by Stanley Burnshaw, T. Carmi, and Ezra Spicehandler. New York: Schocken Books, 1966, 136–47.
Modern Hebrew Poetry: A Bilingual Anthology. Edited and translated by Ruth Finer Mintz. Berkeley: University of California Press, 1960, 252–69.
Voices in the Ark. Edited by Howard Schwartz and Anthony Rudolph. Yonkers, N.Y.: Pushcart Press, 1980, 80–85.

2. *Works by Other Poets*

IN HEBREW

Alterman, Natan. *Shirim.* (Poems). Vols. 1–2. Hakibbutz Hameuchad/Maḥbarot Lesifrut, 1967.
———. *Shirim 1931–1935* (Poems 1931–1935). Hakibbutz Hameuchad, 1984.
Amichai, Yehuda. *Shirim 1948–1960* (Poems 1948–1960). Jerusalem and Tel Aviv: Schocken, 1962.
———. *Akhshav ba-ra'ash* (Now in the Storm). Jerusalem: Schocken, 1968.
Bialik, Ḥayim Naḥman. *Kol shirei* (Complete Poems). Dvir, 1953.
Fogel, David. *Kol ha-shirim* (Complete Poems). Edited by Dan Pagis. Maḥbarot Lesifrut, 1966.

Gilead, Zerubavel. *Ne'urim* (Youth). Bama'ale Publishing, 1936. [Appeared under the authorship of "Zerubavel," Gilead's early pen name.]

———. *Priḥat ha-oranim* (The Blossoming of the Pines). Hakibbutz Hameuchad, 1950.

Gouri, Ḥaim. *Pirḥei esh* (Flowers of Fire.) Tel Aviv and Merḥavia; Hakibbutz Ha'artsi/Hashomer Hatsa'ir, 1949.

———. *Ad alot ha-shaḥar* (Till Dawn). Hakibbutz Hameuchad, 1950.

———. *Shoshanat ruḥot* (Compass Rose). Hakibbutz Hameuchad, 1960.

———. *Tenu'a le-maga* (Movement to Touch). Hakibbutz Hameuchad, 1968.

Greenberg, Uri Zvi. *Eima gedola ve-yare'aḥ* (A Grear Terror and Moon). Hedim, 1925.

———. *Ha-gavrut ha-ola* (Manhood Ascendant). Sadan, 1925.

———. *Anacreon al kotev ha-itsavon* (Anacreon on the Pole of Sadness). Dvir, 1927.

———. *Sefer ha-kitrug ve-ha'emuna* (The Book of Accusation and Belief). Tel Aviv and Jerusalem: Sedan, 1937.

———. *Reḥovot ha-nahar* (Streets of the River), 1951.

Lamdan, Yitsḥak. *Masada.* Dvir La'am, 1927, 1960.

———. *Ba-ritma ha-meshuleshet* (In the Threefold Harness). Berlin/Tel Aviv: Stybel Press, 1930.

———. *Be-ma'ale akrabim* (In the Rise of Scorpions). Mosad Bialik/Dvir, 1944.

Shlonsky, Avraham. *Shirim* (Poems). 2 vols. Merhavia: Sifriat Poalim, 1965.

Tanai, Shlomo. *Erets ha-ḥayim* (Land of the Living). Matspen, 1954.

Tcherniḥovsky, Sha'ul. 1966. *Shirim* (Poems). 2 vols. Dvir, 1966.

Tenne, Binyamin. *Shirim u-fo'emot* (Poems and Narrative [or Long] Poems). Sifriat Poalim, 1967.

Zach, Natan. *Shirim shonim* (Different Poems). Author's publication, 1960. (2nd ed., Alef, 1964. Expanded ed., Hakibbutz Hameuchad, 1974.)

IN YIDDISH

Greenberg, Uri Zvi. *Farnakhtngold* (Twilightgold). Warsaw: Di Tsayt, 1921. Also in U. Z. Greenberg. *Gezamlte verk* (Collected Works). 2 vols. Jerusalem: Magnes Press, 1979.

Katzenelson, Yitshak. *Dos Lid funm oysgehargtn Yidishn folk* (The Song of

the Murdered Jewish People). New York: Ikuf Publishing, 1948.
Papiernikov, Yosef. *Iberblaybn* (Leavings). Warsaw-Tel Aviv: "Aleyn" (self) publishing: 1918–1925. (2nd ed. Tel Aviv, 1949).
———. *In zunikn land* (In the Sunny Land). Warsaw, 1927.
———. "Vayn un vegn" (Tears and Roads), *Literarishe bleter* 18 (May 3, 1935): 573.

3. Selected Writings on Gilboa

Aḥi-Ne'eman, Y. "Hirhurei agav" (Passing Thoughts). *Le-aḥdut ha-avoda,* Mar. 20, 1947.
Akavyahu, Yitsḥak. "Ya'akov avinu ve-taḥarut kaduregel" (Our Patriarch Jacob and a Soccer Match), in *Lifnim mi-shurat ha-shir* (Beyond the Letter of the Poem). Eked Publishing, 1975, 279–81.
Aminadav, S. "Amir Gilboa: Al shirav" (On Gilboa and His Poems). *Ba-maḥane* 42 (June 15, 1950): 10.
Anavi, Aryeh. "*Sheva reshuyot* le-Amir Gilboa" (Amir Gilboa's *Seven Domains). Ashmoret,* Nov. 24, 1949: 13.
Aran, David. "Shira shel ḥiyut enoshit" (A Poetry of Human Vitality). *Al ha-mishmar,* Jan. 1 and Feb. 7, 1964.
Arpali, Boaz. "Ratsiti likhtov siftei yeshenim." *Davar,* Dec. 12, 1971.
Avneri, Shraga. "Shiratenu ha-tse'ira be-mivḥan ha-nose" (Our Young Poetry in the Test of the Topic). *Moznayim* 8, 5–6 (1959): 420–24.
———. "Ha-milim ha-yafot ha-nedushot she-hafkhu mamashut: Al shirei Amir Gilboa" (The Beautiful Common Words That Became Reality). *Al ha-mishmar,* Dec. 31, 1971.
Bahar, Uzi. "Im Amir Gilboa: Gevulot ha-mamlekhet" (With Amir Gilboa: The Borders of the Kingdom). *Siman kri'a* 8 (1978): 332–33.
Balaban, Avraham. [B. Avraham] "Amir Gilboa: 'Zera'im shel oferet'" ("Seeds of Lead"). *La-merḥav,* Mar. 13 and 20, 1970.
———, editor. *Amir Gilboa: Mivḥar ma'amarim al yetsirato* (A Selection of Critical Essays on Gilboa's Writings). Am Oved Publishing, 1972.
———. "Mavo: Kavim be-hitpatḥut bikoret Gilboa" (Introduction: Aspects of the Development of Gilboa Criticism). In *Amir Gilboa: Mivḥar ma'amarim al yetsirato,* 7–39.
Bar-Kadma, Emanuel. "Amir Gilboa: Ha-meshorer ha-lo-Palmaḥnik shel

dor ha-Palmaḥ" (The Non-Palmach Poet of the Generation of the Palmach). *Yedi'ot aḥaronot,* Nov. 9, 1981.

———. "Amir Gilboa: Shirat yaḥid ve-lo shirat yaḥad" (Poetry of the Individual and Not of the Group). *Yedi'ot aḥaronot,* Nov. 13, 1981.

Bar-Ya'akov, M. "Mi-ba'ad le-amud ha-esh" (Behind the Column of Fire). *Ma-ariv,* Dec. 20, 1963.

Bar-Yosef, Ḥamutal. "Meshorer she-hifsik shetikato le-aḥar 10 shanim" (A Poet Who Has Ended His Silence After 10 Years). *Yedi'ot aḥaronot,* Mar. 15, 1963.

———. "'Yitsḥak' le-Amir Gilboa" (Gilboa's "Isaac"). *Yedi'ot aḥaronot,* Mar. 29, 1968. Also in *Yalkut nitukhei shira* (Anthology of Poetry Analyses), edited by Chana Ya'oz. Eked Publishing, 20–22. Also in *Amir Gilboa: Mivḥar ma'amarim al yetsirato,* 184–86.

———. "Sus esh baishan" (A Shy Fiery Horse). *Davar,* Aug. 28, 1987.

Bargad, Warren. "Binary Oppositions in the Poetry of Amir Gilboa." *Association for Jewish Studies Review* 12 (1988): 103–27.

———. "Poems of Saul: A Semiotic Approach." *Prooftexts* 10 (1990): 313–34.

Bartana, Ortsiyon. "Amir Gilboa u-shnei kirkhei shirav" (Amir Gilboa and His Two Volumes [of Collected Works]). *Ma'ariv,* June 19 and 26, 1987. Some of the comments here are noted in Bartana's *Lavo ḥeshbon* (Coming to Account). Alef Publishing, 1985, 39 and 60.

Barzel, Bina. "Ha-ketiva hi tsorekh—kemo le'ehov ve-le'ekhol" (Writing is Necessary—Like Loving and Eating). *Yedi'ot aḥaronot,* June 1, 1973.

Barzel, Hillel. "Alpit shel ha-sa'ar . . . " (One Thousandth of the Storm . . .). *Ashmoret* 6, 5 (1950): 10.

———. "Shir ke-ḥolem" (A Poem Like a Dreamer). *Mevo'ot* 2 (1953): 7–8.

———. "Shira ha-koveshet be-lahata ha-penimi" (Poetry that Conquers with Its Inner Flame). *Yedi'ot aḥaronot,* Dec. 27, 1963.

———. "Amir Gilboa: Tserufim tanakhiyim" (Biblical Combinations), in *Shira u-morasha* (Poetry and Tradition), vol. 2. Eked Publishing, 1971, 11–55.

———. "Ha-tseruf ha-personalisti" (The Personal Combination). *Eked le-shira,* 21 (1971).

———. "Temurot be-shirat Amir Gilboa" (Changes in Gilboa's Poetry). *Moznayim* 60, 5–6 (1975): 379–94. Also in *Meshorerim bi-gedulatam* (Poets in Their Greatness). Yaḥdav Publishing, 1979, 326–52.

———. "Min ha-kolel el ha-mesuyam: Al yesodot ha-poetika shel Amir Gilboa" (From the General To the Particular: On the Foundations of Gilboa's Poetics). *Moznayim* 54, 6 (May 1982): 5–9. Somewhat expanded under the title "Amir Gilboa: Leha'id ba-ḥavaya et ha-ḥushim" (To Testify to the Senses Through Experience), in *Meshorerei besora* (Good News Poets). Yaḥdav Publishing, 1983, 293–317.

———. *Amir Gilboa: Monographia* (Monograph). Sifriat Poalim, 1984.

———. "Amir Gilboa: Shir ne'urim be-Yiddish" (A Youthful Yiddish Poem). *Iton* 77, 52–53 (1984): 12–13.

———. "Amir Gilboa: Shirim aḥaronim" (Last Poems). *Iton* 77, 57 (1984): 6.

Be'er, Ḥayim. "Devarim al Amir Gilboa" (Comments on Gilboa). *La-merḥav,* May 31, 1968. Also in *Moznayim* 29, 3–4 (1969): 236–40, under the title "Shirat ish Yehudi: Al tsad eḥad be-shirei Amir Gilboa" (The Poetry of a Jew: On One Aspect of Amir Gilboa's Poems). Also in *Amir Gilboa: Mivḥar ma'amarim al yetsirato,* 147–57.

———. "Al ha-ikar she-ḥaser" (On the Missing Main Point). *Ha-arets,* Dec. 24, 1971.

Benn [Braun], Menaḥem. "Da'at ha-tseva'im ve-da'at ha-atsvut" (The Knowledge of Colors and the Knowledge of Sadness). *Yedi'ot aḥaronot,* June 21, 1968. Also in *Akhshav* 21–24 (1968): 288–90.

Bernstein, Ory. "Ha-simḥa ve-ha-capriza: Al *Ketaf* le-Amir Gilboa" (Joy and Caprice: On *Balm* by Amir Gilboa). *Yedi'ot aḥaronot,* Nov. 5, 1971.

———. "Ha-iton ve-ha-'musaf'" (The Newspaper and the "Supplement"). *Yedi'ot aḥaronot,* Feb. 23, 1973.

———. "Lilmod mimenu" (To Learn From Him). *Iton* 77 6, 334 (June-Aug. 1982): 36.

Betsalel, Yitsḥak. "Shira be-emet" (Poetry in Truth), *La-merḥav,* Mar. 27, 1964. (See next entry.)

———. "Shira be'emet." *La-merḥav,* January 1, 1969. This interview and a brief excerpt from the 1964 interview (ibid.) are collected in *Ha-kol katuv ba-sefer: Im sofrim ha-kotvim be-Yisrael kayom* (Everything is Written in the Book: With Authors Writing in Israel Today). Hakibbutz Hameuchad, 1969, 183–91.

Carmi, David. "Pitom kam adam ba-boker" (Suddenly a Person Gets Up in the Morning). *Ba-maḥane,* No. 14, 1962.

Carmi, Uri. *"Sheva reshuyot:* Shirim me'et Amir Gilboa" (*Seven Domains:* Poems by Amir Gilboa). *Dorot* 1, 11 (1949): 12–13.

Cohen, Adir. "Shirav ha-ḥadashim shel Amir Gilboa" (Gilboa's New Poems). *Davar,* July 26, 1968.

———. "Shirato shel Amir Gilboa" (Gilboa's Poetry). *Ha-arets,* April 13, 1973.

———. "Be-shulei shirato shel Amir Gilboa" (On the Periphery of Gilboa's Poetry), in *Derekh ha-ru'aḥ: Koḥah ha-meḥanekh shel ha-sifrut* (The Way of the Spirit: The Educational Power of Literature). Yaḥdav Publishing, 1977, 393–401.

Cohen, Yisrael. "Iyun ba-sifrut ha-ivrit le-or mishnato shel Jung" (Discussion of Hebrew Literature in the Light of Jung's Theories). *Moznayim* 44, 5–6 (1977): 330–43.

Dan [sic]. "Le'orer o lehardim?" (To Rouse or To Put to Sleep). *Ba-sha'ar* 14 (1950): 5.

Dor, Moshe. "Pitom kam meshorer" (Suddenly a Poet Arises). *Ma'ariv,* Oct. 21, 1977. Also in *Aval ha-devarim ha-yafim* (But the Lovely Things), edited by R. Gurfein-Ukhmani. Sifriat Poalim, 1980, 19–23.

———. "Gilboa: He'arot muzarot" (Strange Comments). *Ma'ariv,* Jan. 8, 1982.

———. "Goral ve-adama" (Fate and Land). *Al ha-mishmar,* June 3, 1987.

Doron, Daniel. "Shira ve-shivron lashon" (Poetry and the Breakdown of Language). *Al ha-mishmar,* Jan. 1, 1950.

Gilead, Zerubavel. "Al ha-shir ve-ha-shar" (On the Poem and the Poet). *Mi-bifnim* 44, 3–4 (1982): 328–29.

Goren, Natan. "Sifrutenu bi-shenat 1949–50" (Our Literature in 1949–50). *Devar ha-shavua,* October 5, 1950.

Gouri, Ḥaim. *"Keḥulim va-adumim" (Reds and Blues). La-merḥav,* Dec. 6, 1963.

———. "Ha-ish ha-kotev siftei yeshenim" (The Man Who Writes the Lips of Sleepers). *Al ha-mishmar [Ḥotam],* Jan. 1, 1982.

Gurfein, Rivka. "Ḥavayat yaldut shel ha-meshorer" (A Childhood Experience of the Poet). *Devar ha-po'elet,* Mar.-April 1964: 119, 122. Also appeared as "'Sha'ul': Al shir eḥad shel Amir Gilboa" ("Saul": On One of Gilboa's Poems), in *Mi-karov u-me-raḥok* (From Near and Far). Tarbut Veḥinukh Publishing, 1964, 242–46. Also in *Im shir,* (With Song). Eked Publishing, 1967, 38–43. Also as "'Sha'ul'" in *Amir Gilboa: Mivḥar ma'amarim al yetsirato,* 180–83.)

———. "Sifro he-ḥadash shel Amir Gilboa" (Amir Gilboa's New Book).

Moznayim 27, 3–4 (1968): 248–51. Also in *Amir Gilboa: Mivḥar ma'amarim al yetsirato,* 140–46.

———. "Bein me'oravut li-nesiga" (Between Engagement and Retreat). *Al ha-mishmar,* Aug. 24, 1973. Also in *El milim u-me'ever lahen* (Toward Words and Beyond Them), Masada Publishing, 1973, 90–97, under the title *"Ayala eshlaḥ otakh* le-Amir Gilboa" (Gilboa's *Gazelle I Send You).*

Gutkind, Naomi. "Amir Gilboa: 'Lo leshorer, lo leshorer, le'orer'" ("Not To Poetize, Not To Poetize, To Arouse"). *Ha-tsofe,* June 19, 1970.

Ha'efrati, Yosef. "Al shnei shirim shel Amir Gilboa" (On Two Poems by Gilboa), *Akhshav* 7–8 (Spring 1962): 102–12. (Also in *Amir Gilboa: Mivḥar ma'amarim al yetsirato,* 168–79.

———. "Al motiv be-*Ayala eshlaḥ otakh* le-Amir Gilboa" (On a Motif in Gilboa's *Gazelle I Send You). Siman kri'a* 6 (1976): 311–12.

Ḥakak, Lev. "'Malkhut demama' le-Amir Gilboa" (Gilboa's "The Kingdom of Silence"), in *Im arba'a meshorerim* (With Four Poets). Eked Publishing, 1979, 59–101.

Halkin, Shimon. "Kirkhei shira tse'ira ba-shanim ha-aḥaronot" (Volumes of Young Poetry in Recent Years). *Beḥinot* 6 (1952): 6–25. Also in *Derakhim ve-tsidei derakhim* (Ways and Byways), vol. 1. Jerusalem: Akadamon Publishing, 1969, 101–37.

Ḥazak, Yeḥiel. "Mi-ḥerut le-shi'abud" (From Freedom to Slavery). *Al ha-mishmar,* Apr. 1, 1977.

Hurvitz, Ya'ir. "Im Amir Gilboa: Admat ha-tashtit ha-penimit" (With Amir Gilboa: The Inner Basic Earth). *Siman kri'a* 8 (1978): 337–38.

Kahana-Carmon, Amalia. "Mikhtav galuy le-Amir Gilboa im sifro *Ratstiti likhtov siftei yeshenim"* (An Open Letter to Amir Gilboa at the publication of his book *I Wanted To Write the Lips of Sleepers). La-merḥav,* June 14, 1968.

———. "Sefer li ba-bayit" (I Have a Book At Home). *Moznayim* 32 (1971): 147.

———. "Im Amir Gilboa: 'Ḥelkat yam, besarah lisḥot bah'" (With Amir Gilboa: "A Stretch of Sea, Its Flesh To Swim In It"). *Davar,* October 14, 1977. Also in *Siman kri'a* 8 (1977): 331.

———. "'Elḥats kaf yadi el klipat ha-ets'" ("I'd Press My Palm On the Bark of the Tree"). *Siman kri'a* 16/17 (1983): 55–57.

Kalderon, Nissim. "Ha-shira ve-ha-besora: Le-shirato shel Amir Gilboa" (Poetry and Good News). *Kol ha-am,* Aug. 20, 1965.

———. "Ha-paḥad, ha-buz ve-ha-ahava ha-gedola: Le-shirat Amir Gilboa" (Fear, Scorn, and Great Love: On Gilboa's Poetry]. *Kol ha-am,* Aug. 27, 1965.

———. "Elei shira arukat neshima: Le-shirato shel Amir Gilboa" (Toward a Long-winded Poetry: On the Poetry of Gilboa). *Kol ha-am,* Sept. 3, 1965.

Kalinov, Rina. "Gevulot ha-shira" (The Boundaries of Poetry). *Mi-bifnim* 31, 2 (1969): 234–40.

———. "Ḥazara—al rama gevoha yoter" (Once Again—On a Higher Level). *Moznayim* 36, 3 (1973): 231–33.

———. "Divrei petiḥa" (Opening Remarks). *Mi-bifnim* 44, 3–4 (1982): 319–20.

Kartun-Blum, Ruth. *Shira bi-re'i atsmah* (Poetry In Its Own Mirror). Hakibbutz Hameuchad, 1982, 74–75.

Katzenelson, Gideon. "Shirei Amir Gilboa" (Gilboa's Poems). *Ha-arets,* July 24, 1953. Also in *Le'an hem holkhim?: Ḥatakh be-shiratah shel Yisrael ha-tse'ira* (Where Are They Going?: A Cross-section of the Poetry of Young Israel). Alef Publishing, 1968, 110–13, 129–32, 254–58.

Keller, Assaf. "Mahapekha be-shira" (Revolution in Poetry). *Aspaklaria* 48 (Mar. 20, 1947).

Komem, Aharon. "'Im yaruni even': Al Amir Gilboa u-*Keḥulim va-adumim*" ("Should They Show Me a Rock": On Gilboa and *Reds and Blues).* *Moznayim* 58, 5–6 (1984): 19–24.

Kurzweil, Baruch. "Nose ha-akeda be-sifrutenu ha-ḥadasha" (The Subject of the Binding of Isaac in Our Modern Literature). *Davar,* Oct. 2, 1959.

Levin, Yisrael. "Bein dam ve-kotsim, bein leida ve-ḥayim" (Between Blood and Thorns, Birth and Life). *Mi-bifnim* 44, 3–4 (1982): 322–24.

Litvin, Rina. *"Keḥulim va-adumim* va-aḥerim . . . " *(Blues and Reds* and Other [Things] . . .). *Moznayim* 18, 4 (1969): 273–76.

Luz, Tsvi. "Merḥavim u-merkaz—Amir Gilboa" (Expanses and Center), in *Metsi'ut ve-adam ba-sifrut ha-erets-Yisraelit* (Reality and Humanity in Land-of-Israel Literature). Dvir Publishing, 1970, 68–89. Also in *Amir Gilboa: Mivḥar ma-amarim al yetsirato,* 119–39.

Meged, Aharon [M. A.] "Mashehu al Gilboa" (Something About Gilboa). *La-merḥav,* Jan. 27, 1961.

———. "Kama milim al Amir Gilboa" (A Few Words About Gilboa). *La-merḥav,* Oct. 13, 1967.

Meged, Matti. "'Ki az etsak'" ("For Then I'll Scream"). *Al ha-mishmar,* Dec. 23 and 30, 1949.

———. "Mi-*Sheva reshuyot* el Ha-boker" (From *Seven Domains* to the Morning). *La-merḥav,* June 4, 1953.

———. "Mekorot ha-ḥavaya ha-shirit" (Sources of the Poetic Experience). *La-merḥav,* Jan. 7, 1955.

———. "Dovev siftei yeshenim" (Rousing the Lips of Sleepers). *Molad* 2, 7 (1968): 118–23. Also in *Amir Gilboa: Mivḥar ma'amarim al yetsirato,* 158–67.

Mi-bifnim 34, 3–4 (1982): 319–44. Special section in honor of Gilboa's receiving the Israel Prize for Literature.

Mikhali, B.Y. "Shirim be-khol lashon" (Poems in Any Language). *Davar,* July 29, 1955.

———. "Siyuto shel meshorer" (A Poet's Nightmare). *Moznayim* 42, 5–6 (1976): 358–68. Also in *Mishbetsot bikoret* (A Patchwork of Criticism]. Yaḥdav Publishing, 1980, 79–95.

Miron, Dan. "Hirhurim al shirat Gilboa" (Thoughts on Gilboa's Poetry). *Ha-arets,* Apr. 2, 1964, and "Bi-teḥum u-miḥuts la-teḥum: Hirhurim nosafim al shirat Gilboa" (Within and Without the Pale: Additional Thoughts on Gilboa's Poetry). *Ha-arets,* Apr. 24, 1964. Also in *Amir Gilboa: Mivḥar ma'amarim al yetsirato,* 96–119.

———. "Lo makom shel shir" (Not a Place For Poetry). *Akhshav* 31–32 (1975): 227–30.

Mohar, Eli. "Bi-meḥoz ha-shirim shel Amir Gilboa" (In the Realm of Gilboa's Poetry). *Devar ha-shavu'a,* December 24, 1971.

Moked, Gavriel. "Amir Gilboa: Kinus be-tokh esrim shana" (A Collection of Twenty Years). *Ha-boker,* Jan. 17, 31, and Feb. 14, 1964. Also in *Amir Gilboa: Mivḥar ma'amarim al yetsirato,* 86–95.

———. "Amir Gilboa" (Review of *Ratsiti likhtov siftei yeshenim). Yedi'ot aḥaronot,* Jan. 10, 1969.

———. "Pras le-shira bi-gedulata" (A Prize for Poetry in its Greatness). *Yedi'ot aḥaronot,* Nov. 13, 1981.

Nira [sic]. "Pan el pan im Amir Gilboa" (Face to Face With Amir Gilboa). *Ba-mivḥan,* October, 1973.

Peles [Kalinov], Yedidia. "Al hebet aḥer be-shirei Gilboa" (Regarding a Different Perspective on Gilboa's Poetry). *Mi-bifnim* 44 (1982): 320–22.

Rabin, Ozer. "Al shir eḥad mi-shirei Amir Gilboa" (On a Poem by Gilboa).

Iton 77 6,34 (June-Aug. 1982): 36–37.

Ratok, Lili. "'Malkhut demama'" ("Kingdom of Silence"). *Shedemot* 58 (1976): 82–85.

———. "Bein shir le-shir" (Between One Poem and Another). *Iton* 77 6,34 (June-Aug. 1982): 38.

———. "Laga'at ba-mufla" (To Touch the Wondrous). *Al ha-mishmar,* April 27, 1982.

Ravid, Chana [Kliger]. "Mi-pegishot be-yamim mi-she-kvar" (Of Meetings Long Ago). *Mi-bifnim* 44 (1982): 324–26.

Ruebner, Tuvya. *"Ratsiti liktov siftei yeshenim." Moznayim* 32 (1970): 71–72.

Sadeh, Pinḥas. "Kri'at tagar al ha-metsi'ut" (A Call To Arms On Reality), *Ha-arets,* Dec. 30, 1949.

Sandbank, Shimon. "Shirei Gilboa ha-mekubatsim: Kri'a rishona" (Gilboa's Collected Poems: First Reading). *Amot* 2 (1963)3: 102–4.

———. "'Le'aḥar she-hayiti har, le'aḥar she-hayiti yam': Al shirat Amir Gilboa" ("After I Was a Mountain, After I Was a Sea": On Gilboa's Poetry). *Davar,* Oct. 14, 1977. Also in *Ha-shir ha-nakhon* (The Correct Poem). Sifriat Poalim, 1982, 70–75.

Schweid, Eliezer. "El ha-milim ha-peshutot" (Toward the Simple Words). *La-merḥav,* December 12, 1963. Also in *Amir Gilboa: Mivḥar ma'amarim al yetsirato,* 79–85.

Segal, Sarah [Kalinov]. "Bereshit shirato shel he-ḥalutz-ha-meshorer" (The Beginnings of the Pioneer-Poet's Poetry). *Mi-bifnim* 44, 3–4 (1982): 326–28.

Sened, Alexander. "Al Amir Gilboa" (On Amir Gilboa). *Mi-bifnim* 44, 3–4 (1982): 330.

Senunit, Mikhal. "'Ha-kol bi-glal erets Yisrael'—ha-agadot she-od notru" ("It's All Because of Israel"—the Myths That Remain). *Al ha-mishmar,* Dec. 21, 1973.

Sha'anan, Avraham. "Ha-ayala ha-mishtalaḥat" (The Gazelle that is Sent Off). *Davar,* Mar. 2, 1973.

Shaḥam, Ḥaya. "'Lo leshorer—le'orer': Shirat Amir Gilboa be-zika mitamemetet el shirat Alterman" ("Not to Poeticize—To Rouse": Gilboa's Poetry in Its Confrontative Relationship to Alterman's Poetry). *Dapim lemeḥkar be-sifrut* 7 (1990): 37–53.

Shaked, Gershon. "Ḥamisha shirim al ha-melekh Sha'ul" (Five Poems on King Saul), *La-merḥav,* May 16 and 23, 1958.

Shamir, Moshe. "Shoshanim noshmot (Roses Breathing)," *Ba-sha'ar,* Nov. 3, 1949.

———. "Ha'arot le-shirat Amir Gilboa" (Insights Into Gilboa's Poetry), *La-merḥav,* May 13, 1952. Also, in slightly expanded form and entitled "Ha-yotser ve-kibush ha-yotser" (The Creator and the Creator's Conquest), in *Be-kulmus mahir* (With a Quick Pen), Sifriat Poalim, 1960, 130–38. Also in *Amir Gilboa: Mivḥar ma'amarim al yetsirato,* 40–48.

———. "Im shirei A. Gilboa" (With the Poems of Gilboa). *Davar,* May 22, 1953.

———. "Shirat Amir Gilboa" (Gilboa's Poetry). *La-merḥav,* May 16, 1956.

———. "Ko me'at, ko harbe" (So Little, So Much). *Ma'ariv,* Oct. 22, 1971.

———. "Kakh katvu aleihem ha-mevakrim" (That's How the Critics Wrote About Them). *Yedi'ot aḥaronot,* May, 4, 1973.

Shammas, Anton. "Al parparim ve-shira" (On Butterflies and Poetry). *Ha-yom,* May 2, 1969.

Shapir, A.D. "Atik ve-tsa'ir u-molid" (Ancient and Young and Procreative). *Davar,* Dec. 24, 1971.

Shavit, Zohar. *"Amir Gilboa: Mivḥar ma'amarim al yetsirato"* (Review of A. Balaban, ed. *Selected Essays of Gilboa's Works). Moznayim* 36 (1963): 362–64.

Shenhod, Shlomo. "Mikhtav le-turei sifrut" (Letter to the Literary Pages). *Ha-boker,* Mar. 28, 1958.

Sheva, Shlomo. "Ha-masa el ha-olam ha-gadol" (The Journey to the Big World). *Devar ha-shavu'a,* Jan. 10, 1964.

———. "El ha-milim ha-peshutot" (To the Simple Words). *La-merḥav,* Dec. 27, 1963.

Shiffman, Semadar. "Me-ḥatsiva ba-kokhavim li-nesi'a ba-autobus" (From Star Quarrying To Riding On a Bus). *Siman kri'a* 16/17 (1983): 58–63.

Shoḥam, Ḥayim. *"Siftei yeshenim* le-Amir Gilboa" (Gilboa's *Lips of Sleepers). Ha-arets,* July 26, 1968.

Tanai, Shlomo. "Al shirat Amir Gilboa" (On Gilboa's Poetry). *Ba-sha'ar,* 45 (November 17, 1949): 5.

Treinin, Avner. "Gilboa ve-Amiḥai—analiza shel yesodot" (Gilboa and Amichai—An Analysis of Basic Principles). *Ma'ariv,* April 30, 1982.

Tselka, Dan, editor. *Amir Gilboa: Mivḥar shirim u-devarim al shirato* (A Selection of Gilboa's Poems and Comments on His Poetry). Maḥbarot

Leshira Publishing, 1962.
———. "Andarte'ot ha-milim" (Statues of Words). *Ha-arets,* May 7, 1982.
Tsipper, Benny. "Shnei sulamot: Majori u-minori" (Two Scales: Major and Minor). *Ha-arets,* Nov. 13, 1981.
———. "'Retson ha-hisha'arut hu she-madrikh oti'" ("The Will of Constancy Is What Guides Me"). *Ha-arets,* Sept. 9, 1984.
Tsurit, Ida [Meged]. "Shirat Amir Gilboa" (Gilboa's Poetry). *La-merḥav,* May 16 and 18, 1956.
———. *Ha-ḥayim, ha-atsilut: Iyunim be-shirato shel Amir Gilboa* (Spheres of Life and Emanation). Hakibbutz Hameuchad, 1988.
Wechsler, Yitsḥak. "Shirato shel Amir Gilboa" (Gilboa's Poetry). *Niv ha-kevutsa* 13, 3–4 (1964): 675–78.
Wieseltier, Meir. "Im Amir Gilboa: Bemo ani" (With Amir Gilboa: I Myself). *Siman kri'a* 8 (1978): 334–37.
Yaffe, A. B. [A. B. Y.] "Shirei Amir Gilboa" (Gilboa's Poems). *Al ha-mishmar,* July 17, 1953.
———. "Meshorer seva nidudim" (A Poet of Many Wanderings), *Ma'ariv,* October 9, 1953.
———. "Shneihem be-yaḥad ve-khol eḥad leḥud" (The Two of Them Together and Each of Them Alone). *Al ha-mishmar,* Nov. 13, 1981.
Ya'oz, Chana. *Ha-sho'a be-shirat dor ha-medina* (The Holocaust in the Poetry of the Generation of the State). Eked Publishing, 1984, 90–101.
———. "Amir Gilboa: Ha-tse'aka shelo nits'aka" (The Scream That Was Not Screamed). *Iton* 77 52–53 (1984): 14–15, 20.
Yasur, Chava. "Shorsheha shel shira" (The Roots of Poetry). *Al ha-mishmar,* June 15, 1956.
———. "Al shnei sifrei shira: *Keḥulim va-adumim* le-Amir Gilboa" (On Two Books of Poetry: *Reds and Blues* by Amir Gilboa). *Al ha-mishmar [Ḥotam],* no. 18–19, 1964.
Yitsḥaki, Yedidia. "Iyun be-shir 'Kol ze she-holekh' le-Gilboa" (Discussion of Gilboa's poem "All This That Passes"]. *Alei si'aḥ* 10–11 (1981): 31–32.
Zach, Natan. [N. Z.] "Ha-ḥotem hitatesh" (The Nose Sneezed). *Ma'avak* 69, July 31, 1953.
———. "Muvanuto shel Amir Gilboa" (The Comprehensibility of Amir Gilboa), *Davar,* Oct. 25, 1957. Also in *Amir Gilboa: Mivḥar ma'amarim al yetsirato,* 73–78.
Zahavi, Alex. "Leshon ha-remez shel Amir Gilboa" (Gilboa's Allusive

Language). *Yedi'ot aḥaronot,* Jan. 5, 1973.
———. "Be-ḥipus aḥarei ha-aktuali" (In Search of the Real). *Yedi'ot aḥaronot,* Jan. 18, 1974.
———. "Ha-temurot be-shirat Amir Gilboa" (The Changes in Gilboa's Poetry). *Yedi'ot aḥaronot,* April 30, 1982.
[Unsigned interview with Gilboa]. *Ba-maḥane* 44, July 9, 1953.
[Unsigned review of *Shirim ba-boker ba-boker* and interview with Gilboa]. *Ba-maḥane* 44, Sept. 9, 1953.
[Unsigned opinion poll of four poets—Gilboa, Greenberg, Shlonsky, Zach—as to the criteria used to determine the quality of a poem.] *La-merḥav,* April 10, 1959.
[Unsigned review of *Ratsiti likhtov siftei yeshenim.*] "Me'at im u-me'at al Amir Gilboa" (A Bit with and a Bit about Gilboa). *Al ha-mishmar,* Dec. 25, 1971.

4. Related Works

Abrams, Maurice H. *The Mirror and the Lamp: Romantic Theory and the Critical Tradition.* New York: Oxford University Press, 1953.
Arpali, Boaz. *Avotot shel ḥoshekh: Al 'Simḥat aniyim' le-Natan Alterman* (Bonds of Darkness: On Natan Alterman's *The Joy of the Poor).* Hakibbutz Hameuchad, 1983.
———. *Ha-peraḥim ve-ha-agartal: Shirat Amiḥai—Mivne, mashma'ut, poetika* (The Flowers and the Vase: Amichai's Poetry—Structure, Meaning, Poetics). Siman Kri'a/Hakibbutz Hameuchad, 1986.
Baker, Carlos. *The Echoing Green: Romanticism, Modernism, and the Phenomena of Transference in Poetry.* Princeton: Princeton University Press, 1984.
Balzer, Wolfgang, and Heide Gittner. "A Theory of Literature Logically Reconstructed: Reconsideration of the Example—Roman Jakobson." *Poetics* 12, 6 (1983): 489–510.
Bargad, Warren. *Ideas in Fiction: The Works of Hayim Hazaz.* Chico, California: Scholars Press/Brown University, 1982.
Basok, Moshe. *He-ḥalutz ha-tsa'ir: Me'asef* (The Young Pioneer [Organization]: An Anthology). Ein-Ḥarod: Hakibbutz Hameuchad, 1944.
Bialik, Ḥayim N., and Yehoshua H. Ravnitzky. *Sefer ha-agada.* Dvir

Publishing, 1947.

Bloom, Harold. *Romanticism and Consciousness: Essays in Criticism.* New York: W. W. Norton, 1970.

———. *The Anxiety of Influence.* New York: Oxford University Press, 1975.

Burnshaw, Stanley, T. Carmi, Ezra Spicehandler, editors. *The Modern Hebrew Poem Itself.* New York: Schocken Books, 1965.

Cizviskij, Dmitrij. *On Romanticism in Slavic Literature.* The Hague: Mouton & Co, 1957.

Cohen, Ralph, editor. *New Directions in Literary History.* Baltimore: Johns Hopkins University Press, 1974.

Culler, Jonathan. *Structuralist Poetics: Structuralism, Linguistics, and the Study of Literature.* Ithaca: Cornell University Press, 1975.

———. *Ferdinand de Saussure.* New York: Penguin Books, 1977.

———. *The Pursuit of Signs: Semiotics, Literature, Deconstruction.* Ithaca: Cornell University Press, 1981.

———. *On Deconstruction.* Ithaca: Cornell University Press, 1982.

Dan, Yosef, editor. *Sefer Klossova* (The Klossova Book). Beit Loḥamei Hageta'ot and Hakkibutz Hameuchad, 1978.

De Beaugrande, Robert-Alain. "Semantic Evaluation of Grammar in Poetry." *Poetics, Theory, Literature* 3 (1978): 315–25.

Eigner, Hans, editor. *'Romantic' and Its Cognates: The European History of a Word.* Toronto and Buffalo: University of Toronto Press, 1972.

Elgar, Viti. "The Interpretation of Symbols in Literature." *Poetics, Theory, Literature* 4 (1979): 15–30.

Erlich, Victor. *Russian Formalism: History—Doctrine.* 4th edition. Mouton Publishers: The Hague, Paris, New York, 1980.

Even-Zohar, Itamar. "Rashei perakim la-te'oria shel ha-text ha-sifruti" (An Outline of the Theory of the Literary Text). *Ha-sifrut* 3, 3–4 (1972): 427–46.

———. "Ha-sifrut ha-Ivrit ha-Yisraelit—model histori" (Israeli Hebrew Literature—A Historical Model). *Ha-sifrut* 4, 3 (1973): 427–40.

———. "Polysystem Theory," *Poetics Today* 1, 1–2 (1979): 287–310.

Feldman, Yael. *Modernism and Cultural Transfer: Gabriel Preil and the Tradition of Jewish Literary Bilingualism.* Cincinnati: Hebrew Union College Press, 1986.

Fleishman, Lazar. "Problems in the Poetics of Pasternak." *Poetics, Theory, Literature* 4 (1979): 43–61.

Freud, Sigmund. "The Relation of the Poet to Day-Dreaming," in *On Creativity and the Unconscious: Papers on the Psychology of Art, Literature, Love, and Religion.* Selected, with introduction and annotations by Benjamin Nelson. New York: Harper & Row, 1958, 44–54.

Gleckner, Robert F. and Gerald E. Enscoe, editors. *Romanticism: Points of View.* Englewood Cliffs, New Jersey: Prentice-Hall, 1962.

Gouri, Ḥaim, Moshe Shamir and Ḥayim Hazaz. "On the Post-Six-Day War (October 1967) Writers Convocation in Jerusalem." *Moznayim* 35, 3 (Aug. 1967): 169–88.

Guyman, W. "Exercise in Semiotic Analysis." *Journal of Literary Semiotics* 4 (1979): 73–91.

He-atid (The Future). (Special edition on the tenth anniversary of the Hechalutz organization.) Warsaw: March 1928.

———. "Report on the Tenth Anniversary of the *hakhshara* Camp Klossova." Sept. 15, 1934.

Hrushovski [Harshav], Binyamin. "Free Rhythms in Modern Yiddish Poetry," in *The Field of Yiddish: Studies in Yiddish Language, Folklore and Literature,* edited by Uriel Weinreich. *Publications of the Linguistic Circle of New York* 3 (1954): 219–66.

———. "On Free Rhythms in Modern Poetry," in *Style in Language,* edited by T. A. Sebeok. Cambridge, MA: M.I.T. Press, 1960, 173–90.

———. "Al teḥumei mada ha-sifrut" (On the Areas of the Science of Literature). *Ha-sifrut* 1 (1968): 1–10.

———. "Ha'im yesh la-tselil mashma'ut?" (Does Sound Have Meaning?) *Ha-sifrut* 1 (1968): 410–20.

———. "Prosody, Hebrew." *Encyclopedia Judaica,* 1971, vol. 13, 1195–1240.

———. "Poetica, bikoret, mada: He'arot al teḥumav ve-al aḥrayuto shel mada ha-sifrut" (Poetics, Criticism, Science: Comments on the Areas and the Responsibility of the Science of Literature). *Siman kri'a* 6 (1976): 131–38.

———. "The Structure of Semiotic Objects." *Poetics Today* 1, 1–2 (1979): 363–76.

———. "An Outline of Integrational Semantics: An Understander's Theory of Meaning in Context." *Poetics Today* 3, 4 (1982): 59–88.

———. "Poetic Metaphor and Frames of Reference." *Poetics Today* 5, 1 (1984): 5–43.

Iser, Wolfgang. "The Reading Process: A Phenomenological Approach," in

New Directions in Literary History, edited by Ralph Cohen. Baltimore: Johns Hopkins University Press, 1974, 125–45.

Jakobson, Roman. "Aphasia: The Metaphoric and Metonymic Poles," in *The Problem of Style,* edited by J. V. Cunningham. Greenwich: Fawcett Publications, 1966, 260–65.

———. "Closing Statement: Linguistics and Poetics," in *Style in Language,* edited by T. A. Sebeok. M.I.T. Press, 1960, 350–77.

———. "The Poetry of Grammar and the Grammar of Poetry." *Lingua* 21 (1968): 597–609.

———. "Subliminal Verbal Patterning in Poetry," in *Studies in General and Oriental Linguistics,* edited by R. Jakobson and S. Kawamoto. Tokyo: TEC Publishing, 1970, 302–8.

Jauss, Hans Robert. "Literary History as a Challenge to Literary Theory." *New Literary History* 2, 1 (1970): 7–37. Also in *New Directions in Literary History,* 11–41.

Kress, Gunther R. "Poetry as Anti-Language." *Poetics, Theory, Literature* 3 (1978): 327–44.

Kressel, Getzel. *Lexicon ha-sifrut ha-Ivrit ba-dorot ha-aḥaronim* (Lexicon of Hebrew Literature in Recent Generations). 2 vols. Merḥavia: Sifriat Poalim, 1965/67.

Kronfeld, Chana. "Allusion: An Israeli Perspective," *Prooftexts* 5 (1985): 137–63.

———. [Forthcoming] *On the Margins of Modernism.* Berkeley and Los Angeles: University of California Press. [Especially the chapter tentatively entitled "Beyond Language Pains: The Possibility of Modernist Hebrew Poetry"].

Laferriere, Daniel. "The Teleology of Rhythm in Poetry." *Poetics, Theory, Literature* 4 (1980): 411–50.

Lotman, Yuri [Jurij]. *Analysis of the Poetic Text.* Ann Arbor: Ardis Press, 1976.

———. *The Structure of the Artistic Text.* Ann Arbor: Department of Slavic Language and Literature, 1977.

———. "The Text and the Structure of Its Audience." *New Literary History* 14, 1 (1982): 81–87.

———. *The Semiotics of Russian Cultural History,* edited by Alexander D. and Alice C. Nakhimovsky. Ithaca and London: Cornell University Press, 1985.

Margolin, Uri. "Le-va'ayat ha-ḥaluka li-tekufot ba-historia shel ha-sifrut" (On the Problem of Periodization in Literary History]. *Ha-sifrut* 2, 1 (1969): 5–13.

McHale, Brian. *Postmodernist Fiction.* London and New York: Routledge, 1987.

Miron, Dan. "Al ha-musag 'Doro shel Bialik'" (On the Concept "The Generation of Bialik"). *Moznayim* 13, 3–4 (1961): 206–13.

———. *Ha-perida min ha-ani he-ani* (Taking Leave of the Impoverished Self: Ch. N. Bialik's Early Poetry). Open University Press, 1986.

———. *Bo'a laila* (Come, Night: Hebrew Literature Between the Rational and the Irrational at the Turn of the Century: Studies in Ch. N. Bialik and M. Y. Berditchevsky.) Dvir Publishing, 1987.

———. *Bodedim be-mo'adam: Lideyoknah shel ha-republika ha-sifrutit ha-Ivrit bi-teḥilat ha-me'a ha-esrim* (When Loners Come Together: A Portrait of Hebrew Literature at the Turn of the Twentieth Century). Am Oved Publishers, 1987.

Perry, Menaḥem. *Ha-mivne ha-semanti shel shirei Bialik* (The Semantic Structure of Bialik's Poems). Siman Kri'a/Hakibbutz Hameuchad, 1977.

Piekarz [Paikaz], Mendel, editor. *Ha-sho'a u-sefiḥeha be-aspaklari'at kitvei-et Ivriyim: Bibliographia* (The Holocaust and Its Offshoots in the Mirror of Hebrew Periodicals: Bibliography). Jerusalem: Yad Vashem, 1974, vol. 2.

Riffaterre, Michael. "Criteria for Style Analysis." *Word* 15 (1959): 154–74. Also in *Essays on the Language of Literature,* edited by Seymour Chatman and Samuel R. Levin. Boston: Houghton Mifflin, 1967, 412–30.

———. "The Stylistic Approach to Literary History," in *New Directions in Literary History,* edited by Ralph Cohen, 1974, 147–64.

———. "Semantic Overdetermination in Poetry." *Poetics, Theory, Literature* 2 (1977): 19.

———. *Semiotics of Poetry.* Bloomington and London: Indiana University Press, 1978.

———. "Interpretation and Undecidability." *New Literary History* 12, 2 (1981): 227–42.

———. *Text Production.* New York: Columbia University Press, 1983.

Scheindlin, Raymond. *The Gazelle: Medieval Hebrew Poems On God, Israel, and the Soul.* Philadelphia: Jewish Publication Society, 1991.

Scholem, Gershom. "Mitzva ha-ba'a ba-avera" (A Good Deed Through Sin). *Knesset* 2 (1937): 347–92.

———. *Sabbatai Sevi.* Princeton: Princeton University Press, 1973.

Scholes, Robert. *Semiotics and Interpretation.* New Haven and London: Yale University Press, 1982.

Sebeok, Thomas A. *Style in Language.* Cambridge: M.I.T. Press, 1982.

Shamir, Ziva. *Ha-shira me-ayin timatse: 'Ars Poetica' bi-tsirat H.N. Bialik* (Where Shall Poetry Be Found: "Ars Poetica" in Bialik's Works). Papyrus Publishing, 1987.

Shavit, Uzi. "Reshit ha-ritmus ha-ḥofshi ba-shira ha-Ivrit ha-ḥadasha" (The Beginning of Free Rhythm in Modern Hebrew Poetry). *Siman kri'a* 10 (1980): 461–66.

Shlonsky, Avraham. "Al 'Shuv re'itikhem be-kotser yedkhem'" (On [Bialik's poem] "I See You Again in Your Impotence"). *Ketuvim* 6 (1931): 6.

Shklovskii, Viktor. *Theory of Prose,* translated by Benjamin Sher. Elmwood Park, IL: Dalkey Archive Press, 1990.

Shukman, Ann. *Literature and Semiotics: A Study of the Writings of Yu. M. Lotman.* Amsterdam, New York: North Holland Publishing, 1977.

Smith, Barbara Herrnstein. *Poetic Closure: A Study of How Poems End.* Chicago and London: University of Chicago Press, 1968.

Stankiewicz, Edward. "Linguistics and the Study of Poetic Language," in *Style in Language,* edited by T. A. Sebeok, 1960, 69–81.

———. "Poetics and Verbal Art," in *A Perfusion of Signs,* edited by T. A. Sebeok. Bloomington: Indiana University Press, 1977, 54–76.

Tamir-Ghez, Nomi. "Binary Oppositions and Thematic Decoding in E. E. Cummings and Eudora Welty." *Poetics, Theory, Literature* 3 (1978): 235–48.

Todorov, Tzvetan. *Symbolism and Interpretation.* Ithaca: Cornell University Press, 1982.

Tsur, Reuven. *Yesodot romantiyim ve-anti-romantiyim be-shirei Bialik, Tcherniḥovsky, Shlonsky, ve-Amiḥai* (Romantic and Antiromantic Foundations in the Poems of Bialik, Tcherniḥovsky, Shlonsky, and Amichai). Papyrus Publishing, 1985.

Ukhmani, Azriel, Moshe Shamir, and Shlomo Tanai, editors. *Dor ba-arets* (A Generation in the Land). Merḥavia: Sifriat Poalim, 1959.

Wellek, René. *Concepts of Criticism.* New Haven and London: Yale University Press, 1963.

———. *Discriminations: Further Concepts of Criticism.* New Haven: Yale University Press, 1970.

Wimsatt, W. K., Jr. and Monroe C. Beardsley. "The Structure of Romantic Nature Imagery," in *The Verbal Icon: Studies in the Meaning of Poetry,* edited by W. K. Wimsatt and Monroe C. Beardsley. Lexington: University of Kentucky Press, 1954.

Index of Gilboa's Works

General Index

Alterman, Natan, 2, 23–25, 117, 292; *Kokhavim baḥuts* (Stars Outside), 2; *Kol* (Voice), 24, 26, 30–33; *Shirei makot mitsrayim* (Poems of the Plagues of Egypt), 73; *Simḥat aniyim* (Joy of the Poor),
Ambiguous enjambment and ungrammatical syntax, 25, 55–56, 97, 122–25, 129, 144, 177, 210–211, 218, 222, 228–33, 235, 238, 247–48, 258–60, 288
Amichai, Yehuda, 84, 290, 292
Anavi, Aryeh, 58
Antiromantic romantic poetry, 69, 119–20, 165, 199, 257–78
Appelfeld, Aharon, 76

Baal Shem-Tov, Rabbi Israel 145–46, 149
Bartana, Ortsiyon, 290–93
Bar-Yosef, Hamutal, 176, 291–93
Barzel, Hillel, 292
Ben-Amitai, Levi, 10, 18
Bialik, Ḥayim Naḥman, 2, 4–6, 6–10, 51, 62, 68–69, 73, 96, 212–13, 234, 251, 292; *Ba-sade* (In the Field), 37; *Eineha* (Her Eyes), 67; *Ha-einayim ha-re'evot* (The Hungry Eyes), 67; *Metei midbar* (The Dead of the Desert); *Rak kav shemesh ehad* (Only One Beam of Sunlight), 67; *Razei laila* (Night Secrets), 7; *Safiaḥ* (Aftergrowth), 7; *Shirati* (My Song), 146; *Zohar* (Splendor), 7, 212–13
Biblical-theme poems, 137–44; 200–202; 205–207
Bluvstein, Raḥel, 286; *Ve-ulai* (And Perhaps), 18, 22–23
Brenner, Yosef Ḥaim, 5

Cahan, Ya'akov, 2
Child images, 38–39, 41, 97–101, 103, 125, 130, 133–37, 138–
39, 165, 181–85, 186–92
Comic and playful themes, 133, 154–61, 208–12
Creation and cosmic mythology, 20–26, 34–37, 63, 72, 246, 268, 271
Critical response to Gilboa's works, 290–93
Criticism of his works, Gilboa's response to, 42–45, 126, 148, 150, 169–70, 171–73, 205, 276

Dichotomy of styles in Gilboa's works, 2, 30–36, 58, 71, 80–82, 164, 206, 222, 238; compared to Alterman, 30–33, 35; to Bialik, 37; to Shlonsky, 6, 28–29, 33, 36, 42–47
Dreams, in Gilboa's works, 66, 72, 85, 86–89, 99, 101, 136, 200–203, 223–24, 259–61, 271–72; and visionary world of the poet, 197–99, 245–46, 252, 254–56, 286–87

End of the world images, 192–96, 216, 228, 257–78
Even-Zohar, Itamar, 2–3

Feldman, Joshua, 5, 49, 66–67, 78–79, 130, 200–203
Feldman, Moshe, 66

Geisel, Theodor (Dr. Seuss), 160
Gilboa, Amir (Berl Feldman): aliyah to Erets Israel, 1; as editor at Masada Publishing Company, 200; as social critic, 186–92, 222, 276–78; compared to other Holocaust poets, 73–80; death, 279; early life and cultural influences, 4–5; early Zionist affiliation, 4–6, 12, 45; existential fear of death, 214–16, 222–35, 246–50; first poetic responses to learning of his family's fate, 49, 54–60; identification with Azariah de Rossi, 203–5; in British Eighth Army, 3, 48; in Jewish Brigade, 48, 84–93; Israel Prize, 1, 49; North African war experiences, 50–54, 65; overwhelmed by barrage of images,